CENTURY 21 TYPEWRITING

First-Year Course

ISBN: 0-538-20710-8
Library of Congress;
Catalog Card Number: 76-169158

9 10 11 12 H 0 9 8 7

Printed in the United States of America

DR. D. D. LESSENBERRY
Professor of Education, Emeritus
University of Pittsburgh

DR. T. JAMES CRAWFORD
Chairman, Department of Business Education
and Office Management
Graduate School of Business
Indiana University

DR. LAWRENCE W. ERICKSON
Assistant Dean, Graduate School of Education
University of California, Los Angeles

DR. LEE R. BEAUMONT
Professor of Business
Indiana University of Pennsylvania

DR. JERRY W. ROBINSON
Senior Editor
South-Western Publishing Co.

Published by

SOUTH-WESTERN PUBLISHING CO.

Cincinnati   West Chicago, Ill.   Dallas   New Rochelle, N.Y.
Palo Alto, Calif.   Brighton, England

T71

CENTURY 21 TYPEWRITING | CONTENTS

PREFACE

Century 21 Typewriting is a *new* book: *new* in organization, *new* in content, *new* in learning impact, *new* in appearance. Based upon the highly successful Ninth Edition of *20th Century Typewriting*, this textbook represents a careful blending of effective classroom-tested practices and research-supported innovations into a learning system that is readily adaptable to a wide variety of teaching/learning situations.

The organization of the learning materials is based upon two well-known learning phenomena: (1) forgetting and skill attrition begin as soon as learning and skill building end; and (2) skill development and problem solving are ideally undertaken in a simple-to-complex sequence.

Thus it is that **Century 21 Typewriting**, First-Year Course, is comprised of two *cycles* of 75 well-planned 50-minute lessons each. Each *cycle* is subdivided into two or more *phases*, each with a major thrust in emphasis. Each *phase* is further subdivided into from three to six *units*, with varying numbers of lessons per unit. The number of lessons in a unit depends upon two important learning considerations: (1) the difficulty of the typewriting operation to be presented and learned; and (2) the desired level of skill to be developed at that point in the learning continuum.

Cycle 2 builds and enlarges upon the knowledges and skills developed in Cycle 1. This instructional pattern provides not only a review and reinforcement of previous learnings, but also an extension of them to higher performance levels in progressively more complex, realistic application settings. The cyclical sequence assures that at the end of each *cycle* the various typing skills are maximized and all personal and vocational problem-solving competencies are at peak levels. Optimum transfer of learning is thus assured.

In addition to the 150 carefully planned lessons, this textbook contains 21 pages of Supplementary Drills, Timed Writings, and Work Assignments (pages 233-253). These supplementary materials provide meaningful copy for the high achievers to use in class as extra credit work and for the less rapid learners to use as out-of-class self-improvement assignments. The supplementary Work Assignments are particularly useful in those classes that complete the regular lessons before year end and by those students who are to terminate formal typewriting instruction at the end of the year and need or want additional office typing practice.

A 16-page Reference Guide (pages i-xvi) is provided following page 126. The Reference Guide is a look-it-up-yourself section that helps to avoid needless repetition of instructions within the lessons and time-consuming searching through previous lessons for information that may have been forgotten.

CYCLE 1: Basic Typing

Cycle 1 contains two phases. Phase 1 (Lessons 1-39) is devoted exclusively to keyboard learning, technique refinement, and speed/control development because these are prerequisite skills for even the most basic problem applications. The materials designed to build these prerequisite skills are based upon extensive computer analyses of word-frequency studies and are sequenced to result in maximum skill growth in minimum time. They include intensive practice on the letter and number combinations and words that actually occur in a wide range of general and business communications.

Phase 2 (Lessons 40-75) places primary emphasis on the development of knowledges, concepts, and skills required in the efficient completion of personal/business papers: tables, notes, announcements, outlines, themes, and reports. Practice moves quickly from model copy, to semiarranged copy, to hand-corrected copy (script and rough draft). Basic skill improvement receives secondary, but appropriate, emphasis—about a third of the planned class time being devoted to it. Each type of application or basic typewriting operation is presented in its simplest form with a minimum of variation in format.

CYCLE 2: Personal/Business Typing

Cycle 2 consists of Phases 3-5. Phase 3 (Lessons 76-93) emphasizes basic skill improvement (including script, rough-draft, and statistical copy) and related communication skills (capitalization, number usage, and punctuation guides) that are required in the completion of realistic personal and vocational application activities.

Phase 4 (Lessons 94-125) is devoted primarily to the extension of knowledges and improvement of skills required in the typing of correspondence, tabulated reports, and manuscripts.

Phase 5 (Lessons 126-150) includes the typing of special business forms (cards, interoffice memorandums, invoices, and voucher checks), variations in basic communication forms (letters, business reports, and tables), and intensive production skill-building practice followed by production skill measurement.

LABORATORY AND TESTING MATERIALS

Optional (but highly desirable) laboratory materials are available for use with the First-Year Course. These materials include a technique check sheet, progress records, self-improvement acitvities, self-check questions, skill-performance activities, supplementary problems paralleling those in the textbook, business forms, and progress checkups to be completed at strategic points in the course.

In addition, a separate set of 6 achievement tests is available for periodic evaluation.

Lessenberry/ Crawford/ Erickson/ Beaumont/ Robinson

Form 3—Invoice

Problem 3: Invoice

Type an invoice with 1 cc on a plain half sheet. Use the information given below; use the illustration at the left as a model.

INVOICE

Crosswhite Wholesale Suppliers | 499 Alamo Avenue, S.E.
Albuquerque, NM 87102 (505) 271-4431

Sold to: Young Engineering Associates
808 S.W. Broadway
Portland, OR 97205

Date November 19, 19--
Our Order No. GJ-5032
Cust. Order No. H-32068
Shipped Via REA Express

Terms 2/10, n/30

Quantity	Description	Unit Price	Total
2	J-2643 Cylinder grinders	45.32	90.64
12	FH 291 Bushing driver sets	5.98	71.76
24	KX 102 Oil pan gaskets	.75	18.00
1	W 2358 Torque wrench	21.88	21.88
2 doz.	NX 4215 Welder's goggles	30.00 doz.	60.00
2	10-foot Engineer rods	15.00	30.00
1 doz.	50-foot Steel tapes	40.00 doz.	40.00
			332.28

Sold to: King Manufacturing Co. 147 Mill Street Canastota, NY 13032 | Date: December 15, 19-- | Our Order No.: HR-2212 | Cust. Order No.: 76693B | Shipped Via: Our truck | Terms: Net 30 days | Quantity 10 doz. | Description 120 v., 20 amp., fuseless circuit breakers | Unit Price 1.90 | Total 228.00 | Quantity 8 | Description Single-circuit automatic lighting devices | Unit Price 15.00 | Total 120.00 | Quantity 60 | Description 30 amp. brass-end cartridge fuses | Unit Price .15 | Total 9.00 | (Total) 357.00

Form 4—Voucher Check

Problem 4: Voucher Check

Type a voucher check with 1 cc. Use the information given below; use the illustration at the left as a model. **NOTE:** The top part of the form is a standard check. The lower part is for the receiver's records. The carbon is a record of the check and the invoiced items for the sender's files.

young engineering associates

808 S.W. Broadway
Portland, OR 97205

24-320
1230

November 24 19 -- No. 217

PAY to the order of ___Crosswhite Wholesale Suppliers___ $ 839.64

___Eight hundred thirty-nine and 64/100---------------------------___ Dollars

PORTLAND NATIONAL BANK
PORTLAND, OREGON 97203

⑆1230⑈0320⑆ 143 0602 31⑈

Treasurer, young engineering associates

Detach This Stub Before
Cashing This Check

TO Crosswhite Wholesale Suppliers
499 Alamo Avenue, S.E.
Albuquerque, NM 87102

young engineering associates

808 S.W. Broadway
Portland, OR 97205

IN PAYMENT OF THE FOLLOWING INVOICES:

Date	Invoice	Amount
11/19	GJ-5032	332.28
11/20	GJ-5097	524.50
		856.78
	Less 2%	17.14
		839.64

Date: December 29, 19-- | Check No. 315 | To Cortland Wholesale Electrical Supply | Amount 669.50 Six hundred sixty-nine and 50/100 Dollars | TO Cortland Wholesale Electrical Supply 201 Homer Avenue, Cortland NY 13045 | Date 12/10 | Invoice HR-2169 | Amount 31250 | Date 12/15 | Invoice HR-2212 | Amount 357.00 (Total) 669.50

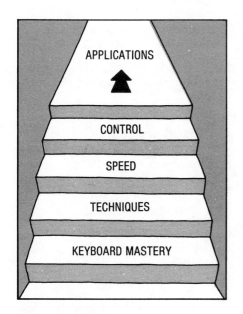

APPLICATIONS

CONTROL

SPEED

TECHNIQUES

KEYBOARD MASTERY

PHASE I: BASIC TYPING SKILLS

■ You are starting to learn a very useful skill. In our modern world most personal and business papers are typed rather than handwritten, for typing is both faster and more legible than handwriting.

■ Before you can put the typewriter to practical use, you must become skilled in operating its various parts.

In Phase 1 (39 lessons), you will learn:

1. To operate the letter, figure, symbol, and service keys by touch.
2. To type words, sentences, and paragraphs with speed and good techniques.
3. To type from printed, handwritten, and corrected copy.

UNIT 1   LESSONS 1-15

The Letter Keys

■ LESSON 1

1A ■ ARRANGE YOUR WORK AREA

1. Clear the desk of unneeded books and papers.
2. Move the typewriter so the front of the frame is even with the front edge of the desk or table.
3. Place this book to the right of the typewriter on a bookholder, or put something under the top of the book to raise it to a good reading position.

1B ■ KNOW YOUR TYPEWRITER

1. Typewriters are similar, but different makes may not have all parts in the same place. When you are asked to find a machine part, look at the illustration, guided by the part number, and find the part there; then locate that part on the typewriter you are to use.
2. Locate the **right platen (cylinder) knob (19)**.

3. **Drill:** Place the right thumb well under the **right platen (cylinder) knob (19)** and the first and second fingers on the top. TWIRL the knob two or three times with a quick movement of the fingers and thumb, without twisting the elbow or making unneeded wrist movements.

Work Assignment 5: Business Forms

Form 1—Postal Cards (5½″ x 3¼″)

HAD YOUR BRAKES CHECKED LATELY, MR. BAXTER?

Dependable brakes are the cheapest insurance around. Stop in soon at our shop or call us at 872-8418 for fast pickup/delivery service.

RADLETT BRAKE SERVICE - 131 S. MAIN
Burbank, CA 91506

Relining (parts and labor)	$10.00
Wheel alignment	7.00
Wheel balancing	6.00
Special for all of above	20.00

Problem 1: Tabulation on Postal Cards

Type 8 cards to the addressees listed below. On the first line on the message side, provide the appropriate title and surname.

Mr. Alan Baxter
3147 Collyer Avenue
Anaheim, CA 92805

Mrs. Boyd Bricker
27534 Cordova Blvd.
Alhambra, CA 91801

Mrs. Leslie Graham
3746 Kellogg Avenue
Glendale, CA 91203

Mr. Gordon Myers
299 North Cedar Street
Glendale, CA 91202

Mrs. Florence Norris
244 Bruce Lane
Burbank, CA 91504

Mrs. Dorothy O'Brien
1788 Bell Cyn Blvd.
Canoga Park, CA 91304

Mr. Al Parker
11402 Bellflower St.
Downey, CA 90241

Miss Jaye Sanders
12 East 25th Way
Long Beach, CA 90806

Form 2—Purchase Order

Problem 2: Purchase Order

Using the information given at the right below and the illustration of a purchase order as a model, type in attractive form a purchase order with 1 cc. Type the cc on a plain half sheet. Since there are only three lines used for the items in the order, type the items with single spacing.

KRAFT *Wholesale Hardware Co.*
Montgomery, OH 45242   (513) 891-6060

Purchase Order

Order No. C-26101

To
Morton and Jones
169 Scott Street
Covington, KY 41011

Date   March 30, 19--
Terms   2/15, n/30
Shipped Via   Truck

Quantity	Cat. No.	Description	Amount
40	AT-15287	Casement adjusters, rod and plate type 17A019	86.80
15	UM-64053	Casement window adjusters--#4703 BF, left hand	90.00
6 sets	YE-21435	#H14716 Stationary plate casters, plate size 2 3/4 in. x 3 3/4 in., rubber wheels	18.84
			195.64

BY_____

PURCHASING AGENT

To: | David Jackson Supply Co. | 719 Cleveland Avenue | Columbus, OH 43201 | *Order No.* 77274B | *Date:* November 23, 19-- | *Terms:* Net 30 days | *Shipped via:* Best way | *Quantity* 3 | *Cat. No.* EH-79531 | *Description* 220 v., 60 c. Emerson water heaters | *Amount* 241.85 | *Quantity* 2 doz. | *Cat. No.* FM-80567 | *Description* 3″ x 3″ x 1½″ y-branch copper fittings | *Amount* 62.40 | *Quantity* 550 ft. | *Cat. No.* RC-19047 | *Description* 3/8″ rigid copper tubing, Type C | *Amount* 148.50 (Total) 452.75

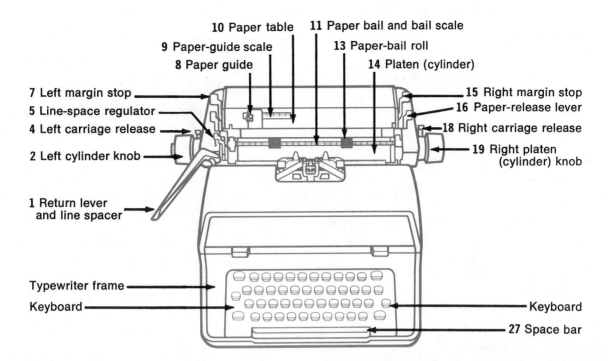

10 Paper table
9 Paper-guide scale
8 Paper guide
11 Paper bail and bail scale
13 Paper-bail roll
14 Platen (cylinder)

7 Left margin stop
5 Line-space regulator
4 Left carriage release
2 Left cylinder knob

15 Right margin stop
16 Paper-release lever
18 Right carriage release
19 Right platen (cylinder) knob

1 Return lever and line spacer

Typewriter frame
Keyboard
Keyboard
27 Space bar

1C ▪ INSERT PAPER

1. Locate on your typewriter the parts identified above (*and on Reference Guide pages i-ii*).

2. Adjust the **paper guide (8)** as directed on Reference Guide page iii, at the back of the book.

3. Place a full-size sheet of paper (8½″ x 11″) on the desk at the left of the typewriter, with the long side facing the front edge of the desk.

4. Pull the **paper bail (11)** forward—toward you—with your right hand.

5. Take a firm hold of the paper with your left hand, your thumb under the sheet and your fingers on the top (first illustration at right); bring the paper to the **platen (14)** and drop it between the platen and

paper table (10), the long edge against the **paper guide (8);** *at the same time,* bring the right hand to the **right platen knob (19)** and twirl knob with a quick movement of fingers and thumb.

6. Push paper bail down to hold paper against platen.

1D ▪ FINGER POSITION

1. Look at the keyboard shown at the right and locate **asdf** (home keys for the left hand) and **jkl;** (home keys for the right hand).

2. Look at your typewriter keyboard and locate the home keys. Place the fingers of your left hand on **asdf** and the fingers of your right hand on **jkl;**. *Keep your fingers curved.*

3. Remove your hands from the keyboard; then place your curved fingers in home position again, holding them lightly just above the keys. *Repeat two or three times.*

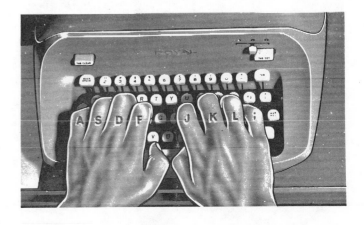

Augustine Insurance Agency

INTEROFFICE COMMUNICATION

TO: B. F. Keifer, NYHO   DATE: December 12, 19--   7

FROM: Don Rives, SERO   SUBJECT: Rowan County Nurses   15

                                    Association   17

The Rowan County Nurses Association ~~has been contacted as~~ *is* a   25
potential group annuity prospect. A review of the Association   38
membership has revealed the following pertinent data: 49

  1. There are over 200 active members.   57
  2. All members are females.   63
  3. The average income if $6,600. *of the members*   69
  4. The average ~~member~~ age is 38.   78
  5. Participation in the pension plan eventually selected   121
     will be mandatory. *by Rowan County, nurses must be*   125
  6. The nurses ~~cannot~~ accept employment, ~~unless they are~~ mem-   90
     bers of the Association.   95
  7. Membership dues are paid to the Association on a monthly   107
     basis.   109

The committee named to select an insurance ~~carrier to~~ under-   135
write *a* pension plan for the association is a strongly supporter of   147
our Company. The committee has *already* ~~prior to this date~~ approved a   157
deferred annuity proposal recommended by this office. The financing   171
of this proposal is to come from the membership dues. By this   183
method the Association can establish a pension plan on a noncon-   196
tributory basis. ~~This procedure would~~ eliminat*ing* much of the   204
clerical work ~~which would be~~ required *with a* ~~were the~~ plan on a contribu-   214
tory basis. ¶ *Regarding* ~~Because of~~ the problem of establishing the employer-   227
employee relationship required by the Internal Revenue Serv. *(spell)* and   240
the State of N.C. *(spell)*, I contacted our legal department and have re-   251
ceived a memo from J. P. Spellman of that department giving their   268
approval of solicitation of this Association as a group annuity   281
prospect. This approval, however, relates only to the legal require-   295
ments of the State of North Carolina. Before *we* proceeding with ~~any~~   307
further solicitation, can you tell me if this basic-type pension   320
plan will meet the IRS requirements, thereby qualifying the   332
Association for tax relief under section 101(c) of the Internal   345
Revenue Code?   348

1E ■ KEY STROKING AND SPACING

NOTE: If you are using an electric typewriter, turn the ON-OFF switch to ON POSITION.

LEARN: Type **f** with the left first finger (the index finger); then type **j** with the right first finger. Strike each key with a quick, snap stroke (see illustration). ▶

DO: Type ffjj three times: ffjjffjjffjj

READ: To space after typing a letter or a word, operate the **space bar (27)** with a quick down-and-in motion of the right thumb.

DO: Operate the space bar once; then TYPE **f j** (with a space after each letter) three times. The completed line should look like this:

ffjjffjjffjj f j f j f j

DO: On the same line on which you typed **f j** type the home keys **asdf jkl;** twice, with a space after each letter group. The completed line should look like this:

ffjjffjjffjj f j f j f j asdf jkl; asdf jkl;

1F ■ CARRIAGE (or Element Carrier) RETURN

■ The **return lever (1)** on a manual typewriter or the **return key (1)** on an electric is used to space the paper up and make the return to the beginning of the line. This return is made as described below and illustrated at the right. ▶

Manual (Nonelectric). Move the left hand, fingers bracing one another, to the carriage return lever and move the lever inward to take up the slack; then return the carriage with a quick wrist and hand motion. Drop the hand to typing position without letting it follow the carriage across.

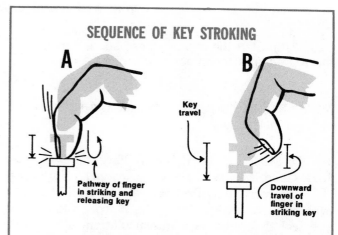

SEQUENCE OF KEY STROKING

A **B**

Key travel

Pathway of finger in striking and releasing key

Downward travel of finger in striking key

A. Strike each key with a firm, sharp stroke and release it quickly. Keep most of the stroking action in the fingers; hold the hands and arms quiet.

B. Snap the finger *slightly* toward the palm of the hand as you release the key. Do not let the finger follow the key all the way down. Striking and releasing a key should be one motion with the release motion started almost at the same instant as the downward motion of the finger.

KNOW YOUR TYPEWRITER: Each work station should be supplied with a pamphlet giving operating instructions for the typewriter to be used. The manufacturers of the typewriters will furnish these to the school. An operating manual is especially useful when the Selectric typewriter is to be used because this machine has some operating features that are not common to other typewriters, either electric or nonelectric (manual).

■ If an operating manual is available, study it carefully and *know your typewriter.*

Electric and Selectric. Reach the little finger of the right hand to the return key, tap the key lightly, release it quickly, and return the finger to its typing position.
■ On the Selectric the return key returns the **element carrier** (not the carriage) to the left margin.

Type the following interoffice memorandums (refer to page 210). Start the heading lines about 1 inch from the top edge of the sheet.

Memo 1 (Plain sheets ▪ 1″ side margins ▪ 1 cc ▪ correct your errors)

Words

TO: **D. M. Fairchild, Chicago Office** │ *FROM:*   9
J. H. Gadd, MWRO │ *DATE: (Current)* │ *SUB-*   17
JECT: **Harper Clinic Proposal** (¶ 1) We have   25
evaluated the proposal for the Harper Clinic   34
and feel that there is a miscalculation in the   43
dependent coverage rate. Our check indicates   52
a rate of $20.19 contrasted with your rate of   62
$18.77. (¶ 2) Will you please check this item   70
so that we can process the proposal.   78

Memo 2 (Plain sheets ▪ 1″ side margins ▪ 2 cc's ▪ correct your errors)

TO: **J. H. Gadd, MWRO** │ *FROM:* **D. M. Fair-**   8
child, Chicago Office │ *DATE: (1 week from*   16
current date) │ *SUBJECT:* **Harper Clinic Pro-**   22
posal, Dependent Coverage Rate (¶ 1) The   29
dependent coverage rate for the Harper Clinic   38
Proposal should have been $20.19, as you indi-   47
cated in your memo to me. I am attaching a   56
corrected proposal to replace the incorrect   64
copy. (¶ 2) Thanks for calling this error to my   73
attention. I am informing the salesman of rec-   82
ord, Hal Drew, of the change. cc H. Drew │   91
Attachment   93

Memo 3 (Plain sheets ▪ 1″ side margins ▪ 1 cc ▪ arrange table in attractive form)

TO: **W. E. Julius, NYHO** │ *FROM:* **J. H. Gadd,**   9
MWRO │ *DATE: (Current)* │ *SUBJECT:* **GAC**   17
#719, Clingman Construction Co. (¶ 1) Mr.   24
P. J. Karg, secretary-treasurer of the Clingman   34
Construction Co., has notified me that several   43
of their employees have decided to join that   52
company's pension plan. (¶ 2) Pertinent infor-   60
mation regarding these applicants is as follows: 70

Name	Sex	Birthdate	Date Hired	Annual Salary	
					72
					84
F. A. Linden	M	1/22/46	10/4/71	5,200	92
Mary Mertz	F	10/4/47	9/11/71	4,900	99
Jean Napier	F	11/29/40	10/31/71	7,200	106
David Phelps	M	6/5/33	9/2/71	5,400	113
J. J. Wolnitzek	F	3/12/38	10/31/71	10,800	122

Words

(¶ 3) Please furnish the total pension costs for   130
each employee, the new monthly estimated   138
stipulated payments required to fund the plan,   148
and the employer and employee contribution   156
split. (¶ 4) Will you please see that the indi-   165
vidual certificates for the employees listed   174
above are sent to Mr. Karg. He will need this   183
information soon, as it takes a week to ten days   193
to make the needed changes in the payroll   201
tapes and forms. I understand that the Cling-   210
man Construction Co. would like to include in   219
their pension plan the employees listed above   229
as soon as the forms can be processed and the   238
necessary payroll record changes made. (¶ 5)   246
Thanks for all your good help.   253

Memo 4 (Plain sheets ▪ 1″ side margins ▪ 1 cc ▪ arrange table in attractive form)

TO: **B. F. Keifer, NYHO** │ *FROM:* **J. H. Gadd,**   9
MWRO │ *DATE:* **November 20, 19——** │ *SUB-*   15
JECT: **GAC #543, Dobson Heat & Air Condi-**   23
tioning Co. (¶ 1) Mr. J. R. Roda, controller   31
of the subject company, called me to say that   40
he was unable to reconcile his records with our   49
monthly estimated stipulated payment due on   58
December 1 to meet the company's pension   66
liability. A service call upon Mr. Roda revealed   76
the following information: (1) There is no   85
disagreement on the payment made on Novem-   93
ber 1, and (2) the source of confusion seems to   103
center around four employees who received   111
wage increases between November 1 and   119
November 15. I, too, was unable to reconcile   128
their records with our statement. (¶ 2) I have   136
persuaded Mr. Roda to send us a check for the   146
full amount that we show due as of December   154
1 with the understanding that we will adjust,   164
in the payment due on January 1, any error   172
discovered meanwhile. (¶ 3) Here is the infor-   180
mation about the employees that you will need   189
for your checkup.   193

Name	Cert. No.	NRD	Former Salary/Wage	Adjusted Salary/Wage	
					198
					211
H. Marazzi	171	1/85	115/wk.	125/wk.	219
D. McDevitt	157	12/81	2.85/hr.	2.95/hr.	227
R. Bahl	231	5/98	95/wk.	99/wk.	233
C. De Haan	112	10/74	12,000/yr.	13,000/yr.	241

(¶ 4) Please send Mr. Roda and me an analy-   247
sis of your findings when you have checked the   257
rate change on these four employees.   265

1G ■ TAKE CORRECT TYPING POSITION as illustrated

1. Body erect; sit back in the chair.

2. Feet on the floor, one just ahead of the other.

3. Fingers curved and upright over second row of keys.

4. Wrists low and relaxed.

5. Forearms parallel to the slant of the keyboard; elbows in a comfortable position at sides of body.

6. Eyes on the copy (at the right of the typewriter).

1H ■ STROKING PRACTICE

TYPE the practice lines twice; then, if time permits, retype the lines, trying to type with smooth, continuous stroking. *Do not type the line numbers or identifications.*

Stroking Cue: With your fingers curved and held lightly in home position, strike and release one key quickly; then strike the next key in the same way.

1	*F*	*J*	ff f ff f jj j jj j ff f jj j fj fj fj ff jj fj fj	*Return without spacing after final stroke in the line*
2	*D*	*K*	dd d dd d kk k kk k dd d kk k dk dk dk dd kk dk dk	
3	*S*	*L*	ss s ss s ll l ll l ss s ll l sl sl sl ss ll sl sl	
4	*A*	*;*	aa a aa a ;; ; ;; ; aa a ;; ; a; a; a; aa ;; a; a;	
5	*Home keys*		fd fds fdsa jk jkl jkl; fd fds fdsa jk jkl jkl; fj	
6	*Home keys*		as ask ask ad lad lad all fall all fall ask a lad;	

1I ■ END-OF-LESSON ACTIVITY: REMOVE THE PAPER; CENTER THE CARRIAGE; TURN ELECTRICS OFF

1. Raise or pull forward the **paper bail (11)**. Operate the **paper-release lever (16)** with your right hand.

2. Remove the paper with your left hand. Return the paper-release lever to its normal position.

3. Depress the **right carriage release (18)** and hold the platen knob firmly. Move the carriage so it is *approximately* centered.

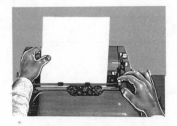 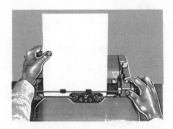 

Problem 3: Employment Form (Type a specimen form; then type the fill-in information appropriate for you.)

Application for
Employment

GENERAL HEATING CORPORATION
Minneapolis, Minnesota

- -

Date_____

Name_____
　　　　　　　　　　Last　　　　　　　　First　　　　　　Middle

Address_____
　　　　Street and Number　　　　City　　　　State　　　　Zip Code

Telephone Number_____ Social Security No._____

Date of Birth_____ Birthplace_____ U.S. Citizen____
　　　　　　　　　　　　　　　　　　　　　　　　　　　　　　　　Yes/No

Age_____ Weight_____ Height_____ 　Male ( ) 　Female ( )

Single ( ) 　Married ( ) 　Widowed ( ) 　Separated ( ) 　Divorced ( )

EDUCATION RECORD

	Name and Address of School	From Year	To Year	Degree or Diploma
Grammar				
High School				
College				
Other				

EMPLOYMENT RECORD
(Show latest employment first)

From Mo. Yr.	To Mo. Yr.	Name and Address of Employer	Position	Salary	Reason for Leaving

PERSONAL REFERENCES*

Name	Address	Occupation

*If you have never been employed, give
names of at least two responsible persons
(not relatives) to whom we may refer.

Signature_____

LESSON 2

2A ■ GET READY TO TYPE

1. Clear the desk of unneeded items.
2. Place this book to the right of the typewriter, the top of the book raised slightly.
3. Have front of typewriter frame even with front edge of desk or table.
4. Pull the **paper bail (11)** forward.
5. Adjust the **paper guide (8)**.
6. Place paper at left of typewriter, long side toward you.
7. Insert paper.

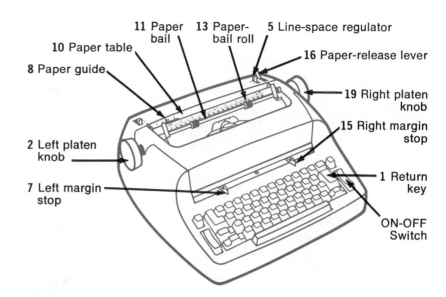

11 Paper bail
13 Paper-bail roll
5 Line-space regulator
10 Paper table
8 Paper guide
16 Paper-release lever
19 Right platen knob
15 Right margin stop
2 Left platen knob
1 Return key
7 Left margin stop
ON-OFF Switch

2B ■ KNOW YOUR TYPEWRITER: LINE-SPACE REGULATOR

■ The **line-space regulator** (5) determines the spacing of typed copy—single, double, or triple spacing. Set the regulator on "1" for single-spacing the lines you are to type in the lessons of this unit.

■ When so directed, set on "2" for double spacing or on "3" for triple spacing.

■ Single-spaced (SS) copy has no blank line space between lines; double-spaced (DS) copy has 1 blank line space; and triple-spaced (TS) copy has 2 blank line spaces between lines.

```
1 SS is used to type this line and the next.
                                              SS
2 DS is used to type this line and the next.
3          (1 blank line space)            DS
4 TS is used to type this line and the next.
5
6          (2 blank line spaces)           TS
7 DS has 1 and TS has 2 blank line spaces.
```

2C ■ TYPING POSITION

1. Body erect; sit well back in the chair.
2. Feet on the floor, one slightly ahead of the other, for better balance.
3. Forearms parallel to slant of keyboard; wrists low and relaxed.
4. Fingers deeply curved and upright over home-row keys.
5. Elbows near (but not "hugging") the body.
6. Eyes on the copy at right of typewriter.

2D ■ CONDITIONING PRACTICE type the lines as shown

LEARN: To double-space (DS) when the line-space regulator is set for single spacing (SS), operate the return lever or key *twice* as you make the return. DS after the second typing of the lines below.

Stroking Cue: Strike and release each key quickly. Snap the finger slightly toward the palm of the hand as you release the key. Do not let the finger follow the key all the way down. (See page 3.)

Spacing Cue: Keep right thumb close to space bar. Space with down-and-in motion.

```
1   fff f jjj j ddd d kkk k sss s lll l aaa a ;;; ; fj
2   fff f jjj j ddd d kkk k sss s lll l aaa a ;;; ; fj
3                                                       DS (double-space)
4   fj dk fj dk fj dk sl a; sl a; sl a; fj dk sl a; fj
5   fj dk fj dk fj dk sl a; sl a; sl a; fj dk sl a; fj
6                                                       DS
7   fasdf j;lkj fasdf j;lkj as ask; ad lad; ask a lad;
8   fasdf j;lkj fasdf j;lkj as ask; ad lad; ask a lad;
```
Space once after ; used as punctuation

Problem 1: Table (Arrange in good form; full sheet; reading position)

			Words
CANFIELD CORPORATION			4
DS			
Income (In Thousands of Dollars) by Major Business			14

	Income *		Words
	1971	**1970**	17 / 21
Agriculture, land development	$ 28,056	$ 22,196	30
Chemicals	14,165	19,290	35
Intergroup sales	---	---	41
Investments	1,592	6,109	46
Manufacturing			49
Portsmouth Shipbuilding	23,394	29,430	57
Gaudin Manufacturing	33,249	27,694	64
J. I. Carter	13,074	3,179	69
Natural gas pipelines	160,521	120,815	77
Oil production, refining, marketing	91,133	77,606	87
Packaging	18,631	18,087	95
Total	$383,815	$324,406	106

109

* Before interest, federal income taxes, outside stockholders' interest, and extraordinary items. Income must be evaluated in terms of capital investment required, which varies widely by type of business.

123
137
150

Problem 2: Table (Arrange in good form; full sheet; reading position)

Pedestrian Actions Resulting in] all caps
Deaths and Injuries

Actions	Pedestrians Killed	Percent	Pedestrians Injured	Percent	Words
					6 / 10 / 24 / 31 / 38 / 52
Crossing at Intersection:					58
With Signal	400	4.4	21,700	7.9	64
Against Signal	770	8.6	26,000	9.5	71
No Signal	670	7.4	22,300	8.1	77
Diagonally	40	.4	1,900	.7	82
Crossing Between Intersections	3,670	40.8	86,800	31.6	93
Standing on Safety Isle			300	.1	99
Getting on or off Other Vehicle	80	.9	4,400	1.6	108
Children Playing in Street	300	3.3	17,300	6.3	118
At Work in Road	250	2.8	5,000	1.8	125
Riding or Hitching on Vehicle			300	.1	132
Coming from Behind Parked Car	620	6.9	46,200	16.8	142
Walking on Rural Highway	1,400	15.6	20,900	7.6	151
Not on Roadway	420	4.7	9,900	3.6	158
Miscellaneous	380	4.2	11,700	4.3	165 / 172
Total	9,000	100.0	274,700	100.0	179 / 193

2E ■ KNOW YOUR TYPEWRITER: MARGIN STOPS

READ: When the **left margin stop (7)** and the **right margin stop (15)** are positioned properly, your typed lines will be centered horizontally on the page. When the right margin stop is set, a bell will ring to warn that the end of the writing line is near.

■ Some typewriters have hand-set margin stops (first three illustrations at the right); other typewriters have key-set margin stops (last illustration).

HAND SET

HAND SET

HAND SET

KEY SET

DO:

1. Compare the illustrations at the left with your typewriter to determine whether it has hand-set or key-set margin stops.

2. Set the **left margin stop (7)** 25 spaces to the left of the approximate center of the paper for the beginning of a 50-space line.

3. Move the **right margin stop (15)** to the end of the scale.

■ You will type the copy in the lessons of the first units of this book line for line and will not need the right margin stop to indicate the end of the line.

2F ■ CONTINUITY PRACTICE   type the lines as shown

Take correct typing position with the fingers curved and held lightly on the home keys.

Practice Cue: Type at a steady, even pace––one stroke after the other without pausing between them.

1		as ask ad fad lad sad asks lads all fall all falls
2		as ask ad fad lad sad asks lads all fall all falls
3		DS (double-space)
4	*Space once*	a lad; a sad lad; a fad; a fall fad; ask all lads;
5	*after ; used*	a lad; a sad lad; a fad; a fall fad; ask all lads;
6	*as punctuation*	DS
7		ask dad; a lad asks dad; ask all dads; a fall fad;
8		ask dad; a lad asks dad; ask all dads; a fall fad;
9		DS
10		all fall; all fall ads; a sad fall; all fall fads;
11		all fall; all fall ads; a sad fall; all fall fads;

2G ■ REMOVE THE PAPER; CENTER THE CARRIAGE; TURN ELECTRICS OFF

1. Raise or pull forward the **paper bail (11).** Operate the **paper-release lever (16).**

2. Remove the paper with your left hand. Return the paper-release lever to its normal position.

3. Depress the right **carriage release (18).** Move the carriage so it is centered.

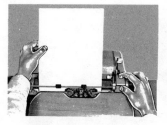

End-of-Lesson Activity	Pick up all waste paper. Push chair to the desk as you leave.

Words

Typist: Bring material from page 1 as necessary. Then type this table in attractive form.

	Social Security Benefit	Salary Continuance Benefit	Total Monthly Income	
				356
				362
DS				371
If single OR				373
if married and				376
wife under age 62	$127	$293	$420	383
If married with				386
one or more children				390
under age 18	254	196	450	395

You are eligible for the plan if you — 402

are a regular full-time salaried employee — 411

whose basic rate of pay is $4,800 a year or — 420

more and if you have completed one — 427

year of service with the Corporation. Date — 436

of eligibility occurs on the first of the — 444

month coinciding with or next following — 452

one full year of employment. — 458

To enroll in the plan, you should — 465

complete and sign the enrollment form — 472

provided for this purpose. — 478

■ LESSON 3

3A ■ GET READY TO TYPE

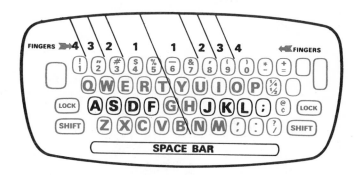

1. **Desk:** Clear it of unneeded books and papers.

2. **Book:** Place it to the right of the typewriter, the top of the book raised slightly.

3. **Typewriter Frame:** Have front frame even with edge of desk.

4. **Paper Guide (8):** Adjust it as directed for your typewriter.

5. **Paper Bail (11):** Adjust it as directed for your typewriter.

6. **Paper:** Place at left of typewriter, long side toward you. Insert as directed on page 2.

7. **Paper Release (16):** Be sure it is in position.

8. **Line-Space Regulator (5):** Set on "1" for single spacing.

9. **Margin Sets:** Set **left margin stop (7)** 25 spaces to left of approximate center of paper; move **right margin stop (15)** to end of scale.

3B ■ CONDITIONING PRACTICE   type the lines as shown

DO: Type each line twice as shown; the first time at an easy pace, the second time more rapidly.

Technique Cue: Curve the fingers; type with quick, snap strokes; keep hands and arms quiet.

1 *Start each*
2 *new line*
3 *without pausing*

```
fa fasdf j; j;lkj fdsa jkl; ff jj dd kk ss ll aa ;
fa fasdf j; j;lkj fdsa jkl; ff jj dd kk ss ll aa ;
```
DS (double-space)

4
5
6

```
fj dk sl a; fa fs fd j; jl jk s l d k f j a;sldkfj
fj dk sl a; fa fs fd j; jl jk s l d k f j a;sldkfj
```
DS

7
8

```
all fall ad lad fad as ask asks all ads ask a lad;
all fall ad lad fad as ask asks all ads ask a lad;
```
TS (triple-space: operate return 3 times)

3C ■ KNOW YOUR TYPEWRITER: PICA AND ELITE TYPE

LEARN: The large letters and figures in the illustrations below are in PICA type; the small, in ELITE type. Look at your typed lines. Does your typewriter have pica type or elite type?

```
1234567890     Pica type has 10 spaces to the horizontal inch.
|. . . . . . . . . .1|    1|       2|       3|       4|       5
|. . . . . . . . . . .1|    1|       2|       3|       4|       5
123456789012   Elite type has 12 spaces to the horizontal inch.
```

LEARN: Pica center, 42; elite, 50.

■ Typing paper is usually 8½ inches wide. It has 85 pica or 102 elite spaces (8½ × 10 = 85; 8½ × 12 = 102). The center of the paper is at 42½ for pica type and at 51 for elite type; but you will *use 42 for pica and 50 for elite center.*

■ By changing the placement of the paper guide, you can insert the paper so that 50 will be the center point for pica as well as for elite type, if you are so directed.

DO:

■ Remove the paper from the machine. Place the top left and right edges together. Make a slight crease at the exact center at the top. Reinsert the paper with the center at 42 for pica or at 50 for elite (or whatever center you are directed to use).

■ Move the paper guide against the left edge of the paper. Check to see that it is in this position at the beginning of each practice period.

Problem 4: Topbound Business Report

Top margin, first page: 2½"

Words

SALARY CONTINUANCE PLAN FOR SALARIED EMPLOYEES) *Center both lines*   9
Tri-State Compressor Corp. DS   16
TS *spell*

¶ What is the Plan?

It is an insured plan that will pay you 70% of the first $750.00 *spell* of your   39

basic monthly earnings in the event ʌ*that* you are disabled for an expended period of   55

time. In addition, it will pay 50% of ʌthe basic monthly earnings in excess of $750. *spell your*   74

Any monthly benefits payable under any applicable federal, state, or muni-   89

ciple workmen's compensation act or occupational ʌ*disease* ideaser law, the Federal   104

Social Security Act, or any similar law will reduce the monthly benefit payable   120

from the ~~salary continuance~~ plan. The maximum benefit payable by this plan   145

shall not exceed: 149

1. $1,500 a month, or   153

2. 75% of employees basic monthly earnings ʌ*less* ~~reduced by~~ the total amount the   169
employee is entitled to receive from total monthly benefits of any federal,   184
state, or municipal compensation act where applicable, whichever is less.   199

The minimum benefit received from this plan shall be $50 *a* ~~per~~ month.

Benefit payments under the plan will begin six months following the date *that*   214

disability originates, ʌ*unless* ~~if~~ you ~~not~~ ʌ*are* receiving sick (-leave) payments from the Corpora-   231

tion, *beyond* ~~past~~ that date. If you ~~do~~ receive sick-leave payments for longer than six   247

months, benefit payments will begin ~~on~~ the first of the month ~~that~~ following the   262

expiration of the sick-leave payments. Benefit payments are payable for life if   278

disability results from an acci*d*ent; to age 65 for disability caused by ʌ*an* illness.   295

To illustrate the plan, let us assume that an employee ʌ*who* earns $600 *a* ~~per~~ month   311

~~and~~ is totally disabled by an accident occur*r*ing off the job. After his sick   325

leave is discontinued or six months after the accident, whichever is ʌ*later* ~~the latest~~,   341

his total monthly disability income would be as follows: 352

Typist: Take to top of page 2 of report as necessary.

3D ■ NEW KEY LOCATION: H, E, LEFT SHIFT KEY

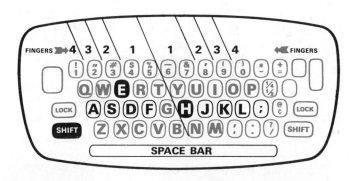

1. Find the new key on the typewriter keyboard chart at the right.
2. Locate the new key on your typewriter keyboard.
3. Study the reach illustration for the new key.
4. Type the reach technique drill on one line.

REACH TECHNIQUE FOR H

Reach the *right first finger* to the left to type **h** without moving the other fingers from their home keys.

```
hj hj hh jhj jhj hh hj hj
hj has had hj has had has  DS
```

REACH TECHNIQUE FOR E

Reach the *left second finger* to **e**, lifting the first finger slightly to free the controlling finger.

```
ed ed ee ded ded ee ed ed
ed led led ed led fed led  DS
```

CONTROL OF LEFT SHIFT KEY

Hold the **left shift key (28)** down with the *left little finger* until the capital letter has been typed. Release quickly.

```
Ha Hal Hall Ha Hale Hakes
Hal Hakes led; Jake fled;  TS
```

3E ■ STROKING TECHNIQUE PRACTICE type 2 copies of the drill as shown

RECALL: Operate the return lever or key twice (double-space) to leave one blank line space between two-line groups, three times (triple-space) to leave two blank line spaces between lesson parts.

Stroking Cue: Snap the finger slightly toward the palm of the hand as you release a key. Do not let the finger follow the key all the way down. Strike and release the key in one continuous motion.

Do not type the line numbers or identifications.

```
1  H              hj hj hh ha has had hal half hall shall hj has had
2                 hj hj hh ha has had hal half hall shall hj has had
                                                                        DS (double-space)
3  E              ed ed ded led fed ee seek safe sale lead jade sell
4                 ed ed ded led fed ee seek safe sale lead jade sell

5  H    E         he he she she heed held head heads heal hale shelf
6                 he he she she heed held head heads heal hale shelf

7  Left shift key Ja Ha La Ja Jake Ha Hal La Lake Jake Hall; Hal Lee
8                 Ja Ha La Ja Jake Ha Hal La Lake Jake Hall; Hal Lee

9                 Jeff Lake has a safe ad; Hal Hall heads all sales;
10  All letters   Jeff Lake has a safe ad; Hal Hall heads all sales;
    learned
    are used
11  in Lines 9-12 He asked Jake Hale; he feels she has a safe lease;
12                He asked Jake Hale; he feels she has a safe lease;
                                                                        TS (triple-space)
```

	Words
neighborhood of a certain plant or	769
office; or near the airport.	775
3. Facilities. Will your employer need to	784
provide a meeting room or to serve	791
refreshments (as formal as a banquet	798
or as informal as a buffet of snacks	806
and beverages).	809

Typing the Itinerary	817

	Words
From your file of confirmed arrangements,	826
type the plans in a complete, accurate, easy-to-	835
read form. List chronologically the events of	845
each day and all important details of each	853
event. Use airline, airport, and railroad station	863
names; flight numbers; exact departure and	872
arrival times, including time zones (4:28 p.m.	883
EST, for instance). With a zone other than	893
yours, state that the time is given in the local	902
(destination) time. Show any arrangements	911
made for connecting transportation and the	920
time required (as Limousine to hotel, 1 hour).	934
State whether tickets are attached or are to be	944
picked up.	946
In listing a meeting, note the exact sched-	955
uled time, the exact location (street address	964
and room number--hotels may have many	972
meeting rooms), and any papers to go to that	981
meeting. Provide an appropriate telephone	989
number whenever you can.	994
The final, extremely important step is to	1003
check your work. Your employer must be able	1015
to depend on your accuracy. He may not have	1024
time to check your plans or, more disastrously,	1033
to correct an error once he finds it. An execu-	1043
tive leaving hastily for a trip has a hundred and	1053
one things on his mind. Give him the confi-	1061
dence of an accurate itinerary.	1068

---

[1] Lois Hutchinson, Standard Handbook for Secretaries (8th ed.; New York: McGraw-Hill Book Co., 1969), p. 550. (32 words)

[2] Official Airline Guide (Chicago: Reuben H. Donnelley Corp., 1972), pp. 2-28. (20 words)

[3] Road Atlas, the United States, Canada, and Mexico (New York: Rand-McNally & Co., 1969), inside back cover. (31 words)

[4] J Marshall Hanna, Estelle L. Popham, and Esther Kihn Beamer, Secretarial Procedures and Administration (5th ed.; Cincinnati:

South-Western Publishing Co., 1968), p. 377. (43 words)

[5] Hotel & Motel Red Book (New York: American Hotel Association Directory Corp., 1971), pp. B1-B112. (26 words)

Problem 2: Outline for Manuscript

Top margin same as Ms. p. 1 ■ 1½″ left margin ■ use vertical spacing style for outlines

	Words
GETTING YOUR BOSS FROM HERE TO THERE--AND BACK	9
I. INTRODUCTION	13
II. PRELIMINARY WORK	17
III. PLANNING AND SCHEDULING THE TRIP	25
A. Air Travel	28
B. Automobile Travel	33
C. Train Travel	37
D. Overnight Accommodations	42
IV. TYPING THE ITINERARY	

Problem 3: Bibliography for Manuscript

Top margin same as Ms. p. 1 ■ 1½″ left margin ■ use heading BIBLIOGRAPHY ■ SS each item ■ DS between items ■ indent second and subsequent lines 5 spaces

	Words
Hanna, J Marshall, Estelle L. Popham, and	8
Esther Kihn Beamer. Secretarial Proce-	19
dures and Administration, 5th ed. Cincin-	32
nati: South-Western Publishing Co., 1968.	41
Hotel & Motel Red Book. New York: Ameri-	53
can Hotel Association Directory Corpora-	61
tion, 1971.	63
Hutchinson, Lois. Standard Handbook for Sec-	77
retaries, 8th ed. New York: McGraw-Hill	87
Book Co., 1969.	90
Official Airline Guide. Chicago: Reuben H.	104
Donnelley Corporation, 1972.	109
Road Atlas, the United States, Canada, and	126
Mexico. New York: Rand-McNally & Com-	135
pany, 1969.	137

■ LESSON 4

4A ■ GET READY TO TYPE 3 *

1. **Paper Guide (8) and Paper Bail (11):** Adjust them as directed for your typewriter.

2. **Paper Release (16):** Be sure it is in position.

3. **Line-Space Regulator (5):** Set on "1" for single spacing (SS).

4. **Margin Stops:** Set **left margin stop (7)** 25 spaces to left of center of paper; move **right margin stop (15)** to end of scale.

5. **Ribbon Control (22):** Set as directed in 4B below.

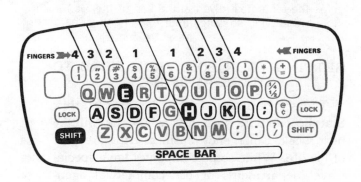

4B ■ KNOW YOUR TYPEWRITER: RIBBON CONTROL 5

■ The **ribbon control (22)** can be set to type on the upper or lower part of the ribbon if there are three adjustments on your typewriter for this control. If there are four adjustments, the typing will be on the upper, middle, or lower part of the ribbon. Set the ribbon control to type on the upper part of the ribbon. Make this a part of your daily Get Ready to Type.

REMEMBER:

1. A full-length line on paper 8½ inches wide has 85 pica or 102 elite spaces. (See illustration on page 7.)

2. There are 10 pica or 12 elite spaces to a horizontal inch; therefore, use 42 for pica or 50 for elite center unless directed to use another center point.

4C ■ CONDITIONING PRACTICE 7 type the copy as shown

First Writing: Type the first line of each pair at a slow, easy pace. Work for precise stroking.

Second Writing: Type the second line of each pair at a quicker pace. Move from key to key quickly; keep the carriage (or carrier) moving.

Technique Cue: Keep the fingers curved and in home-key position except when a reach-stroke is to be made; then extend the controlling finger (relaxing the curvature only as much as you must to reach the key). Make the reach without moving the hand forward or downward.

```
1    fj a; sl dk fj fds jkl fdsa jkl; a;sldkfj a;sldkfj
2    fj a; sl dk fj fds jkl fdsa jkl; a;sldkfj a;sldkfj
```
DS (double-space)

```
3    hj ed he she ads desks feels heed seek shall shale
4    hj ed he she ads desks feels heed seek shall shale
```

```
5  Shift quickly,   Les Lee; Hal Leeds; Jess Lake; Jake Haas; Lee Hess
6  but firmly       Les Lee; Hal Leeds; Jess Lake; Jake Haas; Lee Hess
```
TS (triple-space)

---

*A time schedule for the parts of this lesson and the following ones is given as a guide for your minimum practice. The number of minutes is shown as a figure within a square:
3 If the schedule permits, retype selected lines from the various drills of the lesson.

Problem 1: Leftbound Manuscript

Leftbound style ■ top margins, 1½″ for pica and 2″ for elite ■ SS enumerated items ■ DS between them ■ type the footnotes (given at the end of the Ms.) at the foot of the page on which their reference figures occur

Words

GETTING YOUR BOSS FROM HERE TO THERE--AND BACK — 9

Today's businessman can be sure of this: 18
that he can't be sure just where he will be 27
next week. Emergency business trips are part 36
of his life. While some companies have special 45
travel departments or use commercial agen- 54
cies, many executives must rely on their secre- 63
taries to make their travel arrangements while 72
they themselves are busy elsewhere. The top- 81
notch secretary must be able to do this quickly 91
--and often under pressure. 97

Preliminary Work — 103

When your employer asks you to plan his 111
trip, get then all the information that you will 121
need and avoid later interruptions. Note dates 131
of departure and return, all destinations to be 140
included, and the place and time of all meet- 149
ings or appointments to be included in your 158
plans. Determine the company policy on trans- 167
portation (first class or economy), whether a 176
specific hotel system must be used when pos- 185
sible, your employer's personal preferences, 194
and any special circumstances that would 202
affect your planning. Ask, also, whether your 211
employer will use credit cards (company or 220
personal) or cash and travelers' checks. You 229
will need to know this in making reservations 238
later. 240

As you gather all preliminary information, 248
follow Hutchinson's advice: 254

A trip folder should be started, into 262
which are put timetables; tickets; . . . 270
confirmations; letters and memorandums 277
regarding appointments . . . to be kept, 285
conferences held, topics discussed, mate- 293
rial used, speeches made.[1] 298

Planning and Scheduling the Trip — 311

Air travel. To save time in making airline 322
reservations, subscribe to the Official Airline 335
Guide. The publisher supplies you with cur- 345
rent information on all scheduled flights, fares, 355
and other data. The opening pages of this 363
guide give complete instructions for its use.[2] 373
In selecting a flight, allow enough time to get 382
to and from airports and to transfer to any 391
connecting flights. Note all the necessary data, 401
call the airline reservation desk, and make the 411
final arrangements. 415

Automobile travel. If your employer plans 427
to drive a rented car, he will usually have not 437
only a preference of rental agency but also its 446
credit card. If not, use any of the agencies 455
listed in the Yellow Pages of the telephone 464
directory. Whether driving his own or a rented 475
car, your employer will need to know the best 484
route and the approximate driving time to his 493
destination. An atlas, such as the Rand- 501
McNally Road Atlas, the United States, Can- 516
ada, and Mexico, gives routing information and 529
even approximate driving times.[3] 536

Train travel. While passenger-train use has 547
declined in recent years, some areas (as be- 556
tween Washington, D.C., and New York City) 564
still offer fast, convenient service. Or your 574
employer may want to travel in a sleeping car 583
and arrive in the morning at the center of the 592
city. "Each railroad publishes its own timetable 602
folder and supplies it free to prospective trav- 612
elers and to passengers."[4] 617

Overnight accommodations. Another "must" 630
for your office library is a current copy of the 640
Hotel & Motel Red Book. This book gives you 654
the facts you need for reserving satisfactory 663
accommodations and also, in a special "blue 672
pages" section, lists hotels and motels that pro- 681
vide business meeting facilities.[5] 688

Among the things that you should consider 697
in your choice are these: 702

1. Hotel or motel. Most large cities now 711
   have both conventional hotels and 718
   "motor hotels" in the downtown area. 725
   A small city will likely have downtown 733
   hotels and outlying motels. 739
2. Location. Will your employer need to 747
   stay downtown, near restaurants and 754
   entertainment facilities; in the general 762

4D ■ REINFORCEMENT PRACTICE ☐15 type 2 copies of the drill as shown

Typing One-Hand Words: Type by stroke response (one letter at a time) but pass from one letter to the next quickly. Speed up the typing by eliminating pauses between strokes.

Typing Double Letters: MANUAL (NONELECTRIC)—— Use a short, quick stroke. Do not allow full return of the key between strokes. ELECTRIC——Allow time for key to return to position before striking it again.

Technique Cue: Curve the fingers; keep the hands and arms quiet; let the fingers do the work.

Spacing Cue: Space with a down-and-in motion of the right thumb; don't pause before or after spacing.

```
1        a as ask asks ash hash dash e he she shed led sled
2        a as ask asks ash hash dash e he she shed led sled

3        ale sale kale hale jell fell sell shell self shelf
4        ale sale kale hale jell fell sell shell self shelf

5        a ad had sad fad add jade fade safe heal deal seal
6        a ad had sad fad add jade fade safe heal deal seal

7        ee see seek seeks keel keels feel feels heed heeds
8        ee see seek seeks keel keels feel feels heed heeds
```

4E ■ CONTINUITY PRACTICE ☐20 type 2 copies of the drill as shown

Continuity Cue: Type on, one key at a time; do not pause between strokes. Space quickly.

Return Cue: Return without spacing after last stroke in line; begin the new line without a pause.

```
1        ask a lad; a lad had; he had a sale; he feels hale
2        ask a lad; a lad had; he had a sale; he feels hale

3        a fad; all fall ads; he sells jade; he held a sale
4        a fad; all fall ads; he sells jade; he held a sale

5        add a dash; a lad led; she sees dad; she asks half
6        add a dash; a lad led; she sees dad; she asks half

7        he has a fall sales flash; she has had a jell sale
8        he has a fall sales flash; she has had a jell sale

9        Lee seeks a deed; Hale feels hale; Jeff has a desk
10       Lee seeks a deed; Hale feels hale; Jeff has a desk
```

WHAT TO DO IF KEYS JAM

■ When one key is struck before the preceding one is released, the keys collide and may stick together, or "jam." (*On the Selectric typewriter, jamming is mechanically impossible.*)

■ To correct this stroking fault, align fingers directly over the home keys and improve timing of key strokes.

1. Use the special jammed-key release if your typewriter has this special key.

2. Depress the shift key; this sometimes works.

3. If keys are still tangled, gently flick with your finger the stuck key nearest you; or push keys slightly toward the platen and untangle them.

Modified block; open punctuation ■ date on Line 16 ■ 1 cc ■
envelope ■ use the opening and closing lines given below

	Words			Words
Opening lines: July 15, 19-- | Mr. Ambrose	5	*Closing lines:* Sincerely yours | Jasper M. Pint-		6
Clark 1227 East Oregon Street | Phoenix, AZ	14	ner | Subscription Manager | Enclosures 2		14/59
85014 Dear Mr. Clark	18			

Words

Did you misplace *that we*	
☐ The renewal notice ~~which was~~ sent to you several weeks ago. ~~must~~	15
We have extended	
~~have been misplaced.~~ Your subscription to Sports Today ~~has been con-~~	25
especially	
~~tinued~~ so that you won't miss the fall football preview ~~or any of~~ your	31
Has	
favorite sports stories. ~~Since you have been~~ a subscriber to SPORTS	49
# *c* *and accurate*	
TODAY for many years, you are thoroughly aquainted with its complete	66
coverage. It is a ~~sports magazine that~~ packs an exciting punch. Each	69
SPORTS TODAY	
month between its ~~two~~ covers. As you know, too, SPORTS TODAY is the	90
spell	
sports magazine for every sports-conscious youngster from nine to 90.	105
unless	
☐ Now, ~~if you don't~~ already have your checkbook out, please ~~take~~	116
leave it in its place.	
~~a minute to get it out so that you can send us your check.~~ Attach your	141
check. ~~to the convenient subscription renewal form which is enclosed.~~	143
Use	
~~Put your check and the form in~~ the enclosed postpaid envelope. Drop	151
and	
the envelope in the mail, We'll do the rest.	161

*Just check "Bill me later" on the convenient
renewal form enclosed. Or you may prefer to*

Personal letter style: modified block with 5-space ¶ indentions; mixed punctuation ■ 2 cc ■ envelope ■ type the address in letter body in mailing list order

Words

767 Compton Ridge Drive / Wyoming, Ohio 45215 / May 4, 19-- /	11
Mr. Andrew W. Bond / International Department / Fifth Na-	22
tional Bank / Carew Tower / Cincinnati, Ohio 45202 / Dear	32
Mr. Bond: / (¶1) This letter will confirm our telephone	42
conversation of today. (¶2) On April 4, I gave you my	52
check for $350 and asked you to deposit it in the checking	64
account of my daughter, Mrs. Ellen Crampton / Acct. /	74
No. 20-55472:0042859 / Barclay's Bank, Ltd. / Marble	84
Arch Branch / 19 Great Cumberland Place / London W1,	94
England (¶3) In a letter I received this morning, Mrs.	104
Crampton wrote that as yet she has not received this	115
amount. Please check into this matter at once and	125
transfer the funds by cable. Please let me know as	135
soon as you have effected this transfer of funds.	145
Sincerely yours, Walter Arbrooks	152/172

LESSON 5

5A ■ GET READY TO TYPE [3]

1. **Paper Guide and Paper Bail:** Adjust them as directed for your typewriter.

2. **Paper Release:** Be sure it is in position.

3. **Line-Space Regulator:** Set it on "1" for SS.

4. **Ribbon Control:** Set to type on top half of ribbon.

5. **Margins:** Set *left stop* 25 spaces to left of center of the paper; move *right stop* to end of scale.

5B ■ RECALL [5]

1. The elements of good typing position (page 4).
2. Key stroking and space bar operation (page 3).
3. Center point for pica and elite type (page 7).
4. Electric and nonelectric return techniques (page 3).
5. What to do when keys jam (page 10).
6. Removing paper and centering carriage (page 4).

5C ■ CONDITIONING PRACTICE [7]

DO: Type the first line twice with single spacing; then double-space and type the other lines in the same way. (See the illustration given at the right.)

Practice Cue: Begin to type at a slow, even pace. Strike and release each key quickly. Move from one letter to the next without pausing between strokes. Keep typing, without jerks and pauses.

```
fdsa jkl; fasdf j;lkj a;sldkfj a;sldkfj h e he she
fdsa jkl; fasdf j;lkj a;sldkfj a;sldkfj h e he she

a as all ask she had sale lake jell fell fall jade
a as all ask she had sale lake jell fell fall jade

Hal had a sale; Jeff has all ads; Lee sells desks;
Hal had a sale; Jeff has all ads; Lee sells desks;
```

```
fdsa jkl; fasdf j;lkj a;sldkfj a;sldkfj h e he she

a as all ask she had sale lake jell fell fall jade

Hal had a sale; Jeff has all ads; Lee sells desks;
```

5D ■ NEW KEY LOCATION: I, T, PERIOD (.) [10]

1. Find new key on chart, above.   2. Locate key on keyboard.   3. Study reach illustration.   4. Type the drill.

REACH TECHNIQUE FOR I

Reach the *right second finger* to **i**; lift the right first finger slightly for improved stroking control.

```
ik ik ii kik kik ii ik ik
if ik is his kid aid laid DS
```

REACH TECHNIQUE FOR T

Reach the *left first finger* to **t** without arching the wrist or moving the hand forward.

```
tf tf tt ftf ftf tt tf tf
tf the flat let left that DS
```

REACH TECHNIQUE FOR .

Curl the *right third finger* down to type . (period) without moving the hand or elbow out of position.

```
.l .l .. l.l l.l .. .l .l
adj. del. add. def. hdkf. TS
```

■ This section provides a review of letter styles, rough-draft materials, report manuscripts, tabulations, memorandums, and simple business forms.

Only brief, general directions are given. Place the materials attractively on the page by using your own judgment. Correct your errors.

Work Assignment 1: Business Letters (Plain sheets)

Letter 1

> Modified block; open punctuation ■ 1 cc ■ envelope

Words

June 7, 19-- | Mr. James Cochran | 22 Hitchcock Road | Westport, CT 06897 | Dear Mr. Cochran (¶ 1) After reviewing the reports of your automobile accident of May 18, 19--, we find that our policyholder Mr. Harvey Keithly is entitled to recover from you the cost of repair of damages to his car. We have therefore arranged for this repair. STATEWIDE INSURANCE will pay for the repairs, and our policyholder's right to recover damages will thereby transfer to us. (¶ 2) We shall correspond directly with your insurer on this matter. From the reports, we understand that your insurer is Mid-Eastern Accident and Casualty Insurance Company, Hartford, Connecticut, and that the claims adjuster is Mr. Andrew Josephson. We further understand that your policy number with them is 472-AVC-76659. If this information is incorrect, please jot any corrections at the foot of this letter and return it in the enclosed envelope. If we have not heard from you by June 14, we will initiate correspondence with your insurer. | Sincerely yours | Justin Holcomb, Claims Agent | Enclosure | (184)

8
15
23
32
40
50
59
68
76
85
93
103
112
121
129
138
146
155
165
175
184
193
202
210
211/**222**

Letter 2

> Modified block; 5-space ¶ indentions; mixed punctuation ■ 1 cc ■ envelope ■ center the longer listed item and block the second item under it ■ consider these items when deciding on placement

Words

April 17, 19-- | Mr. J. J. Bush | Route 2, Box 125 | Verona, MO 65769 Dear Mr. Bush: (¶ 1) We have today charged your commercial account No. 515-01088 for $62.50, the amount of the balance due on your installment loan contract No. LL 881-774, completing payment of this contract. (¶ 2) We are enclosing the following papers:

9
16
24
31
41
49
57
62

    Certificate of Ownership No. 472231
    Insurance Policy No. 629290

69
75

(¶ 3) Our interest as legal owner has been released to you on page 2, Line 2, of the certificate of ownership. (¶ 4) Please do not hesi-

82
91
100

tate to call on us for any service we can provide for you. | Sincerely yours, | Mrs. Paula Arrand, Head | Installment Loan Department | Enclosures 2 (92)

109
117
126
129/**139**

Letter 3

> Modified block; mixed punctuation ■ 1 cc ■ envelope

Words

May 5, 19-- | Miss Marcia Hazelton | 112 Breezewood Avenue | Norwalk, OH 44857 Dear Miss Hazelton: | POLICY NO. CCB-9920; ACCIDENT OF FEBRUARY 18, 19-- | (¶ 1) We have been unable to collect from the other party involved in the accident for the damage to your car; therefore, the only course of action open to you now is to file suit as an individual in the Small Claims Court, where the hearing is informal. Each driver and his witnesses merely appear to tell their version of the accident. Attorneys and insurance firm representatives are not allowed to participate. (¶ 2) Please complete the enclosed Small Claims Court affidavit, sign it before a Notary Public, and return it to this office. When a trial date is set, we shall notify you to appear on that day with your witness. If you obtain a judgment in the Small Claims Court, forward the judgment form to us so that we can collect the judgment for you. (¶ 3) We are sorry that you must resort to this action. Please let us help you in any other possible way. Sincerely yours, | MUTUAL INSURANCE GROUP H. J. deWindt | Subrogation Claims Department | Enclosure | We shall pay the notary fee if you will send us the fee slip. (180)

7
15
22
28
35
44
54
64
73
82
92
102
111
118
128
137
147
156
165
175
183
192
202
208
216
225
232/**244**

Letter 4

> Type Letter 2 to **Mr. F. A. Cyphers** | **827 Wind Mill Road** | **Ballwin, MO 63011** | Use account No. **515-01569**, contract No. **LL 881-995**; certificate of ownership No. **482009**, and policy No. **C33347**.

Letter 5

> Type Letter 3 to **Mr. Daniel Dew** | **2814 Silver Lake Road** | **Cuyahoga Falls, OH 44224** | Use the current date for the letter. Use policy No. **CCC-1079** and date of accident 90 days earlier than the current date.

5E ■ STROKING TECHNIQUE PRACTICE [15] type a line twice SS; then DS and type the next line

Technique Cue: Curve the fingers deeply. *Reach* up to type *i* and *t* without moving the hand forward; *reach* down to . without twisting the hand or elbow.

Typing from Dictation: After typing each of the lines twice, type Lines 1, 2, and 3 once more from your teacher's dictation.

1 *i*   i ik if is his did hid aid said sail fail jail ill

2 *T*   t tf jet set left felt at hat that the these takes

3 .   . .l .l La. H. J. Lake; Lee led. He led all fall.

Space once after . following an abbreviation or an initial; twice after . ending a sentence, except at the end of the line

4 *All letters learned are*
5 *used in Lines 4-5*

     if the; ask if the; I hit it. I like it.   It fit.

     I see Jess is at the field. Ike is at Leeds Lake.

5F ■ CONTINUITY PRACTICE [10] type twice; then type Lines 1 and 3 from dictation

1 *All strokes*
2 *learned are used in Lines 1-6*

     if is it fit sit hit lit tide tile site till still
     His desk is filled. He is still at the lake site.

     DS

3
4

     it is she; she is fit; fill the date; a fast field
     Jed sells tile. He filed the list. Kit is a hit.

     DS

5
6

     Jill did take the test late. It is the last test.
     His aides had the lists. His file is at the lake.

     TS

Words | 1 | 2 | 3 | 4 | 5 | 6 | 7 | 8 | 9 | 10 |

■ LESSON 6

6A ■ GET READY TO TYPE [3]

1. Adjust paper guide and bail.
2. Put the paper release in position.
3. Set line-space regulator on "1" for single spacing (SS).
4. Set ribbon control in black position.
5. Set left margin stop 25 spaces to left of the center of paper; move right margin stop to end of scale.
6. Check what to do if keys jam (p. 10).

Typing Position: Sit back in the chair with body erect; feet on floor. Have forearms parallel to keyboard; wrists low and relaxed; fingers curved and upright. When typing, keep eyes on copy.

Technique Cue: Use a quick, snap stroke——snap the finger slightly toward the palm of the hand as you strike and release the key. Do not let the finger follow the key all the way down.

6B ■ CONDITIONING PRACTICE [7] each line twice SS; DS after each 2-line group

All letters learned   he it as is if did kit let ft. jets fits life left   *Eyes on the copy*

Double letters   ill fill till feel feet tall fall jell steel sheet

All letters learned   His is the last set. Keith Jelk said she left it.

Writing 7

¶ 1

	1'	3'	5'
Our news media and editorial writers have made this idea well known:	14	5	3	46
A high school education is not only important--it is almost essential.	28	9	6	49
Most jobs now go to men and women with the skills needed to run our	42	14	8	51
mechanical world of today, skills that almost always must be acquired in	57	19	11	55
high school or college. Jobs for the unskilled dropout are dying out.	71	24	14	57

¶ 2

Very few people are in the position of not having to earn a living	13	28	17	60
for themselves and their families. Moreover, many men and women who have	28	33	20	63
ample sources of income prefer to engage in a job of some kind. Your	42	38	23	66
primary goal, therefore, should be to learn the skills necessary for a	56	42	25	69
career that you will find both pleasant and profitable.	67	46	28	71

¶ 3

We need to emphasize the merit of making our next goal that of	13	50	30	73
learning how to be complete and fulfilled as a person. A student who	27	55	33	76
makes a concentrated effort can, by wisely and sensibly using his time,	41	60	36	79
take not only technical courses but courses that will teach him to think,	56	65	39	82
reason, inquire, evaluate, and enjoy. Indeed, not only his business life	71	70	42	85
but also his social life can be enriched.	79	72	43	87

1' GWAM | 1 | 2 | 3 | 4 | 5 | 6 | 7 | 8 | 9 | 10 | 11 | 12 | 13 | 14 |
3' GWAM | 1 | 2 | 3 | 4 | 5 |
5' GWAM | 1 | 2 | 3 |

Writing 8

¶ 1

	1'	3'	5'
Knowing that there are sixty seconds in every minute and sixty min-	13	4	3	48
utes in every hour, we should be able to schedule our activities into the	28	9	6	51
available time without difficulty. Why, then, do so many people end up	43	14	9	54
rushing around in a frenzy, trying to meet a deadline? The answer is	57	19	12	57
in the psychological aspect of time. When we are enjoying ourselves,	71	24	14	60
time seems to fly away; but time spent on a tedious job seems endless.	85	28	17	62

¶ 2

Do you ever "goof off" for an hour or more with a television program	14	33	20	65
or a visit on the telephone and discover later that you haven't actually	28	38	23	68
enjoyed your leisure? Each nagging little vision of homework or chores to	43	43	26	71
be completed always seems to result in taking the edge off your pleasure.	58	47	28	74
And you still have to finish whatever you postponed--probably in a hurry.	73	52	31	77

¶ 3

If you fit the situation above, don't waste any time feeling guilty;	14	57	34	80
for you have plenty of company! What you should feel is cheated--out of	29	62	37	82
leisure that you didn't enjoy and study time that didn't produce results.	43	67	40	85
Check with a friend who always seems ready for a good time but is also	58	71	43	88
ready for unexpected quizzes. His secret is budgeting his time.	70	76	45	91

1' GWAM | 1 | 2 | 3 | 4 | 5 | 6 | 7 | 8 | 9 | 10 | 11 | 12 | 13 | 14 |
3' GWAM | 1 | 2 | 3 | 4 | 5 |
5' GWAM | 1 | 2 | 3 |

6C ■ NEW KEY LOCATION: R, O, C ☐10

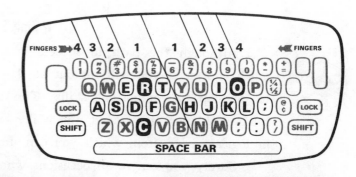

RECALL

1. Find the new key on the keyboard chart.

2. Locate the key on your typewriter keyboard.

3. Study the reach illustration for the new key.

4. Type reach technique drill on one line.

REACH TECHNIQUE FOR R	**REACH TECHNIQUE FOR O**	**REACH TECHNIQUE FOR C**
Reach the *left first finger* up to **r** without moving the other fingers from their home keys.	Reach the *right third finger* up to **o** without moving the hand forward or the elbow outward.	Reach the *left second finger* down to **c** without twisting the elbow in or out or moving the hand down.

rf rf rr frf frf rr rf rf   ol ol oo lol lol oo ol ol   cd cd cc dcd dcd cc cd cd

rf rid ride fir fire tire DS   ol of of old so sold fold DS   cd clad sick cd deck each TS

6D ■ STROKING TECHNIQUE PRACTICE ☐15 each line twice SS; then Lines 1-4 from dictation

1 R   r rf rf rid ride red her here there their fir fire   *Reach the finger, not the hand, to the key*

2 O   o ol ol of to do so dot lot hot host old hold sold

3 C   c cd ce ace act fact call case hack lack lick sick

4 *All letters learned are*   are to do; for her; of their; old case; first call

5 *used in Lines 4-5* Josh has the lock.   Jack is sick.   Joe lacks cash.

6E ■ CONTINUITY PRACTICE ☐15 type twice; then type Lines 1, 3, and 5 from dictation

1 *All strokes*   he told her; the sets are sold; I took their check   *Quick, snap strokes;*

2 *learned are used in Lines 1-6* Let Jeff sort the cards.   Lee Kelch took the case.   *fingers curved and upright*

3   he is here; the old stock; I like Josh; Jo read it

4   He flies a jet.   He asks if the clock is for sale.

5   as she said; he holds the checks; she has the cash

6   He has all the facts.   Jack Orr has her file here.

Words | 1 | 2 | 3 | 4 | 5 | 6 | 7 | 8 | 9 | 10 |

─────────────── **END-OF-LESSON ACTIVITY** ───────────────

■ Pull the paper-release lever forward (toward you) and remove the paper with the left hand.

■ Center the carriage. Pick up all paper. Push the chair to the desk as you leave.

Writing 5

¶1　Although the path to success is usually lengthy, you can make it much shorter if you will set out at the beginning of your business career to develop two important skills. The first is the ability to see and to solve problems; the second, the ability to gather facts and arrange them in logical order, from which you can draw the correct conclusions.

¶2　Surely you can recall occasions when you devoted many hours––even days––to striving unsuccessfully for a goal, and then you happened to see a familiar fact from a new viewpoint. Perhaps you exclaimed to a friend or yourself, "Now I see what the problem is!" And once identified, the problem was easily solved. As you begin work on a project, make your initial step that of seeing the actual problem.

¶3　To solve problems, use all available ways to get the data that you will need. Books and magazine articles give facts and expert opinions, and a request by mail or by telephone may give added help. Enter the data on cards, sort the cards into logical groups, review your work, and apply common sense to reach conclusions that the data support.

GWAM			
1'	3'	5'	
13	4	3	46
28	9	6	49
42	14	8	52
57	19	11	55
70	23	14	58
13	28	17	61
28	33	20	64
43	38	23	66
57	42	25	69
71	47	28	72
80	50	30	74
13	55	33	77
28	59	36	80
42	64	38	82
56	69	41	85
79	73	44	88

1' GWAM | 1 | 2 | 3 | 4 | 5 | 6 | 7 | 8 | 9 | 10 | 11 | 12 | 13 | 14 |
3' GWAM | 1 | 2 | 3 | 4 | 5 |
5' GWAM | 1 | 2 | 3 |

Writing 6

¶1　One of the basic problems that management must solve is that of providing workers with the best possible motivation for doing good work. Some requirements for reaching this goal are to let each employee know just what is expected of him, where he can get any necessary help, and his degree of success at his job.

¶2　In most of us is the potential to work with various degrees of efficiency. Performance is said to depend on such things as the environment of a person, the strength of his motives, his hope of success, and the amount of satisfaction that he expects to get from his success. The force of these factors will vary with each individual.

¶3　Many a worker finds that most of his motivation comes from within, but some may find that they need an extra incentive such as material rewards or prestige. A high achiever, however, may seek no other reward than that of doing a good job. He evidently has no need to symbolize success with material gain, but financial success and prestige are quite likely to come to such a person anyway.

GWAM			
1'	3'	5'	
13	4	3	44
28	9	6	47
42	14	8	50
56	19	11	53
63	21	13	54
13	25	15	57
27	30	18	60
42	35	21	62
56	40	24	65
67	43	26	67
13	48	29	70
27	52	31	73
42	57	34	76
56	61	37	79
70	67	40	82
78	69	42	83

1' GWAM | 1 | 2 | 3 | 4 | 5 | 6 | 7 | 8 | 9 | 10 | 11 | 12 | 13 | 14 |
3' GWAM | 1 | 2 | 3 | 4 | 5 |
5' GWAM | 1 | 2 | 3 |

■ LESSON 7

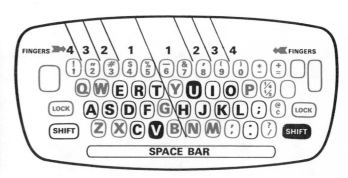

FINGERS ➡4 3 2 1   1 2 3 4 ⬅FINGERS

SPACE BAR

7A ■ GET READY TO TYPE; RECALL [8]

1. Adjust the paper guide and the paper bail.
2. Put the paper release in position; insert paper.
3. Set line-space regulator on "1" for SS.
4. Set ribbon control in black position.
5. Set left margin stop 25 spaces to left of center of paper; move right margin stop to end of scale.

RECALL

1. Correct typing position (p. 4).
2. Key stroking and spacing (p. 3).
3. Pica and elite type center points (p. 7).
4. Spacing after . at end of sentence and after . used with abbreviation or initial (p. 12).

7B ■ CONDITIONING PRACTICE [7] each line twice SS; DS after each 2-line group

Technique Cue: Lift the finger just enough to clear the top of a key in the third row; strike the key quickly; release it instantly.

Spacing Cue: Space with a down-and-in motion of your right thumb. Do not hesitate before the stroke or pause after it. Keep the carriage (carrier) moving.

Reinforcement   ed ee ol oo rf rr ik ii tf tt hj hh cd cc hit core   *Return without pausing; start new line quickly*

R   O   C   ore care took rock joke sort cork coat force stock

All letters learned   Jill Orth is at Lake Heid; she asks for her check.

7C ■ NEW KEY LOCATION: U, V, RIGHT SHIFT [10]

1. Find new key on chart.   2. Locate key on keyboard.   3. Study reach illustration.   4. Type the drill.

REACH TECHNIQUE FOR U

Reach the *right first finger* up to **u** without moving the other fingers from their home keys.

uj uj uu juj juj uu uj uj

uj us used just dust husk *DS*

REACH TECHNIQUE FOR V

Reach the *left first finger* down to type **v**. Hold the elbow in position and the hand in alignment.

vf vf vv fvf fvf vv vf vf

vf vie vie five live have *DS*

CONTROL OF RIGHT SHIFT KEY

Hold the **right shift key (26)** down with the *right little finger* until the capital letter has been typed.

El Al Alf Sal File Stiles

Alf led Sid. Al is sick. *TS*

Writing 3

¶ 1   Communication is a two-way street. Communication, as a matter of fact, does not take place until someone can receive and then react to what has been said, written, or transmitted in some way. Communication can be at the one-to-one level, or it can take place between two of our most powerful nations. And, odd as it may seem, there are many problems that are common to both of these extremes.

¶ 2   A big barrier to real communication is the fact that, even when two people are using the same language, a word may not assume the same meaning for each person. Various factors, such as the tone of the speaker's voice, the expression on his face, or a quick movement of his hand, can determine the meanings that two people apply to a word.

¶ 3   Whether talking at a party or at a high-level meeting, one must use effort and good judgment to select words, tone, and manner conveying exactly what he means. Once we reach the point of being able to communicate on a person-to-person basis, we can start to realize our goal of true friendly relations among the nations of the world.

1'	3'	5'	
13	4	3	46
27	9	5	48
42	14	8	51
56	19	11	54
71	24	14	57
79	26	16	59
14	31	19	61
28	36	21	64
43	41	24	67
57	45	27	70
68	49	29	72
14	54	32	75
28	58	35	78
42	63	38	81
56	68	41	84
67	71	43	86

1' GWAM | 1 | 2 | 3 | 4 | 5 | 6 | 7 | 8 | 9 | 10 | 11 | 12 | 13 | 14 |
3' GWAM | 1 | 2 | 3 | 4 | 5 |
5' GWAM | 1 | 2 | 3 |

Writing 4

¶ 1   Before starting to work as a typist, try to get some work experience on a part-time or temporary basis. After leaving school, you will find it much easier to adjust to the working world if you have some notion of what to expect. If a job of some sort is not practical, a second choice would be the use of the production typing assignments in your textbook to become familiar with the variety of forms you will encounter later.

¶ 2   Here are some hints to help you. Organize your working space to avoid waste motion as you quickly assemble your papers. Always check the copy that you are to type to see that it is accurate in detail and in form; when you finish, make a final check. Complete, reliable forms are essential in an office. Your job is to provide them.

¶ 3   You will find that as you concentrate on typing various record forms you will cut down on your straight-copy speed. Also, it is likely that you will find that some basic techniques will need to be reinforced. So plan to set aside a few minutes every day for intensive practice to keep your skills at a high level, and carry this excellent habit to your job.

1'	3'	5'	
14	5	3	48
28	9	6	51
43	14	9	53
57	19	11	56
72	24	14	59
86	29	17	62
13	33	20	65
27	38	23	67
41	42	25	70
56	47	28	73
64	51	31	75
14	55	33	78
28	60	36	81
43	65	39	84
57	70	42	87
72	75	45	90

1' GWAM | 1 | 2 | 3 | 4 | 5 | 6 | 7 | 8 | 9 | 10 | 11 | 12 | 13 | 14 |
3' GWAM | 1 | 2 | 3 | 4 | 5 |
5' GWAM | 1 | 2 | 3 |

7D ■ STROKING TECHNIQUE PRACTICE ⬚15 each line twice SS; then Lines 1-3 once from dictation

Technique Cue: Make upward and downward reaches without moving the hands out of alignment.

Shifting Cue: Hold the shift key down until the letter key has been struck and released.

1 *U*   uj uj jut just due fur cut our hour full dull rule

2 *V*   vf vf vet have save love vote dive live five serve

3 *U V*   uj vf use vat curve save cause volt four vote true

4 *Right shift* Ro Rose Vi Vic Su Sue Dr. Tod Rike; A. C. Roth Co.   *Remember to space once after . following an initial*

5 *Consolidation* Dru serves our scouts. Ev caused us to vote here.

7E ■ CONTINUITY PRACTICE ⬚10 type twice

1 *All strokes*   to us; save it; this hour; it is out; to serve our   *Space quickly; keep carriage moving*
2 *learned are*   It is ours to save. All four of us have to do it.
   used in Lines 1-6

3   to have it; four or five; a just cause; has a vote
4   Sue has the test file. Ed cashed all five checks.

5   use a true rate; to state the; sit it out; it took
6   Vi or Tess should take the old vase to the school.

Words | 1 | 2 | 3 | 4 | 5 | 6 | 7 | 8 | 9 | 10 |

■ LESSON 8

In this lesson and the remaining lessons of this unit, the time for the Conditioning Practice is changed to 8 minutes. In this time you are to make machine adjustments, get ready to type, and type the lines. As your typing skill increases, more is expected of you. Work quickly and efficiently.

8A ■ CONDITIONING PRACTICE ⬚8 each line twice SS; DS after each 2-line group

All letters learned   Kurt said Jeff or Vic is to sail at Old Hoke Lake.   *Shift firmly*

C   O   V   Viv Koch told us that Ev Drake drove to Cold Cove.

Easy sentence   Sue is to ski at five if her date is here at four.

Words | 1 | 2 | 3 | 4 | 5 | 6 | 7 | 8 | 9 | 10 |

8B ■ MANIPULATIVE PARTS DRILL: SHIFT KEYS ⬚7 each line twice SS; DS after each 2-line group

Shifting Cue: 1. Depress the shift key.   2. Strike the letter.   3. Release the shift key.

Right shift   Dr. Short; St. Charles; Ft. Sill; So. Rholf Drive;   *Abbreviations such as U.S. and N.Y. are usually typed solid (without internal spacing)*

Left shift   Kate Hauss; O. J. Kahle; Hal Oakes; Oak Hills Hall

Both shifts   Dr. Keith C. Virts; Lars J. Houck; U.S. Air Force.

SUPPLEMENTARY ALPHABETIC TIMED WRITINGS

Writing 1

¶ 1 While an office is not always an exciting place, it usually is a busy and interesting place. Letters are sent to and received from far places. With a bit of imagination, you can travel far and wide with the letters. When you answer your telephone, you may hear a voice from next door––or from across the continent. These are the things that make an office a pleasant locale in which to work.

¶ 2 Quite often there will be a day of routine work when a dozen things will demand your attention at the same time––none of them interesting and some actually boring. Some days you will have a rush job to complete and to check for accuracy in the midst of noise and confusion. You must learn to ignore the conversations and the sounds of office machines and concentrate on the job at hand.

¶ 3 Your office life will be whatever you make it; it will reflect your attitudes and your set of values––and should include a fun side as well as a serious, intent one. Every office worker is able to choose his or her own "office life style." Will yours be dreary and uninteresting, or will it be one that offers new challenges and rewards almost daily?

GWAM for Writing 1:

1'	3'	5'	
13	4	3	48
27	9	5	51
41	14	8	54
55	18	11	57
70	23	14	59
79	26	16	61
14	31	19	64
28	36	21	67
42	40	24	70
57	45	27	73
71	50	30	76
78	52	31	77
14	57	34	79
28	62	37	82
42	66	40	85
57	71	43	88
71	76	45	91

1' GWAM | 1 | 2 | 3 | 4 | 5 | 6 | 7 | 8 | 9 | 10 | 11 | 12 | 13 | 14 |
3' GWAM | 1 | 2 | 3 | 4 | 5 |
5' GWAM | 1 | 2 | 3 |

Writing 2

¶ 1 Webster says that a practical joker is one whose humor comes from the tricking of someone who is placed at a disadvantage. If I were able to change people at will, I would surely be happy to change the practical joker. When he is not an actual menace, he is a pest. Rather than giving pleasure, his childish action will merely cause trouble for all.

¶ 2 Of course, most of us feel that there is enough trouble in the world now without our doing anything to add to anyone's share. But there are always a few who are insensitive to the results of their rash actions. A mature person can and does think ahead to the effects of his action, but the immature practical joker will act without thinking and at the expense of his sadder but wiser victim.

¶ 3 It does seem that the practical joker can't learn what those around him so quickly learn––that he is not a bit funny. Anyone who can give people a good laugh is well liked wherever he may go. But that person laughs with people, not at them; his attitude is happy and pleasant, not tricky or mean. Why can't the practical joker see the difference?

GWAM for Writing 2:

1'	3'	5'	
13	4	3	46
28	9	6	49
42	14	8	52
56	19	11	55
71	24	14	58
14	28	17	61
28	33	20	64
43	38	23	66
57	42	25	69
71	47	28	72
79	50	30	74
14	54	33	76
28	59	35	79
42	64	38	82
57	69	41	85
70	73	44	88

1' GWAM | 1 | 2 | 3 | 4 | 5 | 6 | 7 | 8 | 9 | 10 | 11 | 12 | 13 | 14 |
3' GWAM | 1 | 2 | 3 | 4 | 5 |
5' GWAM | 1 | 2 | 3 |

8C ■ STROKING TECHNIQUE PRACTICE [20] type twice; then Lines 4 and 5 from dictation

Lines 1-3: Think vigorously such adjacent-key combinations as **oi** and **re** in Line 1. Make a **direct** reach in consecutive finger reaches such as **hu** and **ce** in Line 2, bypassing the return to home position.

Lines 4-6: Speed up the stroking on easy, balanced-hand sequences such as **if** and **it** in Line 4. Use a short, quick stroke in double-letter combinations as in **all** and **less** in Line 5.

All letters learned are used.

1	*Adjacent keys*	ads oil are here fret jerk art true talk silk last	*Space quickly*
2	*Direct reaches*	hue hurt hush ace face deck cede cease curve serve	*between words*
3	*Consolidation*	Hud serves as host. Sal starts her talk at three.	
4	*Balanced-hand*	if it is to do so or for he the did due held their	
5	*Double letters*	all shall heed seek cuff stuff less fuss foot took	
6	*Consolidation*	Ruth said all of us should heed the call to drill.	
7	*Mixed copy*	Art asked if Ceil sells fresh fruit here for less.	
8	*Mixed copy*	I shall talk to Erv at the Red Hut if he is there.	
9	*Mixed copy*	He did seek aid as that last car crossed the deck.	

| 1 | 2 | 3 | 4 | 5 | 6 | 7 | 8 | 9 | 10 |

8D ■ SENTENCE GUIDED WRITING [15]

1. **Type** each sentence twice; then double-space.
a. First, type at an easy, controlled pace with even, continuous stroking.
b. Then, speed up the stroking. Avoid pausing after strokes and after words––just keep on typing.

2. **Type** each sentence for a half minute, trying to type to the end of the sentence as time is called. The goals are shown as *gwam* (gross words a minute) in the second column at the right of the lines.

3. **Type** each sentence for 1 minute without the call of the line ending. Type until time is called.

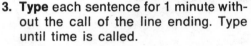

Return Cue	Make the return without looking up from the copy.

All letters learned are used.

		Words In Line *	GWAM 30″ Guide
1	It is this desk file he seeks.	6	12
2	Vic said he likes to do this drill.	7	14
3	Jud asked her if she had the state list.	8	16
4	Have her take all the jade to that lake sale.	9	18
5	Ruth said she asked to take all three field tests.	10	20

| 1 | 2 | 3 | 4 | 5 | 6 | 7 | 8 | 9 | 10 |

*HOW TYPEWRITTEN WORDS ARE COUNTED:

■ Five strokes are counted as one standard typewritten word. The figures in the first column at the right of the drill sentences show the number of 5-stroke words in each of the lines. The scale beneath the copy shows the word-by-word count (5 strokes at a time) for each of the lines.

TO DETERMINE WORDS-A-MINUTE RATE:

■ 1. List the figure at the end of each complete line typed during a writing. 2. For a partial line, note from the scale the figure directly below the point at which you stopped typing. 3. Add these figures to determine the total gross words typed (the same as *gwam* for a 1-minute writing).

SKILL-TRANSFER PARAGRAPHS

STRAIGHT COPY (100% TRANSFER)

¶ 1

When we want to justify an activity that does not conform to the
usual custom, we say, "Rules were made to be broken." Actually, under
special conditions, rules should be broken. For example, in all letter
styles but block, we begin the closing lines at the horizontal center
point of the paper. When a lengthy company name or title occurs in the
closing, we should shift the starting point a little to the left to
avoid the necessity of typing into the right margin.

	1'	3'
	13	4　36
	27	9　40
	41	14　45
	55	18　50
	70	23　55
	83	28　59
	94	31　63

1' GWAM | 1 | 2 | 3 | 4 | 5 | 6 | 7 | 8 | 9 | 10 | 11 | 12 | 13 | 14 |
3' GWAM |　　1　　|　　2　　|　　3　　|　　4　　|　　5　　|

STATISTICAL COPY (90% TRANSFER)

¶ 2

"Men who read more accomplish more" is the conclusion from a study
of 100 men who lead major companies and 100 men of the same general ages
who never succeeded. During the period of the survey, the top 100 men
read 53 books, 338 magazines, and 1,490 newspapers; the other 100 men
read 28 books, 299 magazines, and 853 newspapers. Thus we can affirm
that this is true: The more we read, the better our chances to succeed.

	1'	3'
	13	4　33
	28	9　38
	42	14　42
	56	19　47
	70	23　52
	85	28　56

1' GWAM | 1 | 2 | 3 | 4 | 5 | 6 | 7 | 8 | 9 | 10 | 11 | 12 | 13 | 14 |
3' GWAM |　　1　　|　　2　　|　　3　　|　　4　　|　　5　　|

ROUGH DRAFT (75-80% TRANSFER)

¶ 3

To communicate
~~In communicating~~ with others, we talk, write, read, observe, or
listen. Of the five stated activities, ~~most~~ many people ~~use~~ utilize talk, to the
greatest ~~degree~~ extent. This, however, is not true of, our top businessmen. A Studies
show, that they do more listening than they do talking and writing ~~to-~~
~~gether.~~ combined. We are taught how to read, how (to) write, ~~and~~ how to
~~speak,~~ talk but not how to listen, yet the ability to listen ~~is~~ may be the
most ~~valuable.~~ necessary of all.

	1'	3'
	12	4　33
	27	9　38
	42	14　43
	56	19　47
	68	23　51
	82	27　56
	86	29　57

SCRIPT (90-95% TRANSFER)

¶ 4

Science and industry can provide us with the goods that
we must have, but our ideals and goals for living must come
from other sources--such sources as law and art and literature
and philosophy. It is time for men of thought and action to
bind themselves together for the effective utilization of our
material power for the basic needs of our society.

	1'	3'
	11	4　27
	23	8　31
	36	12　35
	48	16　39
	60	20　44
	70	23　47

LESSON 9

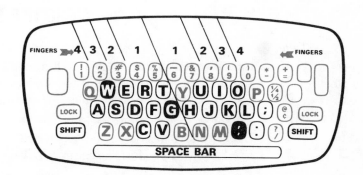

1. *Margins:* left, center point – (minus) 25 spaces; right, moved to end of scale.

2. *Spacing:* drills, single-spaced with double spacing after each 2- or 3-line group.

9A ■ CONDITIONING PRACTICE [8] each line twice SS; DS after each 2-line group

All letters learned	Vic Judd said Lars tied his skiff to the far dock.
Space bar	at to; as so; ad do; far roe; fall lash; half fail
Easy sentence	He has tried to aid that cause; she has tried too.

Eyes on copy as you return carriage

| 1 | 2 | 3 | 4 | 5 | 6 | 7 | 8 | 9 | 10 |

9B ■ NEW KEY LOCATION: W, COMMA (,), G [10]

REACH TECHNIQUE FOR W

Reach the *left third finger* up to type **w** without moving the hand forward or arching the wrist.

ws ws ww sws sws ww ws ws

ws we wit with wish which *DS*

REACH TECHNIQUE FOR , (COMMA)

Reach the *right second finger* down to type **, (comma)**. Space once after a comma in a sentence.

,k ,k ,, k,k k,k ,, ,k ,k

Ike, Kit, or I did do it. *DS*

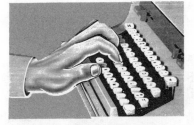

REACH TECHNIQUE FOR G

Reach the *left first finger* to the right to type **g** without moving the other fingers from their home keys.

gf gf gg fgf fgf gg gf gf

gf go got fog log rug jug *TS*

9C ■ STROKING TECHNIQUE PRACTICE [12] each line twice SS; then Lines 2 and 4 from dictation

Technique Cue: Move the fingers, *not* the hands. Keep fingers curved and upright.

Spacing Cue: Make the space bar stroke a part of the stroking of the word that precedes it.

1 *W*	w ws we weld well were law laws was wash wish with
2 *,*	to do, it is, it is his, he did, is due, Co., Ltd.
3 *G*	g gg gf go got fog fig golf flag judge right eight
4 *Consolidation*	he will go, goes to work, a good wage, at what age
5 *Consolidation*	We would give a good wage to the right work crews.

CORRECTIVE SENTENCES
LETTER-CONCENTRATION DRILLS

	Letter	
1A	A	Capable Sandra was awarded a camera for a particular scarlet camellia.
1B	B	Baird Babbitt brought his big box of unbound books to my busy bindery.
1C	C	Cal McCance considers lack of accuracy more costly than lack of speed.
2A	D	Defeated candidates decided to decrease the declaration of deductions.
2B	E	Every effort needs to be expended to see that we get the expected fee.
2C	F	Fred flew five ferry flights to Frankfort after the fifth of February.
3A	G	Engagements gained greatly among the groups of younger girl graduates.
3B	H	When he heard, Hal Heth thought he should either fight or take flight.
3C	I	Irving gained unique standing with his inquiring mind and imagination.
4A	J	Judge Jefferson thought the jury was not prejudiced but just and fair.
4B	K	When you know, know that you know; when you don't know, know that too.
4C	L	Jill and Lloyd Llewellyn left Millvale last fall to live in Hillsdale.
5A	M	Most members must make much more money than Sam Mason made last month.
5B	N	No nation can constantly neglect its neighbors without earning enmity.
5C	O	Opportunity knocks not only once for you, but it knocks over and over.
6A	P	Paul appears to appreciate the opportunity to practice problem typing.
6B	Q	Quent's quarterly quiz questions frequently require quadric equations.
6C	R	Ron's research report correctly describes the problems and procedures.
7A	S	Susan Slusser stressed the necessity of goals for secretarial success.
7B	T	Typewriting teachers attempt to motivate the practice of the students.
7C	U	Unusual but useful is their use of such words as vacuum and continuum.
8A	V	Very few gave such vivid versions of their view of Vesuvius as Vivian.
8B	W	Willing workers who show wisdom and skill will win worthwhile rewards.
8C	X	For example, Alexis expects the expanded X-ray annex to be tax exempt.
9A	Y	You may readily buy a book on the mystery of cybernetics at Youghly's.
9B	Z	Zona amazed Mr. Zazor by organizing and systematizing the zoo records.

| 1 | 2 | 3 | 4 | 5 | 6 | 7 | 8 | 9 | 10 | 11 | 12 | 13 | 14 |

EMPHASIZING LESS FREQUENTLY USED WORDS OF THE FIRST 1,000 MOST-USED WORDS

1A	This particular proposed standard-discount procedure benefits dealers.
1B	The automobile executive reported satisfactory first-quarter earnings.
1C	The treasurer indicated that the industry contributed to the campaign.
2A	Our budget provided for the maximum Christmas bonus for all employees.
2B	Contracts for the promotion of the economic development are requested.
2C	We submitted subscriptions to newspapers serving this particular area.
3A	Arrangements were made for the construction of the community building.
3B	Professor Zane delivered a carefully planned address to the committee.
3C	Endorsement of our latest employment policy was obtained by the union.
4A	The executive personally assured me of excellent display arrangements.
4B	Typing classes learn that daily practice can develop improved control.
4C	The community college administration is advertising for new personnel.
5A	The directors discussed methods to lower the legal charges on housing.
5B	A professor addressed the employees on problems in economic education.
5C	I am providing our representative with figures on that machine design.

| 1 | 2 | 3 | 4 | 5 | 6 | 7 | 8 | 9 | 10 | 11 | 12 | 13 | 14 |

9D ■ CONTINUITY PRACTICE [20] 3 times; then Lines 1 and 3 from dictation

```
1        have to get, wish it were, glad to go, who gave it    Type on;
2        I saw he was a good guide.  We have to get a wage.    avoid pauses

3        who she is; while we are; he ought to; how to work
4        Drew was a guest of the Greggs for the world tour.

5        Rick gave a suit; Harl was there; Gil wrote to Kit
6        If I work for Jack, I shall see what a guide does.
         | 1 | 2 | 3 | 4 | 5 | 6 | 7 | 8 | 9 | 10 |
```

■ LESSON 10

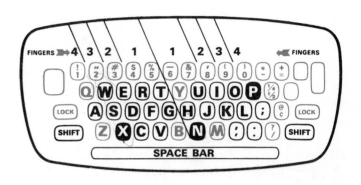

1. *Margins:* left, center point — 25 spaces; right, moved to end of scale.

2. *Spacing:* drills, single-spaced with double spacing after each 2- or 3-line group.

10A ■ CONDITIONING PRACTICE [8] each line twice SS; DS after each 2-line group

All letters learned   Karl West just left for Le Havre with Dick Graves.   *Hold shift key down*

W   ,   G   Lew, Gig, or Drew will have to go with Gil at two.   *until letter has been struck and released*

Easy sentence   Ask the four girls to do the work for us at eight.
                  | 1 | 2 | 3 | 4 | 5 | 6 | 7 | 8 | 9 | 10 |

10B ■ NEW KEY LOCATION: N, X, P [10]

REACH TECHNIQUE FOR N

Move the *right first finger* down to type **n** without moving the other fingers from their home keys.

```
nj nj nn jnj jnj nn nj nj

nj an and an and hand can DS
```

REACH TECHNIQUE FOR X

Reach the *left third finger* down to type **x** without moving the hand downward. Reach with the finger!

```
xs xs xx sxs sxs xx xs xs

xs fix six vex flex sixth DS
```

REACH TECHNIQUE FOR P

Straighten the *right fourth finger* and move it up to type letter **p**. Avoid twisting the elbow out.

```
p; p; pp ;p; ;p; pp p; p;

p; up put par tip top gap TS
```

TECHNIQUE IMPROVEMENT DRILLS

FINGERS CURVED

FINGERS UPRIGHT

FINGER-REACH ACTION

Balanced-hand words (Word-recognition response)

		Words
1A	Their busy social chairman may work with them on their eight problems.	14
1B	It is right for the firm to make a profit when they work for the city.	14
1C	Burns may do a quantity of the civic field work on their land problem.	14

Combination (Variable rhythm)

2A	The union problem case may be referred to the busy firm at this stage.	14
2B	The union may make out a sight draft in the name of the area chairman.	14
2C	Ask their staff to restate the problem and then send us the statement.	14

One-hand words (Stroke response)

3A	*Right hand*	In my own opinion, John's polonium policy is an unlucky monopoly ploy.	14
3B	*Left hand*	Fred exaggerated the fact that few area address cards were ever dated.	14

3C		Ward will join him on the monopoly case that was deferred for opinion.	14
3D	*Left*	The trade union created a minimum reserve fund for extra estate taxes.	14
3E	*and*	Only a minimum number of the oil reserve tax cases are based on facts.	14
3F	*right*	Abstracts on the oil reserve cases stated the exact minimum tax rates.	14

Long reaches—Adjacent-key reaches (Quiet hands)

4A	The unusual weave of that union-made bright green jacket is appealing.	14
4B	Cecile may bring a number of bright new uniforms to the craft exhibit.	14
4C	Many musical numbers have been recorded by the New Brunswick Symphony.	14

Double letters (Uniform stroking)

5A	To the cheers of his winning team, Bill batted the ball over the wall.	14
5B	Allen agreed to appear at the school bazaar to accept the blue ribbon.	14
5C	Betty will tell Matt that it is necessary to accept the bigger drills.	14

Selected-finger drills (Finger-reach action)

6A	*1st finger*	Robert Graham bought many bright trimmings for the big reception room.	14
6B	*2d finger*	Chuck decided to dictate his introduction for the economic conference.	14
6C	*3d finger*	Willard wins the award for his excellent wax replicas of six swallows.	14
6D	*4th finger*	Hazel's pony squashed almost all of Zelda's prize poppies and azaleas.	14

Operative parts (Essential motion patterns)

7A		Space quickly after each word; keep your thumb close to the space bar.	14
7B	*Space bar*	Many of the men may leave the room soon if you ask them for any money.	14
8A		Jack McNary, Allen Fox, and Paul Appel work for McNeil, McAkan & Sons.	14
8B	*Shift key*	Vice-President James V. Hall, of the B & J Company, flew to Las Vegas.	14
9A	*Reading copy*	Try to read	this copy	in word groups.	Return the	carriage quickly	and	14
	and carriage	start	the new line	without a pause.	Try it again	with your eyes	here.	14
	return	You will find	that any new action	takes time to seem	like an easy one.	14

| 1 | 2 | 3 | 4 | 5 | 6 | 7 | 8 | 9 | 10 | 11 | 12 | 13 | 14 |

10C ■ STROKING TECHNIQUE PRACTICE [15] each line twice SS; then Lines 1, 2, and 3 from dictation

1	*N*	nj nj in no not on one an can and hand won now own.	*Finger-action reaches; hands and arms quiet*
2	*X*	xs xs six fix ax wax sax tax lax flax vex text fox	
3	*P*	p; p; up cup par part top stop post past pass step	
4	*All letters learned are*	a new tax; fix the step; one passed; six of us won	
5	*used in Lines 4-6*	I hope the new tax does not pass in the next town.	
6		John paid Lex for the clock; Virg put up the cash.	

10D ■ CONTINUITY PRACTICE [12] type twice; then type selected lines once more

Continuity Cue: Fingers curved; wrists low; eyes on the copy; quick, snappy strokes.

Spacing Cue: Keep the right thumb close to the space bar; space with a down-and-in motion.

1	on hand; torn down; once won; now own; and can now
2	Ann and Jan know that Fran can land the new plane.
3	a tax; wax an ax; fix the sax; a lax law; the text
4	Rex Fox can pick up all the tax rate cards at six.
5	put up, the top post, up to par, keeps up, top pen
6	Pete kept the pen next to the pad on his new desk.

```
| 1 | 2 | 3 | 4 | 5 | 6 | 7 | 8 | 9 | 10 |
```

10E ■ SELF-IMPROVEMENT PRACTICE [5]

■ The letter keys that are paired in the following sentences are sometimes confused because they are adjacent (side by side) on the keyboard.

■ Select the pairs that seem to have been most difficult for you and practice the lines in which those combinations are emphasized.

1	*A S*	Cass at last asked Sal to save on gas at the sale.	*Reach to the keys*
2	*C V*	Vince did count the votes; Vic proved it in court.	*without moving*
3	*D S*	I said she reads ads for leads to goods she needs.	*hands up or down or the elbows in*
4	*E W*	If we were Lew, we would learn a few words a week.	*or out*
5	*F G*	Gif can tee off at five for golf if the fog lifts.	
6	*I O*	I know that the soil at this point is void of oil.	
7	*O P*	Peg has passed up a top spot she won on that show.	
8	*R T*	Trig took a short train trip to a trade arts fair.	
9	*U I*	June said this fruit juice is sure to suit us all.	
10	*All letters learned*	If Ken or Vic Judd got a new set, he paid all tax.	

```
| 1 | 2 | 3 | 4 | 5 | 6 | 7 | 8 | 9 | 10 |
```

PROGRESSIVE-LENGTH STATISTICAL SENTENCES

		Words	15″	12″	10″
			G W A M		
1A	Type: 10, 26, 37, 48, 59, 60.	6	24	30	36
1B	Check Order #3970 (Jay & Co.).	6	24	30	36
2A	Is the number 123, 4,567, or 7,890?	7	28	35	42
2B	The discounts were 2%, 5%, and 10%.	7	28	35	42
3A	Cancel Policy Nos. 123–456 and 78–90–10.	8	32	40	48
3B	The Apollo helicopter sells for $14,500.	8	32	40	48
4A	Deliver Order #937 to 4568 West 120th Street.	9	36	45	54
4B	David's bicycle cost $48.50, less 2/10, n/30.	9	36	45	54
5A	The 1972 average was up 25.3% to a high of $84.50.	10	40	50	60
5B	Sell the #148 J&B tool (heat treated) for $293.50.	10	40	50	60
6A	Quarterly income climbed to $3,856,200 from $2,749,500.	11	44	55	66
6B	Jamison & Company over-the-counter stock sells for $59.	11	44	55	66
7A	1 old 2 was 3 end 4 fur 5 fit 6 jay 7 jam 8 kit 9 old 10 pal	12	48	60	72
7B	"2 @ #3 $4 5% 6¢ 7&8' * (90) Rates increased from 4¼% to 4½%.	12	48	60	72
8A	The F&M average declined from $985.10 to $743.26, or about 24.5%.	13	52	65	78
8B	The inventory shows 1,467 of the #385 item (gross lots @ $92.50).	13	52	65	78

PROGRESSIVE-LENGTH ROUGH-DRAFT SENTENCES

		Words	15″	12″	10″
			G W A M		
1A	I shall [will] not carry the disscussion farther.	8	32	40	48
1B	TWA flight may [will] arrive at 8:30 pm.	8	32	40	48
2A	I [We] plan to attend the game on new Year's day.	9	36	45	54
2B	I will [may] give a report on the holy Roman empire.	9	36	45	54
3A	There were grapes, plums, and peaches in the sack.	10	40	50	60
3B	They will need other data to complete the reports.	10	40	50	60
4A	The title of the book is Business and Society. [required / Caps]	11	44	55	66
4B	Did he [she] read the article "the act of creation?" [FORTUNE]	11	44	55	66
5A	He did not know the facts; consequently, he flunked [failed] the test.	12	48	60	72
5B	If I am elected, I promise to [shall] work for improved teacher salaries.	12	48	60	72
6A	We are using Effective Business English (Robinson) for reference.	13	52	65	78
6B	Au revoir means "good-bye"; laissez faire means "noninterference."	13	52	65	78

■ LESSON 11

Standard Directions for Lessons 11-15

1. *Margins:* left, center point — 25 spaces;
   right, moved to end of scale.

2. *Spacing:* drills, single-spaced; paragraphs,
   double-spaced and indented 5 spaces.

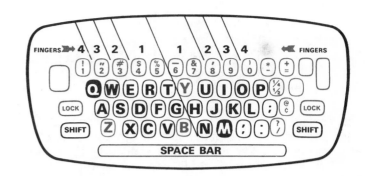

11A ■ CONDITIONING PRACTICE [8] each line twice SS; DS after each 2-line group

All letters learned	Gif will ask Jen to our Hove Park dance next week.
N X P	Pat Nix put the text of the tax plan on tape next.
Easy sentence	It is up to her to see that all this work is done.

`|  1  |  2  |  3  |  4  |  5  |  6  |  7  |  8  |  9  |  10  |`

Return without looking up; start new line quickly

11B ■ NEW KEY LOCATION: Q, M [7]

REACH TECHNIQUE FOR Q

Reach the *left fourth finger* up to type **q** without swinging the elbow out or arching the wrist.

qa qa qq aqa aqa qq qa qa

qa quit quite qa quit qt. *DS*

REACH TECHNIQUE FOR M

Reach the *right first finger* down to type **m**. Do not move the hand down or swing the elbow out.

mj mj mm jmj jmj mm mj mj

mj me map jam ham gum sum *TS*

Spacing Summary: Space once after , and ; and once after . at the end of an abbreviation or following an initial. Space twice after . at the end of a sentence. *Do not space* after any punctuation mark that ends a line.

11C ■ STROKING TECHNIQUE PRACTICE [10] each line twice SS; DS after each 2-line group

1	*Q*	qa quit quick quite quote quell quest squad quaint
2	*M*	mj me men met am same man main make more most must
3	*Q M*	quite quick, meet him, main quest, most quick men,
4	*Q M*	Marv Quinn has quit to move to a quaint farm home.
5	*Consolidation*	Rex Quig used qt. and gal.; J. M. Poe, ft. and in.

Fingers vertical, not slanting, over home keys

SUPPLEMENTARY ACTIVITIES

■ The supplementary drills, timed writings, and problems given on these pages are designed to help students gain additional basic and applied typing skills.

The supplementary drills can be used to force speed, to improve technique patterns, or to build accuracy. A variety of special teaching procedures can be used with these materials.

The supplementary timed writings provide additional copy of increasing difficulty: Syllable intensity, 1.4 to 1.5; average word length, 5.4 to 5.6; and high-frequency words, 85% to 80%.

The problem materials include letters, a manuscript, tables, memorandums, and various business forms in rough-draft, script, and straight-copy form.

SUPPLEMENTARY DRILLS
PROGRESSIVE-DIFFICULTY STRAIGHT-COPY SENTENCES

High-frequency words emphasized

		Words	GWAM 15"	12"	10"
1A	They may go with me to do the work.	7	28	35	42
1B	Did he go to the firm on that date?	7	28	35	42
1C	Were you after a minimum base rate?	7	28	35	42
2A	It is right to make them do their forms.	8	32	40	48
2B	Send this man to our Service Department.	8	32	40	48
2C	We can get only a minimum water reserve.	8	32	40	48
3A	The chairman may wish to sign the right form.	9	36	45	54
3B	The new manager may give you the information.	9	36	45	54
3C	Refer only the extra estate tax cases to him.	9	36	45	54
4A	He, also, may make their six men pay for the form.	10	40	50	60
4B	Send a letter and the check to that firm tomorrow.	10	40	50	60
4C	You were to get my opinion on the estate tax only.	10	40	50	60
5A	When they work with us, then he may sign the amendment.	11	44	55	66
5B	Was the city chairman aware of the fact when he called?	11	44	55	66
5C	Was the oil trade-war case to be read before this date?	11	44	55	66
6A	She may handle a quantity of the problem forms for the firm.	12	48	60	72
6B	The men handle all new orders with extra care and attention.	12	48	60	72
6C	My one regret is that I cannot serve the state area for you.	12	48	60	72
7A	She may pay their men the profit due them if they visit the town.	13	52	65	78
7B	He can handle many of the problems with a minimum of wasted time.	13	52	65	78
7C	Only a few of the extra cases can be referred to you for opinion.	13	52	65	78
8A	The field chairman did half of the problems and cut the profit due me.	14	56	70	84
8B	Please refer many of these amendments to the city chairman for action.	14	56	70	84
8C	In your opinion, are the average water reserves far below the minimum?	14	56	70	84

| 1 | 2 | 3 | 4 | 5 | 6 | 7 | 8 | 9 | 10 | 11 | 12 | 13 | 14 |

11D ■ SENTENCE GUIDED WRITING 17

Exploration (Speed) Level of Practice: When the purpose of practice is to reach out into new speed areas, use the *exploration level*. Take the brakes off your fingers and experiment with new stroking patterns and new speeds.	Control Level of Practice: When the purpose of practice is to type with ease and control, drop back in rate and type on the *control level*. This drop back should be from 4 to 8 words below the exploration (speed) level.

1. Type each line once untimed to explore stroking patterns.
2. Type each line with the 30-second guide call (see p. 16).
3. Type each sentence as a 1-minute writing without the guides.

All letters and punctuation marks learned are used.

		Words in Line	GWAM 30″ Guide
1	Have a goal; work to reach it.	6	12
2	It is how we work that counts most.	7	14
3	She did use a quick stroke at all times.	8	16
4	His work is done as well as he can do it now.	9	18
5	If we do all our work well, we can get to the top.	10	20
6	So do not quit now. Just fix a high goal in mind.	10	20

| 1 | 2 | 3 | 4 | 5 | 6 | 7 | 8 | 9 | 10 |

11E ■ TABULATING PROCEDURE 8

TO CLEAR TAB STOPS
1. Move carriage to extreme left.
2. Depress **tab clear key (31)** and hold it down as you pull carriage all the way to the right to remove all tab stops.

■ *SCM and Olympia typewriters have a Total Tab Clear Key that clears all stops at once.*

TO SET TAB STOPS
■ Move the carriage to the desired position; then depress the **tab set key (23)**. Repeat this procedure for each stop needed.

TABULATING TECHNIQUE
Manual (Nonelectric): Depress and hold the **tab bar (24)** [right first finger] or **key** [right fourth finger] down until the carriage has stopped.

Electric (and Some Nonelectric): Tap the **tab key (24)** [little finger] or **bar** [index finger] lightly; return the finger to home-key position at once.

DO: 1. Clear all tab stops, as directed above.
2. Begin Column 1 at the left margin.
3. **Set tab for Column 2:** 15 spaces beyond left margin.
4. **Set tab for Column 3:** 15 spaces beyond beginning of Column 2.
5. **Set tab for Column 4:** 16 spaces beyond beginning of Column 3.

Type the words as shown DS, tabulating from column to column.

and	*Tab* →	the	*Tab* →	with	*Tab* →	quit
did		jot		gown		make
fix		due		paid		sent
for		cot		have		land

| KEY | 3 | 12 | 3 | 12 | 4 | 12 | 4 |

3. Proofreading Skill Measurement (Alertness Check) (15′)

The "Correct-It-As-You-Type" letter shown below contains many proofreading errors; misspelled words; errors of word division, capitalization, punctuation, and number usage; errors of spacing and paragraphing; omitted words. Follow these steps:

1. Make all necessary proofreading corrections as you type the letter. Be alert.

2. After you have completed the letter, circle any uncorrected proofreading errors you have as your teacher reads the corrections. Mark the necessary corrections on your copy.

3. Score your proofreading skill by deducting 2 points from 100 for each uncorrected proofreading error.

	Words

	Words
Modified block, ¶s indented / Current date on Line 12 / Mixed punctuation / Correct your typing errors	

Mr. Peter Jeffries, Manager │ Student Service Bureau │ Indianapolis — 16

High School │ Indianapolis, IN   46200 — 23

Your letter about the need for proofreeding on the part of all — 36

typist's is a reel concern to us, to. Listed hear are some of the — 49

steps in profreading that we require our typist's to learn and to fo- — 63

llow: — 64

1. Check the placement and general form of the letter: — 76

Is the letter well balanced on the page? Does it look — 87

like a picture in a frame? Have all keys ben struck — 97

with uniform force? Will the leter made a good first — 108

impression. — 111

2. Check the correctniss of all figures and amonts: Is the adress — 125

correct? Are the street name and numbers correct? Has the typist been — 139

consistent in typing figures, such as eight, 26, forty-two. — 150

3. Check the exactness of the content, including the grammer and spel- — 164

ling: does the letter make good cents and does it convay the intend- — 177

ed meaning? Are the werds divided correctly at the ends of lines? — 192

Are their any mispelled words in the letter. are there any errors of — 206

capitalization or punctuation. — 212

dont hesitate to rite to us for any other help we can give you. — 225

I wish you continued success with your student service bureau. — 238

sincerely yurs │ derek e. zahl │ communications consultant │ (215) — 249

4. Spelling Skill Measurement (10′)   (Full sheet; reading position; DS data; 12 spaces between columns)

Arrange the list of words given below in an attractive 2-column table as the words are dictated to you by your teacher. Do this:

1. Determine the vertical and horizontal placement of the table before dictation is started. There will be 25 words in each column. Assume the longest line in each column has 12 letters.

2. Center the main heading; then close your book and type and tabulate from column to column as the words are dictated to you.

3. After the list has been dictated, open your book and check the spelling of each word. Circle each misspelled word.

4. Score your spelling skill by deducting 2 points from 100 for each misspelled word.

Main heading: WORDS FREQUENTLY MISSPELLED │

absence irrelevance │ accommodate liaison │ airmail losing │ argument	
mileage │ attendance miscellaneous │ beginning misspell │ belief ninety │	
believe occasion │ brief occurred │ bureau pamphlet │ business permitted │	
calendar planned │ campaign privilege │ conferring proceed │ cooperate	
profited │ copying quantity │ definite receipt │ definition receive │	
desirable recommend │ difference referring │ enough separate │ existence	
similar │ familiar studying │ government supersede │ intelligence weird │	

■ LESSON 12

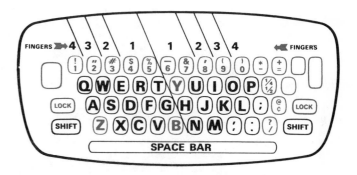

Hand Position: Position the fingers vertically, not slanting, over the home keys. Keep the fingers curved and the wrists relaxed and low.

12A ■ CONDITIONING PRACTICE 8 each line 3 times SS; DS after each 3-line group

First Writing: Type at a well-controlled pace the first time you type each line.

Second Writing: Explore new stroking patterns at a faster pace for the second writing. Force your speed.

Third Writing: Slow up slightly during the third writing of each line. Work for improved control.

All letters learned   Len was quick to send five tax forms to John Page.   *Return without pausing*

Q   M   Ask Sam Quill to meet the squad if Max Quim quits.

Easy sentence   I know it is how I think and what I do that count.

| 1 | 2 | 3 | 4 | 5 | 6 | 7 | 8 | 9 | 10 |

12B ■ REINFORCEMENT PRACTICE 20 each line twice; repeat selected lines as time permits

1   G   N   W   Gene will go to town to get a white gown for Gwen.   *Reduce time lag between strokes*

2   P   V   ,   Dave, Paul, and Vince were put up at a fine place.

3   Q   M   X   Rex will have much more to do if Max Squire quits.

4   T   C   O   Joe told Tom to take these checks to town to cash.

5   I   E   D   Their friends tried to trade eight tires to Keith.

6   U   A   L   Alf and Stu just gave us all their old cuff links.

7   H   S   K   Hank Shore has asked if he can take six weeks off.

8   F   J   .   J. F. Jacques is at Ft. Knox; Joe Fox, at Ft. Dix.

9   All letters learned   Five or six grown men just had to have quick help.

10   Easy sentence   He can lend a hand if that will get the work done.

| 1 | 2 | 3 | 4 | 5 | 6 | 7 | 8 | 9 | 10 |

■ LESSON 150

150A ■ CONDITIONING PRACTICE [5] each line 3 times: slowly, faster, top speed

Alphabet   The quick, ambiguous quiz on job pay vexed all who had studied for it.   *Speed with control*

Figure/symbol   He borrowed $25,600 at 8 3/4% in 1970 under an FHA mortgage (234-560).

Adjacent keys   Robert tired quickly as he tried to remove the five turrethead rivets.

Fluency   Education discloses to the wise not how much they know but how little.
    | 1 | 2 | 3 | 4 | 5 | 6 | 7 | 8 | 9 | 10 | 11 | 12 | 13 | 14 |

150B ■ SKILL MEASUREMENT: EMPLOYMENT TESTING [45]

1. Straight-Copy Skill Measurement (8′)   repeat 149B-1, page 229; **Goal:** to improve your rate

2. Related Learning Measurement (12′)   (74-space line; start first sentence 1″ from top edge of paper)

Type the problem sentences given below, making appropriate corrections at the points of color underlines as the sentences are typed. Follow these steps:

1. Type the number of the sentence; then type the sentence in corrected form. Triple-space after each sentence.

2. Type the sentences from your teacher's dictation as they are dictated with the corrections indicated. Type the dictated sentence on the line below the sentence to which it applies.

3. Mark your sentences for related learning errors. Record number of errors with your name.

1. Colors of a spectrum are violet blue green yellow orange and red.

2. he will meet the governor at the century club on tuesday of next week.

3. As I was washing the sergeant a man no one liked suddenly appeared.

4. I shall be at my office at 10 30 am, and I shall leave at 11 30 am.

5. 8 visitors from the east are here; fifteen or 20 more will arrive soon.

6. Spectrum tables show to a ten-billionth of a millimeter color lines.

7. The letters exhibit 1 and the documents exhibit 13 will be needed.

8. He said, his exact words were I want to go there in a day or two.

9. The letter didnt arrive in fact it couldnt since it wasnt mailed.

10. A boys tricycle was found, but the girls bicycles are still missing.

11. It is difficult to tell your 5s from your 6s. Sell Chicago Fund 4's.

12. Before you leave today, please take the book to Sister Alexis office.

13. Johns class of 67 will meet today. cross your t s and dot your i s.

12C ■ TABULATING PRACTICE 10 · once DS; tab from column to column; return carriage quickly

MARGIN STOP   + 15 spaces = TAB   + 15 spaces = TAB   + 16 spaces = TAB

men	was	them	were
six	dew	take	face
pen	fee	lane	dart
jot	get	have	quit
for	had	will	work
all	can	much	gave
off	put	just	done

KEY | 3 | 12 | 3 | 12 | 4 | 12 | 4 |

12D ■ CONTINUITY (PARAGRAPH) TYPING 12

DO: Clear all tab stops; then set a tab stop for a 5-space paragraph (¶) indention. Use double spacing. Tab to indent the ¶s.

LEARN: To remove a single tab stop without canceling all others, tabulate to the stop and operate tab clear key.

TYPE: The ¶s as shown; then type 1-minute writings on each ¶ as time permits. Ignore your errors temporarily.

All letters learned are used.

GWAM
1' | 2'

¶ 1*   Indent 5 ——→ If I am to win, I must not stop just now. I   9 | 4

must keep on, one quick move at a time. If I can   19 | 9

work on and not lose hope, I will learn.   27 | 13

¶ 2   Indent 5 ——→ I will reach out once more; next time, I can   9 | 18

reach the speed. It is how I work now that means   19 | 23

a lot. If I keep on, I can make a goal at a time.   29 | 28

1' GWAM | 1 | 2 | 3 | 4 | 5 | 6 | 7 | 8 | 9 | 10 |
2' GWAM | 1 | 2 | 3 | 4 | 5 |

---

*COPY DIFFICULTY

■ The ease with which a paragraph can be typed is influenced by three major factors: 1—*Syllable intensity* (SI) or average number of syllables per word; 2—*Stroke intensity* or average word length (AWL); 3—*Percent of high-frequency words* (HFW) from "A Basic Vocabulary for Typewriting." Careful control of these three factors—SI, AWL, and HFW—makes it possible to show the difficulty of the copy selections in this book as very easy (VE), easy (E), low average (LA), average (A), high average (HA), or difficult (D). The difficulty index at the right shows an SI of 1.2 syllables, an AWL of 5.0 strokes, and an HFW of 95%; a composite of VE.

■ Leave your work station in order for the next student who is to use it.

2. Tabulation-Copy Skill Measurement (unarranged copy) (28′) correct errors

Time Schedule	
Planning and preparing	3′
Tabulation production timing . .	20′
Proofreading; determining *n-pram* .	5′

Arrange this problem in proper form as you type it. You will have about 3′ to plan the setup; make pencil notations of the points at which heading lines begin. Stay ALERT as you type. Proofread; determine *n-pram*: total words minus 15 for each error divided by 20.

Full sheet
Reading position
Underline columnar headings
DS columnar data
4 spaces between columns
Longest line in each column is color under-lined

Each figure is used a minimum of 15 times

When a street has a number as its name, separate the house number from the street number by a hyphen preceded and followed by a space.

				Words in Cols.	Total Words
Main heading: NEW INSTALLMENT ACCOUNTS					5
Secondary heading: (Spring Quarter)					8
Columnar headings: Name	Street Address	City and State	ZIP Code		25
Cynthia Bowman	7820 Thurston Circle	Los Angeles, CA	90049	12	37
Ida Cole	848 Allen Street	Hackensack, NJ	07601	21	47
Lucille Faye	63 Sea Cliff Avenue	Sea Cliff, NY	11579	32	57
Marie Gordon	8488 Fenton Street	Denver, CO	80227	42	67
John Hills, Jr.	939 Riverview Drive	Columbus, OH	43202	53	79
Frank B. Johnston	483 Danbury Street	Wichita, KS	67220	65	90
Joseph Long	4659 Portola Drive	San Francisco, CA	94127	76	101
Kevin Maley	5659 E. Upsal Street	Philadelphia, PA	19150	87	112
Wayne McClure, Jr.	8385 Sam Cooper Road	Knoxville, TN	37918	99	124
Peter Mullins	4668 Star Lane, N.E.	Minneapolis, MN	55421	111	136
Darren Paulson	3947 E. Broad Street	Tampa, FL	33610	121	147
Roy W. Roberts	56 Gloucester Street	Boston, MA	02100	132	157
Mark Rogers	3948 W. Elm Street	Greensboro, NC	27406	143	168
Jason Sawatzky	6789 Chicago Avenue	Evanston, IL	60201	154	179
Gary E. Thompson	1391 Fontaine Road	Lexington, KY	40502	165	190
Burt Wieland	4758 Indigo Street	Houston, TX	77035	175	201
Betty Williams	629 – 19th St., N.W.	Oklahoma City, OK	73127	188	213
Scott Zimmer	3465 Clematis Blvd.	Pittsburgh, PA	15235	199	224

3. Envelope Skill Measurement (9′)

a. Type as many small envelopes as you can (using the addresses above) as you are timed for 5′. Start with the first address. Use appropriate titles: *Miss* or *Mr.* with each name.

b. Determine envelope *gwam* by dividing words typed (*Words in Columns* figures) by 5. Put addressed envelopes in order; record your name and rate on first envelope. Put a rubber band around envelopes.

◼ LESSON 13

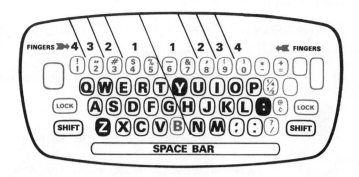

Tabulating Technique: Tap and release the tab bar or key on all electric and *some* nonelectric machines; hold the tab bar or key down on others.

13A ◼ CONDITIONING PRACTICE 8 each line 3 times SS; DS after each 3-line group

All letters learned   Paul has just picked Virg for his next swim squad.   *Eyes on copy*

Long, direct reaches   deck once great large hunt nurse must curve serves

Easy sentence   I paid the men for all their work for these firms.

| 1 | 2 | 3 | 4 | 5 | 6 | 7 | 8 | 9 | 10 |

13B ◼ TABULATING PRACTICE 8 type twice; tab from column to column

MARGIN ↓	+ 15 = TAB ↓	+ 15 = TAB ↓	+ 16 = TAB ↓
all	not	quit	post
off	act	stop	sure
too	two	will	term
odd	vex	joke	high

KEY | 3 | 12 | 3 | 12 | 4 | 12 | 4 |

13C ◼ NEW KEY LOCATION: Y, Z, COLON (:) 10

REACH TECHNIQUE FOR Y

Reach the *right first finger* up to type **y**. Do not arch the wrist or move other fingers from home keys.

yj yj yy jyj jyj yy yj yj

yj yet yj say jay hay may *DS*

REACH TECHNIQUE FOR Z

Reach the *left little finger* down to type **z**. Avoid moving the hand or the elbow in or out.

za za zz aza aza zz za za

za haze zeal za size doz. *DS*

REACH TECHNIQUE FOR :

Depress the left shift key and at the same time strike ; with the *right fourth finger* to type : .

:; :; ;:; ;:; Shift for :

Dear Sir: Dear Mr. Kent: *TS*

1. Straight-Copy Skill Measurement (8')   5' writing; circle errors; determine GWAM

All letters are used.

		G W A M
	1'	5'

¶ 1

	1'	5'	
Some of you may soon be moving from a somewhat structured school	13	3	72
situation to a relatively unstructured work situation. One of your ini-	27	5	75
tial problems may be the wise utilization of your working time. It is	41	8	77
always easy to waste time; this truth becomes even more obvious in the	56	11	80
work situation. For example, most business organizations have a coffee	70	14	83
or rest break in the morning and again in the afternoon. Some employees	85	17	86
may take more than the allotted time for the break. This habit is, in	99	20	89
a very genuine sense, almost the same as stealing from their employer	113	23	92
because the employees are being paid for work time they are not spending	127	25	95
on the job. Your employer has a right to expect that you will use your	142	28	98
work time in a conscientious and responsible manner. One way to do this	156	31	100
is to plan and organize your work so that it can be completed within a	170	34	103
specified time period.	175	35	105

¶ 2

	1'	5'	
Still another distinct problem may be in the human relations domain.	14	38	107
In the world of work you will associate with many different kinds of	28	41	110
people. Some of these persons you may enjoy and others you may dislike;	42	43	113
nevertheless, it is essential that you learn how to get along with those	57	46	116
whom you may not care for as well as with those whom you like. If you	71	49	118
are to promote your relations with others, you often will have to make	85	52	121
an earnest effort to do so. In strained situations, you will learn that	100	55	124
good manners are a positive asset. Also, you should realize that the	114	58	127
irritations and issues of the work situation can readily be transmitted	128	61	130
into curt or impatient dealings with the clients of the company by whom	143	64	133
you are employed. As you can appreciate, your employer has a direct and	157	66	136
distinct concern in how satisfactorily you can get along with others.	171	69	139

1' GWAM	1	2	3	4	5	6	7	8	9	10	11	12	13	14
5' GWAM		1			2			3	

13D ■ STROKING TECHNIQUE PRACTICE 10 Lines 1-3 twice each; then, if time permits, Lines 4 and 5

1 *Y*   y yj yj my may why try yes yet you your yours type   *Fingers curved and upright*

2 *Z*   z za zag zig zip zoo oz. doz. zone jazz size prize

3 *:*   ;: ;: :p: Type: Date: To: From: Dear Mr. Graf: *Space twice after :*

4 *Consolidation*   Type: oz.; doz.; Ky. Type: Zip them to my zone.

5 *Consolidation*   Doug Pitts can have Joy Mack freeze my six quarts.

13E ■ CONTINUITY (PARAGRAPH) PRACTICE 7

1. Type the paragraph once without timing. Note any words that cause stroking difficulty.

2. Practice the difficult words two or three times; then type two 1' writings on the paragraph.

All letters learned are used.

	1' GWAM
I do not need to push if I can just keep on,	9
one key at a time. I shall type a key and let it	19
go at once. I shall not quit, for that will stop	29
my speed gain. I have the zeal to win next time.	39

1' GWAM | 1 | 2 | 3 | 4 | 5 | 6 | 7 | 8 | 9 | 10 |

13F ■ SELF-IMPROVEMENT PRACTICE 7

1. Type the first line of each of the following pairs once without timing. Place a check mark beside those lines that seem most difficult.

2. For each line you checked as difficult, type the line that is paired with it. The second line contains similar stroking combinations.

1 *Adjacent keys*   Wes Pohle said he needs a new pair of walk shorts.   *Keep on typing; do not pause*
2   Franz Yule said he struck oil at three new points.

3 *Direct reaches*   Lum Deece once had a large place in which to hunt.
4   My nurse served him a great lunch on the sun deck.

5 *Balanced-hand*   She did lend a hand when they did the work for me.
6   When I work with good form, I type with speed too.

7 *Double letters*   Lynne did pass the pool as she took off for class.
8   All seem at a loss to know who called at the mill.

9 *Shift keys*   Don Fox and Jo Maze won a large share of the vote.
10   Paul Hakes and Val Quinn go to the dance at eight.

| 1 | 2 | 3 | 4 | 5 | 6 | 7 | 8 | 9 | 10 |

All letters are used.

¶ 1

An average lifespan of 70 years is composed of approximately 25,567 days, or 613,608 hours. About 45.8% of this time is used up in sleeping, eating, and performing other essential biological functions. This time is the equivalent of 11,710 days, or about 32.1 years. Another 34.8% of the total time is spent in what might be labelled leisure- or free-time activities. This time is equal to 8,897 days, or about 24.4 years. If a person works from ages 21 to 67, he spends about 15.6% of his total lifetime at work. This time is the equivalent of 3,988 days, or about 10.9 years. Still another 3.8% of the total lifetime may be occupied in commuting to work (about 972 days, or 2.6 years).

¶ 2

From the beginning of man's life on this earth, it took about 7.9 million years for the population to reach a total of 10 million. Then from the Neolithic age to the time of Christ, a period of some 10,000 years, the population grew to 300 million. From the period of Christ to the days of Columbus (1492), the total population of the earth reached 500 million. In the next 350 years, from the time of Columbus until 1850, the population grew to a total of 1 billion. In just 75 years, from 1850 to 1925, the population soared to 2 billion. In another 37 years, from 1925 to 1962, the population reached 3 billion. It has been estimated that by 1982, in a period of only 20 years, the population will reach 5 billion.

GWAM 1'	5'	
12	2	59
27	5	62
41	8	65
56	11	68
70	14	71
84	17	74
98	20	76
113	23	79
127	25	82
139	28	84
13	30	87
27	33	90
41	36	93
56	39	96
70	42	98
84	45	101
98	47	104
112	50	107
127	53	110
140	56	113
145	57	113

1' GWAM | 1 | 2 | 3 | 4 | 5 | 6 | 7 | 8 | 9 | 10 | 11 | 12 | 13 | 14 |
5' GWAM | 1 | 2 | 3 |

■ LESSON 149

149A ■ CONDITIONING PRACTICE 5 each line 3 times: slowly, faster, top speed

Alphabet   The travel expert frequently amazed us with talks about jungle dances. *Fingers curved and upright*

Figure/symbol   After May 5, Jerry's new address will be 4782 Polk & Fell (ZIP 93106).

Fingers 3, 4   Aza Quando said that Wally saw a plump polo pony down by the aquaduct.

Fluency   The good student is one who reads more, studies more, and thinks more.

| 1 | 2 | 3 | 4 | 5 | 6 | 7 | 8 | 9 | 10 | 11 | 12 | 13 | 14 |

■ LESSON 14

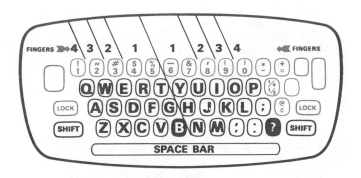

Spacing Technique: Hold the right thumb curved and close to the space bar; use a quick, down-and-in spacing motion (toward the palm).

14A ■ CONDITIONING PRACTICE 〔8〕 each line 3 times SS; DS after each 3-line group

All letters learned   Vern Fox asked Jack to help on my great quiz show.   *Sit erect; do not slouch*

Double letters   all call ill will well too took off scoff see seek

Easy sentence   It is all up to me now. I have to do my own work.
　　　　　　　| 1 | 2 | 3 | 4 | 5 | 6 | 7 | 8 | 9 | 10 |

14B ■ NEW KEY LOCATION: B, QUESTION (?), BACKSPACER 〔10〕

REACH TECHNIQUE FOR B

Reach the *left first finger* down to type **b** without moving the hand from its typing position.

bf bf bb fbf fbf bb bf bf

bf bid but bf big rub rob DS

REACH TECHNIQUE FOR ?

Type **?** with the *right fourth finger*. Remember to shift to type **?**. Space twice after **?** at end of sentence.

?; ?; ?? ;?; ;?; ?? ?; ?;

?; ?; Is he? Is he next? DS

BACKSPACE TECHNIQUE

To fill in an omitted letter or to position the carriage, depress the **backspace key (30)**.

Electric: Reach with the little finger (right or left, depending upon key location); tap and release the key quickly.

Manual (Nonelectric): Reach with the appropriate finger; depress the key firmly; release it quickly.

Tryout Drill: Type **a d** as shown, then backspace twice and fill in the missing letter. Type the other combinations in the same way.

a d t e t h t y o r j u t r
　n　　h　　a　　u　　s　　o

14C ■ STROKING TECHNIQUE PRACTICE 〔10〕 each line twice; backspace to fill in missing letters in Line 3

1 *B*   bf bf by buy boy but box big be bet best rub clubs

2 *?*   ?; ?; Who? What? When? Where? Why? Is it you?   *Space twice after ? at the end of a sentence, once after ? within a sentence*

3 *Backspacer*   Ja k Jon s, Di k S ith, Ral h Ho mes, M ke C arles

4 *Consolidation*   Did Bill Blake lob the ball? or was it Bob Branch?

5 *Consolidation*   Did B. Z. Quinn leave your club at one? or at two?

3. Letter Production Skill Measurement (28′)   (Letterhead or plain paper; 1 carbon copy; correct errors)

Time Schedule	
Planning and preparing	3′
Letter production timing	20′
Proofreading; computing *n-pram* .	5′

Using the ¶s of the rough draft on page 226 as the body of the letter (343 words), type letters as directed below. If you complete the letters before time is up, start over. When time is called, proofread carefully. Subtract 15 words from the total words typed for each *uncorrected* error. Compute *n-pram.*

a. Block style letter (*open punctuation*)

	Words
Opening lines:	
Current date │ Mrs. Barbara Simi, Chairman │	9
Business Education Department │ Indian Hill	17
High School │ Cincinnati, OH 45227 │ Dear	25
Mrs. Simi │	27
(+ Body words)	370
Closing lines:	
Sincerely yours │ Douglas Cords │ Personnel	378
Director │ (xxx)	380

b. Modified block style with 5-space ¶ indentions (*mixed punctuation*)

	Words
Opening lines:	
Current date │ Mr. William Anderson, Chairman │ Business Education Department │ Buena	8
	16
High School │ Ventura, CA 93003 │ Dear	24
Mr. Anderson: │	27
(+ Body words)	370
Closing lines:	
Sincerely yours, │ Douglas Cords │ Personnel	378
Director │ (xxx)	380

■ LESSON 148

148A ■ CONDITIONING PRACTICE [5] each line 3 times: slowly, faster, top speed

Alphabet   A fog-like haze developed quickly just as the workmen left the boxcar.   *Type with continuity*

Figure/symbol A $10 million 25-year 7% debenture was offered at $96 to yield 8 3/4%.

Adjacent key   That very popular but brave aquanaut was not careless in water sports.

Fluency   The full value of happiness is gained through sharing it with someone.
                 | 1 | 2 | 3 | 4 | 5 | 6 | 7 | 8 | 9 | 10 | 11 | 12 | 13 | 14 |

148B ■ TECHNIQUE EVALUATION [15] repeat 146B, page 222; **Goal:** Further refinement of techniques

148C ■ SKILL MEASUREMENT: EMPLOYMENT TESTING [30]

1. Straight-Copy Skill Measurement (10′)
Type a 5′ writing using the paragraphs of 147B-1, page 225.

◆**Goal:** To improve your previous rate, or to reduce the number of errors made.

2. Rough-Draft Skill Measurement (10′)
Type a 5′ writing using the paragraphs of 147B-2, page 226. Compute % of transfer.

◆**Goal:** To exceed your previous rate and to maintain an accuracy goal of not more than five errors.

3. Statistical-Copy Skill Measurement (10′)
Type a 5′ writing on the paragraphs at the top of page 228. Compute % of transfer.

◆**Goal:** To keep your eyes on the copy, to type with continuity, and with not more than five errors.

14D ■ CONTINUITY PRACTICE `15` type the drill 3 times

1 *B Y*   by your; if you buy; best box; big boy; bring back
2   Troy, did you buy the big box of books by my desk?

3 *Z :*   Dear Dr. Zahn: Dear Miss Zier: Dear Mrs. Stoltz: *Space twice*
4   Read the word group: my size; your zoo; try jazz.   *after :*

5 *All letters*   he we up or on be my can lid tax jug ask five quiz
6   If Vic Gould shows up, Jake Zorne may quit by six.
           | 1 | 2 | 3 | 4 | 5 | 6 | 7 | 8 | 9 | 10 |

14E ■ PARAGRAPH (CONTINUITY) TYPING `7` type ¶ once; then type a 1' and a 2' writing

All letters are used.

GWAM
1'   2'

What goal should you go for next: speed? or   9 | 4 | 23

good form? You have to work for both, of course,   19 | 9 | 28

but just one at a time. It is quite right to try   29 | 14 | 33

for the prize of good form first, then speed.   38 | 19 | 38

1' GWAM | 1 | 2 | 3 | 4 | 5 | 6 | 7 | 8 | 9 | 10 |
2' GWAM | 1 | 2 | 3 | 4 | 5 |

■ LESSON 15

15A ■ CONDITIONING PRACTICE `8` each line 3 times SS; DS after each 3-line group

All letters   Zoe Jacks may prep Lew Dove for the next big quiz.   *Return quickly*

B ? :   Do be sure to shift for ? and : but not for ; or .

Easy sentence Try to get one or two of your best men to help us.
                | 1 | 2 | 3 | 4 | 5 | 6 | 7 | 8 | 9 | 10 |

15B ■ MANIPULATIVE PARTS DRILL: REVIEW `10` type twice

Line 1: Set tab stops to have 5 spaces between words; tabulate from word to word.

Line 5: Type **n xt**; backspace and fill in the missing letter. Type other combinations in the same way.

1 *Tabulator*   to   5   and   5   was   5   the   5   you   5   she   5   are

2 *Space bar*   Date: To: From: File: should head my new form.

3 *Left shift*   Have these boys do the work: Jack, Ned, and Matt.

4 *Right shift* Did Frank, Grant, and Carl go to Rome? or to Bern?

5 *Backspacer*   n xt, ca d, qu z, the r, rig t, pr ve, th re, z st
                 | 1 | 2 | 3 | 4 | 5 | 6 | 7 | 8 | 9 | 10 |

2. Rough-Draft Skill Measurement (9') 5' writing; circle errors; determine GWAM

Scan the copy quickly to be sure you understand the
corrections; make indicated corrections as you type.

All letters are used.

¶ 1 (1.5 / 5.6 / A / 80)

Here are some of the ~~things~~ *points* I would ~~point up~~ *emphasize* were I to talk to   13 | 3
who are about to enter the world of work.
your students. First, I would stress the importance of good personal   35 | 7
company
traits. our ~~firm~~ rapidly promot~~es~~ ~~workers~~ *employees* who have a sense of duty,   50 | 10
who can solve problems by themselves,   57 | 11
and who can promptly complete tasks assigned to them ~~and~~ in the   69 | 14
or mode prescribed.
manner ~~in which we want them done.~~ The employee who can wo~~r~~k ~~well~~ *effectively*   83 | 17
who amiable and kind
with other and is ~~tactful and considerate~~ will always be in demand.   96 | 19
Skill in communication
~~The ability to communicate effectively~~ is also very important. I   106 | 21
recommend to a   person   jargon
would like to ~~caution~~ young ~~students~~ that although the ~~"in"~~ vocabulary~~s~~   119 | 24
satisfactory   talk
of the teenager may be a ~~suitable~~ way to ~~communicate~~ with his own   132 | 26
peer group   in
~~fellow students~~ while he is school, it is a poor~~t~~ substitute for   145 | 29
vocabulary   good
the ~~words~~ needed for ~~adequate~~ expression and communication in the   158 | 32
office.
business ~~world.~~   161 | 32

¶ 2 (1.5 / 5.6 / A / 80)

emphasize   concerning
~~Next,~~ I would have to ~~say~~ that attitude ~~about~~ the job and toward   15 | 36

work is exceedingly important. Our company puts a premium on employees   30 | 39
assist
who are willing to ~~help~~ others during a rush period--even though this   44 | 42
now and then d
means working over~~C~~time. We rewar~~e~~ workers who have the ability   59 | 45
a rush job   nonetheless
to do ~~work~~ under pressure and ~~still~~ retain the composure needed to   75 | 48
as it should be done   importance
get the job done. Of equal ~~value~~, too, is the employee who can   93 | 52
regular
understand and follow directions which may not be stated in a ~~straight~~   107 | 54
Spell numbers   be   the employee
(1, 2, 3) sequence; these may directions which require ~~him~~ to make   124 | 58
and then to work his plan if
some decisions, ~~and~~ to plan his work, *he is to get the task completed.*   144 | 62

¶ 3 (1.5 / 5.6 / A / 80)
job
A final ingredient I would label simply as the application of   157 | 64
"common sense" to all work.   162 | 65

¶ I hope these comments will be of some   8 | 67
assistance to you and your students in your   16 | 69
consideration of careers.   21 | 70

15C ■ STROKING TECHNIQUE PRACTICE: REVIEW [15] each line once SS; then type selected lines once more

■ Each sentence below includes *at least four uses* of the letters that sentence is designed to emphasize, thus providing an intensive review of the keyboard. The sentences may be used for selective practice, too, if more practice is needed on a certain letter.

Technique Emphasis: Position the fingers curved and upright over the home keys; keep them there when they are not in use. Strike each key with a quick, snap stroke. Space quickly. Hold the hands and arms quiet, almost motionless.

1	A B	Beth Brach is our best aide; she can do a big job.	*Eyes on copy*
2	C D	Did Clay Cole check the due date on the cost card?	
3	E F	Ed Fisk feels that one file for each firm will do.	
4	G H	Greg is great with weights; Garth, with the rings.	
5	I J	If it is a large jet, Jim will just jump with joy.	
6	K L	Kate Blake keeps all kinds of lists for Mr. Block.	
7	M N	Man is known more for his mind than for his might.	
8	O P	To cop the prize post, you must plan your trip up.	
9	Q R	Be quick to run our queer quartz rock to the quay.	
10	S T	Stu said to be sure to ask the terms of that sale.	
11	U V	Our votes have been pledged but give us your view.	
12	W X	Rex Dow filed the tax of the new wax works at six.	
13	Y Z	Yes, Liz, you won the prize by your zeal and zest.	

| 1 | 2 | 3 | 4 | 5 | 6 | 7 | 8 | 9 | 10 |

15D ■ GROWTH INDEX [10] three 2' writings; determine GWAM

All letters are used.

GWAM
1' | 2'

¶ 1

The way I type has quite a lot to do with my   9 | 4

speed gain. So I must work in just the right way   19 | 9

when I set out to reach a high speed. I will try   29 | 14

for good form, and I will work for it with zest.   39 | 19

¶ 2

If I try in a way that does not work well, I   9 | 24

will not give up. I will use a new plan and make   19 | 29

a new try. The next try with top form may be the   29 | 34

one that will help me reach my new speed goal.   38 | 38

| 1' GWAM | 1 | 2 | 3 | 4 | 5 | 6 | 7 | 8 | 9 | 10 |
| 2' GWAM | | 1 | | 2 | | 3 | | 4 | | 5 |

15E ■ SPEED/CONTROL BUILDING [7] type 1' writings on ¶s 1 and 2 above

LESSON 147

147A ■ CONDITIONING PRACTICE ⑤ each line 3 times: slowly, faster, top speed

Alphabet	Jack will help move the boxes of zinc from the gondola cars at Quincy.
Figure/symbol	The Persian rug (*3758--9' x 12') lists for $640.75 less 15% for cash.
Shift keys	They read the articles "Fatigue," "How to Relax," and "Saving Energy."
Fluency	They had moved to a new address when the statement was mailed to them.

Eyes on copy; quick return

| 1 | 2 | 3 | 4 | 5 | 6 | 7 | 8 | 9 | 10 | 11 | 12 | 13 | 14 |

147B ■ SKILL MEASUREMENT: EMPLOYMENT TESTING 45

Many personnel departments of business firms require an applicant to come for a preliminary interview and to take certain basic skill tests as an initial screening device. If the applicant passes these tests, he is then considered for the position, and he may take other employment tests required by the company.

1. Straight-Copy Skill Measurement (8') 5' writing; circle errors; determine GWAM

All letters are used.

GWAM
1'   5'

¶ 1

	1'	5'
To hunt for a job is a bit of an art. Before you begin, it is	13	3	67
helpful to review your education, work experiences, and skills. Be posi-	27	5	70
tive you understand your goals and what you want to do. Life is too	41	8	73
brief to go through it doing work you really do not like to do. When	55	11	76
you are ready to hunt for a job, organize your approach with care. First,	70	14	79
collect needed personal data; such as your social security number, the	84	17	81
names and addresses of persons whom you can use for reference, and the	98	20	84
dates of your education and work experiences. Next, prepare a data sheet	113	23	87
that lists or sums up your personal characteristics, education, and work	128	26	90
experiences. If you possess special skills, such as typing or shorthand,	142	28	93
be sure to list them. Finally, list the names of two or three persons,	157	31	96
other than relatives, who know something about you.	167	33	98

¶ 2

Now you are ready to hunt for job leads. Inquire among friends,	13	36	101
relatives, and others who may be in a position to assist you. Your	27	39	103
school may have a placement bureau--be sure to utilize it. Examine the	41	42	106
"Help Wanted" advertisements in your newspaper. When you locate a prom-	55	44	109
ising job opportunity, ask by letter or telephone for an interview, unless	70	47	112
you know that you are to go at once for an interview. If you write a	84	50	115
letter of application, realize that it is a mirror of your work habits	98	53	118
and your thinking. The letter should be neatly and correctly typed.	112	56	121
When you are called for an interview, dress simply and in good taste;	126	59	123
exhibit an interest in the company and the job; sell yourself, your skills,	142	62	126
and your abilities; and you will enhance your chances of getting the job.	156	65	129

1' GWAM | 1 | 2 | 3 | 4 | 5 | 6 | 7 | 8 | 9 | 10 | 11 | 12 | 13 | 14 |
5' GWAM | 1 | 2 | 3 |

Improving Stroking Precision

1. Arrange your desk for efficiency.
2. Adjust the paper guide; insert a full sheet of paper.
3. Set left margin stop: center — 25; move right stop to end of scale.
4. SS drills; DS paragraphs.

■ LESSON 16

16A ■ CONDITIONING PRACTICE 8 each line 3 times SS; DS after each 3-line group

Alphabet	Can Jeff Loeb or Zane Quig have my desk top waxed?
B Y Z	Tony Baez may be able to buzz by the zoo for Kyle.
Fluency	Read with more care if you wish to work with ease.

First time, slowly; second time, speed; third time, control

| 1 | 2 | 3 | 4 | 5 | 6 | 7 | 8 | 9 | 10 |

16B ■ MANIPULATIVE PARTS DRILL: SPACE BAR 10 type the drill twice

Lines 1-2: These lines emphasize the ten letters most often used as word endings. Type each word *and space* as a unit. Avoid pausing between words.

Lines 3-4: These lines emphasize the twelve letters most often used as word beginnings. After spacing following a word, type the next word without pausing.

1	Endings	me we she us as was it quit jet or for sir and did
2		an can man my may pay go to zoo of if off all call
3	Beginnings	to the tax am are of own oil is it its we was save
4		see set cut car pet pan for few be but men you yes
5	Beginnings	Don made a cage for his pet owl and for mine, too.
6	and endings	Must we expect a big tax if oil prices rise again?

| 1 | 2 | 3 | 4 | 5 | 6 | 7 | 8 | 9 | 10 |

16C ■ TECHNIQUE PRACTICE: STROKING 12 type the drill twice

Lines 1-3: Place the hands over the home keys—fingers upright, not slanting. Without changing hand position, make low, snappy strokes.

Lines 4-6: Curve the fingers. Without arching the wrist or moving the hand forward, *reach* the controlling finger to the key.

Lines 7-9: Make a direct downward reach to the key without swinging the elbow out or moving the hand out of alignment with the keyboard.

1	Home row	a as ask asks add adds had lad glad all fall shall
2		as a lad; has had; add a dash; had a half; a glass
3		All glad dads had a glass; all glad lads had hash.
4	Third row	it wit we were to too toe tow two top try put your
5		or ore row out route top trip poor pour just quite
6		Did Troy write it to try to quote your witty quip?
7	Bottom row	bag man can van name came cove cave gave hand band
8		ax ox lax mix box excel extend fizz buzz zinc zone
9		Maxim, give me the words for: oz., lb., in., cwt.

| 1 | 2 | 3 | 4 | 5 | 6 | 7 | 8 | 9 | 10 |

*Center heading 1 inch
from top of page
1-inch side margins
Use your judgment in
arranging data*

PERSONAL DATA SHEET
OF
MICHAEL WOODS

Personal Information

Age: 18
Address: 6310 Green Valley Circle
                        Culver City, CA 90230
Telephone: 674-3800
Height and Weight: 6'2", 170 pounds
Health: Excellent

Education

High School: Culver City High School
                        High school diploma, pending graduation
Major: Business-Economic Education--Academic
Grade Average: B+ (Upper 15% of graduating class)

School Activities

Member of varsity track team for two years.

President of Junior Achievement Club during junior year. Organized the Culver High Products Company, which manufactured and
sold tie tacks and decorative pins.

Student body treasurer during senior year. Prepared purchase
requisitions and kept records of receipts and disbursements of
student body funds.

Work Experience

Newspaper route for one year. Delivered 120 papers a day. Made
collections monthly.

Clerk-Typist in an insurance office for two summers. Typed
insurance forms and letters, sorted company mail, and did other
general clerical work.

References (by Permission)

Mr. James Carter, Boys' Adviser, Culver City High School;
4401 Elenda Street; Culver City, CA 90230

Mrs. Rosalyn Kalmar, Business Instructor, Culver City High
School; 4401 Elenda Street; Culver City, CA 90230

Mr. Woodrow Baldwin, Office Manager, Pacific States Insurance
Company; 10202 Washington Blvd.; Culver City, CA 90230

Personal Data Sheet

16D ■ CONTINUITY PRACTICE: GUIDED WRITING [20] ½', 1', and 2' writings as directed

Paragraph 1: Type two 1' writings. Determine *gwam* for the better writing. Use this as your base rate when setting a new goal as directed at the right. *After setting new goal,* type three 1' writings at the new goal rate, guided by the quarter-minute call.

New Goal: Add 2 *gwam* to your base rate. Divide the new goal rate by 4 to determine number of words in each quarter-minute segment. Note these quarter-minute goals in the copy. (Example: Base Rate [14] + 2 = Goal Rate [16] ÷ 4 = 4 words per quarter-minute goal [4, 8, 12, 16]).

Paragraph 2: Type ¶ 2 as directed for ¶ 1.

Paragraphs 1 and 2: Type a 2' writing without the guides. Begin with ¶ 1; then type as much of ¶ 2 as you can. Determine *gwam*. Ignore your errors. If time permits, type a second 2' writing.

All letters are used.

	GWAM 2'	3'
¶ 1 If you are typing with more control now than	4	3
you were last week, you can be quite certain that	9	6
you are growing in typing power. You can improve	14	10
as fast as you desire if you will work with zeal.	19	13
¶ 2 For the next several days, put a little more	24	16
effort into your work; then check the increase in	29	19
speed. You will find that just a bit more effort	34	23
day by day can result in a much higher skill.	38	26

```
2' GWAM |    1    |    2    |    3    |    4    |    5    |
3' GWAM |      1      |      2      |      3      |
```

Word Counts. Each paragraph (¶) is marked with the 4-word count shown in figures and with an in-between count of two words shown by a dot (.) to aid you in noting your goals.

■ The figures in the 2' GWAM column at the right of the ¶s and the first scale beneath the ¶s are to be used in determining the 2' rate. To the figure at the end of the last complete line typed, add the figure beneath the last word typed in a partial line. The total is the 2' *gwam*.

■ The figures in the 3' GWAM column at the right of the ¶s and the second scale beneath the ¶s are to be used in determining the 3' rate in Lesson 17.

■ LESSON 17

17A ■ CONDITIONING PRACTICE [8] each line 3 times SS; DS after each 3-line group

Alphabet   Max Goff will zip his mail to Denver by quick jet.   *Fingers curved, wrists low*

Space bar   Ann said that all your plans had been cut by half.

Fluency   At twenty, we are sure we know more than at sixty.
```
            |  1  |  2  |  3  |  4  |  5  |  6  |  7  |  8  |  9  |  10  |
```

17B ■ SPEED/CONTROL BUILDING [15] use 16D, above, as directed below

1. Type a 1' writing on ¶ 1 of 16D, above. Determine *gwam*; then add 4 *gwam* for a new goal rate, note your quarter-minute goals, and type two 1' writings with the quarter-minute guide call.

2. Follow Step 1 in typing ¶ 2.

3. Type a 3' control (unhurried) writing on ¶s 1 and 2 combined; determine *gwam*. *Use quick, snap strokes; keep the carriage (carrier) moving.*

An Interview

Taking a Typing Test

146C ■ APPLYING FOR EMPLOYMENT [30]

An applicant for employment in a business office may be required to write a letter of application and to complete a data sheet before he is considered for an interview. You will do so now.

Modified block style	Start return address at
Mixed punctuation	center point on Line 10
1½″ side margins	Omit reference initials

1. **Typing a Letter of Application.** The following letter was written in application for a position in a business office. Type the letter as directed; correct all errors.

	Words
6310 Green Valley Circle	5
Culver City, CA 90230	10
Current date	13

Mr. Lee Hein, Personnel Director | Universal 21
Office Systems, Inc. | 12450 Olympic Boule- 30
vard | Los Angeles, CA   90064 | Dear Mr. 37
Hein: (¶1) Mrs. Trudy Saffer, the work- 44
experience coordinator at Culver City High 53
School, told the seniors in our business classes 63
of the office job opportunities for June high 72
school graduates. The opening for general ad- 81
ministrative trainee with your company inter- 90
ests me, and I should like to apply for the 99
position. (¶2) I shall be graduated from Cul- 107
ver City High School in June. My field of 116
study has been business-economic education. 125
My program has included courses in general 133
business, business law, bookkeeping, economics, 143

Words

introduction to data processing, office practice, 153
and typewriting. In addition, I have completed 162
the regular required high school courses. I can 172
type 60 words a minute on straight-copy ma- 181
terials, and I have learned appropriate pro- 190
duction skills. I have been active in school 199
organizations. Last year I was president of 208
the Junior Achievement Club. This year I am 217
student body treasurer. (¶3) The enclosed 224
personal data sheet will give you additional 233
information. I believe my success in my high 243
school subjects, my work experience, and my 251
participation in school activities are an indica- 261
tion that I can succeed in the position for 270
which I am applying. May I come for an inter- 279
view at a time that is convenient for you? My 289
telephone number is 674-3800.   Sincerely 297
yours | Michael Woods | Enclosure (254)   303/325

2. **Typing a Personal Data Sheet.** Type the data sheet (page 224) to enclose with the letter of application. The illustration shows one style that may be used.

3. **Composition.** If time permits, assume you are applying for a job for which you have the requisite skills and education. Prepare a letter of application and data sheet appropriate for you.

17C ■ MANIPULATIVE PARTS DRILL: SHIFT KEYS AND LOCK [10] type the drill twice

Shift Keys: Hold the shift key down until the key for the capital has been *struck*; then release the shift key and return the finger to typing position without pausing.

Shift Lock: Depress the **shift lock (29)** and leave it down until the ALL-CAP combination is typed. Operate the shift key to release the lock. *Be sure to release the shift lock to type* **and** *in Lines 7 and 8.*

1	Left shift	Pam and Jack meet Jane and Hal in the final match.
2		Is the first team Nat, Jake, Matt, Lars, and Pete?
3	Right shift	Elsa had Quincy drive Zoe Spivak to the St. Regis.
4		Al Sparks saw Ellie Epworth in St. Croix in April.
5	Both shifts	Larry and Paul lost the first set to Alan and Sol.
6		Is Meg Spitz a charter member of Alpha Kappa Club?
7	Shift lock	ALL CAP items like these: NSA, CPS, CPA, and AMS.
8		Was that news report carried by NBC, CBS, and ABC?

Keep hands in home key position and reach with the little fingers to shift keys

| 1 | 2 | 3 | 4 | 5 | 6 | 7 | 8 | 9 | 10 |

17D ■ TECHNIQUE PRACTICE: STROKING [12] type the drill twice

Lines 1-3: Adjacent-key controls, such as **ew**, **op**, and **tr**, need special attention. *Think* each letter vigorously; strike it precisely.

Lines 4-6: Make a direct, quick reach from **c** to **e**, **n** to **u**, and the like, without returning the controlling finger to home position.

Lines 7-9: Use a short, quick stroke, especially on the doubled letter, as in **all** and **off**. Keep the stroking action in the fingers.

1	Adjacent keys	new few were base same post hope part trade action
2		we are top upon sale past words truck start builds
3		We will try to view every case with the same hope.
4	Direct reaches	price place check recent must number volume carbon
5		bring branch grade charge serve thus found any why
6		Greg brought a large check for my mutual art fund.
7	Double letters	all call will bill see seem needs keeps free weeks
8		off offer letter little took book less issue happy
9		Bill all books to the class; take off a free copy.

| 1 | 2 | 3 | 4 | 5 | 6 | 7 | 8 | 9 | 10 |

17E ■ SELF-IMPROVEMENT PRACTICE [5]

1. Type each of the following lines once. If any line causes you difficulty, type it until you improve.

2. Select from the drills in 17C and 17D, above, those lines that seemed difficult for you. Type them two or three times each.

B	K	be best base basic keep kind know back banks books
W	N	what note went want news wins won down town wounds
Consolidation		Gib knows he must keep working if he wants to win.

| 1 | 2 | 3 | 4 | 5 | 6 | 7 | 8 | 9 | 10 |

Typing Competence Evaluation

■ In this unit, you will type a letter of application and prepare a data sheet. In addition, various aspects of your typing skill will be measured much as would be done were you to take an employment test for office work. As you do the work called for, type with a purpose and with concentration. Put emphasis on good techniques and typing with continuity, and you will achieve your best skill results. Speed and accuracy of copy are directly related to your use of a pattern of good typewriting techniques. Good luck!

■ LESSON 146

146A ■ CONDITIONING PRACTICE ⑤ each line 3 times: slowly, faster, top speed

Alphabet	New lake equipment may be purchased for the junior magazine executive. *Variable rhythm*
Figure/symbol	His life insurance was under Group Policy #01 7542 65 and #90 4831 56.
Adjacent keys	Were you going to trade a seesaw in the recreation area for the swing?
Fluency	This world is full of good intentions which are waiting to be applied.

| 1 | 2 | 3 | 4 | 5 | 6 | 7 | 8 | 9 | 10 | 11 | 12 | 13 | 14 |

146B ■ TECHNIQUE EVALUATION ⑮ each line 3 times: slowly, faster, top speed

1-2: One-hand words; 3-4: Balanced-hand words; 5-6: *Variable rhythm*
7-8: Space bar; 9-10: Shift key; 11: Carriage return

RESPONSE CUES		EVALUATION CHECKS
1 *Finger-reach*	we are | you imply | union case | rate him | set a date | in my opinion | area oil	*Quick, snap strokes; hands quiet*
2 *action*	John referred a union case on which, in my opinion, we can set a date.	
3 *Think word, and type*	and the | and their | sign the form | they may go with me | eight of the firms	*Speedy, word-level response*
4 *word*	Their map of an ancient land form may aid them when they work with us.	
5 *Combina-tion*	and the date | to their address | give this statement to | it is exaggerated	*Variable rhythm pattern*
6 *response*	On that date, please send this statement to them at their new address.	
7 *Thumb curved and close*	pay them | my key city | map room | the busy firm | many men may | then they can	*Quick, down-and-in spacing motion*
8 *to space bar*	The map of the key city may aid the busy firm when they do their work.	
9 *Little finger shift-key*	Janet Roberts and Paul Dodds work for the South-Western Publishing Co.	*Fingers in typing posi-tion; no pauses*
10 *reach*	J. McNeil ordered HOW TO TYPE FASTER from Black & Lang, New York, N.Y.	
11 *Quick, flick-of-hand motion*	Tab (Center + 10)──►Make a quick, flick return and start the new line without pausing.—Tab──►(Repeat three times.)	*Quick return; eyes on copy*

LESSON 18

18A ■ CONDITIONING PRACTICE 8 each line 3 times SS; DS after each 3-line group

First Writing: Type at an even pace, noting the awkward letter sequences. Practice these as time permits; try to smooth out awkward movements.

Second Writing: Speed up the stroking slightly, but try to work out improved stroking patterns for awkward combinations.

Third Writing: Push yourself a bit for increased stroking speed. Space quickly between words. Keep the carriage moving steadily.

Alphabet　　　Jan glazed my floors with wax after Bev Peck quit.

Shift keys　　Cora wrote to Hans in Oslo and to Vince in Naples.

Fluency　　　Check the paper for any major change in the price.

　　　　| 1 | 2 | 3 | 4 | 5 | 6 | 7 | 8 | 9 | 10 |

Eyes on the copy as you return; start new line without a pause

18B ■ MANIPULATIVE PARTS DRILL: TABULATOR AND RETURN 10 type twice

Machine Adjustments: Clear all tabulator stops; set a tab stop 5 spaces to the right of the left margin; then set three additional tab stops 5 spaces apart.

DO: Begin the first line of the drill at the left margin. Tabulate once (5 spaces) to type Line 2; twice (10 spaces) to type Line 3; and so forth. Learn to tab, release, and type quickly.

↓Margin

1　　　　　　　　　I must get ready to type in the same way each day:

2　*Indent 5*　　Tab once ----→First, I clear my desk of all unneeded items.

3　*Indent 10*　　Tab twice ——→Next, I twirl paper into the typewriter.

4　*Indent 15*　　Tab three times ——→Then, I adjust the machine quickly.

5　*Indent 20*　　Tab four times ——→Finally, I turn to the lesson.

18C ■ TECHNIQUE PRACTICE: STROKING REVIEW 15 type twice

1　*Home row*　　gas jag flag sad had fad hall fall half flash asks
2　　　　　　　　Ladd Lakas has had glass flasks as a fad all fall.

3　*Third row*　　yet tire wire wore tour rout riot port quiet upper
4　　　　　　　　Rita tried to work up to a top speed; so did Paul.

5　*Bottom row*　size cash scan exit mask blank black manage vanish
6　　　　　　　　Alex must give my band a hand; Zahn can help, too.

7　*Adjacent keys*　art buy tree suit stop coin union premium unmanned
8　　　　　　　　Vera did buy a top coin last night at an art sale.

9　*Direct reaches*　once much deck many great humor brave curve nugget
10　　　　　　　Lynn found a gold nugget; it brought a huge price.

11　*Double letters*　seen look tells sorry effort across happen brittle
12　　　　　　　I am sorry, Jeff, that all my letters seem wasted.

　　　　| 1 | 2 | 3 | 4 | 5 | 6 | 7 | 8 | 9 | 10 |

• *Sit erect*
• *Curve the fingers*
• *Use finger motions*
• *Eyes on the copy*
• *Shift firmly*
• *Space quickly*
• *Return without pausing*

■ LESSON 144

144A ■ CONDITIONING PRACTICE [5] each line 3 times: slowly, faster, top speed

Alphabet
Figure/symbol
Related learning
Fluency

H. Weber gives quick, extra quizzes as a means of judging top quality.
Did he order the 16-, 20-, and 24-foot beams (5 7/8″ x 9 3/4″) for us?
Form possessives as follows: boy's hat, men's shirts, but boys' hats.
Can we demonstrate to those who would be careless that life is a gift?
| 1 | 2 | 3 | 4 | 5 | 6 | 7 | 8 | 9 | 10 | 11 | 12 | 13 | 14 |

Quick, snappy keystroking

144B ■ SKILL BUILDING: STATISTICAL COPY [15] two 5′ writings of 100C, page 154, as directed below

1. In the first 5′ writing, try to type at your best rate.
   Goal: not more than 5 errors.

2. In the second 5′ writing, increase your speed if you made the Step 1 goal; if not, decrease it.

144C ■ PRODUCTION TYPING: LETTER STYLE REVIEW [30] (1 carbon; envelopes; correct errors)

Type as many of the problems listed at the right as you can in the time allowed. Make pencil or typed notations of the *problems*, *page numbers*, and *general directions* so you need not refer to this page.

As each letter is typed, evaluate its acceptability: An *acceptable letter* is attractively placed on the page; is typed with uniform (even) keystroking; has

proper word division at ends of lines; and has all errors neatly corrected. It has "eye appeal" and makes a good impression on all who see it.

1. Problem 1, *Style Letter 1*, page 91.
2. Problem 1, *Style Letter 2*, page 93.
3. Problem 1, *Style Letter 3*, page 146.
4. Problem 1, *Style Letter 4*, page 156.

■ LESSON 145

145A ■ CONDITIONING PRACTICE [5] each line 3 times: slowly, faster, top speed

Alphabet
Figure/symbol
Related learning
Fluency

A mad boxer shot a quick, gloved jab to the jaw of his dizzy opponent.
Order #6890 for 2 gross of buttons totals $3.72 (24 doz. @ 15½¢ doz.).
"Will the campaign," the judge asked, "begin this week or next month?"
Try to keep the fingers in typing position when shifting for capitals.
| 1 | 2 | 3 | 4 | 5 | 6 | 7 | 8 | 9 | 10 | 11 | 12 | 13 | 14 |

Finger-reach action; hands quiet

145B ■ SKILL BUILDING: ROUGH DRAFT [15] two 5′ writings of 90D, page 139, as directed below

1. In the first 5′ writing, try to type at your best rate.
   Goal: not more than 5 errors.

2. In the second 5′ writing, increase your rate if you made the Step 1 goal; if not decrease it.

145C ■ PRODUCTION TYPING [30] correct errors

Type as many of the problems listed below as you can in the time allowed. Make pencil or typed notations of the *problems*, *page numbers*, and *general directions* so you need not refer to this page.

As each problem is completed, evaluate it as to its acceptability: (1) placement on the page; (2) uni-

formity of keystroking; (3) neatness of error correction; and (4) thoroughness of proofreading.

1. Problem 1, page 171 (*tabulation*).
2. Problem 1, page 173 (*tabulation*).
3. Problem 9, page 200 (*memorandum*).
4. Problem 11, page 201 (*invoice*).

18D ▪ SKILL-COMPARISON TYPING [12]

1. Type a 1' writing on ¶ 1; determine *gwam*.
2. Type a 1' writing on ¶ 2; determine *gwam*.
3. Type another 1' writing on ¶ 1, trying to equal or better the rate made on ¶ 2.

4. Type a 2' writing on ¶s 1 and 2 combined.
5. Type a 3' writing on ¶s 1 and 2 combined. Try to maintain in the second and third minutes the stroking rate you attain in the first minute.

All letters are used.

	GWAM	
	2'	3'

¶ 1
(LA / 1.4 / 5.4 / 85)

You cannot expect to increase in speed every | 4 | 3

time you practice typing. You can attempt to add | 9 | 6

to some phase of the prized skill, however. Very | 14 | 10

quick effort on just one facet may help. | 18 | 12

¶ 2
(VE / 1.2 / 5.0 / 95)

The first thing one needs to learn in typing | 23 | 15

is the value of good form. Good form is the only | 28 | 19

basis on which top typing skill can be built. If | 33 | 22

you master good form, typing power will come. | 37 | 25

2' GWAM | 1 | 2 | 3 | 4 | 5 |
3' GWAM | 1 | 2 | 3 |

18E ▪ PROOFREADING [5]

PURPOSE: To learn the first step in finding and correcting your errors.

DO:

1. Note the kinds of errors circled in the sample typed lines at the right.

2. Proofread and circle each error you make in a 1' writing of 18D.

The first thing one (neds) to learn in (ty ping)

is the value of (good) form. Good form is (thee) only

basis (in) which (to) typing (skilll) can be (biult). If

you master good form. (typing (powee) will come.

Line 1: (1) Failure to space; (2) omitted letter; (3) faulty spacing.
Line 2: (1) Omitted word; (2) incorrect spacing; (3) added letter.
Line 3: (1) Misstroke; (2) omitted letter; (3) added letter; (4) transposition.
Line 4: (1) Period for comma; (2) strikeover, only one error counted per word.

▪ LESSON 19

19A ▪ CONDITIONING PRACTICE [8] each line 3 times SS; DS after each 3-line group

Alphabet	Virgil Quin has packed twenty boxes of prize jams.
Q X M	Jo Bux made a quick exit to cram for my next quiz.
Fluency	Two of the girls were here at eight to start work.

| 1 | 2 | 3 | 4 | 5 | 6 | 7 | 8 | 9 | 10 |

Maintain correct hand position; reach to the keys

19B ▪ SKILL-COMPARISON TYPING [12] repeat 18D, above; compare rates

■ A typist in the business office is frequently called upon to perform a variety of typing tasks—all of which must be completed with a minimum of confusion and waste motion.

This unit provides a review to help you improve your basic typing skills.

The unit has the following specific objectives:
1. To help you improve your basic typing skills.
2. To help you learn to make notes of and to follow directions without asking unnecessary questions.
3. To help you learn to make critical judgments relating to the usability of your typed work.

■ LESSON 143

143A ■ CONDITIONING PRACTICE ⑤ each line 3 times: slowly, faster, top speed

Alphabet	Quiet Muscovy ducks from Brazil were judged by the experts as winners.
Figure/symbol	Type these figures and symbols: "2," #3, $4, 5%, 6, 7&, 8', (9), (0).
	Electric 2@, #3, $4, 5%, 6¢, 7&, 8*, (9), (0).
Related learning	Remember Maslow's educational dictum, "What a man can be, he must be."
Fluency	Is life so short that we no longer have time for courtesy and a smile?

Fingers curved and upright

| 1 | 2 | 3 | 4 | 5 | 6 | 7 | 8 | 9 | 10 | 11 | 12 | 13 | 14 |

143B ■ SKILL BUILDING: STRAIGHT COPY ⑮ two 5' writings of 88D, page 136, as directed below

1. In the first 5' writing, try to type at your best rate. **Goal:** not more than 5 errors.

2. In the second 5' writing, increase your speed if you made the Step 1 goal.

143C ■ INDEX CARD TABULATION: CLASSIFYING INFORMATION ㉚

1. Type a 5" x 3" index classification card (or use a slip of paper of the same size) from the illustration at the right. Using this card as a guide, type additional index cards for the names contained in 110C, page 169, classified according to *Subject* heading. Arrange the names of the students, their ages, and telephone numbers on the cards in tabulated columns, centered horizontally, with *4 spaces between columns*. In typing the cards, start the columnar headings a double space below the subject heading. Type the subject heading in the upper left corner, ½ inch from the left edge and on the third line from the top edge.

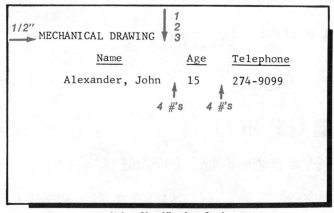

Index Classification Card

2. After you have completed the indexing and tabulating of the names according to the *subject* classification, alphabetize the cards according to the subject classification. Then type an identification card containing the following information, centered vertically and horizontally, and in double-spaced form:

STUDENT TUTORING SERVICE BUREAU | *your name* | *name of your school* | *city and state* in which it is located. Put a rubber band around the cards, or a staple in the lower left corner if slips of paper were used, and submit them to your teacher for evaluation.

19C ■ MANIPULATIVE PARTS DRILL: BACKSPACER/MARGIN RELEASE $\boxed{10}$ (Left: center — 25; Right: center + 25)

use an exact 50-space line

BACKSPACING: To fill in an omitted letter or to position the carriage, depress the **backspace key (30)**. Locate the key on the keyboard.

Electric: Reach with the little finger; make a light quick stroke. Release the key quickly to avoid a double backspace. Hold the key down for repeat backspacing.

Nonelectric (Manual): Straighten the finger slightly and reach it to the backspace key with minimum hand motion. Depress the backspace key firmly; release it quickly.

DRILL 1
1. Type as shown the first word in Line 1 below.
2. Backspace and fill in the missing letter.
3. Type each of the other words in a similar manner.

DRILL 2
1. Depress the **margin release** or **margin bypass (25)** and backspace 5 spaces into the left margin.
2. Type the 60-space sentence (Line 2 below) three times, typing until the carriage locks (ignore the ringing of the bell); then depress the margin release (bypass) and complete the sentence.

1   ja z, up n, un il, jac et, val e, ac uire, vol mes

2   DO: Move right margin stop to end of scale after the drill.

19D ■ TECHNIQUE PRACTICE: STROKING REVIEW $\boxed{12}$ each line 3 times SS; DS after each 3-line group

1	*Home row*	Hal Dallas had a glass as a lass had half a glass.
2	*Third row*	Trudy was just too weary to row to the first pier.
3	*Bottom row*	Max excels at boxing, but Vic is a whiz at soccer.
4	*Adjacent keys*	Sal hopes to use her polo pony as a quick trotter.
5	*Direct reaches*	Merv brought a carbon of my recent service record.
6	*Double letters*	Jeanne needs the letter by noon, but Jess took it.
7	*P O*	Over forty people helped on our new power project.
8	*Q M V*	My seven quaint models are most valuable antiques.
9	*Z J X*	Buy just six jackets to give as prizes at the zoo.

Fingers curved and upright; quick, snap strokes; space quickly after each word

| 1 | 2 | 3 | 4 | 5 | 6 | 7 | 8 | 9 | 10 |

19E ■ SELF-IMPROVEMENT PRACTICE $\boxed{8}$

1. Type the following ¶ at an unhurried pace and with minimum error. Try to work out improved stroking patterns for the awkward combinations.

2. Type the ¶ once or twice at a slightly faster pace. Vary your stroking speed: speed up on the easy combinations; slow up on the difficult ones.

All letters are used.

	1′ GWAM
Typing errors cost money in the office; they	9
require time in school or home. This being true,	19
you must soon strive to get an accurate paper now	29
and then. So just size up the word and type with	39
exact control, using an appropriate rhythm, also.	49
Cut the cost by cutting the errors.	56

1′ GWAM | 1 | 2 | 3 | 4 | 5 | 6 | 7 | 8 | 9 | 10 |

141C ■ BUILDING LETTER PRODUCTION SKILL [30] (Letterheads or plain sheets; 1 cc)

Time Schedule	
Planning and preparing	3'
Timed letter production	20'
Proofreading, determining *gwam*	7'

If you complete the letters before time is called, start over; use plain paper for repeated problems. Do not correct errors. When time is called, proofread your typing; determine *g-pram*.

Problem 1: Modified Block Style, Mixed Punctuation; Return Address on Line 14

	Words
655 Orchard Avenue	Tarzana, CA 91356		8
Current date	Chemical Control Corporation		16
925 Industrial Park Blvd.	So. San Francisco,	25
CA 94080	Gentlemen: (¶ 1) Following a	32
recent household ant invasion, I purchased a	41
can of your all-purpose bug spray. Your tele-	50
vision commercials convinced me of its effec-	59
tiveness. Actual results of using your spray,	68
alas, have been very disappointing. My 9-year-	78
old son informs me that in his room alone we	87
have red ants, black ants, fat ants, and little	96
ants that, according to him, "sting like the	105
dickens." (¶ 2) As a last-ditch attempt to	113
regain control of the situation, I am writing	122
you to ask for either (1) reinforcements (an-	131
other can of spray, if you think I just happened	141
to get a bad batch); or (2) strategy suggestions	151
(unless the printed directions on the can, which	160
I followed to the letter, should have been effec-	170
tive). (¶ 3) Of course, I would appreciate your	179
attending to my request immediately, as the	187
ratio of ants to human beings in my home is	196
approaching the "point of no return." Sincerely	206
yours, (Mrs.) Jeanne Lewis (173)	211/**236**

Problem 2: Block Style; Open Punctuation

	Words
Current date	Mrs. Jeanne Lewis	655 Orchard	9
Avenue	Tarzana, CA 91356	Dear Mrs.	16

	Words
Lewis	(¶ 1) Your clever letter regarding the	24
"ant invasion" arrived this morning. Though it	34
is a rare day when our morning mail contains	43
a customer complaint, yours is (as far as we	52
can recall) the most delightful ever received by	61
this company. (¶ 2) To answer you in the	68
same vein, we read of your troubles with mixed	78
emotions. While we certainly sympathize with	87
your predicament, at the same time we were	96
relieved to hear that there are still some ants	105
left for CHEMICAL CONTROL CORPORA-	112
TION to exterminate; otherwise, we would be	120
out of business! (¶ 3) Seriously, there is an	129
explanation for your poor luck with our bug	138
spray. It's simply that you should have pur-	146
chased our special ant spray. If you will read	159
again the label on your can of bug spray,	167
you'll notice this suggestion in the lower right	177
corner. True, it's in small print! On our newly	187
designed labels, we have made this note much	196
more eye-catching in order to help our cus-	205
tomers make the right choice. (¶ 4) We are	212
sending you one can of our potent special ant	222
spray. In the convenient push-button can,	230
application is so simple that we suggest you	239
enlist the aid of your young son in exterminat-	248
ing his colorful army of ants. We are sure our	258
special ant spray will meet your most exacting	267
expectations. Good luck.	Cordially yours		276
Daryl G. Nichols, Director	Public Relations	284
Division	(253)	287/**298**

LESSON 142

142A ■ CONDITIONING PRACTICE [5] each line 3 times: slowly, faster, top speed

Alphabet	Six big juicy steaks sizzled in a pan as five workmen left the quarry. *Read*
Figure/symbol	The house located at 23968 Richmond Street sold for $14,750 last year. *ahead*
Fingers 3, 4	Aza Q. Popoloux was asked to escort that popular but plump queen home.
Fluency	Some people never escape from the confinement of their own prejudices.

| 1 | 2 | 3 | 4 | 5 | 6 | 7 | 8 | 9 | 10 | 11 | 12 | 13 | 14 |

142B ■ TABULATION TIMED WRITING: SKILL BUILDING [15] repeat 141B, page 218. **Goal:** Improved rates

142C ■ LETTER PRODUCTION SKILL MEASUREMENT [30] repeat 141C, above, but correct errors; compute N-PRAM

LESSON 20

20A ■ CONDITIONING PRACTICE [8] each line 3 times SS; DS after each 3-line group

Alphabet	Martin Fitz quickly proved his big tax was unjust.
Shift keys	Both Nan and Alan plan to attend St. Park College.
Fluency	File all items so that we can find them with ease.

Eyes on copy as you return the carriage (or carrier)

| 1 | 2 | 3 | 4 | 5 | 6 | 7 | 8 | 9 | 10 |

20B ■ MANIPULATIVE PARTS DRILL: REVIEW [10] type twice

Line 1: Set tab stops to leave 4 spaces between words.

Line 5: Type a word as shown; backspace; fill in the missing letter.

Line 6: Begin the line 5 spaces to the left of the left margin setting.

1 *Tabulator*   go 4 also 4 only 4 city 4 upon 4 into 4 ever

Work for improved control of the service keys

2 *Shift keys*   Robbi lives on South James; Marco, on South Paris.

3 *Shift lock*   Ed Parker saw ROMEO AND JULIET; Ann Ames, CAMELOT.

4 *Space bar*   To win the prize of high skill, you must be alert.

5 *Backspacer*   ju t, qui t, ele t, ind x, e tra, let ers, fulfi l

6 *Margin release*   It is how you type, not just how much, that counts most now.

| 1 | 2 | 3 | 4 | 5 | 6 | 7 | 8 | 9 | 10 |

20C ■ TECHNIQUE PRACTICE: STROKING REVIEW [10] type twice

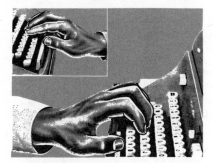
FINGERS: Curved, *Not* Straight

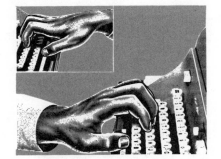
WRISTS: Low, *Not* Arched

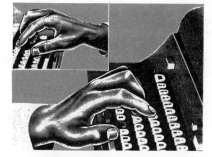
MOTIONS: Finger, *Not* Hand

1 *Third and*   To win my prize, I must give the next job my best.
2 *bottom rows*   I can zip along on many words; on others I cannot.

3 *One-hand*   You set up my tax case only after you saw my card.
4 *words*   I get a grade average only after you read my test?

5 *Easy words*   Toby may go with them to the big town by the lake.
6   I wish to sign the right title forms for the land.

7 *Adjacent keys*   We are free to sort by address a few of the cards.
8   Was her motion based upon a free and open opinion?

9 *Direct reaches*   Cecil must bring a number of my receipts to check.
10   Why must he bring all my carbons to Quincy or Irv?

| 1 | 2 | 3 | 4 | 5 | 6 | 7 | 8 | 9 | 10 |

Letter 2

	Words
Superintendent of Documents │ U. S. Government Printing Office │ Washing-	17
ton, DC 20402 (¶ 1) Enclosed is my check for $1.65. Will you please send	31
me the publications listed below:	38

Your Federal Income Tax	$0.75	44
Tax Guide for Small Business	.75	50
Your Social Security	.15	56
Total	$1.65	61

(¶ 2) I hope you can send these publications to me soon. │ Kenneth Beddow — 75/91
(50)

Letter 3

	Words
Mrs. Alice Pendery │ 826 Barriada Cermica │ San Juan, PR 00917 │ (¶ 1)	15
I have asked our sales representative in San Juan, Mr. Carlos Perez, to contact	31
you about the vacuum cleaner you purchased from us. (¶ 2) We have autho-	44
rized Mr. Perez to make whatever repairs or other adjustments necessary to	59
put your vacuum cleaner in first-class condition. (¶ 3) I am sure you will	73
be pleased with the service Mr. Perez will give you. │ Leslie Wulk, Manager	89/101

(69)

Letter 4

	Words
Mrs. Colette Berman │ 11500 Thurston Circle │ Los Angeles, CA 90049 │	16
(¶ 1) We recently updated your account but unfortunately another bill and	30
collection letter were addressed before the transaction took effect. (¶ 2) We	45
are sorry to have caused you, one of our valued customers, this inconvenience.	60
Your understanding is appreciated. │ BULLOCKS, INC. │ Barbara Simi │	73
Customer Service (44)	77/90

■ LESSON 141

141A ■ CONDITIONING PRACTICE 5 each line 3 times: slowly, faster, top speed

Alphabet
Figure/symbol
Adjacent key
Fluency

The maze box puzzle was quickly solved by the good students from Fiji. *Type*
The 546 copies, priced at $3.78 each, may be shipped on June 19 or 20. *without*
Opportunity comes to a person as a result of dedication and hard work. *pausing*
I will sign a contract by the end of the week so we can test the case.

│ 1 │ 2 │ 3 │ 4 │ 5 │ 6 │ 7 │ 8 │ 9 │ 10 │ 11 │ 12 │ 13 │ 14 │

141B ■ TABULATION TIMED WRITING 15 two 5′ writings; proofread; determine GWAM

Determine quickly needed stops. Do not center vertically—start centered heading about 1″ from top edge.

If you complete table, TS and start over. Try to
improve your rate in the second 5′ writing.

Full sheet
Proper spacing
   between parts
4 spaces between
   columns
DS data in
   columns

			Words
NEW CUSTOMER REPRESENTATIVES			6
Robert Duben	3749 Burning Wood Road	Baltimore, MD 21208	17
Sheldon Eskow	945 Carolynne Drive	St. Louis, MO 63128	28
Henry Fern	3485 Irvington Blvd.	Houston, TX 77009	38
Warren Meyer, Jr.	8564 Lakeshore Drive	San Francisco, CA 94132	51
David Phillips	396 Lehigh Avenue	Louisville, KY 40215	62
Richard Rogers	9046 Cedarhurst Avenue	Memphis, TN 38127	74
Stephen Smith	495 Fernrock Avenue	Concord, NH 03301	84
Walter Winslow	6641 Glacier Drive	Billings, MT 59102	95
Carl Yelland	8936 Plymouth Place	Buffalo, NY 14221	105

20D ■ GROWTH INDEX 9 two 3′ writings; determine GWAM and number of errors on each

All letters are used.

¶ 1

	GWAM	
2′	3′	

We must attempt to do the little things that
come up every day just as if we think them duties
of much importance. Little things may make doing
something very big quite easy later. It is so in
your learning effort now.

2′	3′	
4	3	32
9	6	36
14	10	39
19	13	42
22	15	44

¶ 2

There is a huge difference between doing the
work right and doing it just about right. If you
expect to move up to a fine job, just about right
is not good enough. Recognize this, and begin to
perfect your work habits.

2′	3′	
26	18	47
31	21	50
36	24	54
41	28	57
44	29	59

2′ GWAM | 1 | 2 | 3 | 4 | 5 |
3′ GWAM | 1 | 2 | 3 |

20E ■ SELF-IMPROVEMENT PRACTICE 13

1. Type the following ¶ once at an unhurried pace and with minimum error. Try to work out improved stroking patterns for the awkward combinations.

2. Type the ¶ once or twice at a slightly faster pace. Vary your stroking speed: speed up on the easy combinations; slow up on the difficult ones.

All letters are used.

2′ GWAM

How you type a word depends quite a bit upon ... 5
its size or difficulty. Attempt to type long and ... 10
awkward words letter by letter; short, easy words ... 15
as whole units. Think each word you type; do not ... 20
just read and type the copy without giving it any ... 25
thought. To be exact, learn the vital difference ... 30
between thinking and mere reading and beef up the ... 35
habit of thinking. ... 36

2′ GWAM | 1 | 2 | 3 | 4 | 5 |

140B ■ PRODUCTION TYPING: ITINERARY ☒25

Type the itinerary given below in the form illustrated at the right. Use 1″ margins (approximate) on all sides; center heading lines; 1 carbon copy; correct your errors. If time permits, retype for speed.

An itinerary (a travel schedule) usually includes a chronological listing of departure and arrival times; mode of travel and accommodations; and, often, a listing of scheduled activities.

ITINERARY OF RICHARD WILLIAMS | June 12-16, 19—— | Los Angeles and Honolulu |

SUNDAY, JUNE 12: CHICAGO TO LOS ANGELES

6:45 p.m. Leave O'Hare International Airport on Continental 601 (tickets in travel folder in briefcase).

8:40 p.m. Arrive Los Angeles International Airport. "Guaranteed Arrival" reservation at Century Plaza Hotel, Century City (confirmation in travel folder). Special limousine direct to hotel. *DS*

MONDAY, JUNE 13: LOS ANGELES AND HONOLULU

10:00 a.m. Conference with Dr. John I. Goodlad, Dean, Graduate School of Education, UCLA. Dr. Berry of UCLA will pick you up at 9:40 a.m. at hotel entrance.

11:45 a.m. Luncheon meeting at UCLA Faculty Center to discuss research proposals. Notes are in research folder. Dr. C. Wayne Gordon will preside at meeting.

6:00 p.m. Leave Los Angeles International Airport on United 195 for Honolulu. Limousine service available from hotel at 4:30 p.m. sharp. Check with Mr. Bell at desk.

8:20 p.m. Arrive Honolulu International Airport. Reservation at Colony Surf Hotel. Dr. Dykstra will meet you.

TUESDAY, JUNE 14: WAIKIKI BEACH

The day is yours to rest and relax. Enjoy yourself!

WEDNESDAY, JUNE 15: HONOLULU

8:00 a.m. Visit to Hawaiian Curriculum Center. Dr. Oksendahl will call for you at hotel.

11:00 a.m. You are the scheduled speaker at the East-West Center Conference. Notes for talk in marked folder; also, copy of speech mailed to you at hotel marked, **HOLD FOR ARRIVAL**. Conference chairman: Dr. Henry Illiki.

THURSDAY, JUNE 16: HONOLULU TO CHICAGO

8:30 a.m. Leave Honolulu International Airport on United 114 for return home. Limousine service available at hotel.

11:25 p.m. Arrive O'Hare International Airport. Aloha!

140C ■ LETTER PRODUCTION TYPING: SKILL BUILDING ☒20 (Block style; open punctuation)

Type the following letters. Supply appropriate letter parts as needed. Make 1 carbon copy; address envelopes; erase and correct your errors. **Goal:** To complete all letters in 20 minutes or less.

Letter 1

	Words
Carl E. Hall, President | Rally Products, Inc. | 4698 Calumet Road | Milwaukee, WI 53217 (¶1) Thanks for sending us the cutaway carburetor. This carburetor has been very helpful in our sales demonstrations. (¶2) I understand that you have prepared a single-loop film on the carburetors that you manufacture for sports cars. Can you send us this film so that we can test it at our Divisional Sales Conference next month? Peter Lumsdaine | Sales Manager (64)	17 31 45 60 75 90 92/109

Figures and Basic Symbols

■ In this unit you will learn to type the keys on the top row (the figures and the most frequently used symbols). In addition, you will increase your straight-copy typing skill and will learn to transfer that skill to the typing of statistical copy (paragraph materials containing some figures and symbols).

1. Arrange your work area for efficient typing.

2. Adjust the paper guide and insert a full sheet.

3. Set left margin stop 30 spaces to left of center; move right stop to end of scale.

4. SS drills; DS paragraphs.

■ LESSON 21

21A ■ CONDITIONING PRACTICE 8

■ Eight minutes are provided to *get ready to type* and to type each line of the Conditioning Practice at least twice as directed in Step 1 and to retype selected lines.

1. Type each Conditioning Practice of this unit twice: once at an unhurried pace to feel out appropriate motions, once a bit faster to condition the fingers for speed.

2. As time permits, retype selected lines once more for improved control; or, if your teacher directs, type 1′ writings on selected lines.

Alphabet   If Cy Zin quits, Ray will pick Vic Fox to judge my big show.   *Eyes on copy; return without looking up*

N O R   Neither Rod Norris nor Orin Riggs called Mrs. Norbert today.

Fluency   It is their wish to buy land maps of the eight island towns.
    | 1 | 2 | 3 | 4 | 5 | 6 | 7 | 8 | 9 | 10 | 11 | 12 |

21B ■ FIGURE LOCATION: 1   8 5

1. Find the new key on the typewriter keyboard chart at the right.
2. Locate the new key on your typewriter keyboard.
3. Study the reach illustration for the new key.
4. Type each two-line reach technique drill on one line.

USING LETTER I FOR FIGURE 1

If your typewriter does not have a special key for figure **1**, use the small letter I to type **1**. If your typewriter has a special key for the figure **1**, use the directions in the column at the right.

Double Figures. Experiment with typing double figures, such as **11, 88,** and the like. It is necessary for you to work out the best method of timing the sequence of strokes.

1 .1 111 lol 11 111 111 .1

Did 11 boys work 111 days? *DS*

REACH TO SPECIAL 1 KEY

If your typewriter has a special key for figure **1**, reach up to it with the *left fourth (little) finger.*

Reach Technique. Reach to the top row of keys without moving the hand to the figure row and without twisting the elbow outward or arching the wrist.

◀ Before typing the reach drill, study *Double Figures* at the left.

la 1 ala 11 ala la 111 ala

Did 11 boys work 111 days? *DS*

REACH TECHNIQUE FOR 8

Reach the *right second finger* up to the top row to type **8**. Keep the wrist low.

i8k 8k 8k 8 k8k 88 k8k 888

Were 88 men on Flight 888? *TS*

the point where you could and should recognize a hazard to the point where you do — 788
actually recognize it. This distance varies widely among individuals according — 804
to their alertness. — 808

    A rather grim picture has been presented here; but if it saves the life of — 823
even one person who reads it, then it will have served its purpose. It is too — 839
late to be sorry after an accident occurs. The scars of accidents, like rubbish, — 856
litter our highways. Why take a chance when with the exercise of due care and — 872
caution you can greatly reduce your chances of having an automobile accident. — 887
Always, when you press your foot on the accelerator, ask yourself this question: — 904
Is the time I save by the extra speed worth the chance I may be taking? If you — 920
prefer living to "sudden death," then <u>Drive with Care!</u> Remember: <u>The life you</u> — 941
<u>save may be mine</u>—I'll be walking! — 952

Yours for safe driving, | NATIONAL HIGHWAY SAFETY COUNCIL | Jeffrey — 964
Sellwood, Chief | Traffic Safety | (xxx) | Copy to Mr. Paul Kalmar | A.A.A. — 978
Safety Engineer | — 981/1002

LESSON 139

139A ■ CONDITIONING PRACTICE [5] each line 3 times: slowly, faster, top speed

Alphabet	Six big flaming rocket ships zoomed over the picturesque wooden jetty. *Quick return*
Figure/symbol	The new pool (15′ wide x 60′ long x 7½′ deep) will cost but $3,248.90.
Long words	A habit may be an outgrowth of physiological or psychological motives.
Fluency	The more that is left to chance, the less chance there is for success.

| 1 | 2 | 3 | 4 | 5 | 6 | 7 | 8 | 9 | 10 | 11 | 12 | 13 | 14 |

139B ■ TABULATION SKILL BUILDING [10]

Get ready	2′
Timed writing	5′
Proofreading, determining *gwam* .	3′

Type a 5′ writing on only the columnar data of 138B, page 213. Start about 1″ from the top edge of your page. If you finish the columnar data, double-space and start over.

139C ■ LETTER PRODUCTION TYPING [35] complete the problem of 138D, pages 214-216

LESSON 140

140A ■ CONDITIONING PRACTICE [5] each line 3 times: slowly, faster, top speed

Alphabet	Fill the big jug quickly with five or six pints of Zimmer's Grape Ade. *Quick shift-key reach*
Figure/symbol	Sell the #394 item (nylon) to J&B Company at list—120 gross @ $68.75.
Long words	Propulsion system and applied aerodynamics specialists are needed now.
Fluency	He will sign the contract and take title to the eight docks this week.

| 1 | 2 | 3 | 4 | 5 | 6 | 7 | 8 | 9 | 10 | 11 | 12 | 13 | 14 |

21C ■ STROKING TECHNIQUE PRACTICE 〔10〕 type twice

Technique Cue: Keep the hands and arms quiet; REACH with the fingers.

1 *8*   8k 8 k8 88; 8 qts.; 88 lbs.; 8 ft. 8 in.; 888 Broadway Blvd.
2   Of a class of 88 girls, only 8 made a grade of 88 on June 8.

3 *1*   la al lal 111 .1 11; 11 in.; 11 oz.; Flight 111; Chapter 11.
4   The 111 men and 11 boys go to Miami on July 1 by Flight 111.

5 *Consoli-* Their April 11 test will cover pages 11 to 18 and 81 to 188.
6 *dation*   Paul explained the June 8 quiz which covered pages 18 to 88.
       | 1 | 2 | 3 | 4 | 5 | 6 | 7 | 8 | 9 | 10 | 11 | 12 |

21D ■ TABULATING PRACTICE 〔7〕 type twice (Line: 60; spaces between columns: 8)

Clear and set tabs all	111	ill	888	note	1818	*Return without pausing*
see	181	ink	881	work	8181	
not	818	zoo	811	plan	8118	
for	118	the	181	drop	1881	

KEY | 3 | 8 | 3 | 8 | 3 | 8 | 3 | 8 | 4 | 8 | 4 |

21E ■ IMPROVING KEYBOARD CONTROL 〔15〕

Technique Cue: Curve the fingers; hold the wrists low; eyes on the copy.

1. Type each line once without timing. Work for improved stroking patterns.

2. Type each of Lines 1, 3, 5, and 7 as a ½′ writing. Determine *gwam* on each: words typed x 2.

3. Type each of Lines 2, 4, 6, and 8 as a 1′ writing, trying to equal your ½′ rates.

All letters and all figures learned are used.

1 *Easy words* Try to type easy words as words: She is to do all the work.
2   There is no better time to do all the work in the right way.

3 *Awkward* An executive requested that the unpopular policy be dropped.
4 *reaches* Steve pointed toward a ski slope he had conquered Wednesday.

5 *Long*   Try to get Myrna Brown to take a picture of the old columns.
6 *reaches* A number of my men may need new uniforms for the big parade.

7 *Figure*   Use figures in dimensions; as, 118 ft. 8 in.; 188 lbs. 8 oz.
8 *reaches* Jet Flight 118 to Fort Worth leaves from Gate 8 at 8:11 a.m.
       | 1 | 2 | 3 | 4 | 5 | 6 | 7 | 8 | 9 | 10 | 11 | 12 |

21F ■ SELF-IMPROVEMENT PRACTICE 〔5〕

1. Retype the lines of 21E, above, on which you had the lowest rates.

2. Retype the lines of 21E, above, on which you made the greatest number of errors.

TABLE I. AGE OF DRIVERS IN ACCIDENTS

Age Group	Fatal Accidents	Nonfatal Accidents
Under 24 years	34.8%	35.0%
25-34 years	21.9	22.5
35-44 years	15.3	16.4
45-54 years	12.5	13.3
55-64 years	8.4	8.2
65 and over	7.1	4.6

Since most boys and girls start driving a car at about age 16, and one fifth of all licensed drivers are in this group, this table indicates, in terms of the 8-year span, that the greatest number of fatal and nonfatal accidents occur in the "Under 24 years" age group. The hazard of driving for a young person is indicated by the fact that motor vehicle accidents constitute two thirds of all fatalities among males 15 to 19 years of age!

Because more and more young people will be driving in the years ahead, every effort must be made to make everyone safety conscious so that the trend toward increased "slaughter on the highways" can be reversed or at least halted. SAFETY ON THE HIGHWAYS must begin at home and in our schools if we are to reduce the auto accident rate. Here are some things that you as an individual can do:

1. Learn thoroughly how to operate an automobile with safety. Always follow the best driving practices.
2. Always keep your car in a safe mechanical condition. Be aware of the road conditions as you drive.
3. Set a good example for others by observing all traffic laws and by practicing courtesy on the highways.
4. Keep well within the speed limits at all times.

Accidents are basically the result of a failure to recognize risk. One of the real keys to safe driving is to anticipate danger and to get ready for it while you still have plenty of time to stop. In this way, you can avoid the need for most quick stops. It is well to know, too, the total stopping distance needed when it is necessary to make sudden or quick stops. The following table gives this information.

TABLE II. STOPPING DISTANCE CHART

Miles per Hour	Feet Traveled per Second	Driver Reaction Distance *	Vehicle Braking Distance	Total Stopping Distance
20	29	22	23	45
30	44	33	45	78
40	59	44	81	125
50	73	55	133	188
60	88	66	206	272
70	103	77	304	381

* Based on 3/4-second reaction time.

In normal driving, an extra factor known as Perception Distance must be added to the Total Stopping Distance. Perception Distance is the distance traveled from

(Letter continued on page 216)

Words
295
312
318
322
326
331
335
339
354
372
387
403
420
427
443
458
475
490
506
520
527
541
548
562
569
580
595
610
627
644
659
663
670
676
684
701
704
707
710
713
717
720
724
731
751
772

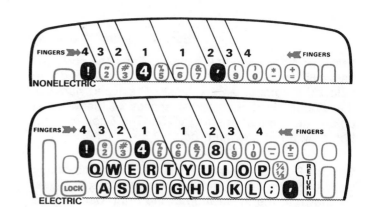

LESSON 22

22A ■ CONDITIONING PRACTICE [8] each line at least twice; as time permits, retype selected lines

Alphabet	Vicki Bold just may win quite a prize for her next pop song.
Q M X	Mamie quickly fixed 18 quarts of the mixture for Max Quimby.
Fluency	Keith may fix the bus panel for the city if the pay is good.

Eyes on the copy as you type

| 1 | 2 | 3 | 4 | 5 | 6 | 7 | 8 | 9 | 10 | 11 | 12 |

22B ■ SYMBOL/FIGURE LOCATION: ' ! 4 [7]

1. Find new key on chart.   **2.** Locate new key on keyboard.   **3.** Study reach illustration.   **4.** Type the drill.

APOSTROPHE '

Nonelectric: Type **'** (the shift of **8**) with the *right second finger*. Type the following drill:

8k 8k'k 8k'k 'k 'k 8k'k 'k

Isn't my pad on Ed's desk? *DS*

➡

Electric: The **'** is to the right of **;** and is typed with the *right fourth finger*. Type the drill:

;'; '; '; '; ';'; ';'; ';'

Isn't my pad on Ed's desk? *DS*

EXCLAMATION !

Type the **'**; backspace, and type the period (!). (If your typewriter has a special ! key—usually the shift of the special figure 1—move the finger to it without moving the elbow outward.) A single exclamatory word may be considered a sentence.

Spacing Rule: *Space twice after ! at end of a sentence.*

Type the following drill:

Fine! I spelled it right!

Eyes front! Type with me! *DS*

REACH TECHNIQUE FOR 4

Reach the *left first finger* to the top row to type **4**. Try to hold the other fingers over their home keys. Type the following drill:

r4f 4f 4f 4 f4f 44 f4f 444

I flew 444 miles on May 4. *TS*

22C ■ STROKING TECHNIQUE PRACTICE [10] type twice

1	**'**	it's; I'll; didn't; Is this book Nan's, Kathy's, or Chuck's?
2		Mrs. O'Malley can't or won't pay for her son's trip to Rome.
3	**!**	Oh! Look! Stop! He loudly commanded: Ready! Aim! Fire!
4		Get set! Begin! You can win if you think you can! Try it!
5	*4*	4f 4f4 44 14 48 148 On May 4 my 14 boys sold 48 sets of R44.
6		Did the 14 boxes Joe shipped on May 4 weigh just 144 pounds?
7	*Consoli-dation*	Isn't that great! The 148 boys from Erie quizzed the 4 men.

| 1 | 2 | 3 | 4 | 5 | 6 | 7 | 8 | 9 | 10 | 11 | 12 |

Step 2: Typing a Company Name in the Closing Lines

Preview: When used in the closing lines, the company name is typed in all CAPITALS on the second line below the complimentary close. The typed name of the dictator is then typed 4 spaces (3 blank lines) below the company name. **NOTE:** The *Copy to* notation may be abbreviated *cc.*

Special Drill: Starting with the last two lines of the body of the letter (page 216), type the closing lines as shown in the illustration at the right. Use 1" side margins and drill paper; leave proper spacing between the various closing parts.

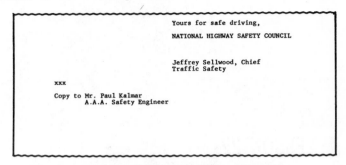

Yours for safe driving,
NATIONAL HIGHWAY SAFETY COUNCIL

Jeffrey Sellwood, Chief
Traffic Safety

xxx
Copy to Mr. Paul Kalmar
        A.A.A. Safety Engineer

**Company Name in the Closing Lines;
Copy to Notation**

138D ■ PRODUCTION TYPING: LETTER 15 additional time is provided in Lesson 139 for completion of letter

Three-Page Letter with Title Line, Tabulations, Enumerated Items, Company Name in Closing Lines, and Copy Notation

Modified block style with 5-space ¶ indentions	Center title line in all capitals with one blank line space
Current date; mixed punctuation	above and one blank line space below the line.
1" side and bottom margins (approximate)	Indent enumerated items (page 215) 5 spaces from left
Horizontal form heading (page 203) for pages 2 and 3	and right margins; DS above and below each item

Words

Current date | Dr. M. E. Oliverio, President | Fairmont Glass, Incorporated | 15
5599 South Indiana Avenue | Charleston, WV 25304 | Dear Dr. Oliverio: | 29

This letter is being sent to all business firms in the United States. Your   44
help is needed. Won't you see that the following portion of this letter is dupli-   60
cated and distributed to all your employees. This is one step your National   76
Council is taking in its efforts to reduce the highway accident rate.   90

DS

SAFETY ON THE HIGHWAYS   94

DS

With most epidemics, our society is very harsh. Offending microorganisms   109
are hit and destroyed with arsenals of wonder drugs and batteries of hypodermic   125
needles. Yet there is one epidemic we permit, almost as if we were unaware   140
of its existence. This is the auto accident plague. Every driver should ask him-   157
self if the minutes saved by excessive speed are worth the consequences of highway   173
accidents––broken bones, disfigured bodies, or even sudden death. Every driver   189
should remember that a car driven at any speed is, in reality, a guided missile, but   206
without built-in and programmed controls. It can be only as safe as the degree   222
of control and caution exercised by the driver.   232

During a recent year, auto accidents took 55,200 lives. The minute you   247
start your car, you have an "accident potential" that varies with your age group.   263
Although all age groups are involved, young people are particularly susceptible   279
as is indicated by the following table.   287

TS

22D ■ TABULATING PRACTICE 7 type twice (Line: 60; spaces between columns: 8)

Reading Cue: Read 3- and 4-digit figures as two groups. For example, read 141 as *one forty-one*; read 1488 as *fourteen eighty-eight*.

Technique Cue: Script copy may be a bit harder to read than print, so keep your eyes on the copy. Tabulate quickly from column to column.

						Words
cut	144	apt	841	vote	1488	5
wit	844	via	114	turn	8418	10
pen	111	3's	184	it's	4481	16
nor	411	I'm	4's	I've	1448	21

KEY | 3 | 8 | 3 | 8 | 3 | 8 | 3 | 8 | 4 | 8 | 4 |

22E ■ SPEED/CONTROL BUILDING: STRAIGHT COPY 12

1. Type a 1′ *control-level* writing on the following ¶. Determine *gwam* and errors.

2. Type another 1′ writing, beginning where you stopped in Step 1. Determine *gwam* and errors.

3. Type a 2′ and a 3′ writing on the ¶. Determine *gwam* and errors.

All letters are used.

	GWAM	
	2′	3′

It is quite necessary for people, old and young alike, to have fun. It is just as crucial for all to realize that having a good time is of secondary importance when there is work to do. People who keep fun and work in proper balance are the ones who have developed a maturity that often leads to success and happiness. Those who see fun in work itself are truly fortunate people, too. For them, work is a great expectation, not a thankless affair.

2′	3′
5	4	34
11	8	38
17	12	42
23	16	46
29	20	50
35	24	54
41	28	58
45	30	60

2′ GWAM | 1 | 2 | 3 | 4 | 5 | 6 |
3′ GWAM | 1 | 2 | 3 | 4 |

22F ■ SELF-IMPROVEMENT PRACTICE 6

1. Type twice each line given below, once for speed and once for control.

2. If time permits, retype 22D, above, or the paragraph in 22E.

Alphabet   Jim Verick was quizzed by Mr. Glade on part of his tax form.

Figure   It's already decided that on August 18 I'll move to 118 Elm!

| 1 | 2 | 3 | 4 | 5 | 6 | 7 | 8 | 9 | 10 | 11 | 12 |

■ LESSON 138

138A ■ CONDITIONING PRACTICE ⑤ each line 3 times: slowly, faster, top speed

Alphabet   The view from the jungle peak was both exciting and amazing to Quincy. *Space*
Figure/symbol   He bought the #39572 die for $84.60, taking an 11% discount of $10.46. *quickly*
Uniform stroking   Don't wonder about your ability; wonder if you are using your ability.
Fluency   You can do the seemingly impossible if you have faith in your efforts.
      | 1 | 2 | 3 | 4 | 5 | 6 | 7 | 8 | 9 | 10 | 11 | 12 | 13 | 14 |

138B ■ BOXED TABULATION ⑮ erase and correct all typing errors

Type the boxed table below (Reference: Page 173). Rule vertical lines with a ball-point pen, estimating center point between columns. **Goal:** To complete table in not more than 15'. Record completion time on paper. Try to work with a minimum of waste time and motion.

> Full sheet ■ reading position ■ DS the data in the columns ■ spaces between columns: 10-6-6-6

NOTE: For best balance, center headings for Cols. 3 and 4 over the columnar items, not over the total below the items.

DAYS OF OCCURRENCE OF AUTOMOBILE ACCIDENTS

(National Average for 1970)

Day of Week	Persons Killed	Per-cent	Persons Injured	Per-cent	Words in Cols.	Total Words
						4
						9
						14
						21
						27
Sunday	9,700	17.6	699,000	13.7	6	33
Monday	6,300	11.4	673,000	13.2	12	39
Tuesday	5,800	10.5	622,000	12.2	19	45
Wednesday	6,200	11.2	683,000	13.4	26	52
Thursday	6,700	12.2	673,000	13.2	32	59
Friday	9,000	16.3	847,000	16.6	38	65
Saturday	11,500	20.8	903,000	17.7	45	72
Total	55,200	100.0	5,100,000	100.0	53	80

138C ■ SPECIAL LETTER PROBLEM APPLICATIONS*: PREVIEW ⑮

Step 1: Typing a Table Within a Letter

a. Special Drill—Table I, page 215. Using 1" side margins and drill paper, type the last two lines of the paragraph preceding Table I. Triple-space; then type Table I according to the special directions given on page 215. Note that in Columns 2 and 3 the data are centered under the columnar headings; be sure to set tab stops for these points. After typing Table I, triple-space and type the first two lines of the paragraph following Table I.

b. Special Drill—Table II, page 215. Using 1" side margins and drill paper, type the last two lines of the paragraph preceding Table II. Triple-space; then type Table II according to the special directions given on page 215. After typing Table II, triple-space and type the first two lines of the paragraph following Table II.

---

*The letter on the following pages is a revision of material appearing in previous editions of this book. Your authors regard the content as having special relevance to all persons who drive cars. In addition, the letter includes many kinds of typing problems encountered in the business office.

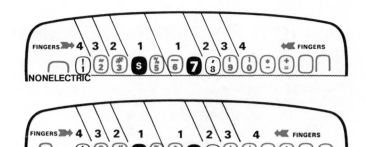

LESSON 23

23A ■ CONDITIONING PRACTICE [8] each line at least twice; as time permits, retype selected lines

Alphabet   Lt. Jack Mix quizzed four vagrant men who slept by the park.

Figures   Mr. O'Neil will be 84 years old on July 14. Isn't he great!

Fluency   The right bid may entitle the girl to the handy ivory forks.
            | 1 | 2 | 3 | 4 | 5 | 6 | 7 | 8 | 9 | 10 | 11 | 12 |

23B ■ SYMBOL/FIGURE LOCATION: $ 7 [7]

REACH TECHNIQUE FOR $

Depress right shift key, then make a low reach with the *left first finger* to the top row to type $ (the shift of 4). *Do not space between $ and the following figure.*

4f 4f$f 4f$f $f $f 4f$f $f

Type: $4.14, $84.48, $84. DS

◀ **NOTE:** Use . (period) to type the decimal point.

REACH TO 7

REACH TECHNIQUE FOR 7

Reach the *right first finger* up to type 7. Try to keep the other fingers in their home position. Keep the wrists low. Make a direct reach to 7 without moving the hand forward.

u7j 7j 7j 7 j7j 77 j7j 777

Tod will be 17 on July 17. TS

23C ■ STROKING TECHNIQUE PRACTICE [10] type twice

All figures and symbols learned are used.

1 $ $f $14 $14 $48 $841 I paid $14.18 for the two copies of X84.
2   Vance Burke owed $144 on March 14 and paid $44 on August 14.

3 7   7j 7j7 77 47 17 147 Did Joan take Flight 147? or was it 187?
4   Andy and I have read 77 of the 177 pages assigned for May 7.

5 Consoli- The 8 men, 17 boys, and 44 girls left for Boston on June 17.
6 dation   Evan's May 7 check should be for $478.48 instead of $748.48!
            | 1 | 2 | 3 | 4 | 5 | 6 | 7 | 8 | 9 | 10 | 11 | 12 |

23D ■ TABULATING PRACTICE [7] twice from copy; once from dictation

							Words
Clear and set tabs	in	47	act	147	door	1.74	$14.18	6
	up	78	tab	718	keep	4.18	$17.48	12
	we	17	set	148	foot	7.71	$47.18	19
	no	74	few	474	boss	8.47	$18.17	25
KEY	2	6	2	6	3	6	3	6	4	6	4	6	6

137B ■ SKILL BUILDING: STATISTICAL ROUGH DRAFT ⟨15⟩ repeat 136B, pages 210-211; **Goal:** improved rates

137C ■ LETTER PRODUCTION SKILL MEASUREMENT ⟨30⟩ (Letterheads or plain sheets; 1 cc; address envelopes)

Time Schedule	
Planning and preparing	3'
Timed letter production	20'
Proofreading; computing *n-pram* .	7'

Type the letters as you are timed for 20 minutes. Erase and correct your errors. When time is called, proofread carefully.

Determine *n-pram* (net production rate a minute—all errors corrected). For each uncorrected error, subtract 15 words from total words typed.

Problem 1

Modified block ■ 5-space ¶ indention ■ mixed punctuation ■ indent the enumerated items 5 spaces from the left and right margins ■ DS above and below each item (Reference: p. 145) ■ use vertical form for second-page heading (Reference: p. 203) ■ omit the official title in second-page heading

	Words
May 25, 19-- │ Mr. John H. Kingston, Chair-	8
man │ Alternative Futures Committee │ 4039	16
Lombardi Lane, Suite 408 │ Denver, CO	23
80215 │ Dear Mr. Kingston: (¶1) Thank you	30
for sending me a copy of your preliminary	39
report, Alternative Futures. I have enjoyed	48
studying it. (¶2) I agree with the committee	56
that we need to attempt to deal, in a system-	65
atic and constructive way, with the many and	74
varied problems before us. In my opinion, pub-	83
lic policy, at the moment, reflects no such ap-	92
proach. We should be looking for basic causes	101
of our problems, and then the effort should be	111
made to eliminate these causes. As was put	120
forth so forcefully in your report, "The net	129
result is that the environment suffers, and the	138
quality of our lives continues to deteriorate."	148
(¶3) Our traditional way of coping with prob-	156
lems has been to attack them separately and	165
individually with little or no consideration of	174
the interrelationships existing between prob-	183
lems. I believe an alternative way of coping	192
with major problems is to seek out these inter-	201
relationships and then attempt to identify	210
some common underlying causes. With this	218
point in mind, I should like to suggest, for con-	228
sideration by the Future's Committee, four	237
underlying causes of disruptions in our society.	247

1. The damaging distribution of popula- 261
   tion. Our population is increasingly 270
   being concentrated in huge urban 276
   centers. 278
2. The damaging patterns of consump- 292
   tion. We need to recognize that we 300
   have only a finite supply of resources. 308
3. The lack of individual economic 322
   strength. Every person should have 331
   more opportunities to exercise his in- 338

	Words
fluence in decisions affecting our	345
economy.	347

4. The lack of individual political 361
   strength. Do some of our elected offi- 370
   cials have a seeming immunity from 377
   effective citizen control? 383

	Words
Even though there is some overlap among	391
these underlying causes of disruption, I be-	399
lieve that Causes 1 and 2 relate most often	408
to our misuse of environmental resources.	417
Causes 3 and 4 relate most often to our misuse	426
of human resources. (¶4) If you believe that	434
these points have sufficient importance to be	443
considered at your Planning Conference, I shall	453
be glad to present them, together with the	462
supporting data. I am pleased that you are	470
meeting to consider ways to solve our many	479
problems. During this decade, we need to be	488
making the decisions which will shape the	496
growth and character of America in the best	505
possible way for all people. We can sit back	514
and do nothing, or we can consciously and de-	523
liberately make alternative choices for a desir-	533
able future. The choice, in my opinion, is ours	542
to make. (¶5) I'll look forward to hearing	550
from you. Thanks, again, for giving me the	559
opportunity to react to your preliminary re-	568
port. │ Sincerely yours, │ Henry Abbott	576/**598**

Problem 2: Block; Open Punctuation

	Words
June 1, 19-- │ Mr. Henry Abbott │ 219 Wana-	8
maker, North │ Philadelphia, PA 19139 │	15
Dear Mr. Abbott (¶1) The Planning Confer-	23
ence agenda has been rearranged. Your presen-	32
tation is scheduled for the Second General	40
Session on Monday, June 15, from 10:00 a.m.	49
to 11:30 a.m. Will you plan to make about a	58
50-minute formal presentation so that we can	67
have a question-and-answer period following	76
it. (¶2) Please send a brief biographical	84
sketch. Also, let me know what audio-visual	93
media you would like for your presentation.	102
(¶3) The Future's Committee is excited about	110
your ideas. We look forward to having you	118
with us. │ Sincerely yours │ John H. Kingston │	126/**139**
(101)	

23E ■ SPEED/CONTROL BUILDING: STATISTICAL COPY 12

1. Type a 1' *control-level* writing on the following ¶. Determine *gwam* and errors.
2. Type another 1' writing, beginning where you stopped in Step 1. Determine *gwam* and errors.
3. Type a 2' and a 3' writing on the ¶. Determine *gwam* and errors.

All letters and all figures learned are used.

GWAM

	2'	3'
Do you realize that lodging and food are two top costs	5	4	27
of business travel? A hotel room that a few years ago cost	11	8	31
just $7 or $8 a day now goes for at least $14, and often as	17	12	35
much as $17 or $18! The cost of food away from home is up,	23	16	39
also. For example, a $4 dinner of the past decade may cost	29	20	43
up to $8 now. Don't you think travel costs are quite high?	35	24	47

2' GWAM | 1 | 2 | 3 | 4 | 5 | 6 |
3' GWAM | 1 | 2 | 3 | 4 |

23F ■ SELF-IMPROVEMENT PRACTICE 6

1. Type the ¶ of 23E, above, trying for improved stroking patterns.
2. Type the ¶ again, untimed. Try to reduce your errors.

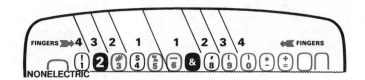

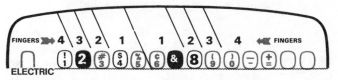

■ LESSON 24

24A ■ CONDITIONING PRACTICE 8 each line at least twice; as time permits, retype selected lines

Alphabet   Paula Judge took my five new girls to lunch at the Quiz Box.

Figure/symbol Jean's weekly pay is $71, but Carl's is between $74 and $78.

Fluency   If they make such a visit, it may end the fight for a title.

| 1 | 2 | 3 | 4 | 5 | 6 | 7 | 8 | 9 | 10 | 11 | 12 |

24B ■ SYMBOL/FIGURE LOCATION: & 2 7

REACH TECHNIQUE FOR & (and)

You typed **7** with the *right first finger*. As & is the shift of **7**, type it with the *same finger. The & is used only in some company names.*

7j 7j&j 7j&j &j &j 7j&j &j

Lane & Lee owe King & Orr. *DS*

REACH TO 2

REACH TECHNIQUE FOR 2

Reach the *left third finger* up to type **2** without moving the elbow outward.

w2s 2s 2s 2 s2s 22 s2s 222

Are 22 boys on Flight 222? *TS*

UNIT 3 (Lessons 21-30) Figures and Basic Symbols

¶2

(A) 1.5 / 5.6 / 80

Communicating with others was a basic *or principal* component of 269 (89.6%) of the 300 jobs in the study. It occurred as a support activity in 31 other jobs. (10.4%) A basic *or principal* component was one that included 5% or more of total job time; less than 5% of the total job time, the work was put in a class called a support activity. Sorting, filing, and retrieving was a principal component of 212 (70.7%) of the 300 jobs. It was a support activity in 40 other jobs. (13.3%) Typewriting was a principal component of 147 jobs (49.0%). It occured as a support activity in 20 other jobs. (6.7%) *From 66% to 68% of the typists reported that handwritten rough drafts were a main source of copy from which they typed.*

	1'	5'
	16 28	83
	34 32	86
	52 36	90
	71 39	94
	84 42	97
	100 45	100
	115 48	103
	128 51	105
	137 53	107
	146 54	109

136C ■ BUILDING LETTER PRODUCTION SKILL [30]

Time Schedule

Planning and preparing . .	3'
Timed letter production . .	20'
Proofreading; determining g-pram	7'

In 20 minutes, type the form letter given below to as many as possible of the names and addresses given on the carbon copy of the memo prepared for 135D, page 210. In the address lines, use the names of your city and state and the ZIP Code for your home address. Supply appropriate salutations. Make the necessary insertions in the first paragraph. *Make other necessary corrections.* Type without waste motions: Fingers close to the keys, eyes on the copy, with the carriage kept moving.

Modified block style ■ mixed punctuation ■ 1 cc ■ address envelopes

Words

August 26, 19-- +*address lines and salutation* 18
(¶1) Did you overlook our recent statement, 26
(*title, last name*)? This statement in the amount 34
of (*give amount*) was sent to you on (*give bill 41
date*). This account now appears on our delinquent or past-due list. (¶2) The low prices 49 / 58
charged at our Fashion Square store are possible because our customers help us keep 66 / 75
billing expenses down by making prompt payment. And, of course, we want to avoid the 83 / 92

necessity of adding costly service charges on 101
merchandise sold on credit. (¶3) Wont you 109
help us by mailing the amount now *past due* 117
as shown on the enclosed duplicate statement. 127
A return envelope is enclosed for your convenience. If you cannot make full payment now 136 / 145
please contact this office. It is extremely important that you do so. Your credit is one 154 / 163
of your most important assets. | Sincerely 171
yours, | Wayne Gordon | Account Manager 179/188
(152)

(For this letter and all remaining letters in Cycle 2 be sure to use your own reference initials.)

■ LESSON 137

137A ■ CONDITIONING PRACTICE [5] each line 3 times: slowly, faster, top speed

Alphabet The quiet king came forth to extend prizes to very bewildered jesters.

Eyes on copy

Figure/symbol I sold Jet Record Nos. 47-2115-B, 86-2735-A, 92-0413-C, and 64-8015-Z.

Related learning He said, "The want of principal is the principal want of many people."

Fluency Often, persons are lonely because they build walls instead of bridges.

| 1 | 2 | 3 | 4 | 5 | 6 | 7 | 8 | 9 | 10 | 11 | 12 | 13 | 14 |

24C ■ STROKING TECHNIQUE PRACTICE 10 type twice

Technique Cue: Keep the hands quiet, almost motionless; the wrists low.

1   *&*   &j &7 j& Ty & Vi's; Childs & Langin; Check Funk & Wagnall's.
2   Lane & Hall merged with Park & North to form Park & Lane Co.

3   *2*   2s 2s2 22 12 27 272 Ray lives at 722 Park Rd.; Lyn, at 1228.
4   Kevin will be 22 years 2 months 22 days old on September 22.

5   *Consoli-*   Of 22 typists 2 typed 72 words, 8 typed 47, and 12 typed 42.
6   *dation*   Hall & Quick's note to Zahl & Fox, due March 4, is for $728.
     | 1 | 2 | 3 | 4 | 5 | 6 | 7 | 8 | 9 | 10 | 11 | 12 |

24D ■ TABULATING PRACTICE 7 twice from copy; once from dictation

							Words
Clear and set tabs at	21	era	272	C+O	8:17	$8.47	6
no	72	car	827	M+M	4:48	$2.48	12
my	12	pop	274	B+G	7:22	$4.87	19
be	28	him	748	A+Z	2:47	$7.14	25

KEY | 2 | 6 | 2 | 6 | 3 | 6 | 3 | 6 | 5 | 6 | 4 | 6 | 5 |

24E ■ IMPROVING KEYBOARD CONTROL 12

1. Type Lines 1, 3, 5, 7, and 9 without being timed. Work at a steady, unhurried pace. Keep the carriage (carrier) moving.

2. Type a 1' writing on each of Lines 2, 4, 6, 8, and 10. Determine *gwam* and errors on each. Compare the *gwam* and error scores line by line.

All letters and all figures learned are used.

1 *Easy words*   an odd city; ditto the proxy; I am sorry; when did it occur?
2   The city auditor may handle the penalty for the island firm.

3 *One-hand*   refer your case; my only regret; minimum wages; tested nylon
4 *words*   My union assessed extra fees after its reserve was depleted.

5 *Alphabet*   Five boys quickly mixed the prizes, baffling one wise judge.
6   JoAnn Vezie quickly won her big chance from DeLuxe Products.

7 *Figures*   All 18 boys climbed 2,487 feet to the peak of that mountain.
8   Flight 27 leaves here at 11:28 a.m.; Flight 74, at 4:12 p.m.

9 *Figure/symbol*   Shift for & and $ as well as for ? and : but not for ; and .
10   McMann & O'Henry Co. offers unique gifts from $12 to $1,478!
     | 1 | 2 | 3 | 4 | 5 | 6 | 7 | 8 | 9 | 10 | 11 | 12 |

24F ■ SELF-IMPROVEMENT PRACTICE 6

1. Type twice each sentence of 24E on which you did not equal your rate on Line 2.

2. If time permits, retype 24D, without dictation.
Goal: To tabulate quickly and without waste motion.

135D ■ MEMORANDUM TYPING: REVIEW [15] (Full sheet; 1" side margins; carbon copy on plain sheet)

Type the following material as an interoffice memorandum (Reference: page 200). If a memorandum form is not available, type the problem on a full sheet with the heading lines starting about 1 inch from the top and left edge of the sheet as shown at the right. Save the carbon copy you make to use in 136C, page 211. Correct your errors.

TO: *Wayne Gordon, Account Manager* FROM: *Jan Parks, Accounting Dept.* DATE: *August 25, 19--* SUBJECT: *Delinquent Accounts*

(¶ 1) Installment accounts that are now more than 30 days past due are shown below. These names

```
TO:     Wayne Gordon, Account Manager
FROM:   Jan Parks, Accounting Dept.
DATE:   August 25, 19--
SUBJECT: Delinquent Accounts

Installment accounts that are now more than 30 days past due are
shown below.  These names are being sent to you so that the regu-
```

are being sent to you so that the regular form letter on delinquent accounts can be sent to them.

(¶ 2) (Triple-space and then type the entire tabulation given in 135C, page 209. Center the table horizontally as directed. In the table, change the month to July, but use the same day as shown.)

■ LESSON 136

136A ■ CONDITIONING PRACTICE [5] each line 3 times: slowly, faster, top speed

Alphabet	Most companies emphasize extra valuable jobs for good quality workers.
Figure/symbol	A 100% hardwood 3-shelf bookcase (38" x 23" x 7 3/4") sells for $9.65.
Fingers 3, 4	A plump yellowtail swallowed the squid as I attempted to set the hook.
Fluency	No job has a future--the future is with the person who holds that job.

Wrists low and relaxed

| 1 | 2 | 3 | 4 | 5 | 6 | 7 | 8 | 9 | 10 | 11 | 12 | 13 | 14 |

136B ■ SKILL-TRANSFER TYPING: STATISTICAL ROUGH DRAFT [15]

1. Type a 5' writing on the ¶s below and on page 211. Type on the *control level* (try to type with fewer than 5 errors).
2. Type another 5' writing. If you made the goal in

Step 1, increase your speed. Compute % of transfer: rough-draft copy rate divided by straight-copy rate. **Goal:** 70-80% of straight-copy rate of 133C, page 207.

All figures are used.

¶ 1

	GWAM	
	1'	5'
The data reported here represent the findings of a 1970 research study of	15	3 | 57
300 different office jobs. These positions were held by employees 16 to 24 years of age.	33	7 | 61
Of the 300 office jobs included in the study, 242 were held by females	47	9 | 64
and 58 by males; 255 of the 300 jobs were in business organizations	61	12 | 67
employing more than 100 workers, and 45 were in business organiza-	74	15 | 69
tions with fewer than 100 workers. There was an average of 3.26 tasks per	89	18 | 72
job with a total of 978 tasks. Each of the 978 job tasks involved for the 300 different jobs	108	22 | 76
a minimum of 6 key steps for a total of approximately	119	24 | 78
5,868 key steps for all the job tasks	126	25 | 80

(Continued on page 211)

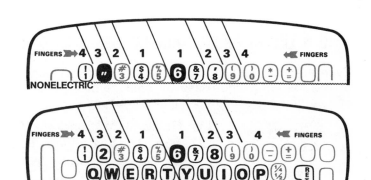

■ LESSON 25

25A ■ CONDITIONING PRACTICE ⑧ each line at least twice; as time permits, retype selected lines

Alphabet   Having pumped in six quick points, Jerry Dow froze the ball.

Figure/symbol   Marie paid Reed & Betz $72 on her August 24 bill of $272.84.

Fluency   A theory the girls wish to make work may throw the chairman.
      | 1 | 2 | 3 | 4 | 5 | 6 | 7 | 8 | 9 | 10 | 11 | 12 |

25B ■ SYMBOL/FIGURE LOCATION: " 6 ⑦

REACH TECHNIQUE FOR " (*quotation*)

Nonelectric: Type " (the shift of **2**) with the *left third finger*.

2s 2s"s 2s"s "s "s 2s"s "s

I said, "He can and will." *DS*

Electric: Type " (the shift of ') with the *right little finger*.

'; ';"; ';"; "; "; ';"; ";

I said, "He can and will." *DS*

REACH TO 6

NOTE: Reach with the controlling finger. Curve the other fingers and try to keep them over their home keys.

▶ **REACH TECHNIQUE FOR 6**

Reach up to **6** with the *right first finger*. Keep the wrist low. Try not to move the hand forward.

Although **6** on some machines may seem nearer the left first finger, use the *right first finger* to type it because the left hand already has a heavier work load than the right.

y6j 6j 6j 6 j6j 66 j6j 666

Read pages 6, 66, and 166. *TS*

25C ■ STROKING TECHNIQUE PRACTICE ⑩ type twice

1 *"*   s" "; 2" "; ";2 2"; Frank said, "Return without looking up."
2   Ken is mixed on "choose" and "chose" and "loose" and "lose."

3 *6*   6j 6j 16 46 116 746 $164; He quoted a price of $64.28 a set.
4   My 66 pupils had a speed range of 16 to 66 on the last test.

5 *Consoli-* His memo read: "I drove Mr. Squibb 264 miles on August 26."
6 *dation* Mat's check to Parker & Owen, dated July 16, is for $276.48.
      | 1 | 2 | 3 | 4 | 5 | 6 | 7 | 8 | 9 | 10 | 11 | 12 |

25D ■ TABULATING PRACTICE ⑦ type twice (Line: 60; spaces between columns: 10)

				Words
Clear and set tabs Sheldon, Inc.	"IPA" Center, Rm. 226	May 17		9
C & O Railway	Gradison Hall, Rm. 87	May 21		17
J. C. Orr Co.	"Walden Pond" Theater	June 2		26
Jantz & Simms	Women's Gym, Rm. 1468	July 8		34
KEY	13	10	21	10	6

134D ■ LETTER PRODUCTION TYPING: SKILL BUILDING (Short Letter) 10 (Plain sheets)

Type the short letter of 134C, page 208, to as many of the following addresses as time permits. Make one carbon copy; address small envelopes.

NOTE: Type each new letter from your previous letter; in this way, you can proofread the previous letter as you type the new letter.

> Block style ■ open punctuation ■ supply appropriate salutations ■ your initials as reference ■ correct your typing errors

(1) Dr. Sarah W. Jones   2190 Notre Dame Avenue   Winnipeg, Manitoba
(2) Mrs. Bea Lux   7468 Old Kings Road   Jacksonville, FL   32217
(3) Dr. George P. Grill   9417 Ashbury Chapel Road   Charlotte, NC   28213
(4) Mrs. Marilyn Hunter   2000 E. Main Street   Danville, IL   61832
(5) Mr. John F. McCreary, Sr.   3700 Sutherland Avenue   Knoxville, TN   37919
(6) Miss Elizabeth Scott   29580 Bellfield Lane   Cincinnati, OH   45238

■ LESSON 135

135A ■ CONDITIONING PRACTICE 5 each line 3 times: slowly, faster, top speed

Alphabet	Jerome quickly realized that six lively polliwogs would soon be frogs. *Quick, snap stroke*
Figure/symbol	We will ship your Order #35790 for 126 boxes and 48 cartons on Monday.
Reach drill	z/a; x.sl c,dk vmfj bngh z/a; x.sl c,dk vmfj bngh z/a; x.sl c,dk vmfj
Fluency	Actions speak louder than words--it is by our deeds that we are known.

| 1 | 2 | 3 | 4 | 5 | 6 | 7 | 8 | 9 | 10 | 11 | 12 | 13 | 14 |

135B ■ LETTER TIMED WRITING 10 5' writing; follow directions of 134D, above; omit envelopes

135C ■ TABULATION TIMED WRITING 20 two 5' writings of unarranged table below; proofread; determine GWAM

Arrange table in proper form. You will have 3' to 4' to determine left margin stop and tab stops for columns. Determine, also, points at which main heading and columnar headings start. Make pencil notations of these points.

> Full sheet ■ reading position ■ 4 spaces between columns ■ DS data of columns

Each figure is used a minimum of 10 times.

When a street has a number as its name, separate the house number from the street number by a hyphen preceded and followed by a space.

				Words
Main Heading: **DELINQUENT INSTALLMENT ACCOUNTS**				6
Columnar Headings: Name	Address	Bill Date	Amount	18
Thomas Adams, Jr.	993 North 15th Street	June 15	$62.78	29
Milton Balzac	8 El Dorado Plaza	June 20	$64.49	38
William Boccacio	9366 Del Mar Avenue	June 25	$74.20	48
(Mrs.) Ray Brady	1680 Corso di Napoli	June 15	$47.83	59
Lee Coleridge	One Hillside Lane	June 10	$75.60	68
James Macaulay	6347 Driftwood Drive	June 25	$81.90	79
Douglas Poynter	3889 Constitution Lane	June 15	$73.46	89
Karl Sandhurst	26790 Cahuenga Blvd.	June 25	$93.10	100
Randy Sims, II	10382 Sandwood Drive	June 25	$46.79	110
Victor Thoreau	2039 Corinthian Walk	June 20	$56.74	120
(Miss) Joy Vale	37484 Vicente Avenue	June 20	$96.15	130
Emile Zins	1927 – 34th St., N.W.	June 15	$47.83	140

25E ■ GROWTH INDEX: STRAIGHT COPY [10] two 3' writings; determine GWAM and errors

All letters are used.

		1'	3'
GWAM			

¶ 1　　　　If you desire to develop the power to get things done, 　11　4 | 32

choose a field to which you can devote your top thought and 　23　8 | 36

effort.　Study or practice until you master all there is to 　35　12 | 40

know; then just continue to excel. 　42　14 | 42

¶ 2　　　　Your typing power will be quite an asset in almost any 　11　18 | 46

field of work you choose.　In fact, you will no doubt prize 　23　22 | 50

this new skill even though you use it only to type personal 　35　26 | 54

papers.　Typing is writing power. 　42　28 | 56

1' GWAM | 1 | 2 | 3 | 4 | 5 | 6 | 7 | 8 | 9 | 10 | 11 | 12 |
3' GWAM | 1 | 2 | 3 | 4 |

25F ■ SELF-IMPROVEMENT PRACTICE [8]

1. Type ¶ 1 of 25E with control (minimum errors).
2. Repeat Step 1 with ¶ 2.

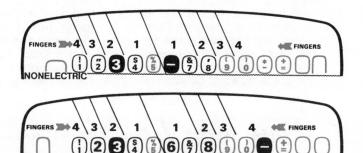

■ LESSON 26

26A ■ CONDITIONING PRACTICE [8] each line at least twice; as time permits, retype selected lines

Alphabet　　Dave Gibson will quickly explain what Janet made for prizes.

Figure/symbol　Lance & Lane's Order 621 reads, "26 boxes of K47 at $18 ea."

Fluency　　Fix in mind just what it is you want; then work hard for it.

　　　| 1 | 2 | 3 | 4 | 5 | 6 | 7 | 8 | 9 | 10 | 11 | 12 |

26B ■ SYMBOL/FIGURE LOCATION: _ (UNDERLINE) 3 [7]

REACH TECHNIQUE FOR _ (*underline*)

Nonelectric: Type _ (the shift of **6**) with the *right first finger*. Hold the wrist low; *reach* with the finger.

6j 6j_j 6j_j _j _j 6j_j _j

Electric: Type _ (the shift of the hyphen key in the top row) with the *right fourth finger*.

p_; p_; _; _; p_; _; _; _; DS

TO UNDERLINE A WORD: Backspace (or move carriage by hand) to the first letter of the word. Shift. Type the underline once for each letter in the word.

TO UNDERLINE SEVERAL WORDS: Depress the **shift lock (29)** and type an unbroken line. To release the shift lock, depress the shift key.

REACH TECHNIQUE FOR 3

Reach up to **3** with the *left second finger*. Avoid arching the wrist or changing hand position.

e3d 3d 3d 3 d3d 33 d3d 333

The 33 men sent 333 cards. TS

LESSON 134

134A ■ CONDITIONING PRACTICE [5] each line 3 times: slowly, faster, top speed

Alphabet Invaluable new zoning rules were quickly expedited by the junior firm. *Finger-reach action*

Figure/symbol Special sale items are identified by the *; as, 10*, 631*, 792*, 845*.

Reach drill qpa; wosl eidk rufj tygh qpa; wosl eidk rufj tygh qpa; wosl eidk rufj

Fluency True merit is like a river--the deeper it is, the less noise it makes.

| 1 | 2 | 3 | 4 | 5 | 6 | 7 | 8 | 9 | 10 | 11 | 12 | 13 | 14 |

134B ■ SKILL BUILDING: STRAIGHT COPY [15]

1. Type a 5′ writing on the ¶s of 133C, page 207, at the *control level* (try to type with fewer than 5 errors).

2. Type another 5′ writing. If you made the goal of Step 1, increase your speed on this writing.

134C ■ LETTER SKILL BUILDING [20] (Block style; open punctuation; 2″ margins; date on Line 20)

1. Type a 3′ writing on the letter to establish a base rate. If you finish before time is called, start over.
2. Determine *gwam*. To this rate add 8 *gwam* to set a new goal. Divide the goal rate into four equal segments; note these quarter-minute check points for guided writings.
3. *Leave proper spacing between let-*

ter parts, but begin the letter (date-line) near the top of the sheet. Beginning with the date, type three 1′ guided writings on the opening parts of the letter and ¶1. Begin the second and third writings a double space below the last line of the previous writing.
4. Repeat Step 3, using ¶2 and the

closing lines of the letter.
5. Type another 3′ writing on the complete letter. Try to maintain your new goal rate for this writing. Do this by using good techniques and by typing with continuity. Determine *gwam* and compare it with the rate you attained in Step 1.

RECALL: *Block style—all lines start at the left margin. Reference: p. 156.*

	Words	3′ GWAM
May 10, 19-- / Mrs. Walter Cummins / 15867 Lakeview Drive	11	4 | 47
Washington, DC 20031 / Dear Mrs. Cummins /	19	6 | 50
(¶1) The excellent way in which you have handled your	29	10 | 53
credit account with us is sincerely appreciated. We want	40	13 | 57
you to know that serving you has been a genuine	50	17 | 60
pleasure. Thank you for giving us this opportunity to	61	20 | 64
be of service.	64	21 | 65
(¶2) Although your account is paid in full, please do not	75	25 | 68
feel that it is closed. Your account is open in our files,	87	29 | 72
ready to serve you. We hope you will use it often.	97	32 | 76
Your credit record now entitles you to make purchases	108	36 | 79
with no down payment. We shall look forward to	118	39 | 83
seeing you.	120	40 | 83
Cordially yours / Marilyn North, Credit Manager / rjm	130	43 | 87

26C ■ STROKING TECHNIQUE PRACTICE [10] type twice

DO: Use the shift key to underline isolated words, as in Line 2.

DO: Use the **shift lock (29)** to underline a continuous series of words, as in Lines 5 and 6.

All letters and all figures learned are used.

```
1 _      _j _; _j_ _;_ 6_ 2846; He added:  "Rush!  This is an order!"
2        Curve your fingers.  Keep your wrists low, your hands quiet.

3 3      3d 3d3 37 3 834 326 $6.36; I missed Questions 3, 13, and 33.
4        Just 33 of the 333 boys had read pages 33 to 333 by March 3.

5 Consoli-  Type a book title in caps, EXODUS; or underlined, The Prize.
6 dation    They sent us 136 copies of Modern Economics at $6.33 a copy.
           |  1  |  2  |  3  |  4  |  5  |  6  |  7  |  8  |  9  |  10  |  11  |  12  |
```

26D ■ SKILL-TRANSFER TYPING [15]

1. Type a 2' writing on ¶ 1. Determine *gwam*.

2. Type a 2' writing on ¶ 2. Determine *gwam*. Compare *gwam* on the two ¶s.

3. Type two additional 2' writings on ¶ 1; then a final 2' writing on ¶ 2.

4. Type a 1' writing on ¶ 1, then on ¶ 2. Determine *gwam* and compare rates.

All letters and all figures learned are used.

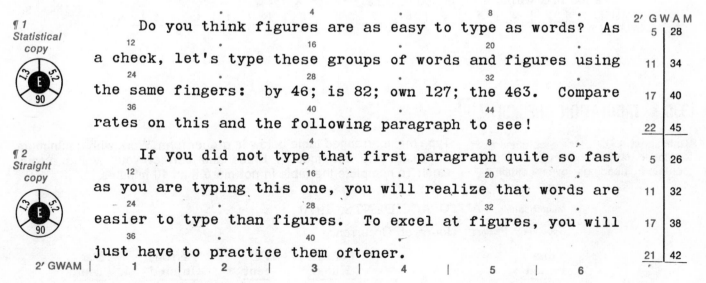

	2' GWAM
¶ 1 *Statistical copy* Do you think figures are as easy to type as words? As	5 | 28
a check, let's type these groups of words and figures using	11 | 34
the same fingers: by 46; is 82; own 127; the 463. Compare	17 | 40
rates on this and the following paragraph to see!	22 | 45
¶ 2 *Straight copy* If you did not type that first paragraph quite so fast	5 | 26
as you are typing this one, you will realize that words are	11 | 32
easier to type than figures. To excel at figures, you will	17 | 38
just have to practice them oftener.	21 | 42

2' GWAM | 1 | 2 | 3 | 4 | 5 | 6

26E ■ GUIDED WRITING [10]

1. Type two 2' guided writings on ¶ 1 of 26D, above, for speed improvement.

2. Type two 2' guided writings on ¶ 2 of 26D, above, for speed improvement.

133C ■ GROWTH INDEX: STRAIGHT COPY ⌷15⌷ two 5' writings; proofread; determine GWAM; record your better score

All letters are used.

	1'	5'

¶ 1   What are a few of the basic components of office work which are   13 3 | 51
made up of the variety of tasks performed by a new office worker? One   27 5 | 54
of the main or most important components is what might be called the   41 8 | 57
ability to communicate effectively. All office workers need to work   55 11 | 60
with others so as to complete many of the tasks which make up the work   69 14 | 62
of the office. Next, every office worker may have to perform tasks which   84 17 | 65
require some skill in sorting, filing, and retrieving. Typewriting, too,   98 20 | 68
continues to be a basic component of office work. In a recent study of   113 23 | 71
new office workers, nearly half of the workers were required to perform   127 25 | 74
tasks involving the use of the typewriter.   136 27 | 76

¶ 2   Good proofreading skill is a big part of nearly all work in the   13 30 | 78
office, and it is a part of the basic component of checking, computing,   27 33 | 81
and verifying of work. Other components of office work include such   41 35 | 84
things as collecting and distributing of items, the use of office machines   56 38 | 87
such as the ten-key adding machine, and in a few cases the analyzing of   70 41 | 90
work procedures. Just about all of these basic components require accu-   85 44 | 93
racy, the need to understand and follow directions, and the need to finish   100 47 | 96
a job task within a set period of time.   108 49 | 97

1' GWAM | 1 | 2 | 3 | 4 | 5 | 6 | 7 | 8 | 9 | 10 | 11 | 12 | 13 | 14 |
5' GWAM | 1 | 2 | 3 |

133D ■ TABULATION CHECKUP ⌷10⌷

Half sheet ■ DS data in columns ■ 4 spaces between columns ■ center columnar headings over columns

Type the unarranged table below in proper form. Work with a minimum of waste time and motion. Erase and correct your typing errors. **Goal:** To complete the table in not more than 10 minutes.

Main Heading: AUTO ACCIDENTS, 1970

Secondary Heading: Hours of Occurrence

NOTE: For best balance, center headings for Cols. 3 and 5 over the columnar items, not over the total below the items.

Time Period	Persons Killed	Per-cent	Persons Injured	Per-cent
12:00 a.m. – 6:00 a.m.	11,900	21.6	602,000	11.8
6:00 a.m. – 12:00 noon	8,600	15.6	1,056,000	20.7
12:00 noon – 6:00 p.m.	15,700	28.4	2,040,000	40.0
6:00 p.m. – midnight	19,000	34.4	1,402,000	27.5
Total *Use ratchet release*	55,200	100.0	5,100,000	100.0

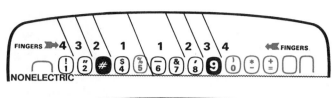

LESSON 27

27A ■ CONDITIONING PRACTICE 8 each line at least twice; as time permits, retype selected lines

Alphabet   Casey Vale asked Max Johns to bring all quiz papers forward.

Figure/symbol   Is Pam's Check 136 for $738.46 to Wells & Pont dated May 23?

Fluency   Mr. Naylor may amend the audit form if it is right to do so.
                  | 1 | 2 | 3 | 4 | 5 | 6 | 7 | 8 | 9 | 10 | 11 | 12 |

27B ■ SYMBOL/FIGURE LOCATION: # (NO., LBS.) 9 7

■ Before a figure, # is the symbol for *Number*; after a figure, it
is the symbol for *pounds*. See Line 2 of the drill at the left.

REACH TECHNIQUE FOR #

You learned to type **3** with the *left second finger*. As # is the shift of **3**, move the same finger up to type it.

3d 3d#d 3d#d #d #d 3d#d #d

Ship Order #6131 for 174#. DS

REACH TO 9

REACH TECHNIQUE FOR 9

Reach the *right third finger* up to type **9**. Avoid swinging the elbow out. Keep the wrist low. *Reach!*

o91 91 91 9 191 99 191 999

Study pages 9, 91, and 99. TS

27C ■ STROKING TECHNIQUE PRACTICE 10 type twice

1 #   #d #d# 3# #d 33 #33 Here is Check #133.   Order 36# of #1284.
2   We shipped Order #634 on August 17; Order #637 on August 28.

3 9   91 919 49 9 297 839 All 29 of the boys typed 99 lines today.
4   Our building lease for 99 years will be up on June 29, 1999.

5 *Consoli-* Order #931 from Zenith & Weaver is for 197# of #9X Compound.
6 *dation*   Prepare Invoice #289 for 19 copies of <u>Impact</u>; total, $63.49.
              | 1 | 2 | 3 | 4 | 5 | 6 | 7 | 8 | 9 | 10 | 11 | 12 |

27D ■ TABULATING PRACTICE 5 twice from copy; once from dictation

							Words
in	92	per	#49	size	1:28	$29.47	6
on	36	net	93#	jump	4:46	$84.16	12
of	12	tow	#87	move	6:37	$79.96	18
KEY	2 6 2 6 3 6 3 6 4 6 4 6 6

Letters / Reports / Tables

■ LESSON 133 (Basic Skill)

133A ■ CONDITIONING PRACTICE ⑤ each line 3 times: slowly, faster, top speed

Alphabet	Six flying fish whizzed quickly over my jigs as a big tuna approached.
Figure/symbol	The new prices are as follows: 12 @ $25.50; 24 @ $48.95; 36 @ $70.50.
Long reaches	She executed many zany swan dives at the aquacade dedication ceremony.
Fluency	It is easier to make the figure-key reaches if the fingers are curved.

Fingers curved and upright

| 1 | 2 | 3 | 4 | 5 | 6 | 7 | 8 | 9 | 10 | 11 | 12 | 13 | 14 |

133B ■ IMPROVING SPEED/ACCURACY ⑳

1. **Speed Jump—Set 1.** Starting with Sentence 1, Set 1, gradually increase your speed as you type each new sentence as the 15″, 12″, or 10″ guide is called by your teacher. Move from one sentence to the next when the "return" is called. Push your speed to its highest possible level.

2. **Accuracy Drive—Set 2.** Starting with Sentence 1, Set 2, gradually increase your speed on each new sentence as the 15″, 12″, or 10″ guide is called by your teacher. Your goal is errorless writing on each sentence; if you make an error, stay on that sentence until you type it without error.

3. **Speed and Accuracy—Set 3.** Type each sentence of Set 3 as a 1′ writing at a guided rate determined by the call of the 15″, 12″, or 10″ *return* guide. Start at a slow rate and gradually increase this rate on each new timing; try to type with not more than 1 error on each writing.

SET 1	High-frequency balanced-hand words emphasized	Words	GWAM 15″	12″	10″
1	He may also make me go with them to do their work.	10	40	50	60
2	They may sign the city amendment form for the chairman.	11	44	55	66
3	The firm may make a profit if the men do a quantity of work.	12	48	60	72
4	Their wish is to do the problem and then visit the city chairman.	13	52	65	78
5	It is their wish to pay the firm for the work so it may make a profit.	14	56	70	84

| 1 | 2 | 3 | 4 | 5 | 6 | 7 | 8 | 9 | 10 | 11 | 12 | 13 | 14 |

SET 2	High-frequency one-hand words emphasized	Words	15″	12″	10″
1	After you rate him, read only a few reserve cases.	10	40	50	60
2	John can get you only a minimum tax rate on the estate.	11	44	55	66
3	We regret that you were referred to him for the tax opinion.	12	48	60	72
4	The average reserve tax rate is greater than the minimum you set.	13	52	65	78
5	Were you to refer all or only a few area tax cases to him for opinion?	14	56	70	84

| 1 | 2 | 3 | 4 | 5 | 6 | 7 | 8 | 9 | 10 | 11 | 12 | 13 | 14 |

SET 3	High-frequency two- and three-letter combinations emphasized	Words	15″	12″	10″
1	When are you and she going to the station for her?	10	40	50	60
2	During this testing session, you will be on your honor.	11	44	55	66
3	The youth will go to the area to seek the title to the tent.	12	48	60	72
4	When they leave at the end of this hour, are you going with them?	13	52	65	78
5	You and I were to go there to do the work before the end of this week.	14	56	70	84

| 1 | 2 | 3 | 4 | 5 | 6 | 7 | 8 | 9 | 10 | 11 | 12 | 13 | 14 |

27E ■ IMPROVING KEYBOARD CONTROL ▣14

1. Type Lines 1, 3, 5, 7, and 9 without being timed. Work at a steady, unhurried pace. Keep the carriage (carrier) moving.

2. Type a 1' writing on each of Lines 2, 4, 6, 8, and 10. Determine *gwam* on each. Compare the *gwam* scores line by line.

All letters and all figures learned are used.

1	*Easy words*	auto body; firm bid; world title; usual vigor; they spent it
2		Rush the auto title for the city auditor to sign with a pen.
3	*One-hand*	were ever; join a union; acted upon; trade war; best opinion
4	*words*	John Starr awarded him a minimum wage after a severe debate.
5	*Alphabet*	Jack Hopkins and Van Wexler must face a big grand jury quiz.
6		B. J. and S. G. Maxim will plan to leave quickly for Zurich.
7	*Figures*	12 13 14 92 93 94 82 83 84 72 73 74 62 63 64 992 336 227 136
8		Type these numbers with quiet hands: 99, 128, 364, and 927.
9	*Figure/symbol*	Try Rey & Dye. Ticket #39462 cost $7. He shouted, "Bravo!"
10		The Tyson & Link note for $2,364 is due on January 27, 1978.

| 1 | 2 | 3 | 4 | 5 | 6 | 7 | 8 | 9 | 10 | 11 | 12 |

27F ■ SELF-IMPROVEMENT PRACTICE ▣6

1. Type at least twice each sentence of 27E on which you did not equal your rate on Line 2.

2. If time permits, retype those sentences on which you made the greatest number of errors.

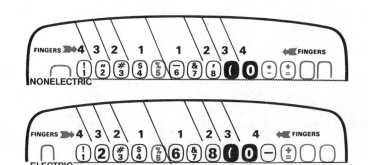

■ LESSON 28

28A ■ CONDITIONING PRACTICE ▣8 each line at least twice; as time permits, retype selected lines

Alphabet   Jeffrey G. Dixon has been quick to try with zeal to improve.

Figure/symbol   Nick's order of April 29 to Howe & Neff is for 436# of Q781.

Fluency   Type one key at a time; then go to the next key and type it.

| 1 | 2 | 3 | 4 | 5 | 6 | 7 | 8 | 9 | 10 | 11 | 12 |

28B ■ SYMBOL/FIGURE LOCATION: (0 ▣7

REACH TECHNIQUE FOR (

You typed **9** with the *right third finger.* Since **(** is the shift of **9**, use the same finger to type it.

91 91(1 91(1 (1 (1 91(1 (1

The (is part of a symbol. *DS*

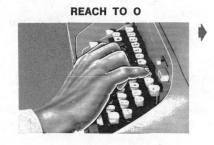

REACH TO 0

REACH TECHNIQUE FOR 0

Reach the *right fourth (little) finger* up to type **0**. Avoid moving the hand or swinging the elbow out.

p0; 0; 0; 0 ;0; 00 ;0; 000

Add 3, 30, 40, 60, and 70. *TS*

Over 300 students met and discussed the kinds 429
of businesses they would like to set up and run 439
themselves. The ideas flowed. The merchan- 447
dising company agreed to supply the facilities, 457
merchandising counseling, and investment 465
capital for each student-operated company. 474
(¶ 5) All this involvement has meant a lot of 482
work for this company. The company now 490
sponsors each year, at each of its retail outlets, 500
a Summer Youth Fair. The shops and services 509
comprising the Summer Youth Fair are 517
planned and managed by high school students 526
and are operated in the parking lots of the 534
company's retail outlets. The shops and ser- 543
vices run the gamut from ice cream parlors to 553
bakeries to handicrafts to candle shops to flea 562
markets. Each of the entrepreneural activities 572
has its own student manager and staff mem- 580
bers. All profits are divided among the young 590
employees. But, in addition, these student 598
workers get much, much more. They get the 607
actual and invaluable experience of planning 616
and operating a small business enterprise. 625
(¶ 6) And what does the merchandising com- 632
pany get from all this? Well, mostly a lot of 641
competition and no money. But as the presi- 650
dent of the company has said, "We have gained 659
a sense of satisfaction in helping young people 669
work within the system in their own way. And 678
who knows . . . from this small beginning might 688
even come a few future vice-presidents of our 697
company." "But it hasn't been all one-sided 706
either," he hastened to add, "we've received 715
much favorable publicity, and, often, the addi- 724
tional customers who come to patronize the 733
Summer Youth Fair booths drop in our stores 742
and spend additional monies. The increase in 751
our retail sales attests to this fact." (¶ 7) So 760
there you have the story of the experience of 769
one company in the Youth Work Experience 777
Program. We'd like to add you to our nation- 786
wide list of participating companies in the pro- 796
gram. Why not return the enclosed card today 805
and we'll have an educational representative 814
from your community call on you to help you 823
plan your participation in the program. I can 832
assure you the rewards will be many. Further- 841
more, you will be participating in the excite- 851
ment of helping young people get a better edu- 860
cation. Sincerely yours, Executive Secretary 869
RJRogers/1e Enclosure   (¶) We shall send 876
you our Youth Work Experience Program bro- 885

chure soon. This brochure shows, in concise, 894
pictorial form, the highlights of the program. 904
You'll enjoy thumbing through it. 910

Problem 18: Letters on Half Sheets
(Review of Letter Styles)

In this problem, you will use two types of stationery often used for short letters (8½″ x 5½″ and 5½″ x 8½″). Address the letters as directed in Steps 1 and 2, **Attention Public Relations Director**. Use **Gentlemen** as a salutation.

1. Type letters on 8½″ x 5½″ paper (long side up) to the first two addressees on your mailing list.

> Modified block style ■ mixed punctuation ■ 1″ side margins ■ date March 10, 19−− on 4th line from top edge ■ space down 3 lines and type the address ■ address small envelopes

2. Type letters on 5½″ x 8½″ paper (short side up) to the next two addressees on your list.

> Block style ■ open punctuation ■ ½″ side margins ■ date March 10, 19−− on 10th line from top edge ■ space down 4 lines and type the address ■ address small envelopes

Words

Date, address, attention line, salutation (¶ 1) Our 26
Youth Work Experience Program brochure 34
is in the mail. As you thumb through it, 42
note the variety of work-experience opportuni- 51
ties that the companies participating in the 60
program provide. Notice, also, the concentra- 69
tion on the faces of the young workers. (¶ 2) 77
Your participation in our Youth Work Experi- 86
ence Program will make similar opportunities 95
and experiences available to other high school 104
youth. Remember, they need your help now! 113
Sincerely yours Executive Secretary RJ 121
Rogers/le (88) 123/144

Problem 19: Composing Thank-You Letters

The first two companies on your mailing list have agreed to participate in the Youth Work Experience Program. Compose a brief thank-you letter to each firm. Indicate how much their participation will mean to high school students. In your first draft, x-out your errors. Make needed corrections with a pen or pencil and retype the letter. Use the date March 20, 19−−. Address a small envelope for each letter.

28C ■ STROKING TECHNIQUE PRACTICE `10` type twice

1 (9((1 (1 9((9 1(1 The (is the shift of 9, so <u>shift for it.</u>
2   As (is the shift of 9, use the same finger to type (and 9.

3 0   0; 0;0 30 40 10 120 Lee will be 20 years old; Ceil, just 10.
4   They had 600 employees in 1970; they may have 1,000 by 1980.

5 *Consoli-* Shift for (and # and $ but not for 112, 94, 36, 40, and 78.
6 *dation* My 12 men got $20 a day <u>each</u> for 10 days, a total of $2,400.
       | 1 | 2 | 3 | 4 | 5 | 6 | 7 | 8 | 9 | 10 | 11 | 12 |

28D ■ TABULATING PRACTICE `5` twice from copy; once from dictation

							Words
go	20	lb.	30#	cwt.	10:40	8,137	6
me	46	oz.	#82	a.m.	12:09	6,470	12
re	73	in.	49#	"76"	11:20	3,490	18

KEY | 2 | 6 | 2 | 6 | 3 | 6 | 3 | 6 | 4 | 6 | 5 | 6 | 5 |

28E ■ SENTENCE GUIDED WRITING `15`

1. Type Line 1 as a 1' writing with your teacher calling the line-ending guide for an appropriate speed. Then, try to type Line 2 at the same rate. Push your speed on the figure/symbol line.

2. Type each of the other pairs of lines in the same way. The figure/symbol lines are arranged in difficult-to-easy order to aid you in reaching your increasing goals.

All letters and all figures learned are used.

		G W A M	
		30″	20″
1	Are Polly and Wes to play Zoe and Maxim?	16	24
2	Fill this order: 136# of #79 at $18.24.	16	24
3	Art's tax was up this year, Fred. Was yours?	18	27
4	Jane's speed is 70; Bob's, 69; and Ken's, 64.	18	27
5	Type easy words fast. Slow down for awkward ones.	20	30
6	Rex cashed the Quig & Uhl check, #890, for $73.62.	20	30
7	If you don't succeed at first, don't give up. Keep on!	22	33
8	Joe's sale of 284 shares of Lynn & Orr stock was at 72.	22	33
9	"Well enough" is never good enough for "the man at the top."	24	36
10	Mat may lend Rod $27 to pay on his last month's bill of $84.	24	36

| 1 | 2 | 3 | 4 | 5 | 6 | 7 | 8 | 9 | 10 | 11 | 12 |

28F ■ SELF-IMPROVEMENT PRACTICE `5`

1. Type Lines 2, 4, 6, 8, and 10 of 28E at an easy pace. Try for precise control.

2. If time permits, retype the tabulating practice of 28D, above.

Step 3: Learning to Type Closing Lines with Special Variations

Preview: The closing lines illustrated below introduce three business letter variations:

1. The typing of only the title below the complimentary close.

2. The typing of the name of the dictator and the typist's initials in the reference notation.

3. The typing of a postscript beginning on the second line below the last item of the closing lines.

NOTE: A postscript may be preceded by the letters P.S. (postscript), but the modern trend is to omit this abbreviation.

```
be many.  Furthermore, you will be participating in the excitement
of helping young people get a better education.

                            Sincerely yours,



                            Executive Secretary

RJRogers/le

Enclosure

        We shall send you our Youth Work Experience Program brochure
soon.  This brochure shows, in concise, pictorial form, the high-
lights of the program.  You'll enjoy thumbing through it.
```

Closing Lines with Special Variations

Special Drill: Starting with the last lines of the body of the letter, type three copies of the closing lines with special variations (given in unarranged form below). Arrange the material according to the illustration. Leave proper space between the various parts. After the first typing, DS, and repeat. Use 1" side margins.

be many. Furthermore, you will be participating in the excitement of helping young people get a better education. Sincerely yours, Executive Secretary RJRogers/le Enclosure (¶) We shall send you our Youth Work Experience Program brochure soon. This brochure shows, in concise, pictorial form, the highlights of the program. You'll enjoy thumbing through it.

Problem 17: Two-Page Form Letter

Type the letter with one carbon copy to the first addressee on your mailing list (prepared in Problem 6, page 198). As time permits in these lessons, type the letter (one cc) to as many additional addressees as possible. For each new letter, use your typed copy of the preceding letter as the copy from which you type; thus you can proofread the previous letter as the new letter is typed. Correct your errors. As you type each new letter, try to reduce your letter typing time.

> Modified block with 5-space ¶ indentions ■ mixed punctuation ■ 1" side margins ■ approximately 1" bottom margin ■ horizontal form second-page heading ■ address large envelopes

Words

February 21, 19-- ARA Services, Inc. 2503 — 8
Lombard Street Philadelphia, PA 19146 — 16
Attention Public Relations Director Gentle- — 25
men: YOUTH WORK EXPERIENCE PRO- — 31
GRAM (¶ 1) There are thousands of students — 39
in our high schools today who need summer — 47
jobs, part-time jobs, and on-the-job work expe- — 56
rience. The Youth Work Experience Program — 72
is emerging as one of the leading educational — 81
tools through which school curriculum planners — 90
can develop a viable educational program for — 99
today's youth. It is a nationwide program de- — 108
signed to involve business and industry in the — 118
work of our schools, and we need your help. — 127
(¶ 2) What can a Youth Work Experience — 133
Program do for young people and for your — 142
company, you might ask. For one thing, the — 150
program is designed to introduce students to — 159
the world of work, and most young people — 168
prefer working to loafing. All they ask is an — 177
opportunity to work. In addition, work experi- — 186
ence helps students develop the job attitudes, — 196
job knowledges, and requisite skills needed for — 205
a job. For these young persons, on-the-job — 214
work experience in their areas of career inter- — 224
est causes education to take on added rele- — 232
vance. For business and industry, the program — 242
helps to provide a pool of qualified, potential — 251
employees. (¶ 3) But the Youth Work Experi- — 259
ence Program does much more as is evidenced — 268
by the following experience of a large West — 276
Coast company that is currently participating — 286
in the program. Sometime ago, a group of — 294
executives of this company were considering — 303
the obligation of business and industry to co- — 312
operate with our schools by providing work — 321
experience opportunities for students. "There — 330
are a lot of students who need summer jobs," — 339
said one executive, "what can we do for them?" — 349
"We always hire students to work in our retail — 358
outlets," replied another executive. "But we — 367
can do something more," suggested a third, — 376
"why not help them set up and run their own — 385
owned-and-operated, income-producing busi- — 393
ness?" (¶ 4) And then the wheels began to — 400
turn. High schools near each of the retail out- — 410
lets of this merchandising firm were contacted. — 420

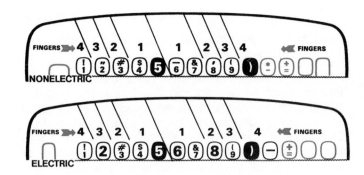

LESSON 29

29A ■ CONDITIONING PRACTICE 8 each line at least twice; as time permits, retype selected lines

Alphabet   John Fox left my quiz show and gave back a prize he had won.

Figure/symbol Isn't Check #230 for $476? Can Pete type 9 and (with ease?

Fluency   Strike figure keys with the hands quiet, the fingers curved.
| 1 | 2 | 3 | 4 | 5 | 6 | 7 | 8 | 9 | 10 | 11 | 12 |

29B ■ SYMBOL/FIGURE LOCATION:) 5 7

REACH TECHNIQUE FOR)
The) is the shift of **0**, and both are typed with the *right little finger*. Hold the elbow in position—reach to **0** and **)**.

0; 0;); 0;););); 0;););

The ")" is the shift of 0. DS

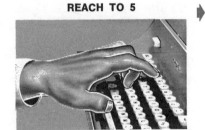

REACH TO 5

REACH TECHNIQUE FOR 5
Type **5** with the *left first finger* without moving the other fingers from their home keys or moving the hand forward. Keep the wrist low.

t5f 5f 5f 5 f5f 55 f5f 555

Are 55 boys on Flight 155? TS

29C ■ STROKING TECHNIQUE PRACTICE 10 type twice

1)   ););))0 9) () (1) Use the left shift to type both (and).
2 '   As) is the shift of 0, use the same finger to type 0 and).

3 5   5f 5f5 55 58 15 152 The 5 men and the 25 boys left at 5 p.m.
4   Judge Young's talk is at 2:55 p.m. in Room 515 of Town Hall.

5 *Consoli-*); 5f5 5) (15) (25) The papers are due next week (April 25).
6 *dation*   Mrs. Nunn sent Check #850 (for $645.95) to Quenton J. Mazor.
| 1 | 2 | 3 | 4 | 5 | 6 | 7 | 8 | 9 | 10 | 11 | 12 |

29D ■ TABULATING PRACTICE 5 type twice

							Words
ad	15	ft.	3's	e.g.	(295)	$1.05	6
ah	50	qt.	4's	i.e.	(158)	$3.52	12
as	65	mi.	5's	etc.	(637)	$8.15	19
at	80	yd.	6's	p.m.	(415)	$7.20	25
an	35	pt.	7's	doz.	(550)	$1.59	31

KEY | 2 | 6 | 2 | 6 | 3 | 6 | 3 | 6 | 4 | 6 | 5 | 6 | 5

Problem 16: Special Business Letter Variations (Plain sheets)

Step 1: Learning the Placement of Attention and Subject Lines

Preview: Study the illustration. Note that the *attention line* is typed on the second line below the last line of the address. In the block and modified block letter styles, the attention line begins at the left margin. The *subject line* is typed on the second line below the salutation. It may be centered, as illustrated, or typed at the left margin. Also, the word SUBJECT (all capitals or first word capitalized) may be used as a heading for the line.

SUBJECT: Youth Work Experience Program

The trend in business offices is to omit the word *Subject*.

Special Drill: Type the opening parts of a business letter (given below in unarranged form) as follows: (1) Arrange the material in proper letter form; set stops for 1″ side margins; space 4 times (3 blank lines) between the date and the address; (2) after the first typing, DS, and repeat the lines two times.

February 21, 19-- ARA Services, Inc. 2503 Lombard Street Philadelphia, PA 19146 Attention Public Relations Director Gentlemen: YOUTH WORK EXPERIENCE PROGRAM (¶) There are thousands of students in our high schools today who need summer jobs, part-time jobs, and on-the-job work experience.

Step 2: Learning to Type the Heading for the Second Page of a Two-Page Letter

Preview: Two forms that may be used for the heading of the second page, as well as additional pages, of a letter are illustrated at the right. These headings are started about an inch from the top of the page. Two blank lines are left between the heading and the first line of the body of the letter. The second page is typed on plain white paper of the same quality as that used for the letterhead sheet.

Special Drill: Type three times each (using 1″ side margins) the heading and the opening lines of the second page (given in unarranged form at the right) in both forms illustrated. After the first typing, DS, and repeat twice.

February 21, 19--

ARA Services, Inc.
2503 Lombard Street
Philadelphia, PA 19146

Attention Public Relations Director

Gentlemen:

YOUTH WORK EXPERIENCE PROGRAM

There are thousands of students in our high schools today who need summer jobs, part-time jobs, and on-the-job work experience. The Youth Work Experience Program is emerging as one of the leading educational tools through which school curriculum planners can develop a viable educational program for today's youth. It is a nationwide program designed to involve business and industry in the work of our schools, and we need your help.

What can a Youth Work Experience Program do for young people and for your company, you might ask. For one thing, the program

Modified Block Style with an Attention Line and Centered Subject Line

---

ARA Services, Inc.
Page 2
February 21, 19--

like to set up and run themselves. The ideas flowed. The merchandising company agreed to supply the facilities, merchandising counseling, and investment capital for each student-operated company.

All this involvement has meant a lot of work for this company. The company now sponsors each year, at each of its retail outlets,

Page 2 Heading, Vertical Form

ARA Services, Inc.   2   February 21, 19--

like to set up and run themselves. The ideas flowed. The merchandising company agreed to supply the facilities, merchandising counseling, and investment capital for each student-operated company.

All this involvement has meant a lot of work for this company. The company now sponsors each year, at each of its retail outlets, a Summer Youth Fair. The shops and services comprising the Summer

Page 2 Heading, Horizontal Form

Note: With the *horizontal* form, the dateline ends even with the right margin; the page number is centered.

Heading: ARA Services, Inc. | 2 | February 21, 19--

like to set up and run themselves. The ideas flowed. The merchandising company agreed to supply the facilities, merchandising counseling, and investment capital for each student-operated company.

29E ■ SKILL-TRANSFER TYPING [15]

1. Type a 2' writing on ¶ 1. Determine *gwam*.
2. Type a 2' writing on ¶ 2. Determine *gwam*. Compare *gwam* on the two ¶s.
3. Type two additional 2' writings on ¶ 2, trying to

equal or exceed your ¶ 1 rate; then a final 1' writing on ¶ 2.
4. As time permits, type 1' guided writings on each ¶: first for speed, then for control.

All letters and figures are used.

		2' GWAM
¶ 1 Straight copy	Do you attend class each day? When you try to develop	5 | 26
	typing power, a daily workout is vital. Every day provides	11 | 32
	a new chance to reach your goal. So be quick to realize it	17 | 38
	and take this route to excellence.	21 | 42
¶ 2 Statistical copy	Express amounts in figures; as, 50 jumpers, 28 quarts,	5 | 29
	317 miles. Express sums of money (whether in dollars or in	11 | 35
	cents) in figure form; as in $195 or in 46 cents. Type the	17 | 41
	day as a figure if it follows a month; as in April 4, 1972.	23 | 47

2' GWAM | 1 | 2 | 3 | 4 | 5 | 6 |

29F ■ SELF-IMPROVEMENT PRACTICE [5]

1. Type ¶ 2 of 29E, above, without timing. Try to improve your control of figures and symbols.

2. If time permits, retype the tabulating practice of 29D, page 50.

■ LESSON 30

30A ■ CONDITIONING PRACTICE [8] each line at least twice; as time permits, retype selected lines

Alphabet   Pam was quite excited when Jack Fyle bought the bronze vase.

Figure/symbol Did Mr. Ott's May 25 order (#4630) come to $1,789 or $1,987?

Fluency   Learn to make the reach to the shift key with proper timing.
                 | 1 | 2 | 3 | 4 | 5 | 6 | 7 | 8 | 9 | 10 | 11 | 12 |

30B ■ SPEED/CONTROL BUILDING [10]

1. Type two 1' speed writings on ¶ 1 of 29E, above. Determine *gwam*.
2. Subtract 4-6 *gwam* from your top rate in Step 1,

set quarter-minute goals, and type a 1' guided writing on ¶ 1 for control.
3. Repeat Steps 1 and 2 with ¶ 2.

```
young engineering associates                                    24-320
                                                                -------
808 S.W. Broadway                                                1230
Portland, OR 97205
                                 November 24    19 --  No.  217

PAY to the order of   Crosswhite Wholesale Suppliers      $ 839.64

Eight hundred thirty-nine and 64/100--------------------------------- Dollars

PORTLAND NATIONAL BANK
PORTLAND, OREGON 97203

⑃1230⑃0320⑃ 143 0602 31⑃          Treasurer, young engineering associates
- - - - - - - - - - - - - - - - - - - - - - - - - - - - - - - - - - - -
Detach This Stub Before
Cashing This Check

  TO   Crosswhite Wholesale Suppliers   IN PAYMENT OF THE FOLLOWING INVOICES:
       499 Alamo Avenue, S.E.
       Albuquerque, NM  87102

young engineering associates
```

Date	Invoice	Amount
11/19	GJ-5032	332.28
11/20	GJ-5097	524.50
		856.78
	Less 2%	17.14
		839.64

808 S.W. Broadway
Portland, OR 97205

NOTE: One part of a voucher check is a standard check; the other part lists or explains items covered by the check.

Problem 13: Voucher Check

Type a voucher check based on the illustration. If the printed form is not available, type a specimen form; then type the appropriate information on the ruled lines and on the check stub. Correct errors as you type.

Problem 14: Voucher Check

Type a voucher check using the firm names shown in the illustration above: December 15, 19--; Check No. 982; $236.96. Invoices: 12/6, GJ-6894, $156.72; 12/8, GJ-7014, $85.08; total, $241.80; Less 2%, $4.84; Net, $236.96.

Problem 15: Justifying the Right Margin (Line: 32; spacing: SS; ¶ indention: 3)

■ Copy may be typed with the right margin even (justified). Newspapers published by schools are often typed in this manner so the duplicated copies will have the appearance of copy on a printed page. First, a stencil is typed from the master copy, and then the desired number of copies are duplicated. A stencil is always typed with the ribbon disengaged.

Except for the last line of a paragraph, the words in each line are spaced so that the right margin will be even. This is done by adding extra spaces between words to fill out short lines, and using half spaces between words to squeeze words on lines.

You are to type the two ¶s at the left in two columns. Leave 4 spaces between columns; do not space between paragraphs.

1. Type the *work copy* with the / to show needed variable spacing for each line.

2. Retype the copy in two columns (count lines used and put half in each column), making the line endings uniform. Center the heading, COPY WITH EVEN RIGHT MARGIN, on the third line above the columns and about 1½" from top edge. Erase and correct all typing errors.

Part of the *work copy* and *final copy* are shown at the right. Lines 1

through 5 require extra spacing. Line 6 is just right. To get the right margin even, the typist has to use judgment and distribute the spaces so they are least noticeable.

```
//////////////////////////////////
   Copy may be typed with the///
right margin even (justified).//
Newspapers published by schools/
are often typed in this manner//
so the duplicated copies will///
have the appearance of copy on a
```

Work Copy

```
   Copy may be typed with the
right margin even (justified).
Newspapers published by schools
are often typed  in this manner
so the duplicated copies will
have the appearance of copy on a
```

Copy with Even Right Margin

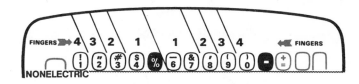

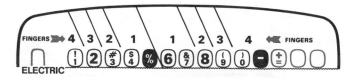

30C ■ SYMBOL LOCATION: % – 7

REACH TECHNIQUE FOR %

You typed **5** with the *left first finger.* As **%** is the shift of **5**, type it also with the *left first finger. Do not use* **%** *for c/o (In care of).*

5f 5f%f 5f%f %f %f 5f%f %f

Charge Ed 5% for the loan. **DS**

REACH TECHNIQUE FOR – (hyphen)

Type – (hyphen) with the *right little finger.* Reach with the finger. Avoid swinging the elbow out. *Note: Type 2 hyphens to make a dash: ––.*

p-; -; -; - ;-; -- ;-; -;-

It is an out-of-date list. **TS**

REACH TO HYPHEN

30D ■ STROKING TECHNIQUE PRACTICE 10 type twice

1 %   %f %f% 5% 8% 9% 55% We offer discounts of 10%, 15%, and 20%.
2   Change the 6% rate on Wirtz & Lang's note (due May 3) to 5%.

3 –   -; - co-op; 5-cent; up-to-date edition; He works as a co-op.
4   Were the up-to-date plans mailed to the out-of-town speaker?

5 -- -- --;-- --:-- That speed--65 <u>gwam</u>--ought to handle the job.
6   PRICED TO SELL: Objets d'art, antiques--Telephone 251-4690.

2 hyphens make a dash

| 1 | 2 | 3 | 4 | 5 | 6 | 7 | 8 | 9 | 10 | 11 | 12 |

30E ■ GROWTH INDEX: STRAIGHT COPY 10 two 3' writings; determine GWAM and errors

All letters are used.

	GWAM
	1'	3'

¶ 1   Because the main emphasis in this unit has been on the   11   4 | 32

handling of figures and symbols, your speed on regular copy   23   8 | 36

will not have increased greatly. In ten days, however, you   35   12 | 40

may have moved up by a word or two.   42   14 | 42

¶ 2   To realize your speed goal by the end of this phase of   11   18 | 46

the course, you must work with a little extra effort during   23   22 | 50

these next few days. Do not stop now. Just try quickly to   35   26 | 54

improve your regular work patterns.   42   28 | 56

1' GWAM | 1 | 2 | 3 | 4 | 5 | 6 | 7 | 8 | 9 | 10 | 11 | 12 |
3' GWAM | 1 | 2 | 3 | 4 |

30F ■ SELF-IMPROVEMENT PRACTICE 5 type the ¶s of 30E; Goal: no more than 3 errors per ¶

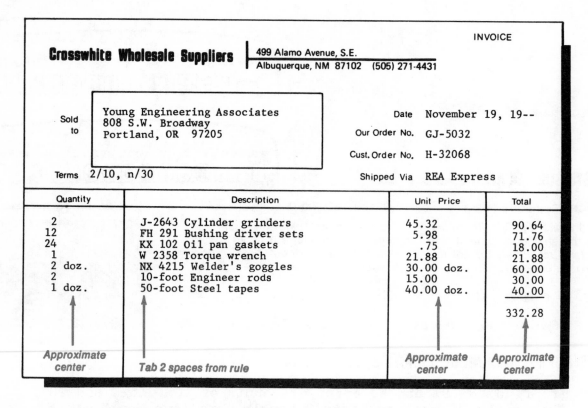

INVOICE

Crosswhite Wholesale Suppliers | 499 Alamo Avenue, S.E.
Albuquerque, NM 87102 (505) 271-4431

Sold to
Young Engineering Associates
808 S.W. Broadway
Portland, OR 97205

Date November 19, 19--
Our Order No. GJ-5032
Cust. Order No. H-32068
Shipped Via REA Express

Terms 2/10, n/30

Quantity	Description	Unit Price	Total
2	J-2643 Cylinder grinders	45.32	90.64
12	FH 291 Bushing driver sets	5.98	71.76
24	KX 102 Oil pan gaskets	.75	18.00
1	W 2358 Torque wrench	21.88	21.88
2 doz.	NX 4215 Welder's goggles	30.00 doz.	60.00
2	10-foot Engineer rods	15.00	30.00
1 doz.	50-foot Steel tapes	40.00 doz.	40.00
			332.28

Approximate center   *Tab 2 spaces from rule*   *Approximate center*   *Approximate center*

Problem 11: Invoice

An invoice is a business paper billing a customer for merchandise purchased. Type an invoice based on the illustration above. If a printed form is not available, type only the typewritten material; arrange it in the same style as the insertions on the printed form.

Set tab stops for the items to be typed. In typing an invoice, type across the line, using the tab key or bar to move from column to column. In the Total column underline the last amount, then double-space to type the total figure.

Proofread and correct the copy before removing it from the typewriter.

Fold the invoice for a window envelope (See Reference Guide, page vi).

Problem 12: Invoice

2 cc's on plain sheets ■ correct your errors

Sold To Young Engineering Associates
808 S.W. Broadway
Portland, OR 97205
Terms 2/10, n/30

Date November 20, 19--
Our Order No. GJ-5097
Cust. Order No. H-32086
Shipped Via Red Ball Express

Quantity	Description	Unit Price	Total
10 cases	10W-30 quart cans Modern motor oil	13.95	139.50
2 C	CX 4139 Plastic funnels	20.00 C	40.00
1 M	1/2-inch, Galvanized reducing elbows	100.00 M	100.00
5 C	1 1/2-inch, 45° Elbows for drainage	12.00 C	60.00
10	60-ft. coils 3/8-inch Copper tubing	10.00	100.00
3 M	3/8-inch Coupling--Copper to copper	20.00 M	60.00
50 rolls	KC 91, 1-inch Clear repair tape	.50	25.00
			524.50

Reading/Typing Response Patterns

1. Arrange your work area neatly.
2. Adjust the paper guide and insert a full sheet of paper.
3. Set left margin stop: center — 30; move right stop to end of scale.

4. SS drills; DS paragraphs.

NOTE: Even though the copy is set in printer's type, type it line for line.

■ LESSON 31

31A ■ CONDITIONING PRACTICE 8 each line 3 times SS; DS after each 3-line group

Alphabet	Jack Nix hopes to quit my show and give Buzz Rolfe a chance.
Figures	Master these figure reaches now: 1, 26, 47, 38, 29, and 50.
Figure/symbol	Change the 7% rate on Fitz & Buck's note (due May 10) to 6%.
Fluency	If it were up to me, I would make him pay you half the rate.

First time, slowly; second time, speed; third time, control

| 1 | 2 | 3 | 4 | 5 | 6 | 7 | 8 | 9 | 10 | 11 | 12 |

31B ■ MANIPULATIVE PARTS DRILL 10 each line twice SS; for Line 6 set right margin stop at center + 30

1 *Tabulator*   1 4 28 4 50 4 37 4 12 4 485 4 563 4 415 4 402 4 592   *Tab and return without pausing*

2 *Space bar*   Many a boy has money to pay cash but prefers to buy on time.

3 *Shift keys*   Willie and Mae played Neil and Jenny a fast game of canasta.

4 *Shift lock*   Gary Betz announces for WLW-TV; Lori Michaels sings on WKRC.

5 *Backspacer*   It is important to watch my xyz's as well as my p's and q's.

6 *Margin release*   ←—In golf the ball usually lies poorly and the player usually lies well!

31C ■ TECHNIQUE PRACTICE: RESPONSE PATTERNS 15 Lines 1-6 twice from dictation, Lines 7-9 for 1' writings

Word Response: Some short, frequently used words (such as those in Lines 1, 4, and 7) are so easy to type they can be typed as words instead of letter by letter. So *think and type the word.*

Letter Response: Many words (such as those in Lines 2, 5, and 8) are not so easy to type even though they are often used. Such words are usually typed letter by letter.

Combination Response: Most normal copy (as in Lines 3, 6, and 9) is composed of both word- and letter-response sequences that require variable speed: high speed for easy words, lower speed for hard ones.

1 *Word*   of to is it or by if us an do so me he am go the and for may

2 *Letter*   as in at my be no we on ax up oh are get you was few him tax

3 *Combination* of no by be us my go at if on am up or we an as so in to tax

4 *Word*   to do | it is | of it | to us | do so | by me | he is | of it | if he | he may

5 *Letter*   be in | my ax | in no | as we | in my | be on | as in | up in | at no | we are

6 *Combination* to be | is up | is my | if no | or be | if we | go up | by my | an ax | he was

Do not type the vertical lines that separate the 2-word groups

7 *Word*   If I am to go by air, he is to go, too. Is she to go, also?

8 *Letter*   As you saw, my tax rate was up. Get a rate card on my case.

9 *Combination* Did you lay my man off? If so, did you pay him a good rate?

| 1 | 2 | 3 | 4 | 5 | 6 | 7 | 8 | 9 | 10 | 11 | 12 |

Problem 8: Addressing Small Envelopes—3′ writing

1. Type as many small envelopes as you can in 3 minutes. Use the addresses on your mailing list prepared in Problem 6, page 198. Arrange the envelopes for easy pickup: Envelopes on left; flaps down and away from you, face up.

2. Count the number of envelopes addressed. Record this information with your name in the upper left corner of the first envelope or on a separate slip of paper. Put the addressed envelopes in order, and put a rubber band around them.

Problem 9: Interoffice Memorandum (Half sheet)

Type the interoffice memorandum as illustrated below. Make a carbon copy. Use 1″ side margins; correct all errors that you make. Type on the control level. Leave two blank lines after the heading lines.

Crosswhite Wholesale Suppliers

INTEROFFICE COMMUNICATION

TO: Kay Price, Steno. Dept.   DATE: November 18, 19--

FROM: Rita Curtin, Manager   SUBJECT: Letter Styles

Effective December 1, all our letters are to be typed in the <u>block style</u> (all lines flush with the left margin). Will you please announce this policy change to all members of your department.

We are making this style letter change because research conducted in the Sales Department during the past three months has indicated that the use of this style enables typists to produce letters more quickly. The net result has been an amazing reduction in letter typing production costs.

Also, will you please assume responsibility for the retraining program that may be needed to familiarize our typists with the <u>block letter style</u>.

jd

Problem 10: Interoffice Memorandum (Full sheet; DS; 1″ side margins; ¶ indention: 5)

TO: All Staff Typists | *FROM:* D. J. Anders, Supervisor | *DATE:* November 18, 19-- | *SUBJECT:* Changing Typewriter Ribbons (¶ 1) These are the basic steps to follow in changing the ribbon on most standard typewriters: (¶ 2) 1. <u>Wind the ribbon on one spool.</u> Adjust the ribbon-reverse lever and wind the ribbon on the right spool, unless the spools are interchangeable. Observe the direction of travel of the ribbon. (¶ 3) 2. <u>Press down the shift-lock key, and move the ribbon-indicator lever to the position for typing on the lower portion of the ribbon.</u> Depress any two central keys, such as <u>y</u> and <u>u</u>, and lock the two type bars in front of the printing point. This will raise and lock the ribbon carrier so that the old ribbon can be removed easily and the new ribbon inserted. Observe how the ribbon is threaded through the ribbon-carrier mechanism. (¶ 4) 3. <u>Remove the ribbon from the carrier and remove both spools.</u> Check the way each spool is attached to its hub, and how the ribbon is attached to the empty spool. (¶ 5) 4. <u>Hook the new ribbon to the empty spool and wind several inches of the new ribbon on it.</u> Be sure to wind this ribbon in the right direction. Place both spools on their holders and thread the ribbon through the ribbon carrier. (¶ 6) 5. <u>Release the shift-lock key and return the ribbon indicator to the position for typing on the upper portion of the ribbon.</u> Unlock the two type bars that were used to raise the ribbon carrier, and the typewriter will be ready for use. (xxx)

31D ■ SKILL-TRANSFER TYPING [17]

1. Type a 1' writing on ¶1; determine *gwam*.
2. Type a 1' writing on ¶2, then on ¶3; determine *gwam* on each.

3. Divide your ¶3 *gwam* by your ¶1 *gwam* to determine *percentage of transfer*; do likewise for ¶2.
4. Type ¶s 2 and 3 twice; try to increase speed.

All letters and figures are used.

2' GWAM

¶1 Straight copy

You are moving right along now in your quest for typing · 6 | 28
power. You know how to use the major service keys; you have · 12 | 34
good control of the letters, figures, and basic symbols; you · 18 | 40
also exhibit good form. You zip right along. · 22 | 45

¶2 Statistical print

Almost everyone can write with pen and ink at nearly 25 · 6 | 29
words a minute. Most of you have been writing for over 8 or · 12 | 35
9 years. After just 6-7 weeks of typing, your stroking rate · 18 | 42
is 23-40 words a minute on normal copy for short intervals. · 24 | 47

¶3 Statistical script

Figures are not so easy to type as words. They can, in · 6 | 30
fact, reduce your speed 25-40%--from 35 to 21 gross words in · 12 | 36
a minute--depending upon how many occur in a copy selection. · 18 | 42
You may lose another 10-15% on handwritten copy with figures! · 24 | 48

2' GWAM | 1 | 2 | 3 | 4 | 5 | 6 |

■ LESSON 32

32A ■ CONDITIONING PRACTICE [8] each line 3 times SS; DS after each 3-line group

Alphabet	Glenn Dovey was quick to jump for the box but lost his zest.	*Eyes on copy; return quickly*
Figures	Order these records: 10 Motown 2849; 5 King 367; 3 Dot 628.	
Figure/symbol	I can take Delta #31 at 8:25 a.m. or United #47 at 6:09 p.m.	
Fluency	It was then up to him to set the book rate on the small box.	

| 1 | 2 | 3 | 4 | 5 | 6 | 7 | 8 | 9 | 10 | 11 | 12 |

32B ■ SKILL-TRANSFER TYPING [17] type 31D, above, as directed below

1. Type ¶1, above, as a 1' writing; determine *gwam* and errors.
2. Using ¶1 *gwam* as a base rate, divide the rate by 4 to determine your quarter-minute goal for ¶2. Note your quarter-minute check points in ¶2, using the superior dots and figures.

3. Type two 1' guided writings on ¶2, trying to reach your goal rate.
4. Type ¶3 in the same way.
5. Type a 2' unguided writing on each of the three ¶s.
6. Determine *gwam* on each 2' writing; determine percentages of transfer.

ADDRESSING ENVELOPES

1. **Envelope Address:** Set a tab stop (or margin stop if a number of envelopes are to be addressed) 2½" from the left edge for a small envelope or 4" from the left edge for a large envelope. Start the address here 2" from the top edge of a small envelope and 2½" from the top edge of a large one.

2. **Style:** Type the address in *block style*, single-spaced, without punctuation at the ends of lines, except when an abbreviation ends a line. Type the city name, state name or abbreviation, and ZIP Code on the last address line. The ZIP Code is usually typed 2 spaces after the state name.

3. **Addressee Notations:** Type addressee notations, such as *Hold for Arrival*, *Please Forward*, *Personal*, etc., a triple space below the return address and about 3 spaces from the left edge of the envelope. These notations may be underlined or typed in all capitals; the latter style provides adequate attention-getting value with fewer typing strokes.

    If an *attention line* is used, type it immediately below the company name in the address lines.

4. **Mailing Notations:** Type mailing notations, such as AIRMAIL, SPECIAL DELIVERY, and REGISTERED, below the stamp and at least 3 line spaces above the envelope address. Type these notations in all capital letters.

5. **State Abbreviations:** U.S. Postal Service encourages the use of the 2-letter ZIP abbreviations for state names (without periods or spaces). However, these abbreviations may be used only with ZIP Codes.

6. **Folding the Letter:** Letter folding procedures for large envelopes are illustrated at the right (for small envelopes, see page 96).

    Step 1: With the letter face up, fold slightly less than one third of the letterhead up toward the top.

    Step 2: Fold down the top of the letterhead to within ½ inch of the bottom fold.

    Step 3: Insert the letter into the envelope with the last crease toward the bottom of the envelope.

When addressing an envelope, observe the amount of space to be left above and to the left of the address. Learn to judge by *eye measurement* the proper point for starting the first line of the address.

Small Envelope

The small envelope shown above has the return address typed on second line from top edge and three spaces from left edge. HOLD FOR ARRIVAL and *In Care of* (c/o) notations are typed in recommended positions.

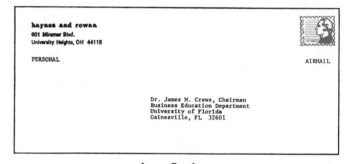

Large Envelope

The large envelope shown above has AIRMAIL and PERSONAL notations typed in recommended positions.

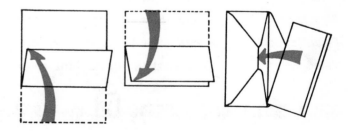

Problem 7: Addressing Large Envelopes

Type 12 large envelopes to the first 12 addresses of the mailing list you prepared in Problem 6. Use the following line for the first line of the envelope address: **Public Relations Director.**

NOTE: Beginning office typists should be able to type about two envelope addresses a minute. Try to meet this standard. Do this by pre-positioning the envelopes for easy pickup: *Flaps down, face up.*

32C ■ TECHNIQUE PRACTICE: RESPONSE PATTERNS [13]

Lines 1-6 twice from dictation;
Lines 7-9 for 1' writings

1 *Word* but due own men did box big end six she cut with their forms
2 *Letter* set war oil far act car age bad fee dear best only date area
3 *Combination* due bad men age big oil own act sir set but war end car they

Speed up on the easy words; slow down for the difficult ones

4 *Word* by six | for me | due us | and the | for us | may go | to them | did do it
5 *Letter* my car | we care | in fact | act upon | face him | ever be | as you read
6 *Combination* the act | did you | due him | may face | big case | did save | firm base

7 *Word* If he is to do the big sign, is she to lend a hand for half?
8 *Letter* In fact, I set a few base fees after you read my data cards.
9 *Combination* If you sign the rate form by noon, you may save the big tax.

| 1 | 2 | 3 | 4 | 5 | 6 | 7 | 8 | 9 | 10 | 11 | 12 |

32D ■ SPEED/CONTROL BUILDING [12]

1. Type a 1' speed writing on ¶ 1; determine *gwam*.
2. Type a 1' speed writing on ¶ 2; determine *gwam*.
3. Compare rates on the two ¶s.
4. Type a 1' control writing on each ¶. Proofread and compare number of errors on the two ¶s.
5. Type two 1' guided writings on each ¶ (the first writing for speed, the second for control).

All letters are used.

¶ 1
Balanced-hand words = 60%

If I do all of my work in the right way, in due time I may learn to handle such words as he, do, for, and the with high speed. I may also handle such words as cozy and eight quickly. It is a good goal, and it may pay me to try.

¶ 2
One-hand words = 60%

As soon as you add to your rate on easy words, you can set a faster rate on such words as at, in, be, up, and was. Test a safe rate next, then edge up only a few strokes at a time. Add just a few strokes as you save on waste motions.

■ LESSON 33

33A ■ CONDITIONING PRACTICE [8] each line 3 times SS; DS after each 3-line group

Alphabet Virgil, Janie, and Bix had perfect papers on my weekly quiz.
Figures He ordered two-suiter No. 14839M and overnighter No. 27560W.
Figure/symbol Her pay is $85 a week, less $4.42 FICA and $9.30 income tax.
Fluency Reserve six seats for him on the aisle near the center exit.

Shift quickly but firmly

| 1 | 2 | 3 | 4 | 5 | 6 | 7 | 8 | 9 | 10 | 11 | 12 |

33B ■ TECHNIQUE PRACTICE: RESPONSE PATTERNS [15] type 32C, above, as directed there

Problem 4: Centering, Aligning, and Fill-Ins

1. Center vertically and horizontally the following copy (double-spaced) on each of eight 5″ x 3″ cards (or slips of paper), long side up.

BUSINESS EDUCATION SERVICE AWARD

to

Type a 30-space underline

for

OUTSTANDING ACHIEVEMENT

2. On the cards prepared in Step 1, type the following names, correctly centered and in proper relation to the underline.

Andrew Chin	Susan Plotz
Barbara Ann Grayson	James R. Reynolds, Jr.
Rudolph E. McNeeley	Signe Thompson
Simon K. Mencher	Samantha Zimmerman

Problem 5: Typing on Postal Cards

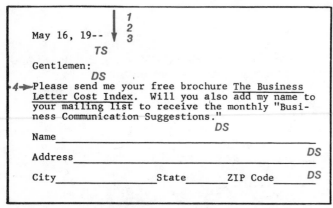

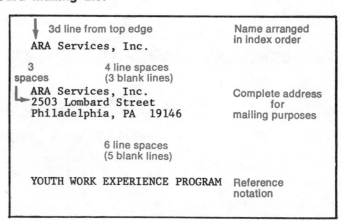

1. Type the message side of four postal cards (or use paper cut to 5½″ x 3¼″) as illustrated above.

Mr. Christopher Chialtas	Mr. Kouchiro Isshiki
29576 Breakers Avenue	24578 San Remo Way
Fort Lauderdale, FL 33308	Bakersfield, CA 93306

2. Type the following names and addresses on the blank lines of the postal cards typed in Step 1.

Mrs. Ruth E. Piaz	Mr. Robert L. Vesco
4567 Barcelona Road	6789 Fairway Terrace
Denver, CO 80229	Cedar Rapids, IA 52403

---

3. Type the appropriate *return address* on each of the cards; then address each card to the company named at the right.

Communication Associates, Inc.
5621 North Michigan Avenue
Chicago, IL 60615

Problem 6: Index Card Mailing List

Mailing lists, as well as other reference items, are frequently typed on 5″ x 3″ index cards.

1. Type a 5″ x 3″ index card (or paper cut to that size) from the illustration. Type a similar index card for each of the firms given on page 177.

2. Arrange the typed cards in alphabetic order by firm name. Identify your index card mailing list by typing and centering vertically and horizontally the following information, double-spaced, on another index card: MAILING LIST | *your name* | *name of your school* | *city and state*. Put a rubber band around the completed cards and save them for later use.

33C ■ GROWTH INDEX [9] two 3' writings; determine GWAM and errors

All letters are used.

GWAM
| | 2' | 3' |

¶1 You can now type many of these words as words, without   5 | 4 | 33

fixing every letter in mind. For other words, however, you   11 | 8 | 37

must adjust your reading and typing pace to a letter level.   18 | 12 | 41

They do need extra effort as well as caution.   22 | 15 | 44

¶2   Just keep the fingers moving over the keys with speedy   28 | 18 | 48

control, being certain not to pause after words or letters.   34 | 22 | 52

Really drive for speed, then slow up to build good quality;   40 | 26 | 56

and go after a top prize of real typing power.   44 | 30 | 59

2' GWAM | 1 | 2 | 3 | 4 | 5 | 6 |
3' GWAM | 1 | 2 | 3 | 4 |

33D ■ SPEED/CONTROL BUILDING: GUIDED WRITING [8]

Type three 1' guided writings on each ¶ above: two for speed and one for control.

Technique Cue: Both paragraphs contain a number of high-speed words. Speed up your stroking on them.

33E ■ SELF-IMPROVEMENT PRACTICE [10]

1. Type each of the following lines once, noting those sentences that are difficult or that contain awkward stroking combinations.

2. For each sentence identified as difficult, practice the difficult words two or three times.
3. Type each of the difficult lines two or three times.

1 *Word*   I may sign the forms if the city pays the firm for the work.
2 *Letter*   We start a dated test on gas war taxes only in my base area.
3 *Combination*   It is great for him to be able to serve, to handle my cases.

4 *Word*   Their firm may own the six big signs down by the town field.
5 *Letter*   In my opinion you gave only a few facts in my wage tax case.
6 *Combination*   He stated the rates to be paid on the world trade agreement.

7 *Word*   It is right to pay half the profit if they wish to visit us.
8 *Letter*   My case was based on average water rates set up on my tract.
9 *Combination*   They held six extra forms to refer my tax case to the state.

10 *Word*   Both of them may aid the busy auditor with the island firms.
11 *Letter*   As you saw, my award was based upon a faster rate on a test.
12 *Combination* In their opinion the tax case signals a return to high risk.

| 1 | 2 | 3 | 4 | 5 | 6 | 7 | 8 | 9 | 10 | 11 | 12 |

Problem 2: Squeezing Letters (Line: 65; DS; center vertically on half sheet)

Certain corrections may be made by squeezing letters into half spaces, or by squeezing or spreading the letters of an entire word into the available space.

Type the sentences (with numbers) as given below; then make the corrections shown in parentheses. Use as a heading: PROBLEM 2: ERROR CORRECTIONS

As typed 1. This sentence has an omitte letter at the end of a word. *(Squeeze "d" into*
As corrected This sentence has an omitted letter at the end of a word. *the half space.)*

As typed 2. This sentence has an omitted letter at the eginning of a word. *(Squeeze "b" into*
As corrected This sentence has an omitted letter at the beginning of a word. *the half space.)*

As typed 3. This sentence has a leter omitted within a word. *(Erase "leter" and*
As corrected This sentence has a letter omitted within a word. *type "letter.")*

As typed 4. This sentence has a lettter added within a word. *(Erase "lettter"*
As corrected This sentence has a letter added within a word. *and type "letter.")*

SOLUTIONS

Lines 1 and 2—What to Do: (a) With your left hand hold the carriage (or element); as you (b) move carriage (or element) a half space before or after the word; then (c) type the omitted letter at the half-space point.

Lines 3 and 4—What to Do: (a) Erase mistyped word; (b) return carriage to typing position.

For omitted letter: (c) move carriage (or element) to space following last word before erasure; (d) hold carriage (or element) with your left hand, then operate space bar to move to the half space; (e) type first letter

of word to be squeezed; then type other letters of word at each half-space point.

For added letter: (c) move carriage (or element) to space following last word before the erasure; space once; (d) hold carriage (or element) with your left hand, then operate space bar to move to the half space; (e) type first letter of word to be squeezed; then type other letters of word at each half-space point.

NOTE: If your typewriter has a half-space mechanism, use it as you position the carriage for typing at the half-space point.

Problem 3: Aligning and Centering on Lines (Half sheet; top margin: 1″)

Formula for Finding Center of Paper	
Scale reading at left edge of paper	10
+ Scale reading at right edge of paper	70
Total ÷ 2 = Center Point	80 ÷ 2 = 40

Formula for Finding Center of a Line or Column	
Scale reading at first letter or item	31
+ Scale reading at last letter or item	49
Total ÷ 2 = Center Point	80 ÷ 2 = 40

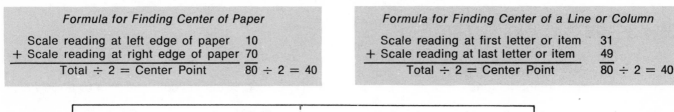

↓ Center of a Column ↓

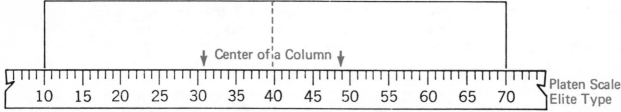

Platen Scale
Elite Type

1. Type a 25-space underline starting 1″ from the left edge of your paper.

2. Center and type your full name on the underline typed in Step 1. Determine center of underline according to formula given above.

Philip Maechling

3. Study relationship of typed letters to underline; the downstem letters barely touch the line. Note

that only a slight space separates the letters of your name from the underline. Note, also, the relationship of the typed letters and underline to the Aligning Scale (33).

4. Space down about 2″ and type a 35-space underline starting 1½″ from the left edge of your paper. Remove the paper.

5. Reinsert the paper. Center and type your name in proper relation to the underline of Step 4.

Special Symbols

■ You will now learn to type special symbols and to type from rough draft (corrected copy). In addition, you will further increase your skill in typing from both straight and statistical copy.

Self-Improvement Practice is not timed as part of these lessons. Materials for self-improvement, however, appear on page 63.
1. Arrange your work area for efficient typing.
2. Adjust the paper guide and insert a full sheet.
3. Set left margin stop 30 spaces to left of center for a 60-space line; move right stop to end of scale.
4. Use single spacing (SS) for drills; double spacing (DS) for paragraphs, unless otherwise directed.

■ LESSON 34

34A ■ CONDITIONING PRACTICE 8

For Each Conditioning Practice in This Unit
1. First writing: Type at a comfortable pace.
2. Second writing: Try to improve stroking technique.
3. Third writing: Emphasize continuity of stroking.

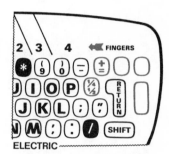

NONELECTRIC   ELECTRIC

Alphabet	Will Dot have Chuck Glanzer fix Jen Quayle's big map for us?
Figures	Terry set the tab stops as follows: 25, 36, 48, 59, and 70.
Figure/symbol	Ball & Cook's long-term bonds (due in 1987) pay 4% interest.
Easy	The ancient jewel at the downtown store was worn by a queen.

Reach to the figures and symbols

| 1 | 2 | 3 | 4 | 5 | 6 | 7 | 8 | 9 | 10 | 11 | 12 |

34B ■ SYMBOL LOCATION: / (DIAGONAL) * (ASTERISK) 7

REACH TECHNIQUE FOR /

Type **/** (end key in first row) with the *right fourth finger. Space between a whole number and a fraction typed with the diagonal (/).*

;/; /; 2/3 5/8 6 2/3 7 5/8

Use / to type 2/3 and 5/8. DS

REACH TECHNIQUE FOR *

Nonelectric. The * is the shift of - (hyphen) and is typed with the *right little finger.* Make the reach to * without moving the elbow in or out.

-; -;*; -;*; *; *; -;*; *;

Type * with this footnote. TS

Electric. Type * (shift of **8**) with the *right second finger.* Keep the wrist low as your finger moves up to type *; avoid moving the elbow out.

8k 8k*k 8k*k *k *k 8k*k *k

Type * with this footnote. TS

34C ■ STROKING TECHNIQUE PRACTICE 10 type at least twice

1	/	/; /; /? 3/5 5/6; Use / to type a "made" fraction; as, 9/16.
2		My stock (bought on July 19 at 36 5/8) sold today at 47 3/4.
3	*	*8 *; 8* ;* *k *- The * (asterisk) is often called the star.
4		He typed * for the first footnote and ** for the second one.
5	*Consolidation*	The * or / is not used often; both * and / appear in tables.
6		Lenz & Buckley drew Contract #49560 (dated 3/18/72) for $75.

| 1 | 2 | 3 | 4 | 5 | 6 | 7 | 8 | 9 | 10 | 11 | 12 |

All figures are used.

GWAM
1' | 5'

¶ 1 the ~~jumps~~ *increase* in family ~~earnings~~ *income* for 1969-70, the ~~latest~~ *most recent* years for   14 | 3 | 51

which ~~figures~~ *data* are ~~available~~ *current*, ~~continued~~ *kept* the ~~general trend~~ *upward course* in family   25 | 5 | 54

income of the ~~previous~~ *past* 22 years. ~~Between~~ *From* 1947-48 ~~and~~ *to* 1969-70,   36 | 7 | 56

median family income in ~~today's~~ *current* dollars tripled, a ~~rising~~ *gain* from *about* $3,000   51 | 10 | 59

to $9,400. ¶ In terms of constant (1969) dollars, me₎dian money income   65 | 13 | 62

in₍creased from ~~about~~ $5,000 in 1947-48 to $9,400 in 1969-70, or *about*   78 | 16 | 64

$200 *each year* ~~annually~~. There was a *drop* ~~decline~~ in the percent of *all* families with   92 | 18 | 67

in comes below $~~3~~,000 *(constant 1969 dollars)*. In 1969-70, 15% of *all* families had incomes   110 | 22 | 71

below $4,000 *compared with 37% of all families in 1947.*   121 | 24 | 73

¶ 2 Projections of trends *those* ~~noted~~ in ~~preceding materials~~ *shown the paragraph above* indicate   13 | 27 | 76

that, by 1980, over 60% of all families ¶ will have incomes of $10,000   27 | 30 | 78

and higher *(in dollars of 1968 value)*, compared to approximately 45% at the pre sent time. In   46 | 33 | 82

1956, the income bulge was in the $5,000 to $10,000 *range* ~~categories~~ (in   58 | 36 | 84

dollars of 1968 value), *with 45.6% of all families in this classification.* In 1968, the bulge was in the $7,000 to   81 | 40 | 89

$15,000 ~~categories~~ *distribution*, and this range included 48.3% of all families.   95 | 43 | 92

By 1980, an inverted pyramid is suggested with   104 | 45 | 94

33.5% of all families above the $15,000 plane   114 | 47 | 96

and with 27.5% in the $10,000 to $15,000 range.   123 | 49 | 97

126F ■ SKILL APPLICATIONS (Lessons 126 to 132) [30]

Problem 1: Alertness Training

The two paragraphs below contain many errors—misspelled words, errors in word division, capitalization, punctuation, and number usage.
1. Make needed corrections as you type the copy.

2. After you complete the typing of the paragraphs, circle any uncorrected errors in your copy as your teacher reads or otherwise indicates the corrections that should have been made.

Center on half sheet ■ type heading: CORRECT IT AS YOU TYPE ■ use a 70-space line ■ DS ■ erase and correct your typing errors

(¶ 1) Dooble spaced tiped matereal must have the furst line of each paragraph endented; otherwise it will be necessary to leeve a a tripl space between paragraphs so that the paragrafing will be cleer to the reeder.

(¶ 2) remember, to, to type figures in a consistant form. the customary practise in the bisiness office is to type all figures as figures rather than to spel them (Example: 2, 9, 18, twenty-one, 47).

34D ■ TABULATING PRACTICE [10] twice from copy; once from dictation

								Words
Clear and set tabs	14	59	10%	5/8	#50*	1 3/4	$9.50	6
	20	73	25%	2/3	#94*	6 5/8	$1.35	12
	75	48	30%	4/5	#25*	8 3/4	$7.05	19
	90	32	95%	7/8	#78*	4 2/3	$9.98	25
KEY	2│ 6	│2 │ 6	│3 │ 6	│3 │ 6	│4 │ 6	│5 │ 6	│5	

34E ■ STATISTICAL TYPING [15] three 1' writings on each ¶; then a 3' writing on ¶s 1 and 2 combined

All figures are used.

	GWAM	
	1'	3'
The 50 most-used words account for 46% of the total of	11	4 │ 34
all words used in a study of 4,100 business letters, memos,	23	8 │ 38
and reports. The first 100 account for 53%; the first 500,	35	12 │ 42
71%; the first 1,000, 80%; and the first 2,000, 88%.	45	15 │ 46
Of the first 7,027 most-used words (accounting for 97%	11	19 │ 49
of all word usage), 209 are balanced-hand words (26% of all	23	23 │ 53
uses) and 284 are one-hand words (14% of all uses). So you	35	27 │ 57
see, drill on such words should add greatly to your skill.	47	31 │ 61

1' GWAM | 1 | 2 | 3 | 4 | 5 | 6 | 7 | 8 | 9 | 10 | 11 | 12 |
3' GWAM | 1 | 2 | 3 | 4 |

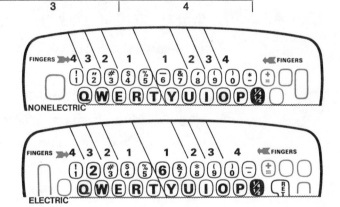

NONELECTRIC

ELECTRIC

■ LESSON 35

35A ■ CONDITIONING PRACTICE [8] each line 3 times

Alphabet	Tim's job is to check liquids forwarded by Getz Express Van.	*Return quickly*
Figures	What is the total of 23 and 45 and 67 and 89 and 90 and 100?	
Figure/symbol	Ed's Order #541 (3/16/72) is for 8 doz. ** Pens at 90 cents.	
Easy	In mixed copy, slow up for symbols and speed up for figures.	

| 1 | 2 | 3 | 4 | 5 | 6 | 7 | 8 | 9 | 10 | 11 | 12 |

35B ■ SYMBOL LOCATION: ½ ¼ [7]

REACH TECHNIQUE FOR ½
Reach the *right fourth finger* up to type ½ without swinging the elbow out. Keep the wrist low.

;½; ½;½; ½;½; ½; ½;½; ½;½;

I typed ½, 2½, 3½, and 4½. DS

REACH TECHNIQUE FOR ¼
The ¼ is the shift of ½ and is typed with the *right fourth finger*. Remember: Shift to type ¼.

;½; ½;¼; ½;¼; ¼; ½;¼; ½;¼;

We used ¼, 3¼, 4¼, and 5¼. DS

Spacing Rules: Type a whole number and a "key" fraction (as, 6½) without spacing between them. Type a whole number and a "made" fraction (made with /) with a space between (as, 6 2/3).

Type 1/2, not ½, with 3/4.

¶ 3
Statistical
rough draft

Surveys ~give evidence~ ~~indicate~~ that 64% of all households own the housing | 13

unit ~in which they live;~ ~they occupy.~ Home ownership ~may vary~ ~~varies~~ from about 50% for | 25

households with # incomes under $3,000 to nearly 85% ~with~ incomes ~~above~~ ~of~ | 39

~or over.~ $15,000 About 42% of every household with a head under 39 years | 54

~of age~ ~~old~~ own their own homes. *Ownership rate for the above-39* | 66

age group is about 70% or over. | 72

126C ■ FIGURE/SYMBOL REVIEW (Lessons 126, 129, 132) [5] (Line: 70; 4 spaces between cols.) each line twice

| Manual | 22 | " " | 33 | ## | 44 | $$ | 55 | % % | 66 | _ | 77 | && | Tab |
| Electric | 22 | @@ | 33 | ## | 44 | $$ | 55 | % % | 66 | ¢¢ | 77 | && | quickly |

| Manual | 88 | ' ' | 99 | ((| 00 |)) | -- | ** | 1½ 1½ | 1¼ 1¼ | ¢¢ | @@ |
| Electric | 88 | ** | 99 | ((| 00 |)) | -- | _ | 1½ 1½ | 1¼ 1¼ | ' ' | " " |

| Both | == | ++ | 11 | !! | // | ?? | 2" | 2@ | 3# | $4 | 5% | 6¢ |
| | 7& | 8' | 8* | 9(| 0) | -- | ** | _ | == | ++ | 1½ | 1¼ |

126D ■ GROWTH INDEX: STRAIGHT COPY (Lessons 127, 130) [15] two 5′ writings

All letters are used.

¶ 1

| | GWAM 1′ | 5′ |

The telephone in a business office can be a useful tool of communi- | 13 | 3 | 52
cation. Unless the telephone is used correctly, however, much time can | 28 | 6 | 55
be wasted. Most business offices have prescribed ways for answering | 42 | 8 | 58
incoming calls, but then effective telephone procedures may break down. | 56 | 11 | 61
For example, if you get a telephone request for some specific data, try | 71 | 14 | 64
to ascertain quickly how long it may take you to get the data. If it | 85 | 17 | 67
takes more than just a few seconds, rather than to keep the caller wait- | 99 | 20 | 69
ing, it is part of good telephone courtesy to get his name and number | 113 | 23 | 72
and to tell him that you will call him soon. | 122 | 24 | 74

¶ 2

If an outside caller has been placed on your line in error, you can | 14 | 27 | 77
be helpful if you try to ascertain the nature of the call so that it can | 28 | 30 | 80
be referred to the proper person. The caller may be unfamiliar with your | 43 | 33 | 83
organization so any help you can give him will be appreciated. It is | 57 | 36 | 85
always frustrating to a caller to be switched to many different exten- | 71 | 39 | 88
sions within a business office without results. Such callers will be | 85 | 41 | 91
grateful to anyone within the office being contacted if he can help | 99 | 44 | 94
him identify the proper person to whom he should speak. Such courtesy | 113 | 47 | 97
will help avoid frayed nerves and will increase company goodwill. | 126 | 50 | 99

| 1′ GWAM | 1 | 2 | 3 | 4 | 5 | 6 | 7 | 8 | 9 | 10 | 11 | 12 | 13 | 14 |
| 5′ GWAM | | | 1 | | | | 2 | | | | 3 | | | |

35C ■ STROKING TECHNIQUE PRACTICE [10] type at least twice

1	½	½; ½;½ 7½ Use ½. We reach with the <u>little finger</u> to type ½.	Eyes on copy
2		The interest rate on my $250 note is changed from 6% to 7½%.	
3	¼	¼; ¼;¼ 6¼ Use ¼. You must use the left shift key to type ¼.	
4		Type fractions in the same way: 1/4 and 2/3--not ¼ and 2/3.	
5	Consoli-	Al wired: "Offer 200 Lobox at 90½ and 100 Square Z at 68¼."	
6	dation	Dr. Kerr moved to 271½ West 86th Street, New York, New York.	

| 1 | 2 | 3 | 4 | 5 | 6 | 7 | 8 | 9 | 10 | 11 | 12 |

35D ■ SENTENCE GUIDED WRITING [7] each line once with the 30" and once with the 20" guide call

	G W A M
	30" 20"
Item 48* on page 156 costs $90 (less 2% for cash).	20 30
Dodson's check is for $2,137.95, but he owes $2,173.85!	22 33
Order #890 for Royal "WQ" totals $567.21 (less 2% discount).	24 36

| 1 | 2 | 3 | 4 | 5 | 6 | 7 | 8 | 9 | 10 | 11 | 12 |

35E ■ TYPING FROM ROUGH DRAFT [18]

LEARN: Copy that is corrected with pencil or with pen and ink is called *rough draft*. Some common marks that proofreaders use for correcting copy are presented at the right. Study them before typing the rough draft given below. Begin on Line 7 on a half sheet.

DO: Type the copy line for line DS on a half sheet. No changes in margin settings are needed.

⌒	Close up	#	Add space	[	Move left
∕	Delete	¶	Paragraph	]	Move right
⊙	Insert period	___	Underline	l.c. or /	Lower case
∧	Insert	∪	Transpose	≡ or Cap.	Capitalize

Rough Draft. Copy ~~Work~~ that has been corrected with pencil

or pen and ink is known as <u>rough draft.</u> Working ~~Typing~~ from rough

draft is a frequent activity in the business ~~company~~ office (well as)

as in the personal applications of typewriting, skill.

¶ Variable <u>Line Endings.</u> In the first paragraph, ~~given above,~~ all lines

(except the last) ends at the same point when correctly typed.

[In this paragraph, however ~~though,~~ some lines ~~may be~~ are longer than others.

This is typical of most of the work you will complete ~~type~~ on the

typewriter, and you will soon learn to type within a range of
acceptable line length.

PHASE 5: OFFICE PRODUCTION SKILLS

■ The primary objectives of Phase 5 are (1) to build your speed and accuracy to the highest possible levels, (2) to increase your application skill, and (3) to improve your production typing rates. You can achieve these goals if you type with good techniques and if you plan your work and then work with a minimum of waste motion and time. Always try to use most of your class time for typing. Work for improvement.

UNIT 20 LESSONS 126-132

Special Office Applications

■ LESSONS 126-132

126A ■ CONDITIONING PRACTICE (Lessons 126-132) ⑤ each line 3 times: slowly, faster, top speed

Alphabet
Figure/symbol
Fingers 3, 4
Fluency

Jack Culep admired the vivid, waxy sheen of a Guatemalan quetzal bird.
The #5346 item will cost Oakley & Company $921.78 (less 10% for cash).
The zealous politician was appalled by the losses in the wool markets.
In life, your position is not nearly so important as your disposition.

Type without breaks or pauses

| 1 | 2 | 3 | 4 | 5 | 6 | 7 | 8 | 9 | 10 | 11 | 12 | 13 | 14 |

126B ■ SKILL-TRANSFER TYPING (Lessons 126, 129, 132) ⑩ (Line: 70)

1. Type two 1' writings on each ¶: the first for speed; the second for control. Record your rates, and try to improve your rates as you repeat timings.

2. Determine percent of transfer. **Goals:** Script rate, 90-100% of your straight-copy rate; statistical-rough-draft rate, 75-85%.

All letters and figures are used.

	1' GWAM

¶ 1
Straight
copy

It really is amazing how quickly our typing rate will improve if   13
we will just remember to type with precise motion patterns. This pat-   27
tern of proper techniques means that every finger is curved and upright,   42
and that we try to keep nearly all the keystroking action in the fingers.   57
In addition, we should try to use every machine part with little or no   71
waste motion.   73

¶ 2
Script copy

The history of this country has been one of intensified use of our   13
natural resources without serious concern for the consequences of these   28
acts. There are persons who would place the blame on "The Establishment."   43
But the truth of the matter is that we are not so much beset by an estab-   58
lishment as we are by the lack of one. Our society has not exactly been   72
organized to control itself effectively.   80

1' GWAM | 1 | 2 | 3 | 4 | 5 | 6 | 7 | 8 | 9 | 10 | 11 | 12 | 13 | 14 |

(Please see page 195 for ¶ 3.)

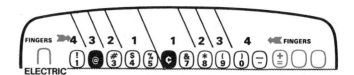

LESSON 36

36A ■ CONDITIONING PRACTICE 〔8〕 each line 3 times

Alphabet	Did Max give J. B. Lowe's check to Fran Quimby as the prize?	*Shift quickly but firmly*
Figures	Fill in the Social Security Number (217-48-3690) on Line 15.	
Figure/symbol	He sold 205 of Rahe & Kahn 3½% Pfd. (bought 4/17/69) at 86¼.	
Easy	The good workman does his work better than just well enough.	

| 1 | 2 | 3 | 4 | 5 | 6 | 7 | 8 | 9 | 10 | 11 | 12 |

36B ■ SYMBOL LOCATION: ¢ (CENT OR CENTS) @ (AT) 〔7〕

REACH TECHNIQUE FOR ¢ and @ (Nonelectric)

Reach the *right fourth finger* to the right to type ¢. The shift of ¢ is @. Make the reach to ¢ and @ without moving the other fingers from their home keys.

;¢; ¢; ¢;@; ¢;@; ¢;@; ¢;@;

I sold 2 dozen @ 69¢ each. *TS*

REACH TECHNIQUE FOR ¢ and @ (Electric)

The ¢ is the shift of the figure **6** and is typed with the *right first finger*. The @ is the shift of the figure **2** and is typed with the *left third finger*.

6j 6j¢j ¢j 2s@s @s 2s@s ¢j

I sold 2 dozen @ 69¢ each. *TS*

> **SPACING RULES**
>
> **1.** Space before and after typing @.
> **2.** Do not space between ¢ and the figure it follows.
>
> These spacing directions apply when the symbols are used in a sentence or in typing bills, but not when used in reach-stroke drills such as the first line of the symbol-location drill.

36C ■ STROKING TECHNIQUE PRACTICE 〔10〕 type at least twice

1	¢	6¢; 11¢; 16¢; Do not space between ¢ and a preceding figure.
2		John paid 98¢ for the ball-point pen and 16¢ for the pencil.
3	@	2# @ $1.59; #11 @ $2.37; Request #121 @ $1.69; #139 @ $2.39.
4		Dorothy bought 10 7/8 yards @ $4.75 and 9 3/4 yards @ $5.25.
5	Consoli-	Vera sold a pen @ 98¢, pad @ 36¢, and 24 pencils @ 15¢ each.
6	dation	The * before Item 29, page 306, indicates a decrease of 68¢.

| 1 | 2 | 3 | 4 | 5 | 6 | 7 | 8 | 9 | 10 | 11 | 12 |

36D ■ TABULATING PRACTICE 〔7〕 twice from copy; once from dictation

							Words
Clear and set tabs	mine	406	sun	12½	72¢	air-	5
	line	957	far	10¼	45¢	for-	10
	gets	284	him	16½	63¢	A-A1	15
KEY	4	8 3 8	3 8	3 8	3 8	3 8	4

125C ■ PRODUCTION MEASUREMENT: TABULATING

Time Schedule

Planning and preparing . .	3'
Timed production writing .	20'
Proofreading; computing	
n-pram	7'

You are to type the table below as you are timed for 20 minutes; if you finish the table, start over on a new sheet. Correct your errors. When time is called, proofread your work. Deduct 15 words from total words typed for each uncorrected error; divide remainder by 20 to determine *n-pram* (net production rate a minute). Work without waste motions.

Full sheet ■ reading position ■ DS the columnar entries ■ 2 spaces between columns

NOTE: In Columns 2 and 3, use the columnar headings as the longest lines; then center entries under these headings, and change tab stops.

				Words
WESTSIDE REALTY BOARD				4
Recent Sales				7
Address	**Listing No.**	**List Price**	**Realtor**	22
616 Fifth Avenue	7610	$164,500	Lelah T. Pierson Realty	33
2524 La Mesa Drive	7578	129,500	Philip Norton, Inc.	44
1700 Stone Canyon	8019	112,500	Fred Sands Associates	54
763 N. Kenter Avenue	7744	94,500	Harleigh Sandler Co.	64
337 – 26th Street	8076	88,000	Philip Norton, Inc.	74
856 Teawood Road	7583	79,500	Harleigh Sandler Co.	84
2216 Duxbury Circle	7560	74,500	Harleigh Sandler Co.	95
1117 Roscomare Road	7613	74,500	Harleigh Sandler Co.	105
15549 Hamner Drive	7796	74,500	Fred Sands Associates	116
2532 La Condessa	8035	73,900	Harleigh Sandler Co.	126
320 S. Westgate Dr.	7795	67,500	Fred Sands Associates	137
1966 Westridge Rd.	7304	67,500	Lelah T. Pierson Realty	148
2865 Motor Avenue	7223	65,000	Helen Meigs Realty	158
2484 Banyan Drive	7512	64,500	Fred Sands Associates	168
1957 Linda Flora	7511	62,500	Fred Sands Associates	178
10415 Troon Avenue	7725	62,500	Helen Meigs Realty	188
10846 Holman Avenue	7606	61,000	Zel Mann Realty	198
10702 Stradella Ct.	8023	57,950	Fred Sands Associates	208

When a street has a number as its name, separate the house number from the street number by a hyphen preceded and followed by a space.

1. Type the rough-draft copy given below, making the indicated corrections. Read carefully and type with minimum error.

2. Remove your paper from the typewriter and proofread it, using proofreaders' marks to indicate corrections needed in your copy.

3. If time permits, retype the copy *from your own rough draft*, not from the copy in the textbook. Type with control.

	GWAM
	1′ / 3′

FACTS ABOUT PAPER: A full sheet (8½ by 11 inches)   10 | 3

has 36 lines for typing; a half sheet (8½ by 5½ inches),   21 | 7

h as only 33 lines. Each line on a ~~full~~ sheet 8½" *inches* wide   33 | 11

has 100 *elite* spaces or 85 pica spaces (on the basis of ~~the~~   44 | 15

12 elite spaces or 10 pica spaces to the inch). Try to   55 | 18

remember these important facts about ~~typewriting~~ paper.   64 | 21

SOME FACTS ABOUT TYPEWRITERS: Most typewriters are set   10 | 25

~~to have~~ *for* 6 lines to a vertical inch; ~~but~~ *However,* some are not.   22 | 28

To check how many lines your typewriter *has* ~~gets~~ to an inch,   33 | 32

type figures 1 through 6 in a single-spaced *list* ~~column~~ at the   44 | 36

~~right~~ *left* margin and measure the space used. Most American   55 | 40

made ~~machines~~ *typewriters* can be ~~geared~~ *set* to type 6 lines to an inch.   66 | 43

Some of the machines imported from europe, however, are   78 | 47

set differently and can not be ~~made~~ *adjusted* to fit precisely   89 | 51

the spacing of american machines and *of the* ruled forms ~~that are~~   100 | 55

designed *for* ~~to~~ completion on those machines.   108 | 57

LESSON 37

37A ■ CONDITIONING PRACTICE 8 each line 3 times

Alphabet	Did Burt Jackson say Liza wove queer hex signs for Mr. Depp?
Figures	She said, "Study the charts on pages 45, 189, 206, and 370."
Figure/symbol	Order 125 of #384B @ 89¢ each and 160 of #7501 @ $1.05 each.
Fluency	Faith, hope, and hard work will help a man to win much more.

Reach to the figures and symbols

| 1 | 2 | 3 | 4 | 5 | 6 | 7 | 8 | 9 | 10 | 11 | 12 |

37B ■ TYPING FROM ROUGH DRAFT 15

1. Type two 1′ *exploration-level* writings on each ¶ of 36E, above. Push for speed.

2. Type two 3′ *control-level* writings on the ¶s of 36E, above. Begin with ¶ 1 and type as far as you can.

LESSON 125

125A ■ CONDITIONING PRACTICE [5] each line 3 times: slowly, faster, top speed

Alphabet	The quiet, still life was movingly executed on canvas by Jack Z. Parr.	*Quick, snappy keystroking*
Figure/symbol	A $50 million 12-year 6 3/4% debenture was offered at $98 to yield 7%.	
Long words	Democracy is based upon the extraordinary possibilities in each of us.	
Fluency	Keep the stroking action in the fingers to increase your typing skill.	

| 1 | 2 | 3 | 4 | 5 | 6 | 7 | 8 | 9 | 10 | 11 | 12 | 13 | 14 |

125B ■ SKILL-TRANSFER TYPING: STATISTICAL ROUGH DRAFT [15] (Line: 70) two 5' writings; proofread; determine GWAM

All figures are used.

GWAM
1' | 5'

¶ 1 (A 1.5 5.6 80)

Approximately ~~one fifth~~ *20%* of the population of the united States is — 11 | 2 | 51

14-24 years, *old* ~~of age.~~ These young people, *presently number* ~~currently tally~~ about 40 — 25 | 5 | 54

million and are expected to increase to over 45.4 million. *by 1980* The popul- — 40 | 8 | 57

lation, *expansion* ~~growth~~ in the, *decade* ~~years~~ ahead will be, *most* rapid for the 22-24-year-olds — 56 | 11 | 60

and ~~are~~ much slower for the younger age groups. All this is a reflection — 70 | 14 | 63

(since World War II) in the birth rate. Between 1969 and 1980, the, *accounting* ~~number~~ of persons at ages — 89 | 18 | 67

22-24 is expected to increase by 33 1/3% (from 9,400,000 to 12,500,000), — 103 | 21 | 69

and those at ages 18-21 by ~~a fifth.~~ *20%* ← — 119 | 24 | 73

¶ 2 (A 1.5 5.6 80)

Currently, *at* ~~age~~ ages 18-24, nearly 32 *%* ~~percent~~ of the *males* ~~men~~ and 26 *%* ~~percent~~ — 12 | 26 | 75

of the *females* ~~women~~ have finished at least 1 year of college. *Conversely,* ~~On the other~~ — 26 | 29 | 78

~~hand,~~ only 7% of the men and 6% of the women have not completed 1 year — 39 | 31 | 80

of high school. *Approximately %* ~~Almost 90 percent~~ of the boys and girls *aged 16-17* attend school. — 55 | 35 | 84

ages At 18-19, approximately 52 *%* ~~percent~~ of the males are still registered — 69 | 37 | 86

(with most in college.) in formal classes, Over 16 2/3% of the *males* ~~men~~ at ages 22-24 are enrolled *(as college students)* — 92 | 42 | 91

Of the young women, the *ratio* ~~proportion~~ attending college is 33 1/3% at — 105 | 45 | 93

ages 18-19, and *about* ~~almost~~ 25% at 20-21 years. *In the 22-24 age bracket,* — 118 | 47 | 96

however, only 1 in 12 is in college. — 126 | 49 | 98

(Only a 3% rise is anticipated at ages 14-17.)

37C ■ GROWTH INDEX 13

1. Type two 3′ writings on both ¶s for *control*. Circle errors. Determine *gwam* on each writing.

2. Type a 1′ *exploration-level* guided writing on each ¶. Push for speed.

All letters are used.

	GWAM		
	2′	3′	

¶ 1 A man who has pencils but no erasers must never make a 5 | 4 | 42
mistake. Of course, he must never attempt anything of much 11 | 8 | 46
importance either. Don't be ashamed of making an error now 17 | 12 | 50
and then, but do try to avoid making the same one again and 23 | 16 | 54
again. Use this excellent measure of a careful worker. 29 | 19 | 58

¶ 2   As you try to improve your typing power, you will make 34 | 23 | 62
quite a few errors when you try out new or improved methods 40 | 27 | 66
of stroking. Just as in other skills, though, many of your 46 | 31 | 70
errors will drop away as you perfect your motions. Realize 52 | 35 | 74
that even the best typist often uses his typing eraser. 58 | 39 | 77

2′ GWAM | 1 | 2 | 3 | 4 | 5 | 6 |
3′ GWAM | 1 | 2 | 3 | 4 |

37D ■ STATISTICAL TYPING 14

1. Type a 1′ *exploration-level* writing on each ¶. Determine *gwam* on each writing.

2. Type two 3′ writings on both ¶s for *control*. Circle errors. Determine *gwam* on each writing.

All letters and figures are used.

	GWAM		
	1′	3′	

When you were just 9 years old, you thought a person in 11 | 4 | 35
the upper teens "old," one in his 20's "antique." But since 23 | 8 | 40
you're now 14, 15, or maybe even 16 or 17, an individual who 36 | 12 | 44
is 20 doesn't seem old; but one in his 30's creaks with age! 48 | 16 | 48

     You might now consider your sister of 12 "a pest" and a 11 | 20 | 51
brother of 13 "a brat" and believe you cannot expect a great 23 | 24 | 55
deal of them. After you become 18 or 19, however, these two 36 | 28 | 59
"children" at your current age will seem amazingly grown up! 48 | 32 | 63

1′ GWAM | 1 | 2 | 3 | 4 | 5 | 6 | 7 | 8 | 9 | 10 | 11 | 12 |
3′ GWAM | 1 | 2 | 3 | 4 |

Problem 1

Words

Current date | Mr. Paul Le Poullouin | New   8
Century Products, Inc. | 5670 Hemingway   16
Avenue | Detroit, MI 48239 | Dear Mr. Le   24
Poullouin | (¶ 1) Have you stayed at the Bay-   31
shore Inn lately? We try to promote the Inn   40
as a sensible hotel for the busy executive who   50
is stopping in Vancouver on business. But,   59
frankly, it's been a losing battle because the   67
Bayshore Inn simply doesn't look like a sensi-   77
ble hotel. It looks like a place you'd find in Rio   88
or Acapulco. (¶ 2) The Bayshore Inn is built   96
on the lee shore of a yacht harbor, and the   104
mountains are so near you can smell the ever-   113
greens on their slopes. The Inn is only four   123
blocks from the heart of Vancouver; but if you   132
look out your window, you'd think you were   141
in a mountain retreat. A walk in the gardens   150
of the hotel is an adventure, and lunch at   158
Trader Vic's is a reward. (¶ 3) The only   166
sensible thing about the Bayshore Inn is the   175
price. Single rooms start at $16. Busy execu-   184
tives keep coming back here again and again.   193
They tell us it is the sensible place to stay.   203
Perhaps you should stop at the Inn the next   212
time you're in Vancouver. We'd like the oppor-   221
tunity to pamper you, too. | Sincerely yours | 230
Derek Zahl, Manager | xxx | (199)   235/**252**

Problem 2

Current date | Mrs. Rosalyn Kalmar, Purchasing   10
Agent | Stone Mountain Products, Inc. | 1568   18
Peach Tree Avenue | Atlanta, GA 30309 | 25
Dear Mrs. Kalmar | (¶ 1) Some people work   32
well at desks piled high with papers. Others   41
work equally well at neat, uncluttered desks.   51
Is someone right and someone wrong? (¶ 2)   58
With Gibralter desks, you're right either way.   68
Uncluttered, a Gibralter desk pays dividends   77
in good looks. It combines functional efficiency   87
with smart, contemporary styling. Cluttered   96
with a mountain of paper work, a Gibralter   105
desk is a bulwark of quality construction. It is   115
made to take rough use. (¶ 3) There is Gibral-   123
ter furniture for every office need. The next   132
time you need furniture, why not make it   140
Gibralter. You'll be right in your choice. | 149
Sincerely yours | Z. S. Dickerson | Sales Man-   158
ager | xxx | (120)   159/**181**

Problem 3

Words

Current date | Mr. Howard Zorba, Office Man-   9
ager | Western States Life Insurance Com-   17
pany | 4856 River Forest Road | Portland, OR   25
97222 | Dear Mr. Zorba | (¶ 1) It has often   32
been said that "the spinal curve is directly re-   42
lated to the efficiency curve." In other words,   52
a seated worker's "slump" leads to excessive   61
fatigue and a "slump" in production. It is a   70
matter of record, too, that correct posture   79
increases speed, reduces fatigue, and improves   88
efficiency and morale. (¶ 2) But don't take our   97
word for these statements. Just mail the en-   106
closed card for two new publications which are   115
of interest to any forward-looking person. One   125
publication discusses the value of correct sit-   134
ting posture; the other describes the new   142
Modern Posture Chairs. The Modern Posture   151
Chairs encourage sustained and accurate work.   160
The self-adjusting backs give the utmost in   169
correct body support. What's more, there is a   179
Modern Posture Chair for every executive and   188
general office need. (¶ 3) Be sure to mail the   196
postpaid card today. The two new publica-   204
tions will reach you promptly. | Sincerely   213
yours | Mark Palmer | Sales Manager | xxx | 220
Enclosure (180)   222/**245**

Problem 4

Current date | Mr. John R. Perry | 1502 Cedar   9
Street | La Grande, OR 97850 | Dear Mr.   17
Perry | (¶ 1) We have continued your sub-   23
scription beyond the date of its expiration. We   33
did this because of the importance of uninter-   42
rupted service to you. (¶ 2) Each issue of THE   51
NATIONAL OBSERVER forwarded to you   58
has contained valuable news, original informa-   67
tion, editorials, and interpretative articles that   77
you would not want to miss. You can get such   86
information nowhere else at such nominal cost.   96
(¶ 3) If your check is not handy, your word as   104
to payment is as good as your bond with us.   113
Just return the enclosed card now. | Sincerely   122
yours | Arthur Pollyea | Circulation Manager | 131
xxx | Enclosure (101)   133/**144**

SELF-IMPROVEMENT PRACTICE

DO: Set the left margin 30 spaces to the left of the center of the paper; move the right margin to the end of the scale. Set the line-space regulator on "1" for single spacing.

TYPE: Each line three to five times each; first for technique improvement, next for speed of stroking, and then for more precise control of finger motion patterns.

High-Frequency Words

■ All 107 *different* words that are used in the following drills are among the 500 most-used words in the English language. In a study of 600,000 words in a large number of letters, memos, and reports, these 107 words accounted for more than 40 percent of all word occurrences. Thus, they are important to you in perfecting your typewriting skill. Practice them frequently for both speed and control.

Balanced-hand words of 2 to 5 letters

EMPHASIZE
Finger reaches; speedy stroking; quick spacing

1 of to is it or by if us an do so me he am go the and for may
2 but sir pay due own men did box with they them make than when
3 work such form then wish paid name held both their city also
4 of it, it is, for us, with them, both of, or me, it is right,
5 and the, may go to, due the men, to do it, and do so, by them
6 He may pay the six men for the work they did by the big box.
7 They did the work right and paid the dues on the city field.
| 1 | 2 | 3 | 4 | 5 | 6 | 7 | 8 | 9 | 10 | 11 | 12 |

One-hand words of 2 to 5 letters

Finger action; uniform stroking

8 we in be on as no at up my are you was get him tax few set
9 dear were best only date card area upon case ever rate fact
10 get at, you were, tax him, after my, after rates, great state
11 rate card, tax case, in no, we are, at only, as in, are ever
12 As you are on my state tax case, get a few tax rates set up.
13 Only a few tax rates were ever set in my area after my case.
| 1 | 2 | 3 | 4 | 5 | 6 | 7 | 8 | 9 | 10 | 11 | 12 |

Double-letter words of 3 to 5 letters

Quick stroking of double letters

14 all see too will been good need full well call feel soon week
15 free book less keep fill bill shall three offer books issue
16 too small, all will, shall still, still small, all too soon,
17 feel well, need less, three books, shall see, will call all,
18 The three books will fill the need; so issue the offer soon.
19 He will keep all books, too; do feel free to issue the bill.
| 1 | 2 | 3 | 4 | 5 | 6 | 7 | 8 | 9 | 10 | 11 | 12 |

Balanced, one-hand, and double-letter words of 2 to 5 letters

Continuity of stroking

20 of we to in or on is be it as by no if at us up an my he am
21 and all him for see you men too are may get but was pay tax
22 work will best then been rates such good were wish need only
23 right small state field offer rates their three great after
24 it is up to all, if you are free, he is less, offer to state
25 it was too soon, for all the men, he may call for, do keep it
26 It was then up to him to set the book rate on the small box.
27 On the rate card he saw the due date, the date he is to pay.
| 1 | 2 | 3 | 4 | 5 | 6 | 7 | 8 | 9 | 10 | 11 | 12 |

Performance Evaluation

Lessons 124-125 provide activities that will help you make a more nearly complete evaluation of your typing skill. Do your best work.

■ LESSON 124

124A ■ CONDITIONING PRACTICE 5 each line 3 times: slowly, faster, top speed

Alphabet | The reporters quickly recognized the vexing problems of judging flaws. *Space*
Figure/symbol | This rug (12′ x 13′6″) was $417.90, but it is now on sale for $381.50. *quickly*
Continuity | It will help to remember that anger is but one letter short of danger.
Fluency | They expect to make the audit of the offices at the end of this month.

| 1 | 2 | 3 | 4 | 5 | 6 | 7 | 8 | 9 | 10 | 11 | 12 | 13 | 14 |

124B ■ GROWTH INDEX: STRAIGHT COPY 15 two 5′ writings; proofread; determine GWAM

All letters are used.

GWAM
1′ 5′

¶ 1

It often is so easy to take many things for granted. Consider for   13 3 51
a moment what amazing equipment our hands really are. Just think of the   28 6 54
many exacting things, often without conscious thought, our hands do for   42 8 57
us every day. We utilize our hands for clapping approval, for waving   56 11 59
goodbye, for tugging at zippers, buttoning buttons, fumbling for door   70 14 62
keys, or for the quick and skillful operation of the keys of a typewriter.   86 17 65
Our hands and fingers do all these things for us and we hardly ever give   102 20 68
a thought to their wonder and adaptability. It is so easy to do this.   114 23 71

¶ 2

Yet there is more to hands than mere utility. Our hands and fingers   14 26 74
are used to express the deepest of human emotions. Our fingers touch   28 28 77
the strings of a guitar or the keys of a piano to express our mood and   42 31 79
feeling. Our hands are used in communicating with another individual,   56 34 82
whether verbally or in writing. We use our hands to draw and to paint,   71 37 85
and man has developed beautiful and individual works of art with his   84 40 88
hands. Combined with our mind, our hands are one of the principal meth-   99 43 91
ods we use for learning. A youngster touches and feels everything to   113 45 94
gain knowledge about it, and the process is continued for a lifetime.   127 48 96

1′ GWAM | 1 | 2 | 3 | 4 | 5 | 6 | 7 | 8 | 9 | 10 | 11 | 12 | 13 | 14 |
5′ GWAM | 1 | 2 | 3 |

124C ■ PRODUCTION MEASUREMENT: LETTERS 30 (Block style; open punctuation; type on control level)

Time Schedule	
Planning and preparing	3′
Timed production writing . . .	20′
Proofreading; determining *n-pram* .	7′

Type each letter on page 191, properly placed, on a letterhead or a plain sheet. Correct your errors. When time is called, proofread each letter. Deduct 15 words from total words typed for each uncorrected error; divide remainder by 20 to determine *n-pram*. Use your initials for reference.

Evaluating Basic Typing Skills

■ LESSON 38

38A ■ CONDITIONING PRACTICE [8] each line 3 times

Alphabet	Joe Bair quickly wrote the zoology exam for advanced pupils.	Body erect;
Figures	In 1968 that school had 175 boys, 234 girls, and 20 faculty.	fingers curved
Figure/symbol	Study Figures 3-5 (page 86), 4-2 (page 90), 10-3 (page 375).	
Fluency	All the men said they would fight for what is right for all.	

| 1 | 2 | 3 | 4 | 5 | 6 | 7 | 8 | 9 | 10 | 11 | 12 |

38B ■ SKILL-TRANSFER TYPING [12]

1. Type a 1' *exploration-level* writing on each of the following paragraphs. Compare *gwam*.

2. Type an additional 1' writing on each ¶ on which the *gwam* was lower than that on ¶ 1.

All letters and figures are used.

GWAM
1' | 3'

¶ 1 Straight copy

An ideal kind of practice is that done with a purpose. — 11 | 4
It helps very little just to jam the paper with words. Try — 23 | 8
to get your fingers to move quickly when working for speed. — 35 | 12
For typing precision, lower the rate a little to develop an — 47 | 16
easy, accurate motion in every finger action. — 56 | 19

¶ 2 Statistical copy

People dislike high prices, but they like high wages-- — 11 | 22
except when having to pay them! Many were critical in 1930 — 23 | 26
when a dozen eggs cost only 28¢; a pound of potatoes, 4¢; a — 35 | 30
pound of bacon, 35¢. We will not like 1976 prices either! — 47 | 34

¶ 3 Rough draft

[If you aspire to do something, get up and do it. Quit — 11 | 38
whinning about not having a change. Create your own chance. — 23 | 42
Take advantage of all opportunities that come to you; don't — 35 | 46
[merely covett them when they pass by. — 42 | 48

¶ 4 Script copy

You don't have to agonize over speed to develop skill. — 11 | 52
You can improve in power without speeding up the fingers by — 23 | 56
using each machine part with exact control. The proper use — 35 | 60
of the space bar will in fact help. — 42 | 63

1' GWAM | 1 | 2 | 3 | 4 | 5 | 6 | 7 | 8 | 9 | 10 | 11 | 12 |
3' GWAM | 1 | 2 | 3 | 4 |

TO DETERMINE PERCENTAGES OF TRANSFER:
Divide your straight-copy rate into (1) your statistical-copy rate, (2) into your rough-draft rate, and (3) into your script-copy rate. How much did you transfer?

◼ LESSON 122

122A ◼ CONDITIONING PRACTICE 5 each line 3 times: slowly, faster, top speed

Alphabet	The Aztec jewelry makes an exquisite gift of which everybody is proud.	*Eyes on*
Figure/symbol	The new prices are as follows: 12 @ $25.50; 24 @ $48.95; 36 @ $70.50.	*copy*
Long words	Electro-mechanical devices and servomechanisms solve systems problems.	
Fluency	They paid for the gowns with the money she received for her handiwork.	

| 1 | 2 | 3 | 4 | 5 | 6 | 7 | 8 | 9 | 10 | 11 | 12 | 13 | 14 |

122B ◼ LEFTBOUND MANUSCRIPT WITH FOOTNOTES 45 continue 119C, pages 184-188

◼ LESSON 123

123A ◼ CONDITIONING PRACTICE 5 repeat 122A, above

123B ◼ GROWTH INDEX: STRAIGHT COPY 15

Type two 5′ writings on 116B, page 178: **Goal:** improvement.

123C ◼ LEFTBOUND MANUSCRIPT WITH FOOTNOTES 30

Complete manuscript report, 119C, pages 184-188.

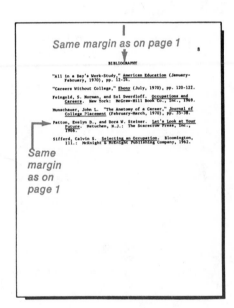

Problem 1: Bibliography

Type the bibliography, which is a listing of references used in the manuscript report. The entries illustrate one form that may be used in typing a bibliography.

Number this page to follow the last page of the report.

> Top margin, same as on page 1 ◼ left margin, 1½″ ◼ right margin, 1″ ◼ center heading over line of writing ◼ start first line of each entry at left margin ◼ indent second and succeeding lines 5 spaces ◼ SS each entry ◼ DS between entries

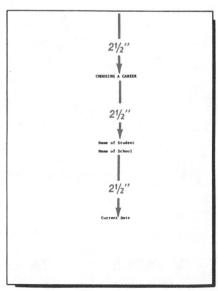

BIBLIOGRAPHY

"All in a Day's Work-Study," <u>American Education</u> (January-February, 1970), pp. 12-14.

"Careers Without College," <u>Ebony</u> (July, 1970), pp. 120-122.

Feingold, S. Norman, and Sol Swerdloff. <u>Occupations and Careers.</u> New York: McGraw-Hill Book Co., Inc., 1969.

Munschauer, John L. "The Anatomy of a Career," <u>Journal of College Placement</u> (February-March, 1970), pp. 35-38.

Patton, Evelyn D., and Dora W. Steiner. <u>Let's Look at Your Future.</u> Metuchen, N. J.: The Scarecrow Press, Inc., 1966.

Sifferd, Calvin S. <u>Selecting an Occupation.</u> Bloomington, Ill.: McKnight & McKnight Publishing Company, 1962.

Problem 2: Manuscript Title Page

1. Center title over the *line of writing*, 2½″ from top of the page.

2. Type your name 2½″ below title;

DS; type name of your school.

3. Type the current date 2½″ below the name of your school.

38C ■ GROWTH INDEX $\boxed{10}$

1. Type two 3' writings on the two paragraphs that follow.

2. Determine *gwam* and errors on each writing. Record the better writing.

All letters are used.

		GWAM	
		2'	3'
¶ 1	Record every problem that limits your typing facility;	5	4 / 32
	then look at each as squarely as you can and mark those you	11	8 / 36
	will solve alone. Decide upon a course of action to remedy	17	12 / 40
	them. Finally, put the plan to work.	21	14 / 42
¶ 2	Now, note those problems that remain unchecked on your	27	18 / 46
	index. Discuss each of them with your teacher, and realize	33	22 / 50
	the great help he can offer you in your efforts to excel in	39	26 / 54
	typing power. It takes but a jiffy.	42	28 / 56

2' GWAM | 1 | 2 | 3 | 4 | 5 | 6 |
3' GWAM | 1 | 2 | 3 | 4 |

38D ■ SPEED/CONTROL BUILDING $\boxed{20}$

1. Type two 1' guided writings on ¶ 1, 38C, for speed; then type a 1' guided writing for control.

2. Type two 1' guided writings on ¶ 2, 38C, for speed; then type a 1' guided writing for control.

3. Type two 3' writings on the two paragraphs of 38C combined.

■ LESSON 39

39A ■ CONDITIONING PRACTICE $\boxed{8}$ each line 3 times

Alphabet	Zeb Shaw did quick, exceptional engraving work for Jim Raye.	*Type without*
Figures	He has 30 cartoons, 86 charts, 157 graphs, and 249 pictures.	*pauses between*
Figure/symbol	She ordered 150 yds. #13947-C @ 78¢; 130 yds. #6284-M @ 74¢.	*strokes or words*
Fluency	Fuel for their giant plant was sent via motor freight today.	

| 1 | 2 | 3 | 4 | 5 | 6 | 7 | 8 | 9 | 10 | 11 | 12 |

39B ■ TABULATION CHECKUP $\boxed{5}$

DO: Set tabulator stops to leave 6 spaces between words and groups of figures.

TYPE: Two copies of the tabulated columns. **Goals:** (1) properly aligned columns; (2) no more than 4 errors per copy.

1 *Words*	go	all	add	inn	ball	been	issue
2 *Figures*	28	405	361	272	4036	9568	34127
3 *Figures/symbols*	#9	75¢	16%	$20	83–M	(45)	R & D
KEY	2	6	3	6	3	6	3	6	4	6	4	6	5

Summary

Successful career planning includes three important steps. The first step is to understand and appraise yourself; the second is to investigate careers and compare requirements with your personal characteristics and abilities; and the third is to organize the means to achieve your career goal. There is the right career for you if you plan and prepare for it. If you are honest with yourself and follow the steps given in this brief report, you will increase your potential for experiencing the satisfaction of a career that "fits."

LESSON 120

120A ■ CONDITIONING PRACTICE [5] each line 3 times: slowly, faster, then at top speed

Alphabet	The explorer quickly adjusted the beams as the freezing wave hit them.	*Quick, shift-key reach*
Figure/symbol	Type: "2," #3, $4, 5%, 6¢, 7&, 8'*, (9), (0); 1 + 2 = 3; $\frac{1}{2} + \frac{1}{4}$ = 3/4.	
Shift key	Jack LeConte and Mary O'Brien accepted jobs with S. & J. Wooland, Inc.	
Fluency	Some frustration in life may help us develop a better sense of values.	
	| 1 | 2 | 3 | 4 | 5 | 6 | 7 | 8 | 9 | 10 | 11 | 12 | 13 | 14 |	

120B ■ IMPROVING SPEED: PROGRESSIVE-DIFFICULTY SENTENCES [12]

Type two 1' writings on each sentence for speed. **Goal:** Try to equal Sentence 1 rate on 2, 3, and 4.

		High-frequency words emphasized	*EMPHASIZE*
1	*Balanced-hand*	The field chairman may make them do their work and then sign the form.	*Word response*
2	*Combination*	Will you deliver the statement and the contract to them for signature?	*Variable rhythm*
3	*One-hand*	I regret that you gave only a minimum opinion on the extra water case.	*Quiet hands*
4	*Figures*	A customer ordered 123 boxes, 456 metal forms, 78 books, and 90 desks.	*Finger reaches*
		| 1 | 2 | 3 | 4 | 5 | 6 | 7 | 8 | 9 | 10 | 11 | 12 | 13 | 14 |	

120C ■ LEFTBOUND MANUSCRIPT WITH FOOTNOTES [33] continue 119C, pages 184-188

LESSON 121

121A ■ CONDITIONING PRACTICE [5] each line 3 times: slowly, faster, top speed

Alphabet	The new Zula and Jaguar sports cars were moved quickly from a box car.	*Return quickly*
Figure/symbol	The 5 reams of $8\frac{1}{2}$" x 11" paper (No. 24) on Order #79 will cost $16.30.	
Adjacent keys	Rewards received for services rendered are related to effort expended.	
Fluency	An efficient secretary paid the busy clerks for the eighty handy pens.	
	| 1 | 2 | 3 | 4 | 5 | 6 | 7 | 8 | 9 | 10 | 11 | 12 | 13 | 14 |	

121B ■ IMPROVING ACCURACY [12] repeat 120B but with emphasis on accuracy: not over 1 error each minute

121C ■ LEFTBOUND MANUSCRIPT WITH FOOTNOTES [33] continue 119C, pages 184-188

39C ■ SKILL-COMPARISON TYPING 10

1. Type a 1' *exploration-level* writing on each of the following ¶s. Compare *gwam*.

2. Type two additional 1' writings on each ¶ on which the *gwam* was lower than that on ¶ 1.

All letters are used.

¶ 1

	GWAM		
	1'	3'	
I know it is quite all right for you to get your speed	11	4	47
as high as you can. Just as soon as you end your drive for	23	8	51
speed, though, you should drop back a few words to work for	35	12	55
good form. It may take a while, but you can do it.	45	15	58

¶ 2

Are you able to type with speed and good form? If so,	11	19	62
you must work next for reach control. Practice on an easy,	23	23	66
precise style of typing. Tell the hands what to do and let	35	27	70
them do it. Work with proper zeal.	42	29	72

¶ 3

You are about ready to begin putting your new skill to	11	33	76
work in the typing of realistic problems: tables, letters,	23	37	80
and reports. You will work from the simple to the complex.	35	41	84
Thus, the task will be easy for you.	42	43	86

```
1' GWAM |   1   |   2   |   3   |   4   |   5   |   6   |   7   |   8   |   9   |   10  |   11  |   12  |
3' GWAM |          1          |          2          |          3          |          4          |
```

39D ■ GROWTH INDEX 10

1. Type two 3' writings on the two paragraphs that follow.

2. Determine *gwam* and errors on each writing. Record the better writing.

All letters are used.

¶ 1

	GWAM	
	1'	3'
The shortest distance between two points is a straight	11	4	41
line, according to an old axiom. Quite as true is the idea	23	8	45
that the quickest route to the prize post in business is to	35	12	49
develop the knowledge and skill that many a company may pay	47	16	53
top dollar to get when staffing its offices.	56	19	56

¶ 2

Will you be ready for the interview when it is time to	11	22	60
locate a job, whenever that is? Many applicants aren't but	23	26	64
expect to be hired simply because they are next of a number	35	30	68
of applicants. Decide soon the field you want; develop the	47	34	72
skills needed; get ready for the job interview.	56	37	75

```
1' GWAM |   1   |   2   |   3   |   4   |   5   |   6   |   7   |   8   |   9   |   10  |   11  |   12  |
3' GWAM |          1          |          2          |          3          |          4          |
```

39E ■ SPEED/CONTROL BUILDING 17

1. Type two 1' writings on ¶ 1, 39D, for speed; then type a 1' writing for control.

2. Type two 1' writings on ¶ 2, 39D, for speed; then type a 1' writing for control.

3. Type two 3' control writings on the two paragraphs of 39D combined.

Titles. This government publication describes more than 35,000 jobs and lists their titles. The U.S. Government Printing Office also publishes a document entitled Career Guide for Demand Occupations. This guide lists occupational titles, helpful high school subjects, special characteristics needed for the occupation, educational requirements, and useful selected references. When you have identified those careers which interest you and which seem to match your qualifications, you should consult the Occupational Outlook Handbook. This handbook is revised and reissued every two years. Copies are available in most libraries. The handbook gives the qualifications and education required for entry into a particular career as well as the opportunities and trends for that career. Presently, one of the major occupational trends is toward the service occupations, which include many opportunities in the clerical and office work area.

After completing these steps, you should try to narrow your selection to a few career choices—those that most nearly match your abilities and interests. Now you are ready to compile detailed information on the specific careers you have selected. Look in the library card catalog and the indexes under the titles of your proposed careers, or career. You can find information also under such headings as "Careers," "Professions," "Occupations," and "Vocational Information." Many trade and professional associations have published career materials which may be helpful to you in matching your self-inventory to occupational requirements. Magazines are another source of up-to-date career information. Patton and Steiner remark that "a magazine article is as fresh as the new material which it offers." [6] Some magazine articles contain personal accounts of young people and their career choices. One such article describes young people in challenging jobs that do not require a college degree. [7]

Means to Achieve Your Career Goal

In his discussion of career planning, Munschauer noted that "when goals have been set, and ends determined, there is the matter of means." [8] The major means to achieving your career goal will be

getting the education required for it. In your study of careers and the matching of your abilities and interests to career requirements, you should have determined the kind of education you will need. You should have asked yourself these very important questions: What am I willing to do in preparation for a career? Am I willing to make the sacrifice that a good education requires?

Once you have narrowed your career choices, you should plan your educational program in relation to this career choice. If your career goal requires a college education, you must be sure to include in your high school program those courses necessary to meet the admission requirements of the college or university of your choice. You should consider at least three colleges or universities which are accredited in your special career program, for, as Patton and Steiner have noted, "You may not be accepted by your first choice." [9]

Lack of needed funds should not discourage you from seeking the education or training necessary to a career. Available student aid is an important part of career planning for many young people. Every year millions of dollars in scholarship money is not used because young people do not know about it. Academic scholarships are available at most colleges and universities. Many industrial and fraternal organizations award college scholarships. Some government scholarships are available. In addition, student loans are growing in importance as an aid to young people in their efforts to get the education and training needed for a career. The importance of loans in career planning is emphasized in the following statement:

> The growth of educational loans ranging from small private loan funds, as well as those loans offered through the National Defense Education Act (NDEA), has made it possible for hundreds of thousands of young people to borrow their way to a college, business school, or vocational education. [10]

A magazine article describes the Work-Study Program in which "students earn while they learn." [11] There are nearly a half-million students working on or off campus in this program, which is jointly supported by the Federal Government, colleges, and off-campus employers. (continued)

---

[6] Evelyn D. Patton and Dora W. Steiner, Let's Look at Your Future (Metuchen, N.J.: The Scarecrow Press, Inc., 1966), p. 243.

[7] "Careers Without College," Ebony (July, 1970), pp. 120-122.

[8] Munschauer, p. 38.

[9] Patton and Steiner, p. 233.

[10] Feingold and Swerdloff, p. 71.

[11] "All in a Day's Work-Study," American Education (January-February, 1970), p. 13.

PHASE 2: BASIC TYPING APPLICATIONS

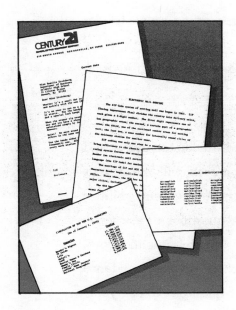

■ The major objectives of Phase 2 are to learn to center copy attractively, to arrange and type tables, to compose as you type, to type personal/business letters, to prepare outlines, and to arrange and type manuscripts of both informal and formal reports. In addition, you will improve basic skills, learn how to erase and correct errors, to divide words, to prepare carbon copies, to type special symbols, and to apply your skill in typing script and rough-draft problems.

Standard Machine Adjustments:

1. Line: 70 (left margin, center — 35; right, at end of scale).
2. Spacing: SS sentence drills; DS ¶s; space problems as directed.

UNIT 7 — LESSONS 40-51

Centering / Tabulating / Composing

■ LESSON 40

40A ■ CONDITIONING PRACTICE 8 at least twice SS; then 1' comparative writings on Lines 1 and 4

Alphabet	We have checked the six very old quill pens Jan bought from Ziegler's.
Figures	I said, "The quiz will be on May 6 covering pages 35-149 and 168-270."
Figure/symbol	Ed paid a $72.90 premium on a $5,000 insurance policy (dated 4/13/68).
Fluency	A man is at his best when he is doing his best at work he can do best.

Return without looking up

| 1 | 2 | 3 | 4 | 5 | 6 | 7 | 8 | 9 | 10 | 11 | 12 | 13 | 14 |

40B ■ HORIZONTAL CENTERING: LINES 15 twice (Half sheets; DS; begin on Line 9)

Get Ready to Center

1. Insert paper with left edge at zero.
2. Move left margin stop to 0, right margin stop to end of scale.
3. Clear all tab stops.
4. Set a tab stop at horizontal center of paper.

How to Center

1. Tabulate to center of paper; from center, backspace *once* for each *two* letters, figures, spaces, or punctuation marks in the line: as ST (backspace) EP (backspace) S space (backspace).
2. Do not backspace for an odd or leftover stroke.
3. Begin to type where the backspacing ends.

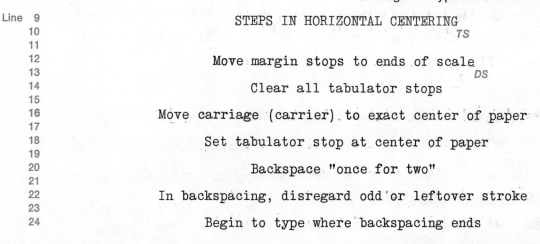

```
Line  9          STEPS IN HORIZONTAL CENTERING
     10                                          TS
     11
     12          Move margin stops to ends of scale
     13                                          DS
     14              Clear all tabulator stops
     15
     16      Move carriage (carrier) to exact center of paper
     17
     18          Set tabulator stop at center of paper
     19
     20              Backspace "once for two"
     21
     22      In backspacing, disregard odd or leftover stroke
     23
     24           Begin to type where backspacing ends
```

To triple-space when the machine is set for double spacing, (1) operate the carriage return once and (2) space forward one line space by hand, using the cylinder knob.

the circumstances under which you will live. There are three prime requisites for a career decision. The first requisite is self-understanding; the second is to know the requirements of the career in which you have an interest; and the third is to take the steps to achieve your career goal.

Understanding Yourself

If you could see yourself as others see you, the task of self-understanding would not be so difficult. Writing down facts and opinions about yourself will make your task easier. This listing will enable you to compare your characteristics and abilities more objectively with the requirements of a career. Pertinent questions to ask yourself, according to Sifferd, include those of physical fitness, mental qualifications, educational qualifications, and personality.[4] Also, your teachers or your guidance counselor should be able to help you with some of the specific questions to ask yourself. There are "choosing-a-career" books in most libraries. Such books often contain questionnaires which may guide you in your self-analysis. These books are listed in the card catalog under such titles as "Vocational Guidance," "Careers," or "Occupations."

Aptitude tests have been designed to help you look within yourself for career clues. Such tests can provide valuable information about such things as your aptitudes, abilities, skills, and interests. All test results, however, should be evaluated with caution. Feingold and Swerdloff indicate that "No tests, by themselves, will tell you what you should do . . . . Tests can, however, provide clues to narrow down the possible fields."[5] In other words, tests are tools for guidance, not answers. Your teacher or counselor may utilize these tools in assisting you with your self-appraisal. In addition, there are testing services which are available to you; however, they usually charge a fee for their services. In making your self-analysis, be sure (1) to consider actual work experiences you may have had and (2) to talk, if possible, with persons doing work in which you are interested.

When you have completed your self-inventory, you are ready to compare your personal characteristics, interests, and aptitudes with occupational or career requirements.

Career Requirements

Your next step in choosing a career is to investigate the careers which seem to match your self-inventory. A good place to start may be the <u>Dictionary of Occupational</u>

——————————————— DS   SS

[4] Calvin S. Sifferd, <u>Selecting an Occupation</u> (Bloomington, Ill.: McKnight & McKnight Publishing Company, 1962), p. 130. DS

[5] Feingold and Swerdloff, p. 15.

40C ■ PROBLEM TYPING: CENTERED ANNOUNCEMENTS [17] (Half sheets)

1. Place typed copy of 40B, page 67, beside your typewriter for easy reference.
2. Follow those steps in typing Problems 1 and 2.

Problem 1: On a half sheet, center each line of the announcement at the right. Begin on Line 13. Use single spacing (SS).

Problem 2: Repeat Problem 1, double-spaced (DS). Begin on Line 11. TS after heading.

	Words
WALNUT CREEK PLAYERS	4
TS	
announce casting tryouts for	10
"Sound of Music"	13
3:30-5:30 p.m. in the	18
Little Theater of the Music Building	25
Monday-Friday, October 2-6	30

40D ■ HORIZONTAL CENTERING: COLUMNS [10] twice (Drill sheet)

LEARN: Columns in tables can be spaced and centered horizontally in the same way individual lines are centered. Think of the columns of words in the drill below and the spaces between columns as *one continuous line of letters and spaces to be centered.*

GET READY TO TYPE: Center and type the following columns of words, leaving 6 spaces between columns. Follow these steps:

1. Move margin stops to ends of scale and clear all tabulator stops.

2. Move carriage (carrier) to center of paper; from that point backspace *once* for each *two* letters and each *two* spaces (#'s) in Line 1, as follows:

ke | ep | ## | ## | ## | yo | ur | ## | ## | ## | ey | es | etc.

3. Set left margin stop where backspacing ends.

4. From left margin, space forward *once* for *each* letter in Col. 1 and for each space to be left between Col. 1 and Col. 2. Set tab stop there for Col. 2. Set remaining tab stops in the same way.

keep	your	eyes	here	each	time
were	they	take	four	send	name

KEY | 4 | 6 | 4 | 6 | 4 | 6 | 4 | 6 | 4 | 6 | 4 |

■ LESSON 41

41A ■ CONDITIONING PRACTICE [8] at least twice SS; then 1' comparative writings on Lines 2 and 3

Alphabet	Jane Peyton was quite lax about the exact zone marking for deliveries.	*Body erect;*
Figures	My car license is 8640BB and my Social Security number is 728-15-3935.	*fingers curved*
Figure/symbol	Section 4, pages 230-259, of Volume XV (6/18/71), covers those points.	
Fluency	It is now your duty to find a remedy for each of your typing problems.	

| 1 | 2 | 3 | 4 | 5 | 6 | 7 | 8 | 9 | 10 | 11 | 12 | 13 | 14 |

41B ■ HORIZONTAL CENTERING [10] (Half sheets; DS; begin each drill on Line 12)

Drill 1

QUEEN CITY CHOIR
TS

offers folk music concert

November 1, 8:30 p.m.

Emery Auditorium

Student Admission: $1.25

Drill 2

						Words
EASY WORDS						2
TS						
to	do	am	work	name	turn	7
so	by	an	male	hand	town	12
it	me	go	lend	with	kept	17
is	or	us	form	pair	down	21

KEY | 2 | 6 | 2 | 6 | 2 | 6 | 4 | 6 | 4 | 6 | 4 |

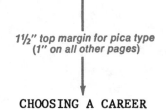

1½" top margin for pica type
(1" on all other pages)

CHOOSING A CAREER

One of life's greatest satisfactions is a career that "fits." In choosing your career goal, therefore, you should 1½" "be honest with yourself." Munschauer supports this state- 1" ment when he says, "Of all the things that comprise a career choice, the human factors and attitudes shouldn't be over-looked."[1] It is important that you choose a career you like.

You cannot expect to drift into a career that fits. You must choose it deliberately. You will need to match your ap-titudes, interests, and personal qualifications with a career that requires your abilities and interests. Feingold and Swerdloff emphasize this point in the following statement:

Indent 5 spaces from left and right margins; SS

> Before you can choose anything intelligently, you must have some basis for your choice. Choos-ing without knowing is merely taking a chance, as you do when you reach into a grab bag for a prize. Given several opportunities, you must know enough about each to select the one that suits your needs better than the others, stimulates your interest, and tests your sense of values. Otherwise, you will choose blindly.[2]

They suggest, also, that choosing a career "may be the first really complex adult decision you will be called upon to face."[3] This decision will determine the pattern of your life, the type of friends you have, where you will live, and

---

[1]John L. Munschauer, "The Anatomy of a Career," Journal of College Placement (February-March, 1970), p. 35.

[2]S. Norman Feingold and Sol Swerdloff, Occupations and Careers (New York: McGraw-Hill Book Co., Inc., 1969), p. 2.

[3]Feingold and Swerdloff, p. 2.

Approximately 1"

1

½"

PICA

41C ■ BELL CUE DRILL 〔12〕 (Half sheet; SS; begin on Line 7)

1. Set the margin stops for an *exact* 60-space line (left: center − 30; right, center + 30).
2. Type the sentence below at a slow rate in a single line; stop as soon as the typewriter bell rings. Instead of typing the remainder of the sentence, type the figures 12345 (etc.) until the carriage locks.

    Set stop for bell to ring 3 spaces
    before desired line ending.

3. To set the right margin stop so the bell will ring as a warning signal 3 spaces before the desired line ending, move the right margin stop to the right as many spaces as necessary (usually exact line ending plus 3 to 7 spaces). REMEMBER THIS NUMBER.
4. Type the sentence again to check the accuracy of the setting of the right margin stop.
5. Using the same margin settings, type the following ¶. Be guided by the bell to return. If the carriage locks, depress the margin-release key and complete the word; then return. *The line endings will not be the same as those below.*

Typewriters vary greatly in the number of strokes that can be typed between the point where the bell rings and where the carriage locks. Soon you will learn to divide words at line endings; but for now, you will release the margin, if necessary, and complete the word at the end of the line. A word of one to five letters can be added if the bell rings at the end of a word.

41D ■ PROBLEM TYPING: SYLLABLE IDENTIFICATION 〔20〕 twice (Half sheets; SS; begin on Line 11)

■ It is often necessary to divide words at line endings to aid in maintaining a fairly even right-hand margin. The first step in word division is syllable identification.

1. Move margin stops to ends of carriage scale; clear all tabulator stops.
2. From horizontal center, backspace *once* for each *two* letters in longest word in each column and for each *two* spaces to be left between columns. *Set left margin stop at this point.*
3. From the left margin, space forward *once* for *each* letter in the longest word in Column 1 and *once* for *each* space to be left between Columns 1 and 2. Set a tab stop for Column 2 where the forward spacing ends. Set other tab stops in the same way. *Check your tab stop settings with the key beneath the problem.*
4. Center and type the heading; then triple-space.
5. Type the first word in Col. 1; tabulate to Col. 2 and type the first word with the diagonals to show division points between syllables; tabulate to Col. 3 and type the first word; tabulate to Col. 4 and type the first word of Col. 3 but *with the diagonals between syllables.*
6. Type the remaining words in a similar manner.
7. Verify syllable identification with the dictionary or with your teacher. Make handwritten corrections. Retype the problem.

SYLLABLE IDENTIFICATION

TS

				Words
				5
accomplish	ac/com/plish	acceptance	ac/cep/tance	14
betterment	bet/ter/ment	bottleneck		24
certified	cer/ti/fied	considers		33
misspelled	mis/spelled	different		42
multiplied	mul/ti/plied	filmstrips		51
producing	pro/duc/ing	happiness		60
restaurant	res/tau/rant	journalist		70
submitted	sub/mit/ted	management		79
vacations	va/ca/tions	transistor		88
waterworks	wa/ter/works	usefulness	use/ful/ness	97
KEY	10	6	12	6	10	6	12

119B ■ SKILL-TRANSFER TYPING: STATISTICAL ROUGH DRAFT [15] (Line: 70) two 5' writings; proofread; determine GWAM

	GWAM	
	1'	5'

¶1 A study of 225 ordinary ∧copy 5' writings of second-~~half~~ *semester* first-typing year ~~typewriting~~ students has shown a total of 1,673 errors, of which *and 315 were errors in another area* 1,358 were keyboard errors. Of the 1,358 keyboard errors, 56.1% *(and 43.9% were right-hand.)* were left-hand errors, ~~Approximately~~ 48.5% of the 1,358 keyboard *Generally,* errors were made on the third bank, 30.5% were made on the home bank, and 21.0% were made on the first bank. Of the 315 other area errors, 60.3% were ~~space~~ *spacing*, 19.4% were ~~shift key~~ *shifting*, and another 19.4% were *various* ~~miscellaneous~~ reading errors *of one kind or another.*

13 / 3 49
26 / 5 52
46 / 9 56
64 / 13 59
78 / 16 62
93 / 19 65
105 / 21 67
115 / 23 69

¶2 The fact that *many* students do not type with *proper* form ~~was probably a~~ *may be an explanation* ~~reason~~ for a sizeable percentage of the 1,358 keyboard errors. In particular, 27.4% of these were adjacent-key errors, of which 65.7% were made with the left *hand* and 34.3% were made with the right hand. *or uniform keystroking* Not using even ~~stroking~~ pressure was a reason for 12.7% of the errors, *inferior* and ~~poor~~ typing response patterns ~~probably were a cause of~~ *may have been a reason for* another 20.9%. *Students may not realize that such errors as these may be the result of hand-and-arm movement which forces the fingers out of proper position.*

13 / 26 72
28 / 29 75
41 / 31 78
82 / 40 86
101 / 43 90
116 / 46 93
117 / 46 93

119C ■ LEFTBOUND MANUSCRIPT WITH FOOTNOTES* [30]

Full sheets ■ center heading over line of writing ■ top margin first page, 1½″ pica or 2″ elite ■ top margin second and succeeding pages, 1″ ■ left margin, 1½″ ■ right margin, 1″ ■ bottom margin, about 1″ ■ number all pages in proper position ■ correct your errors

*You are not expected to complete the report in this lesson; additional time is provided in Lessons 120-123.

Type in leftbound manuscript form the report given on the following pages. The first page of the manuscript in pica type is shown in arranged form on page 185; other pages are given in printed form.

One acceptable form for typing footnotes is illustrated. Number the footnotes as shown in the report. (Footnotes may be numbered consecutively or started anew on each page.)

NOTE. To save space for the footnotes and leave an inch for the bottom margin, *do this:* Make a light pencil mark at the right edge of the sheet about 1″ from the bottom. As you type each footnote reference, place another pencil mark 3 or 4 spaces above the previous mark. This will reserve about 3 spaces for typing each footnote. Erase these pencil marks when the page has been completed.

LESSON 42

42A ■ CONDITIONING PRACTICE 8 at least twice SS; then 1' comparative writings on Lines 1 and 4

Alphabet	With superb form, five or six good ski jumpers whizzed quickly by Nan. *Wrists low*
Figures	The store moved from 3948 North 56th Street to 1270 Degas Place, West.
Figure/symbol	His 4/8/72 wire read: "36 copies Modern Math (Stock #958)––less 10%."
Fluency	That man who keeps both his feet firmly on the ground never falls far.

| 1 | 2 | 3 | 4 | 5 | 6 | 7 | 8 | 9 | 10 | 11 | 12 | 13 | 14 |

42B ■ BELL CUE DRILL 5 (Drill sheet; line: 60; DS; ¶ indention: 5; begin on Line 7)

1. Set the margin stops for a 60-space line (left: center − 30; right: center + 30 + 3 to 7 spaces [according to your own typewriter]).

2. Type the following ¶. To return, listen for the bell. Use margin release if necessary. Do not divide words.

To avoid having the right margin ragged, you must often divide words *Wrists low* at line endings. You should, nevertheless, divide words only when absolutely necessary. You should avoid dividing words at the ends of more than two consecutive lines, and you should not divide the last word on a page.

42C ■ VERTICAL CENTERING 20 twice (Half sheets; line: 60; SS)

VERTICAL CENTERING: MATHEMATICAL METHOD

1. Count the lines and blank line spaces needed. (Count 2 blank line spaces for triple spacing after main or secondary heading and 1 blank line space between double-spaced lines.)

2. Subtract lines needed from 66 for a full sheet or from 33 for a half sheet.

3. Divide remainder by 2 to get top and bottom margins. If a fraction results, disregard it. Space down from top edge of paper *1 more than number of lines to be left in top margin.*

NOTE: For *reading position,* which is above exact vertical center, subtract 2 from exact top margin.

DO: Type the guides at the right, line for line, in the general style shown at the right.

1. Center the list vertically, following the method given above.

2. Center horizontally and type the main heading in ALL CAPS.

3. SS the enumerated items; DS between them.

4. After typing "1." in Item 1, reset the margin stop as indicated. Use the margin release; backspace four times to type remaining numbers.

Problem Solution:

Lines available:	33
Lines used:	16
For top and bottom margins:	17

17 ÷ 2 = 8 (disregarding the fraction); therefore, start heading on Line 9.

Line	
9	
10	**GUIDES FOR ERASING**
11	*2 spaces* TS
11	┌──Reset margin
12	1. Use a plastic shield and a typewriter (hard) eraser.
13	DS
14	2. Lift the paper bail and turn the paper forward if the
15	error is on the upper two thirds of the page or backward
16	if it is on the lower third.
17	
18	3. Move the carriage (carrier) to the left or right as far as
19	you can so the eraser crumbs will not clog the mechanism.
20	
21	4. Erase lightly––don't "scrub" the error. Blow eraser par-
22	ticles away as you erase.
23	
24	5. Return the paper to writing position and type.

118C ■ TECHNIQUE IMPROVEMENT: READING THE COPY [9] type 3 times; then three 1' speed writings

Try to read | and type | this copy | in these | word groups. | Make a quick
typing response | to each | word group. | Think the | word groups | as they
are typed. | This is | another way | to force | your speed | to higher levels.

118D ■ LEFTBOUND MANUSCRIPT WITH FOOTNOTES [30]

1. Study the illustration and the paragraphs on footnote form.
2. Type the following 1-page leftbound manuscript.
3. Proofread; correct; retype from your rough draft.

Full sheet: Center heading over line of writing
TS after heading; DS copy
Margins—
Left: 1½″; Right: 1″
Top: 1½″—if pica type is used
        2″—if elite type is used
SS before and DS after the underline separating copy
and footnotes

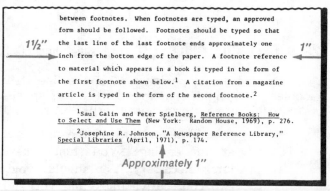

Footnote Placement and Style

FOOTNOTE FORM REVIEW

In school, you will often have to prepare themes, reports, or term papers which require library research. When you quote from the written material of others or use ideas of an author, you must acknowledge the source of your information. This is done by means of a footnote reference with the footnote itself usually appearing at the bottom of the page on which the reference is made.

In this brief manuscript page, you will review the proper order and form of footnotes by typing the two footnotes listed below. Note that the footnotes are separated from the manuscript by a dividing line 1½ inches long. The first line of a footnote is indented to the paragraph point and is preceded without spacing by a reference figure raised one-half line space. Footnotes are single-spaced with double spacing between footnotes. When footnotes are typed, an approved form should be followed. Footnotes should be typed so that the last line of the last footnote ends approximately one inch from the bottom edge of the paper. A footnote reference to material which appears in a book is typed in the form of the first footnote shown below.[1] A citation from a magazine article is typed in the form of the second footnote.[2]

[1] Saul Galin and Peter Spielberg, Reference Books: How to Select and Use Them (New York: Random House, 1969), p. 276.

[2] Josephine R. Johnson, "A Newspaper Reference Library," Special Libraries (April, 1971), p. 174.

■ LESSON 119

119A ■ CONDITIONING PRACTICE [5] each line 3 times: slowly, faster, top speed

Alphabet   Jolly housewives made inexpensive meals using quick-frozen vegetables.   *Uniform (even)*
Figure/symbol   The test for April 8 will cover pages 64-75, 98-130, 152-239, and 402.   *stroking*
Adjacent keys   As we drew near, a weaverbird wasted little time in vacating her nest.
Fluency   Keep the right thumb close to the space bar in order to space quickly.
| 1 | 2 | 3 | 4 | 5 | 6 | 7 | 8 | 9 | 10 | 11 | 12 | 13 | 14 |

42D ■ PROBLEM TYPING: SYLLABLE IDENTIFICATION [17] twice (Half sheets; SS)

1. Review the steps for placement of columns in 41D, page 69. Then determine and set stops for horizontal placement of the following columns.
2. Review the steps in vertical centering given in 42C, page 70. Then determine the line on which to center and type the heading of the problem.
3. Center and type the heading; then triple-space.
4. Type the first word in Col. 1; tabulate to Col. 2 and type the first word with diagonals to show division points between syllables; type Cols. 3 and 4 in a similar manner.
5. Type the remaining words in the same way.

SYLLABLE IDENTIFICATION

TS

				Words
				5
advertised	ad/ver/tised	accounting	ac/count/ing	16
chalkboard	chalk/board	beginning		23
difference	dif/fer/ence	candidate		33
emphasized	em/pha/sized	deductions		42
hundredth	hun/dredth	financial		51
newspapers	news/pa/pers	happened		59
possessed	pos/sessed	lubricants		68
recommends	rec/om/mends	microfilms		78
succeeding	suc/ceed/ing	opponents		87
supersedes	su/per/sedes	photostats	pho/to/stats	97

KEY	10	6	12	6	10	6	12

■ LESSON 43

43A ■ CONDITIONING PRACTICE [8] at least twice SS; then 1' comparative writings on Lines 2 and 3

Alphabet	The audience was quite amazed by the report Felix Kline gave the jury.
Figures	Flight 690 with 74 men was due at 10:58 p.m. but arrived at 12:34 a.m.
Figure/symbol	Brown & Decker's C.O.D. Order #809-6 (dated 10/23) amounts to $746.59.
Fluency	All workers can do a lot more through push than they can through pull.

Quick, snap strokes

| 1 | 2 | 3 | 4 | 5 | 6 | 7 | 8 | 9 | 10 | 11 | 12 | 13 | 14 |

43B ■ VERTICAL CENTERING [15]

Type the problem of 42D, above, on a full sheet, double-spaced, in reading position. (See 42C, page 70, for *reading position* placement.)

43C ■ ERASING DRILL [10] (Line: 60; DS)

Type the sentences as they are shown below; do not type the numbers. Then study the guides for erasing given at the right. Erase and correct each error in your copy.

1 Draw a blueprint fro superiority.

2 Get ready to wrok promptyl.

3 Always practice wiht a purpose.

4 Learn ot wokr with control.

5 Accuracy is needed by all workres.

GUIDES FOR ERASING

1. Use a plastic shield and a typewriter (hard) eraser.
2. Lift the paper bail and turn the paper forward if the error is on the upper two thirds of the page or backward if it is on the lower third.
3. Use the margin release, and move the carriage to the left or right as far as you can so eraser crumbs will not clog the mechanism. (Ignore this step on the Selectric.)
4. Erase lightly––don't "scrub" the error. Blow eraser particles away as you erase.
5. Return the paper to writing position and type.

typing that is not to be erased. If the erasure is to be made on the upper two thirds of the paper, turn the cylinder forward; if on the lower third of the paper, turn the cylinder backward so that the paper will not slip out of the typewriter as you erase the error.

Disadvantages. A rubber eraser must be used with care as it is possible to rub a hole in the paper. Also, eraser crumbs must be brushed away from the typewriter because if they fall into the type basket they can cause sticky key action.

Correction Paper

Process. Correction paper covers (masks) the error with a powder-like substance. Correction paper comes in colors to match the kinds of paper commonly in use in the business office—white, blue, pink, yellow, etc.

Types of correction paper. Correction paper is available in several types, among which are the following: (1) correction tape (reel-type dispensers) and (2) correction paper strips. A slightly different type of correction paper is available for making corrections on carbons. The latter type of correction paper also is available in a variety of colors.

Method to use. Follow the steps outlined below:
1. Backspace to the beginning of the error.
2. Insert the correction tape or paper strip behind the typewriter ribbon and in front of the error.
3. Retype the error exactly as you made it. In this step, powder from the correction paper is pressed by force of the keystroke into the form of the error, thus masking it.
4. Remove the correction paper; backspace to the point where the correction is to be made and type the correction.

Disadvantages. The powder correction can rub off and expose the original error. Also, at the present time, correction-paper corrections may not be satisfactory when copies are to be made of an original by a photocopy process. In some instances, the original error may show through on the copies.

Correction Fluid

Process. Correction fluid covers or masks the error with a penetrating liquid which leaves an opaque enamel-like substance on the paper. Correction fluid is available in colors to match paper commonly in use in the business office.

Type. Correction fluid is packaged in a small bottle with an applicator brush attached to the inside of the cap. A thinner liquid can be used for thinning the correction fluid if it thickens.

Method. Here are the steps to follow when correction fluid is used:
1. Turn the paper up a few spaces.
2. Shake the correction fluid bottle; then remove the applicator from the bottle; daub excess liquid on inside of bottle opening.
3. Apply liquid sparingly to error by a touching action so as to cover entire error.
4. Return applicator to bottle and tighten cap; blow on error to speed drying process.
5. When liquid is dry, type the correction.

Disadvantages. With the passage of time, the enamel mask may crack or peel, exposing the error or, even more serious, causing the correction to be lost. For this reason, this error correction method is not acceptable for copy that is to be stored for long periods of time, such as in the archives of a library. Correction liquid must be dry before the correction is typed, or the liquid will stick to the type face and clog it.

■ LESSON 118

118A ■ CONDITIONING PRACTICE [5] each line 3 times: slowly, faster, top speed

Alphabet	Jack, Roxanne, and Pam will study vigorously for the big zoology quiz. *Finger-reach action*
Figure/symbol	The purchase price is $14,675.89 plus 3% sales tax and 20% excise tax.
Shift keys	Refer the papers to Miss Jan Q. O'Brien, secretary to McCrae & McGill.
Fluency	One of the heaviest loads to carry may be a bundle of bad work habits.

| 1 | 2 | 3 | 4 | 5 | 6 | 7 | 8 | 9 | 10 | 11 | 12 | 13 | 14 |

118B ■ IMPROVING ACCURACY [6] type a 1' writing on each line of 118A, above, for accuracy

43D ■ PROBLEM TYPING: WORD DIVISION [17] (Full sheet; line: 60; SS)

1. Type the main heading centered horizontally on Line 14 *(reading position)*.
2. After typing "1." in Item 1, reset the margin 2 spaces to the right of the period. To type the remaining numbers, depress the margin release and backspace 4 spaces into the left margin. *Erase and correct any errors you make as you type.* If time permits, retype the problem.

Words

GUIDES FOR WORD DIVISION   6

2 spaces   —Reset margin   TS

1. Divide a word between syllables only; as in-ter-views,   20
will-ing, suc-cess-ful, fea-si-ble. To indicate the   37
division of a word, type a hyphen at the end of the line;   49
type the rest of the word on the following line.   59

Use margin release and backspace →
2. Do not divide a word of five or fewer letters; as, enter.   73

3. Do not divide from the remainder of the word: 84

2 spaces
     a. A one-letter syllable at the beginning or end of a   94
        word; as, across, steady.   101

     b. A two-letter syllable at the end of a word; for exam-   112
        ple, greater, friendly.   119

4. If the final consonant in a word is doubled when adding a   132
suffix, divide between the double letters; as in begin-   143
ning, admit-ted. Divide between the double letters, also,   156
when a root word ends in a doubled letter and one of those   168
letters becomes a part of the final syllable when adding   179
a suffix; as in exces-sive, discus-sion.   189

5. Divide after a one-letter syllable within a word, as sepa-   203
rate, unless the word ends with able, ible, or ical (two-   218
syllable endings that must be kept as a unit); as, depend-   230
able. If two one-letter syllables come together, however,   242
divide between them; as, evalu-ation.   252

6. Avoid dividing initials, numbers, or abbreviations. Ini-   265
tials or a given name may be separated from a surname,   276
and a date may be separated between the day and the year.   288
In these instances, however, the hyphen is not used.   299

NOTE: For more complicated division problems, refer to a handbook, such as *Word Division Manual* by Silverthorn and Perry, which shows appropriate points for word division.

ORAL CHECKUP ON WORD DIVISION

According to the word division guides given above, where would you divide these words?

above	beauty	financial	unified
abrupt	controlling	providing	uniforms
anywhere	deduction	rewritten	vigorous
assessing	economical	forward	within

Center (METHODS OF CORRECTING ERRORS   *∠Triple-space*

In most typewritten ~~work~~ *copy*, errors should be corrected.   Several

methods, *or procedures* that may be used for error correction are given in brief form in

this ~~report~~ *short* report.   *∠Triple-space*

<u>Rubber Typewriter Eraser</u> *underline*

<u>Process</u>.   *By an abrasive action,* The rubber eraser actually removes the typed error from

the paper.

<u>Types of rubber erasers</u>.   Rubber *typewriter* erasers are avail able in several

types: (1) wheel type, with or without a brush *for removing the eraser crumbs from the paper*; (2) pencil types--one

type has a rubber eraser on one end with a brush on the other; another

has a regular *typewriter* eraser on one eid with a *softer* rubber eraser on the other end

for use with carbon copies; *and* (3) electric erasers *similar to those used by draftsmen.*

<u>Method to use</u>.   These are the steps to follow in making error

corrections: *with a rubber eraser :*

1.   Turn the platen or cylinder forward; *(a few spaces)* then move the carriage toe

the extreme right or left. *So that the eraser crumbs will not fall into the machine.*

2.   Move the paper bail out of the way.   pull the *original* sheet forward and place

a card (5 x 3 inches) *or slightly larger* in front of, not behind, the first carbon to protect

the copy from smudges. *as the erasure is made on the original sheet*

3.   Flip the *original* sheet back and made the errasure with a hard eraser.

Brush *or blow* the eraser crumbs off the paper.

4.   Move the *protective* card to a position in front of the second carbon, if

more than one copy is being made. Erase the error on the first carbon

copy, ~~and~~ erase all other errors in a like manner.

5.   Remove the card and type the correction.

When you erase, be careful that your fingers do not smudge the copy as

you hold the paper.   Some typist use an erasure shield to protect the

LESSON 44

44A ■ CONDITIONING PRACTICE 8 at least twice SS; then 1' comparative writings on Lines 1 and 4

Alphabet	James Wexford gained amazing typing skill by improving his techniques. *Quiet hands and arms*
Figures	Jean studied pages 95-170 of Section 2 and pages 184-260 of Section 3.
Figure/symbol	Thea & Lowen's Invoice #873 for $641.50 (less 2%) was paid on the 9th.
Fluency	The auditor is right to make the men pay for the damage to the chairs.

| 1 | 2 | 3 | 4 | 5 | 6 | 7 | 8 | 9 | 10 | 11 | 12 | 13 | 14 |

44B ■ VERTICAL AND HORIZONTAL CENTERING 10

1. Move margin stops to ends of carriage scale; clear all tab stops; set a tab stop at horizontal center.

2. Center the problem vertically (single-spaced) on a half sheet; center each line horizontally.

3. Repeat the problem but center it vertically (double-spaced) on a half sheet; center each line horizontally.

	Words
TIPS FOR TYPISTS *TS*	3
Head up; eyes on copy; feet on floor	11
Wrists relaxed and low; fingers curved	19
Hands hovering quietly over home row	26
Thumb close to or lightly on space bar	34
Quick, snap key stroke and release	41

44C ■ WORD DIVISION AND ERASING 12 (Full sheet; DS)

1. Center the lines vertically (*reading position*), double-spaced. Follow the directions given in Step 2 at the right. *Erase and correct any errors you make as you type.*

2. Type the heading centered horizontally. Type the words in Columns 1 and 2 as shown, in Column 3 with the hyphen to show only acceptable division points.

			Words
WORD DIVISION *TS*			3
ability	a/bil/i/ty	abil-ity	8
amazingly	a/maz/ing/ly		15
chemical	chem/i/cal		21
deductible	de/duct/i/ble		29
erasure	e/ra/sure		34
featuring	fea/tur/ing		41
identify	i/den/ti/fy		47
likelihood	like/li/hood		55
meaningful	mean/ing/ful		62
overloaded	o/ver/load/ed		69
resistance	re/sis/tance		77
successful	suc/cess/ful		84
transcribing	tran/scrib/ing		92
transferring	trans/fer/ring		101
unwritten	un/writ/ten	un-writ-ten	108

KEY | 12 | 8 | 14 | 8 | 14 |

Page Numbers

The first page may or may not be numbered. The number, if used, is centered and typed one-half inch from the bottom edge. Other page numbers, as a general rule, are typed on the fourth line in the upper right corner so that they are approximately even with the right margin; however, if the manuscript or report is to be bound at the top, the page numbers are typed in the first-page position.

Other General Guides

As a general rule, avoid ending a page with one line of a new paragraph, or carrying one line of a paragraph to a new page. This general rule, however, is no longer strictly enforced, even in formal writing.

The regular word-division rules govern the division of words at the ends of lines. Avoid, if possible, dividing words at the ends of more than two consecutive lines, or at the end of a page.

■ LESSON 117

117A ■ CONDITIONING PRACTICE 5 each line 3 times: slowly, faster, top speed

Alphabet	The queerly boxed package of zinc mixtures was delivered just in time.	*Wrists low*
Figure/symbol	Type $4 and 5% and 6¢ and 8' and (90); 123 + 17 = 140; 6 3/4%; 10 7/8.	*and relaxed*
Fractions	Type the following fractions and mixed numbers: ½, ¼, 5¼, 7½, and 9¼.	
Fluency	The chairman of the firm suggested that the statement be mailed to us.	

| 1 | 2 | 3 | 4 | 5 | 6 | 7 | 8 | 9 | 10 | 11 | 12 | 13 | 14 |

117B ■ IMPROVING SPEED/ACCURACY: STATISTICAL COPY 10

1. Type two 2' writings for speed. Compute your average *gwam* rate.
2. Deduct 4 words from your average rate; then type two 2' guided writings at this new rate for control (not more than 1 error in each writing).

All figures are used.

	2' GWAM
An inch of rain over an acre, which is equal to 43,560 square feet,	7
amounts to 6,272,640 cubic inches of water. A gallon contains 231 cubic	14
inches. Therefore, a rainfall of 1 inch over an acre will mean a total	21
of 27,154 gallons of water. A gallon of water weighs about 8.3 pounds.	29
A cubic foot weighs about 62.4 pounds. The weight of a uniform fall of	36
1 inch of rain over an acre is about 226,621 pounds, or 113.3 tons. An	43
inch of snow falling on an acre of ground is equal to about 2,900 gallons	50
of water, the figure varying according to the wetness of the snow.	57

117C ■ UNBOUND MANUSCRIPT: ROUGH DRAFT 35

Full sheets ■ carbon pack ■ DS the ¶s ■ 5-space ¶ indention ■ top margin first page, 1½" ■ side margins, 1" ■ bottom margin, about 1" ■ top margin second and succeeding pages, 1" ■ number all pages in proper position

NOTE: When enumerated items are typed in double-spaced form, they are typed as illustrated on page 181.

1. Study copy on correcting errors (pages 181-182).

2. Assemble a carbon pack (original, carbon paper, and copy sheet).

3. Type material in unbound manuscript form. Make corrections indicated in the copy on next page. Erase and correct all errors.

44D ■ GROWTH INDEX 20 (Line: 70; DS; ¶ indention: 5; type line for line)

1. Type a 3' *control-level* writing. Circle errors. Determine *gwam*.
2. Type a 1' *exploration-level* (speed) writing on each ¶. Determine *gwam*.
3. Type a 1' *control-level* writing on each ¶. Circle errors.
4. Type a 5' *control-level* writing. Circle errors. Determine *gwam*.

All letters are used.

GWAM
3' | 5'

¶ 1
Writing is just one of the many avenues through which we convey our   5 | 3 | 34
ideas to others. The writing process enables us to elicit a desired   9 | 5 | 36
action from people who read what we have written. If we do not obtain   14 | 8 | 39
the desired response, our effort is ineffective.   17 | 10 | 41

¶ 2
The better we put our thoughts into words, the more likely we are   21 | 13 | 44
to persuade the reader to do what we want. If our messages ramble, are   26 | 16 | 47
not clear, or include poor grammar, we increase the chance of having our   31 | 19 | 50
reputation jeopardized and our ideas rejected.   34 | 21 | 51

¶ 3
The final copy of a message must quickly convey its basic thought   39 | 23 | 54
in a clear, exact manner. No reader should have to puzzle over its   43 | 26 | 57
meaning. All features of style and presentation ought to be designed to   48 | 29 | 60
enhance the meaning instead of to distract from it.   51 | 31 | 62

3' GWAM | 1 | 2 | 3 | 4 | 5 |
5' GWAM | 1 | 2 | 3 |

■ LESSON 45

45A ■ CONDITIONING PRACTICE 8 at least twice SS; then 1' comparative writings on Lines 2 and 3

Alphabet	C. J. Downey asked to be given a week to reply to their tax quiz form. *Finger-action stroking*
Figures	We sold 825 typing, 630 bookkeeping, and 147 shorthand books on May 9.
Figure/symbol	Order #1896 (File 754-2) must be shipped to Day and O'Dell by June 30.
Fluency	Keith can handle all the problems of the formal visit of the chairman.

| 1 | 2 | 3 | 4 | 5 | 6 | 7 | 8 | 9 | 10 | 11 | 12 | 13 | 14 |

45B ■ WORD DIVISION AND ERASING 12

1. Type ¶s 1 and 2 of 44D, above, with the margins set for an exact 60-space line, dividing words and correcting your errors as necessary.

2. Using a 60-space line, type a 5' writing on the ¶s of 44D. Be guided by the bell to make the return. Divide words as necessary.

116C ■ UNBOUND MANUSCRIPT WITHOUT FOOTNOTES 30

1. Study the illustrations and the paragraphs on manuscript or report form on this page and page 180.
2. Type the unbound manuscript as directed at the right. Indent the enumerated items 5 spaces from the left and right margins; space them as illustrated.

NOTE: Make a light pencil mark at the right edge of the page about 1″ from the bottom edge (and again at 1½″) or use a lined backing sheet to remind you to leave a 1″ bottom margin.

> Full sheets ■ DS the ¶s ■ 5-space ¶ indention ■ top margin first page, 2″ ■ side margins, 1″ ■ bottom margin, about 1″ ■ top margin second page, 1″ ■ type page numbers in proper position

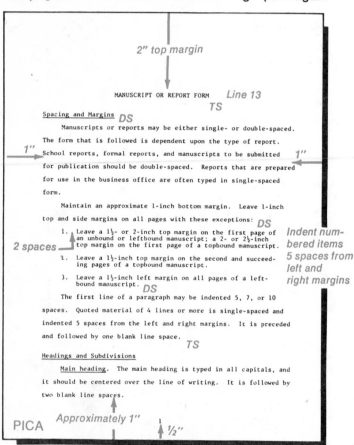

**First Page of Unbound Manuscript
Without Footnotes**

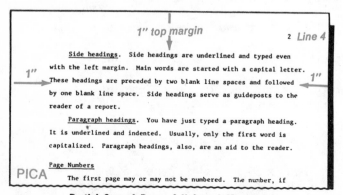

Partial Second Page of Unbound Manuscript

MANUSCRIPT OR REPORT FORM TS

Spacing and Margins DS

Manuscripts or reports may be either single- or double-spaced. The form that is followed is dependent upon the type of report. School reports, formal reports, and manuscripts to be submitted for publication should be double-spaced. Reports that are prepared for use in the business office are often typed in single-spaced form.

Maintain an approximate 1-inch bottom margin. Leave 1-inch top and side margins on all pages with these exceptions:

1. Leave a 1½- or 2-inch top margin on the first page of an unbound or leftbound manuscript; a 2- or 2½-inch top margin on the first page of a topbound manuscript.
2. Leave a 1½-inch top margin on the second and succeeding pages of a topbound manuscript.
3. Leave a 1½-inch left margin on all pages of a leftbound manuscript.

The first line of a paragraph may be indented 5, 7, or 10 spaces. Quoted material of 4 lines or more is single-spaced and indented 5 spaces from the left and right margins. It is preceded and followed by one blank line space.

Headings and Subdivisions TS DS

Main heading. The main heading is typed in all capitals, and it should be centered over the line of writing. It is followed by two blank line spaces.

Side headings. Side headings are underlined and typed even with the left margin. Main words are started with a capital letter. These headings are preceded by two blank line spaces and followed by one blank line space. Side headings serve as guideposts to the reader of a report.

Paragraph headings. You have just typed a paragraph heading. It is underlined and indented. Usually, only the first word is capitalized. Paragraph headings, also, are an aid to the reader.

45C ■ PROBLEM TYPING: TWO- AND THREE-COLUMN TABLES ☐30

SUMMARY OF GUIDES FOR HORIZONTAL PLACEMENT OF COLUMNS

1. Preparatory Steps

a. Move margin stops to ends of scale.

b. Clear all tabulator stops.

c. Move carriage (carrier) to center of paper.

d. Decide spacing between columns (if spacing is not specified)—preferably an even number of spaces (4, 6, 8, 10, 12, etc.)

2. Set Left Margin Stop

From center of paper, backspace once for each 2 characters and spaces in longest line of each column and for each 2 spaces to be left between columns. Set the left margin stop at this point.

If the longest item in a column has an uneven number of spaces, couple the last letter of the item with the first space between the columns when backspacing by 2's; as in refer (4) man (4) half:

re|fe|r#|##|#m|an|##|##|ha|lf

3. Set Tabulator Stops

From the left margin, space forward once for each letter, figure, symbol, and space in longest line in the first column and for each space to be left between first and second columns. *Set tab stop at this point for second column.* Follow similar procedure when additional columns are to be typed.

Problem 1: Two-Column Table

Use a half sheet; SS; use the key beneath the problem to check the placement of columns.

Center:

the problem vertically (see p. 70)
the heading horizontally (see p. 67)
the columns (see Guides 2 and 3 above)

		Words
TELEPHONE LIST		3
TS		
Mark C. Alberts	(205) 271-4185	9
Leotis Jackson	(315) 446-7139	15
Bobbi Jo Scott	(806) 742-2172	21
Donna Jean Smith	(815) 753-1177	28
Alex K. Young	(319) 353-4905	33

KEY	16	10	14

Problem 2: Three-Column Table

Use a half sheet; SS; 6 spaces between columns. Center the problem vertically, the heading horizontally, the columns horizontally.

Technique Cue: *Reach* to the tab bar or key without moving the hand out of position. Tabulate from column to column *without looking up.*

			Words
ADDRESS LIST USING TWO-LETTER STATE ABBREVIATIONS			10
	2 spaces TS		
Raymond Childs	2714 Crescent Drive	Erie, PA 16506	20
Marilyn Dawson	3948 Granada Blvd.	Miami, FL 33146	30
Bart Gregory	1438 South Delaware Pl.	Tulsa, OK 74104	41
Becky Izen	2947 Liverpool Road	Gary, IN 46405	51
Matt Liston	1900 East Florence Dr.	Tucson, AZ 85719	61
Mary Riga	One Akers Avenue	Akron, OH 44312	70
Barry Rost	P.O. Box 103	Zap, ND 58580	78
Jerry Tolliver	1756 Hampden Lane, N.E.	Salem, OR 97303	89
Kent Wallace	R.R. 1, Box 48	Huron, SD 57350	98
Marge Xylon	31 Eastover Road	Troy, NY 12180	107

KEY	14	6	23	6	17

Manuscripts / Reports

One of several acceptable ways of typing footnotes is illustrated in this unit. The lessons are designed to help you gain skill in arranging copy in manuscript or report form.

■ LESSON 116

116A ■ CONDITIONING PRACTICE [5] each line 3 times: slowly, faster, top speed

Alphabet	Six women in the valley heard piercing squawks of dozens of blue jays.
Figure/symbol	Was the total of Hartley & Mann's bill $1,586.73, or was it $2,490.75?
Fingers 3, 4	Was it Polly who saw Paul quizzing Wally about eating all the loquats?
Fluency	Try to let the fingers do the typing and your skill will grow rapidly.

Fingers curved and upright

| 1 | 2 | 3 | 4 | 5 | 6 | 7 | 8 | 9 | 10 | 11 | 12 | 13 | 14 |

116B ■ GROWTH INDEX: STRAIGHT COPY [15] two 5' writings; determine GWAM; proofread and circle errors

All letters are used.

	GWAM		
	1'	5'	

¶ 1

What are some of the criticisms that are frequently made of the new office employee? An executive of an insurance company said that nearly ninety percent of all the new employees they hired were poor spellers. This executive indicated, too, that most of these new employees had poor vocabularies. Another frequent criticism was that many young employees often did not do a fair day's work for a fair day's wage. There is no secret to success. Success is the result of doing more than is required by the immediate task. It has frequently been said that the employee who never does any more than he gets paid for, will never get paid for any more than he does.

14	3	53
28	6	56
42	8	59
57	11	62
71	14	65
86	17	68
100	20	71
114	23	73
128	26	76
133	27	77

¶ 2

Other executives said that many workers did not know how to use a dictionary, and they did not proofread all copy carefully before giving it to the employer. These executives said that the new employees did not have desirable work habits, and they often did not take pride in doing a good job. Employers indicated, too, that new typists had poor tabulating skills and did not recognize a need for good English skills. These employers said that they did not expect a young office employee to have all the qualities needed for good job performance, but they would be happy if he had some of them.

14	29	80
28	32	83
43	35	86
58	38	89
73	41	92
86	44	94
101	47	97
114	49	100
120	51	101

1' GWAM | 1 | 2 | 3 | 4 | 5 | 6 | 7 | 8 | 9 | 10 | 11 | 12 | 13 | 14 |
5' GWAM | 1 | 2 | 3 |

LESSON 46

46A ■ CONDITIONING PRACTICE [8] at least twice SS; then 1' comparative writings on Lines 1 and 4

Alphabet   Ron Plevin quickly amazed all of us by his exact knowledge of jujitsu.   *Return quickly without pausing*

Figures   The 175 to 200 young men worked from 8:15 to 6:30 p.m. on May 4 and 9.

Figure/symbol He said, "Study Sections 4-5, pages 230-259, of Volume XVI (6/18/71)."

Fluency   The man who is sure he is right usually speaks with a quiet authority.
               | 1 | 2 | 3 | 4 | 5 | 6 | 7 | 8 | 9 | 10 | 11 | 12 | 13 | 14 |

46B ■ BELL CUE AND WORD DIVISION [7]

1. Type the following ¶ with a 70-space line, double-spaced. Be guided by the bell to return. Divide words as necessary. *Erase and correct errors.*

2. Type the following ¶ with a 50-space line, double-spaced. Be guided by the bell to return. Divide words as necessary. *Erase and correct errors.*

When you compose at the typewriter, x-ing out words is more efficient than erasing them. So when you are asked to compose, x-out and retype words in which you make errors. After your theme, memo, letter, or report is complete, you can type a final copy with errors erased.

46C ■ PROBLEM TYPING: TWO- AND THREE-COLUMN TABLES [23]

Problem 1: Two-Column Table

Center the following problem vertically on a half sheet of paper, single-spaced. Use the key at the foot of the table as an aid in placing the columns.

Problem 2: Three-Column Table

Follow the directions given for Problem 1 at the left. Since the heading is unusually long, type it in two lines centering one beneath the other, SS.

		Words
COMMON BUSINESS ABBREVIATIONS		6
acct.	account	9
bal.	balance	11
b/l	bill of lading	15
cat.	catalogues	18
C.O.D. (cod)	cash on delivery (collect)	26
cwt.	hundred weight	30
dept.	department	34
f.o.b.	freight on board	38
mdse.	merchandise	41
misc.	miscellaneous	45
whsle.	whole sale	49

15	6	26

			Words
ZIP CODE PREFIXES AND TELEPHONE (AREA CODES) FOR MAJOR U.S. CITIES			9 / 13
New York	100	212	16
Chicago	660	312	20
Los Angeles	900	213	24
Philadelphia	119	215	28
Detroit	482	322	31
Houston	770	731	34
Baltimore	202	310	38
Dallas	726	214	41
Washington, D.C.	200	202	46
Indianapolis	363	217	50

16	10	3	10	3

NOTE: The longest entry in each column is color underlined. Do not type the underline.

SELECTED BUSINESS FIRMS

(Home Offices) _TS_

DS

Name	Street	City and State	ZIP Code	Words in Cols.	Total Words
					5
					8
					21
ARA Services, Inc.	2503 Lombard Street	Philadelphia, PA	19146	12	24
Admiral Corporation	3800 Cortland Street	Chicago, IL	60647	24	46
Alexander & Baldwin, Inc.	822 Bishop Street	Honolulu, HI	96813	37	58
The Bendix Corporation	The Bendix Center	Southfield, MI	48075	49	71
Bobbie Brooks, Inc.	3830 Kelley Avenue	Cleveland, OH	44114	61	82
Bristol-Myers Co.	345 Park Avenue	New York, NY	10022	71	93
Capitol Industries, Inc.	1750 N. Vine Street	Los Angeles, CA	90028	85	106
Century Paper Co.	281 Summer Street	Boston, MA	02210	95	117
Control Data Corp.	8100 - 34th Avenue, S.	Minneapolis, MN	55420	108	129
Daniel Industries, Inc.	9720 Katy Road	Houston, TX	77024	119	141
Essex International, Inc.	1601 Wall	Ft. Wayne, IN	46804	130	152
Evans Products Co.	1211 S.W. Salmon St.	Portland, OR	97205	142	163
Florida Steel Corp.	1715 Cleveland Street	Tampa, FL	33606	154	175
Genesco, Inc.	111 Seventh Avenue	Nashville, TN	37206	164	186
Green Giant Company	1100 Summit Avenue	Le Sueur, MN	56058	176	197
Hart Schaffner & Marx	36 S. Franklin	Chicago, IL	60606	187	208
Hercules, Inc.	9th & Market Streets	Wilmington, DE	19801	198	220
Heublein, Inc.	330 New Park Avenue	Hartford, CT	06106	209	230
Hughes Tool Co.	5425 Polk Avenue	Houston, TX	77023	219	241
Kimberly-Clark Corp.	North Lake Street	Neenah, WI	54956	231	252
Lenox, Inc.	Prince & Meade	Trenton, NJ	08638	240	261
Meredith Corporation	1716 Locust Street	Des Moines, IA	50503	252	273
Miles Labs, Inc.	1127 Myrtle	Elkhart, IN	46514	261	283
Northern Natural Gas Co.	2223 Dodge	Omaha, NE	68102	272	293
Ramada Inns, Inc.	3838 E. Van Buren	Phoenix, AZ	85008	282	304
Russell Aluminum Corp.	5761 N.W. 37th Ave.	Miami, FL	33142	294	316
Stokely-Van Camp, Inc.	941 N. Meridian	Indianapolis, IN	46204	307	328
The Tappan Company	180 Park Avenue	Mansfield, OH	44902	318	339
Telephone Utilities, Inc.	Box E	Ilwaco, WA	98624	327	349
Upjohn Co.	7000 Portage Road	Kalamazoo, MI	49002	337	358
VCA Corporation	1720 Fairfield Avenue	Bridgeport, CT	06605	349	370
Varadyne, Inc.	1547 - 18th Street	Santa Monica, CA	90404	359	381

46D ■ COMPOSING AT THE TYPEWRITER [12] (Drill sheet; line: 50; DS)

Drill 1: Type the following sentences, filling in the missing information. X-out and retype words in which you make errors. (See page 76.)

1. My name is (*first, middle, last*).

2. I live in (*names of city and state*).

3. My address is (*house number and street name*).

4. I am (*years and months*) old.

5. I am taking typing in the (*grade in school*).

Drill 2: Answer the following questions, each with a complete sentence. X-out and retype words in which you make errors.

1. What is your favorite sport?

2. Who is your favorite singer?

3. What do you do as a hobby?

4. When do you expect to finish high school?

5. Upon graduation, what do you plan to do?

■ LESSON 47

47A ■ CONDITIONING PRACTICE [8] at least twice SS; then 1' comparative writings on Lines 2 and 3

Alphabet	Cletus W. Knox puzzled us by endeavoring to qualify for the high jump. *Fingers curved and upright*
Figures	Over 290 attended my 3-, 5-, and 7-day workshops on June 4, 8, and 16.
Figure/symbol	Dr. Thomas Keller's contract (#38490) for <u>Finance</u> draws a 15% royalty.
Fluency	Some men profit from experience; others never seem to recover from it.

| 1 | 2 | 3 | 4 | 5 | 6 | 7 | 8 | 9 | 10 | 11 | 12 | 13 | 14 |

47B ■ COMPOSING AT THE TYPEWRITER [10] (Drill sheet; line: 60; DS)

1. Type the ¶ as given at the right. Proofread your copy; circle errors.

2. Without referring to your copy or the textbook, summarize in three or four lines the idea the paragraph conveys. X-out and retype words in which you make errors.

Words

There is value in work--value to the worker as well as — 11
to the one for whom the work is done. The worker who takes — 23
pride in a worthwhile job well done rarely has the desire — 35
to look for bizarre ways to occupy his mind, his hands, or — 46
his leisure hours. — 50

47C ■ CENTERING COLUMNAR HEADINGS [12] once on drill sheet

TO DETERMINE CENTER OF COLUMN: From point at which column begins, space forward *once* for each *two* letters, figures, or spaces in the longest line (the line that requires the most strokes to type). Disregard a leftover character.

TO TYPE COLUMNAR HEADING: From center of column, backspace *once* for each *two* spaces in heading. Begin to type where backspacing ends.

DO: Type the two drills given at the right. Use double spacing. Center drills horizontally.

Drill 1: Spaces between columnar items: 6

<u>Name</u>	<u>Date</u>
C. Paul McCarthy	September 1, 19--

Drill 2: Spaces between columnar items: 10

<u>Bridge</u>	<u>Location</u>
Golden Gate	San Francisco Bay

Problem 3: Special 3-Column Table

Full sheet ■ reading position ■ arrange data as shown ■ 6 spaces between columns

Alertness Cues: Remember to reset tab stops and to forward-space and back-space as needed.

			Words
TEEN-AGERS' INCOME AND SPENDING HABITS			8
(Weekly Average)			11
Classification	Girls	Boys	21
Income	$20.35	$19.15	25
Spending			27
Indent 3 → Clothing	4.50	3.20	31
Grooming	5.00	1.05	34
Movies, dates, etc.	2.05	4.60	40
Cars, gas	1.50	3.40	44
Jewelry, notions	1.55	––	49
Records	.95	.65	53
Magazines, paperbacks	.85	.60	59
Candy, ice cream, etc.	.45	1.20	65
Hobbies	––	.80	69
Miscellaneous	.25	.30	73
Savings	3.25	3.35	77
			81
Source: Rand Youth Poll.			86

■ LESSON 115

115A ■ CONDITIONING PRACTICE [5] each line 3 times SS: slowly, faster, in-between rate

Alphabet Fay saw many zebra and quaint pink ducks in the exciting jungle movie. *Return quickly*

Figure/symbol Send Order #1280-YL ($4,936.70 less 15%) for 4¼ C&B Pine via C&NW R.R.

Quiet hands This is my translation: The incurable itch of writing possesses many.

Fluency It is by our daily work that we make our future what we want it to be.
| 1 | 2 | 3 | 4 | 5 | 6 | 7 | 8 | 9 | 10 | 11 | 12 | 13 | 14 |

115B ■ GROWTH INDEX: STRAIGHT COPY [15]

1. Type a 5′ writing on the ¶s of 114B, page 174, on the *control level* (try to type with not more than 5 errors).

2. Type another 5′ writing. If you made the goal of Step 1, increase your speed on this writing, but try to maintain good control.

115C ■ TABULATING PRODUCTION MEASUREMENT [30]

Time Schedule

Planning and preparing . .	3′
Timed tabulating production .	20′
Proofreading; determining *n-pram*	7′

You are to type the table on page 177 as you are timed for 20 minutes; if you finish the table, start over on a new sheet. Erase and correct all errors you make as you type the table. Proofread your work. Deduct 15 words from total words typed for each uncorrected error; divide remainder by 20 to determine *n-pram* (net production rate a minute).

47D ■ VERTICAL CENTERING: BACKSPACE-FROM-CENTER METHOD ☐10

VERTICAL CENTERING: BACKSPACE-FROM-CENTER METHOD

Basic Rule: From vertical center of paper, roll platen (cylinder) back once for each two lines, two blank line spaces, or line and blank line space to be centered vertically. Ignore odd or leftover line.

1. *To move paper to vertical center,* space down from *top* edge of paper (move paper up):
   a. *Half sheet:* Down 6 TS — 1 SS (Line 17)
   b. *Full sheet:* Down 11 TS + 1 SS (Line 34)

2. *From vertical center:*
   a. *Half sheet,* SS or DS: Follow Basic Rule (back 1 for 2).
   b. *Full sheet,* SS or DS: Follow Basic Rule (back 1 for 2); then back 2 SS for *reading position.*

NOTE: The mathematical method of vertical centering is taught on page 70.

Drill 1: On a half sheet of paper, type the table in exact vertical center, double-spaced, 8 spaces between columns. Use backspace-from-center method for vertical centering.

Drill 2: On a half sheet of paper, type the table in exact vertical center, single-spaced.

CLASS OFFICERS		Words
		3
President	Dan Gezymalla	8
Vice-President	Kathy Kucharski	14
Secretary	Carol Safer	18
Treasurer	Carl Lammers	23

47E ■ PROBLEM TYPING: TABLE WITH COLUMNAR HEADINGS ☐10 (Full sheet; DS; 8 spaces between columns)

Type the following problem in *reading position.* Use either the mathematical method or the backspace-from-center method for vertical centering. *Erase and correct errors.*

			Words
ACADEMY AWARDS IN MOTION PICTURES *TS*			7
Year	Picture	Company *DS*	15
1950	an American in Paris	MGM	21
1952	Greatest Show on Earth	Paramount	28
1953	From Here to Eternity	Columbia	35
1954	On the Waterfront	Columbia	42
1955	Marty	United Artists	47
1956	Around the World in 80 Days	United Artists	57
1957	The Bridge on the River Kwai	Columbia	65
1958	Gigi	MGM	68
1959	Ben-Hur	MGM	71
1960	The Apartment	United Artists	78
1961	West Side Story	United Artists	85
1962	Lawrence of Arabia	Columbia	92
1963	Tom Jones	UA-Lopert Pictures	99
1964	My Fair Lady	Warner Brothers	105
1965	The Sound of Music	20th Century-Fox	114
1966	A Man for All Seasons	Columbia	121
1967	In the Heat of the Night	United Artists	130
1968	Oliver	Columbia	134
1969	Midnight Cowboy	United Artists	141
1970	Patton	20th Century-Fox	147

114C ■ BUILDING SUSTAINED TABULATING SKILL 30

Time Schedule
Planning and preparing . . . 5′
Timed tabulating production . 20′
Proofreading; determining
  g-pram . . . . 5′

Directions for each problem are given with that problem. If you complete the problems before time is called, start over. Plan and prepare for each problem with a minimum of waste time. Have the materials needed ready so that you can move quickly from one problem to the next.

Problem 1: 4-Column Table

Full sheet ■ reading position ■ DS data ■ 4 spaces between columns or headings as noted below

NOTE: In Cols. 3 and 4, use columnar headings as longest lines when backspacing for horizontal centering. When typing table, center columnar entries under the headings.

Alertness Cues: If you are using an electric typewriter, remember to release shift lock when typing apostrophe in the heading line.
  Change tab stops in Cols. 3 and 4 as needed.

WORLD'S HIGHEST BUILDINGS

Building	Location	Height in Feet	Stories	Words
				5
				21
World Trade Center*	New York City	1,353	110	30
Empire State Building	New York City	1,250	102	39
Standard Oil Building*	Chicago	1,136	80	47
John Hancock Center	Chicago	1,107	100	54
Chrysler Building	New York City	1,046	77	63
60 Wall Tower	New York City	950	67	70
Bank of Manhattan	New York City	900	71	77
RCA Building	New York City	850	70	84
U.S. Steel Building	Pittsburgh	841	64	92
Chase Manhattan Plaza	New York City	813	60	102
Pan Am Building	New York City	808	59	108
First National Bank	Chicago	800	60	115
Woolworth Building	New York City	792	60	123
Gaspar Libero	Sao Paulo	787	60	129
				133

* Under construction in 1970.   138

Problem 2: 3-Column Table

Full sheet ■ reading position ■ DS data ■ 8 spaces between columns except as noted below

NOTE: In Col. 3, use columnar heading as longest line when backspacing for horizontal centering; then center columnar entries under heading.

MAJOR WORLD LANGUAGES

Language	Chief Location	Speakers*	Words
			4
			17
Chinese	China	700	21
English	U.S., U.K., Canada	300	27
Russian	U.S.S.R.	200	31
Spanish	Spain, Latin America	165	38
Hindi	India	165	41
Japanese	Japan	100	45
German	Germany, Austria	100	50
Arabic	Middle East	100	55
Bengali	Bangladesh	100	59
Portuguese	Portugal, Brazil	90	66
French	France, Canada	75	71
Italian	Italy	55	74
			78

*In millions.   80

LESSON 48

48A ■ CONDITIONING PRACTICE [8] at least twice SS; then 1' comparative writings on Lines 1 and 4

Alphabet	Boyd Nixon just gave a quick report on rockets that amazed Frank Lowe. *Shift quickly but firmly*
Figures	The data are given in Figures 26 and 27 of Part 14, Unit 39, page 658.
Figure/symbol	As she directed on May 5, I have been typing 1/2 and 1/4--not ½ and ¼.
Fluency	Boredom is not in the work we do, but in ourselves as we do that work.
	| 1 | 2 | 3 | 4 | 5 | 6 | 7 | 8 | 9 | 10 | 11 | 12 | 13 | 14 |

48B ■ COMPOSING AT THE TYPEWRITER [10] (Drill sheet; line: 60; DS)

1. Type the ¶ as given at the right. Proofread your copy; circle errors.

2. Without referring to your copy or the textbook, summarize in three or four lines the idea the paragraph conveys. X-out and retype words in which you make errors.

Words

The needs of society are many and varied. These needs — 11
account in large measure for the jobs that must be done. — 23
While some jobs require more training and skill than others, — 35
it would be wrong to say that the job of the garbage col- — 46
lector is less necessary than that of the stockbroker. — 57

48C ■ ALIGNING FIGURES [10] twice as shown

LEARN: To align columns of figures at the right, space forward or backward as necessary. Set a tab stop for the digit in each column (after the first) that requires the least forward and backward spacing. Do not consider fractions as part of the column; let them extend into between-column space.

MARGIN	+ 17 spaces = TAB	+ 19 spaces = TAB	+ 17 spaces = TAB
↓	↓	↓	↓
604	1483	350	9102
492	→730	314	→627
→65	→45 2/3	→90 5/8	→88
109	2037	←2503	1029
KEY | 3 |	14 | 4 |	14 | 4 |	14 | 4 |

48D ■ SPACING MAIN AND SECONDARY HEADINGS [8] center vertically and horizontally on half sheet

Spacing Main and Secondary Headings: Double-space between main and secondary headings if both are used; triple-space between the last line of the heading (whether main or secondary) and the first line of the columns (or columnar headings).

DO: Have 10 spaces between columns. Set margin and tab stops (see page 75). Center headings horizontally.

TYPE: Drill as given at right.

Main heading

THE SMALLEST AND THE LARGEST STATE
DS

Secondary heading

Land Area (Sq. Mi.) and Capital
TS

Rhode Island	1,214	Providence
Alaska	586,400	Juneau

LESSON 114

114A ■ CONDITIONING PRACTICE [5] each line 3 times SS: slowly, faster, in-between rate

Alphabet   Exquisite rings were made quickly by the jovial friends on the piazza.   *Continuous stroking—*

Figure/symbol   He thought $24.36 too much for a 150# bag of sugar and offered $18.79.   *no pauses*

Concentration   He asked us to translate "Tenet insanable multos scribendi cacoathes."

Fluency   To type rapidly, hold your arms quiet and let the fingers do the work.
                  | 1 | 2 | 3 | 4 | 5 | 6 | 7 | 8 | 9 | 10 | 11 | 12 | 13 | 14 |

114B ■ GROWTH INDEX: STRAIGHT COPY [15] two 5′ writings; determine GWAM; proofread and circle errors

All letters are used.

		GWAM	
		1′	5′

¶ 1

If you were to ask an employer what one quality he considers of | 13 | 3 | 57
most importance in an employee, evidence indicates that he would say | 27 | 5 | 60
dependability. To be able to depend on an employee is of importance | 40 | 8 | 63
to an employer who has to plan the work so that it will be completed | 54 | 11 | 65
properly and on time. If the employer isn't sure that the employee | 68 | 14 | 68
will be on the job and that he can do the tasks assigned, his problems | 82 | 16 | 71
increase tremendously. Another source of concern is the employee who | 96 | 19 | 74
arrives at work ten to fifteen minutes late. All workers should recog- | 110 | 22 | 77
nize that this practice does not make a good impression. Dependability | 125 | 25 | 80
starts with being at work every day and being there on time. | 137 | 27 | 82

¶ 2

Just being at work, however, is only a beginning on the road to | 13 | 30 | 84
dependability. The employer also considers how thoroughly you do your | 27 | 33 | 87
work and the manner in which you do it. If he can assign an exacting | 41 | 36 | 90
task to you and depend on your doing the task in the proper way and on | 55 | 38 | 93
schedule, you should quickly become a very valued employee. If you are | 70 | 41 | 96
the type, however, who can never quite complete an assigned task without | 84 | 44 | 99
coming back for additional instructions, or if the task sometimes must | 98 | 47 | 102
be corrected by someone else, watch out. Your type can be replaced-- | 112 | 50 | 104
and probably soon will be. Make it a practice to be a dependable em- | 126 | 53 | 107
ployee and you can depend on continuous employment. | 136 | 55 | 109

1′ GWAM | 1 | 2 | 3 | 4 | 5 | 6 | 7 | 8 | 9 | 10 | 11 | 12 | 13 | 14 |
5′ GWAM | 1 | 2 | 3 |

48E ■ PROBLEM TYPING: TABLES WITH SECONDARY AND COLUMNAR HEADINGS [14]

Problem 1

Use a half sheet; SS; 6 spaces between columns. Center the problem vertically, the headings and columns horizontally. *Erase and correct errors.*

		Words
HEISMAN TROPHY WINNERS *DS*		5
1963-1971 *TS*		7
Roger Staubach, QB	Navy	11
John Huarte, QB	Notre Dame	17
Mike Garrett, HB	USC	21
Steve Spurrier, QB	Florida	27
Gary Beban, QB	UCLA	31
O. J. Simpson, RB	USC	35
Steve Owens, RB	Oklahoma	40
Jim Plunkett, QB	Stanford	45
Pat Sullivan, QB	Auburn	50

18	6	10

Problem 2

Use a half sheet; SS; 14 spaces between columns. Center the problem vertically, the headings and columns horizontally. *Erase and correct errors.*

		Words
CIRCULATION OF LEADING U.S. MAGAZINES		8
(As of December 31, 1970) *DS*		13
Magazine *TS*	Copies *DS*	19
Reader's Digest	17,930,403	24
TV Guide	15,419,537	28
Life	8,510,686	31
McCall's	7,913,859	35
Look	7,369,393	38
Ladies' Home Journal	6,969,326	44
Good Housekeeping	5,804,909	49
Time	4,259,046	53
Newsweek	2,597,807	56

20	14	10

■ LESSON 49

49A ■ CONDITIONING PRACTICE [8] at least twice SS; then 1' comparative writings on Lines 2 and 3

Alphabet	Marnie sold a dozen copies of Harvey Dixon's new book, JUDGE THE QUIZ.
Figures	Paul must study Section 2, pages 75-190, and Section 3, pages 246-380.
Figure/symbol	On August 19 she paid $2,640.78, with 3% sales tax and 15% excise tax.
Fluency	Many of their problems need to be thought through to a final solution.

| 1 | 2 | 3 | 4 | 5 | 6 | 7 | 8 | 9 | 10 | 11 | 12 | 13 | 14 |

49B ■ CENTERING MAIN, SECONDARY, AND COLUMNAR HEADINGS [8] (Drill sheet)

Beginning on the third line below the last line of the Conditioning Practice, arrange and type the headings and the first two lines of tabulated items of Problem 1 of 48E, above. Then triple-space and type the headings and first two lines of items of Problem 2 in a similar way.

49C ■ CENTERING ON SPECIAL-SIZE PAPER [10]

LEARN: To determine the center of special-size paper (or card), follow these steps:

1. Read and add the numbers on the cylinder scale (or paper-bail scale) at each edge of paper.
2. Divide the sum by 2 to find the center of the paper.

DO: 1. Insert a half sheet (5½" x 8½") with the long edge at the left (short side up).
2. Use double spacing and a 2½" top margin.
3. Determine the horizontal center of the half sheet. Set tab.

4. Center and type each line of the announcement.

	Words
CENTRAL BUSINESS CLUB	4
will hold its monthly meeting	10
Wednesday, December 1, 3:30 p.m.	17
Building C, Room 215	21
Topic: Managing Your Money	27

Problem 1: Boxed Tabulation

Full sheet ■ reading position ■ type data as shown in table ■ spaces between entries in columns: 10-6-6-6

Type the table as if there were no rulings. After it has been typed, type an underline one-half space above and below the columnar headings, and below the last line of the table.

NOTE: Center the years over the 2-digit entries in each column.

The vertical lines may be ruled with a ball-point pen without removing the paper; use the automatic line finder (ratchet release) and roll the paper forward to rule the lines. (See Reference Guide, page xi.)

To type the vertical lines, indicate with an apostrophe where each of these lines should be typed. Remove the paper; reinsert it with the long side up, and type the vertical lines with the underline.

Problem 2: Boxed Tabulation

Full sheet ■ reading position ■ DS data ■ 4 spaces between columns

Center primary columnar headings (Male, Female) over the three columns to which each applies.

NOTE: In the 1980 columns, do not consider the asterisk (*) in determining placement.

	Words In Cols.	Total Words
OCCUPATIONAL DISTRIBUTION OF EMPLOYED PERSONS		9
(In Percent)		12

Classification	1950	1960	1970	1980*	Words In Cols.	Total Words
						19
White-collar	37	43	47	50	5	24
Professional, technical	9	11	14	16	12	31
Proprietary, managerial	9	11	10	10	19	38
Clerical, sales	19	21	23	24	25	44
Blue-collar	41	36	36	33	30	49
Skilled	14	13	13	13	34	53
Semiskilled	21	18	18	16	39	58
Unskilled	6	5	5	4	43	62
Service	10	13	13	14	47	66
Farm	12	8	4	3	50	69
All workers	100	100	100	100	57	76

Indent 3 → Professional, technical

SS
DS

*Estimated projection.   80
+ Rules   145

	Words In Cols.	Total Words
LABOR MARKET PARTICIPATION BY AGE AND SEX		8
(In Percent)		11

Age	Male			Female			Words In Cols.	Total Words
	1960	1970	1980*	1960	1970	1980*		13 / 14 / 21
16-19	58.6	58.4	56.7	39.1	44.0	41.5	7	28
20-24	88.9	86.6	83.0	46.1	57.8	57.6	14	35
25-34	96.4	96.6	96.0	35.8	45.0	45.7	22	42
35-44	96.4	97.0	96.1	43.1	51.1	53.3	29	49
45-54	94.3	94.3	94.0	49.3	54.4	54.8	36	57
55-64	85.2	83.0	80.5	36.7	43.0	45.2	43	64
65-up	32.2	26.8	22.0	10.5	9.7	8.7	50	71
All ages	82.4	80.6	79.2	37.1	43.4	43.0	58	79

*Estimated projection.   83
+ Rules   172

49D ■ PROBLEM TYPING: TABLES ON SPECIAL-SIZE PAPER ◼24

Problem 1

On a half sheet of paper (5½″ x 8½″) inserted with the long side at the left, type the following table in double-spaced form. Center the problem vertically in *reading position*. Leave 14 spaces between columns. *Erase and correct your errors.* QUESTION: How many lines are available for typing? Check answer below problem if you do not know.

		Words
POPULATION OF MAJOR CANADIAN CITIES		7
(Including Metropolitan Area)		13
City	Persons	18
Montreal	2,553,000	22
Toronto	2,316,000	26
Vancouver	980,000	30
Winnipeg	534,000	33
Ottawa	527,000	36
Hamilton	479,000	40
Edmonton	437,000	43
Quebec	430,000	46
Calgary	375,000	49
Windsor	223,000	52

9	14	9

(ANSWER: 51)

Problem 2

On a sheet of paper cut to 7¼ x 10½ inches inserted with the long side at the left, type the following table in double-spaced form. Center the problem vertically in *reading position*. Leave 8 spaces between columns. *Erase and correct your errors.* QUESTION: How many lines are available for typing? Check answer below problem if you do not know.

			Words
POPULATION OF CANADIAN PROVINCES			7
(Estimated June 1, 1970)			12
Province	Persons	Capital	21
Alberta	1,600,000	Edmonton	26
British Columbia	2,137,000	Victoria	34
Manitoba	891,000	Winnipeg	39
New Brunswick	625,000	Fredericton	46
Newfoundland	518,000	St. John's	53
Nova Scotia	766,000	Halifax	59
Ontario	7,647,000	Toronto	64
Prince Edward Is.	110,000	Charlottetown	73
Quebec	6,013,000	Quebec	78
Saskatchewan	942,000	Regina	83

17	8	9	8	13

(ANSWER: 63)

Problem 3

On a half sheet (short side at the left), center the problem vertically single-spaced. Center columns horizontally with 6 spaces between columns. Type the symbols in Column 3 as directed in Column 2.

			Words
SPECIAL SYMBOLS			3
	TS		
		next	
Insert	Diagonal (/); roll platen back one line	my/day.	15
In care of	Small c; diagonal; small o	c/o	23
Carbon copy	Small letter c typed twice	cc	32
English pound	Capital L; backspace; f	£	40
Equals	Two hyphens, one slightly below the other	=	50
Plus	Diagonal; backspace; hyphen	+	58
Division	Colon; backspace; hyphen	÷	65
Subscript	Letter; cylinder forward slightly; figure	H_2O	72

13	6	41	6	7

Problem 3: 3-Column Table

Full sheet ■ reading position ■ DS data ■ 8 spaces between columns ■ *Be alert:* Change tab stops as needed in typing columnar entries

Problem 4: Skill Building

Retype Problem 3 with these changes: add new Column 1 as shown below ■ 6 spaces between columns

Rank
1
2
3
4
5
6
7
8
9

NOTE: Use margin release when backspacing for new Column 1 heading.

			Words In Cols.	Total Words
BEST SELLERS OF U.S. GOVERNMENT PRINTING OFFICE				10
(1970)				11
Title	Unit Cost	Number Sold		22
Infant Care	$0.20	14,824,275	6	27
Your Federal Income Tax	.75	12,984,830	14	35
Prenatal Care	.20	8,913,527	19	41
Your Child From 1 to 6	.20	6,627,022	27	48
Your Child From 6 to 12	.55	3,183,627	34	56
Tax Guide for Small Business	.75	3,171,326	43	64
Strictly for Teen-agers	.05	2,977,650	50	72
Your Social Security	.15	2,149,205	57	79
Rescue Breathing	.05	1,954,850	63	85

■ LESSON 113

113A ■ CONDITIONING PRACTICE [5] each line 3 times SS: slowly, faster, in-between rate

Alphabet	Six juicy steaks sizzled over a big wood fire as the quaint men slept.
Figure/symbol	Order #2856 for 30 chairs and 47 desks will be shipped on November 19.
Long words	Systems engineers had complete responsibility in space communications.
Fluency	The simple way to better our lot in life is to try to do a lot better.

Uniform (even) keystroking

| 1 | 2 | 3 | 4 | 5 | 6 | 7 | 8 | 9 | 10 | 11 | 12 | 13 | 14 |

113B ■ TECHNIQUE IMPROVEMENT [17] each line 3 times; then a 1' writing on each line

EMPHASIZE

1	*Finger 1*	Five hungry men helped James save a battered boat from further damage.
2	*Finger 2*	Dick decided to dedicate his new musical work to an educational group.
3	*Finger 3*	An old wax sample was used by Wally Olds to wax those new wood floors.
4	*Finger 4*	Aza Quinn quizzed a popular polo player about scaling the Alpine peak.
5	*One hand*	Are you going to send an abstract of the monopoly case to him by noon?
6	*Long reaches*	Many economy-minded union men are numbered among Mr. Bright's friends.

Fingers upright; close to keys

Finger-reach action; quiet hands

Quick, snap strokes

| 1 | 2 | 3 | 4 | 5 | 6 | 7 | 8 | 9 | 10 | 11 | 12 | 13 | 14 |

■ LESSON 50

50A ■ CONDITIONING PRACTICE [8] at least twice SS; then 1' comparative writings on Lines 1 and 4

Alphabet   May Johns planned to have exquisite views of Nick Zale's big art show.   *Reach to the figure/symbol keys*

Figures   The decorator chairs we back-ordered are Nos. C2175, K4038, and Z6395.

Figure/symbol   Ship by C.O.D. express Order #7541-2 for 8½ doz. of #6307 @ 89¢ each.

Fluency   It is a part of the work of a proficient typist to proofread the work.

| 1 | 2 | 3 | 4 | 5 | 6 | 7 | 8 | 9 | 10 | 11 | 12 | 13 | 14 |

50B ■ SKILL-TRANSFER TYPING: STRAIGHT COPY AND STATISTICAL COPY [12]

1. Type two 1' speed writings on ¶ 1. Determine average *gwam*.

2. Type two 1' speed writings on ¶ 2. Determine average *gwam*.

3. Type two 1' and one 2' speed writings on ¶ 2; try to equal ¶ 1 *gwam*.

All letters and figures are used.

¶ 1

	GWAM 1'	2'
In a discussion of the generation gap, each faction is quick to	13	6	56
point up its own successes and the failings of the other. It is time to	27	14	63
take a more positive view. Those who came before us needed to concen-	41	21	70
trate on necessary things––at first, on just eking out a living and,	55	28	77
later, on the major economic changes of their times. Each generation	69	35	84
leaves its successor with something on which to build. Your generation	84	42	91
may well be free to examine and solve the social problems that concern us.	98	49	98

¶ 2

Your grandparents started the organization of labor. In 1914, one	13	7	55
company raised its basic wage from $2.40 for a 9-hour day to $5 for an	27	14	62
8-hour day. Without the current level of education, your parents were	42	21	69
able to support the research that has led to the control of most diseases	57	28	76
and, in 1969, put man on the moon. A recent survey reveals that in 51%	71	36	84
of the schools polled, 42.37% of their graduates continue on to college.	86	43	91
Among the last 3 generations, where will yours rank?	96	48	96

1' GWAM | 1 | 2 | 3 | 4 | 5 | 6 | 7 | 8 | 9 | 10 | 11 | 12 | 13 | 14 |
2' GWAM | 1 | 2 | 3 | 4 | 5 | 6 | 7 |

50C ■ CENTERING/TABULATING/COMPOSING: REVIEW [30]

Make a list of the following page numbers and problem and drill references. Place the list alongside your typewriter for easy reference. Type once as many of the items as you can in 20 minutes. Proofread; circle errors.

Page 67, 40B
Page 70, 42C
Page 73, 44C
Page 80, 48E, Problem 2
Page 81, 49D, Problem 3

Compose and type complete sentence answers to these questions:

1. How many lines can you type in a vertical inch?

2. What is the centering point on your typewriter?

3. How many spaces can be typed in a horizontal inch on your typewriter?

4. What is the size (in inches) of a standard sheet of typewriting paper?

5. How many lines are available on a full sheet of typewriting paper?

LESSON 112

112A ■ CONDITIONING PRACTICE ⑤ each line 3 times SS: slowly, faster, in-between rate

Alphabet   Jack Waxlof made amazing progress by using improved typing techniques. *Quick shift-key reach*

Figure/symbol   McNeil, Jones & Sons refused to pay invoice #63405 dated May 18, 1972.

Double letters   Three letters will go to Bill and Betty Ott about the Tennessee deeds.

Fluency   It is a good plan to do your very best on each typing job that you do.
                  | 1 | 2 | 3 | 4 | 5 | 6 | 7 | 8 | 9 | 10 | 11 | 12 | 13 | 14 |

112B ■ IMPROVING ACCURACY ⑦ 1' writing on each sentence of 112A; **goal:** not over 1 error each writing

112C ■ TABULATING SKILL BUILDING ⑧ 3' writing on data in columns only, plus leaders, in Problem 1 below

1. Determine quickly left margin stop and tab stops for columns. Do not center vertically.

2. Start writing about 1" from top edge of sheet. If you complete columns, start over.

112D ■ TABULATING SKILL APPLICATIONS ㉚

Problem 1: Table with Leaders*

Full sheet ■ reading position ■ space data as shown ■ 20 spaces between columns ■ leave 2 spaces after last leader

Problem 2: Skill Building

Retype Problem 1 with these changes: half sheet ■ short side up ■ 10 spaces between columns ■ omit leaders

		Words In Cols.	Total Words
EDUCATION AND LIFETIME EARNINGS			6
DS			
(Earnings from Age 18 to 64)			12
TS			
Grade Completed	Earnings		22
DS			
Elementary School:		4	26
Indent 3 → Less than 8 years	$192,023	13	35
8 years	246,375	22	44
DS			
High School:		25	47
1 to 3 years	273,079	34	56
4 years	328,233	44	65
College:		46	67
1 to 3 years	370,306	55	77
4 years	510,077	64	86
5 years or more	548,070	73	95
All Education Groups	323,035	83	105
SS			108
DS			
Source: Bureau of Census.			114

Leaders (made by alternating the period and the space) are sometimes used to connect typed material, as shown in the table of Problem 1. When typing leaders, check on the line-of-writing scale whether the first period is struck on an odd or an even number; then strike all additional lines of leaders on either the odd or the even number so as to align the leaders vertically. Use left first finger on space bar.

LESSON 51

51A ■ CONDITIONING PRACTICE [8] at least twice SS; then 1′ comparative writings on Lines 2 and 3

Alphabet	Joseph's high quiz marks excelled those of Frank McGow by five points.
Figures	ZIP Codes 45207, 95180, and 60634 must appear on mail to our branches.
Figure/symbol	Order #514-B for 18 2/3 doz. of Item #607 @ 98¢ ea. was shipped C.O.D.
Fluency	When money talks, it seems to do so without saying much of importance.

| 1 | 2 | 3 | 4 | 5 | 6 | 7 | 8 | 9 | 10 | 11 | 12 | 13 | 14 |

51B ■ TECHNIQUE PRACTICE: REVIEW [9] type twice

| 1 | *Space bar* | am my by way may day pay you fly buy try many stay from only form your | *Down-and-in* |
| 2 | | am you buy my may say try us stay here from you buy yours fly you home | *motion of thumb* |

| 3 | *Shift keys* | Rick's, Inc.; Tuesday, August 12; One Fifth Avenue; Las Vegas, Nevada; | *Finger reaches* |
| 4 | | Paul and Della will have lunch with Jerry and Ann at Eddie's Hideaway. | *to shift keys* |

| 5 | *Stroke* | anxious averages general interest previous probably secretary standard | *Quick, snap* |
| 6 | *response* | A secretary with top references will probably get the standard salary. | *strokes* |

| 7 | *Word* | when wish visit usual turn title their spent small right profit handle | *Speedy, word-* |
| 8 | *response* | He may visit the firm to work with the title forms they handle for us. | *typing response* |

| 1 | 2 | 3 | 4 | 5 | 6 | 7 | 8 | 9 | 10 | 11 | 12 | 13 | 14 |

51C ■ GROWTH INDEX [8] type a 5′ writing; determine GWAM; proofread and circle errors

All letters are used.

		GWAM		
		1′	5′	

¶ 1

The use of the typewriter in school goes back many years. Its use — 13 | 3 | 34
with younger pupils, however, has only recently become widespread. In — 28 | 6 | 37
the lower grades boys and girls alike now have an opportunity to learn — 42 | 8 | 39
how to typewrite. It is amazing to see them work. — 52 | 10 | 41

¶ 2

Not only are pupils of ten or eleven years of age able to type at — 13 | 13 | 44
quite high speeds, but they are also able to type with acceptable accu- — 27 | 16 | 47
racy many of their personal letters, themes, notes, and cards. In the — 42 | 19 | 50
process they improve their knowledge of language. — 51 | 21 | 52

¶ 3

If such results are possible from using the typewriter in the fifth — 14 | 23 | 54
or sixth grade, you also should be able to improve your command of lan- — 28 | 26 | 57
guage by the use of the typewriter. In addition, you can build the — 41 | 29 | 60
foundation for a very important future job skill. — 51 | 31 | 62

1′ GWAM | 1 | 2 | 3 | 4 | 5 | 6 | 7 | 8 | 9 | 10 | 11 | 12 | 13 | 14 |
5′ GWAM | 1 | 2 | 3 |

LESSON 111

111A ▪ CONDITIONING PRACTICE [5] each line 3 times SS: slowly, faster, in-between rate

Alphabet	Quick, lively jazz and wailful blues excite the progressive music fan.
Figure/symbol	Order the #38, #56, and #79 dies and the #1204 (Diamond) machine tool.
Long words	These laboratories specialize in solid-state space propulsion systems.
Fluency	Regrettably, nuances of techniques may be lost in the drive for speed.

Good typing position

| 1 | 2 | 3 | 4 | 5 | 6 | 7 | 8 | 9 | 10 | 11 | 12 | 13 | 14 |

111B ▪ SELECTED-GOAL PRACTICE: PROGRESSIVE-DIFFICULTY SENTENCES [15]

1. Select a speed goal and type each sentence 3 times on the call of the 20-, 15-, or 12-second return guide, as directed by your teacher. Pause briefly after each spurt writing to relax.

2. Type a 1′ writing on each sentence. Type on the *speed level*. Work for continuity and rhythm.

NOTE: The figures above the copy indicate the 1′ rates in terms of the guide call.

GWAM
20″ Guide	3	6	9	12	15	18	21	24	27	30	33	36	39	42
15″ Guide	4	8	12	16	20	24	28	32	36	40	44	48	52	56
12″ Guide	5	10	15	20	25	30	35	40	45	50	55	60	65	70

1	Balanced hand	They paid for the maps of the ancient land forms with their endowment.
2	Combination	Most of the statements are mailed by the staff at the end of each day.
3	One hand	Only a few of your cases on monopoly were referred to the union staff.
4	Figures	He sold 126 bats, 573 balls, 48 gloves, and 90 Dopp-Kits to the teams.
5	Long words	Specialists are needed in magnetohydrodynamics and telecommunications.
6	Shift key	Jack A. MacDuff, President of MacDuff & O'Brien, lives in Walla Walla.

| 1 | 2 | 3 | 4 | 5 | 6 | 7 | 8 | 9 | 10 | 11 | 12 | 13 | 14 |

111C ▪ TABULATING SKILL APPLICATIONS [20]

Problem 1: Learning

Half sheet ▪ long side up ▪ center vertically ▪ SS data ▪ 4 spaces between columns

NOTE: Use line finder (ratchet release) to position the paper for typing the double underline.

Alertness Cue: Reset tab stops for Cols. 2 and 3 for most frequently occurring items; then remember to forward space or backspace as required.

Problem 2: Skill Building

Retype Problem 1 with these changes: full sheet ▪ reading position ▪ DS data ▪ 6 spaces between columns

			Words in Cols.	Total Words
AVERAGE ANNUAL LIVING COST SS				5
IN SELECTED UNITED STATES CITIES*				12
DS				
(Family of Four)				15
TS				
<u>Item</u>	<u>Amount</u>	<u>Percent</u>		23
		DS		
Food and Beverages	$1,778	27.1	6	29
Housing	1,384	21.1	10	33
Clothing and Personal Care	780	11.9	17	40
Personal Taxes	619	9.4	22	44
Medical Care	539	8.2	26	49
Transportation	484	7.4	31	53
Other Goods and Services	320	4.9	37	60
Misc. (Life Insurance, etc.)	663	10.0	45	68
		DS	48	70
Indent 5 → Total	$6,567	100.0	50	73
		SS	55	78

*Estimate of dollar amount required to maintain a "modest but adequate" level of living.

	81
	91
	99

111D ▪ TABULATING SKILL BUILDING [10] two 3′ writings on Problem 1, using only the column entries; 6 spaces between columns; start typing on Line 7

51D ■ PROBLEM TYPING MEASUREMENT: CENTERING/TABLES [25] erase and correct errors

Problem 1

On a half sheet of paper with the short side at the left, center and type in exact vertical center the following problem in double-spaced form.

		Words
SPACING SUMMARY FOR TYPEWRITING		6
Pica spaces to the horizontal inch	10	14
Elite spaces to the horizontal inch	12	22
Pica spaces to an 8½-inch line	85	29
Elite spaces to an 8½-inch line	102	36
Lines to a vertical inch (pica and elite)	6	45
Vertical lines to an 11-inch sheet	66	53
Vertical lines to a 5½–inch (half) sheet	33	61

41	6	3

Problem 2

On a half sheet of paper with the long side at the left, type the following table in exact vertical center. Use DS. Type the heading in two lines, SS.

		Words
THE WORLD'S TEN MOST POPULOUS URBAN AREAS		6 / 8
Urban Area	Population	17
Tokyo, Japan	14,770,727	22
New York, U.S.A.	11,528,649	28
Buenos Aires, Argentina	8,408,930	34
Paris, France	8,196,746	39
London, England	7,948,270	44
Osaka, Japan	7,781,000	49
Moscow, USSR	7,061,000	54
Los Angeles, U.S.A.	7,032,075	60
Chicago, U.S.A.	6,978,947	65
Shanghai, China	6,977,000	70

23	10	10

NOTE: Certain typewriters, particularly foreign makes, do not have exactly 6 lines to the inch.

Problem 3

On a full sheet of paper, center in *reading position* the following table in double-spaced form.

Correct all errors marked in the copy. In addition, erase and correct any errors you make as you type.

Center each line

			Words
TEN 10 MOST RECENT U. S. PRESIDENTS			6
(1913 to 1973) TS			9
President	Party	Birthplace	20
Woodrow Wilson	Democart	Virginia	26
Warren F. Harding	Republican	Ohio	33
Clavin Coolidge	Republicane	Vermnt	40
Herbert C. Hover	Democrat	Iowa	47
Frankling D. Roosevelt	Republican	Missouri	55
Harry S Truman	Democrat	New York	61
Dwight D. Eisenhower	Republicane	Texas	69
John F. Kenedy	Democart	Masachusets	77
Lyndon G. Johnson	Democrat	Texas	83
Richard M. Nixon	Republican	California	91

Center over column

21	6	10	6	13

LESSON 110

110A ■ CONDITIONING PRACTICE [5] each line 3 times SS: slowly, faster, in-between rate

Alphabet   Liquid oxygen fuel was used to give this big jet rocket amazing speed. *Sharp, down-and-in keystroking action*

Figure/symbol   A 100% hardwood 3-shelf bookcase (38″ x 23″ x 7 3/4″) sells for $9.65.

Adjacent keys   John asked Fred to cover the boxes for the six men before you came in.

Fluency   When typing the top-row figures, keep the reach action in the fingers.

| 1 | 2 | 3 | 4 | 5 | 6 | 7 | 8 | 9 | 10 | 11 | 12 | 13 | 14 |

110B ■ SKILL BUILDING: STRAIGHT COPY [15]

1. Type a 5′ writing on the ¶s of 109B, page 167, on *control level* (try to type with 5 or fewer errors).

2. Type another 5′ writing. If you made the goal of Step 1, increase your speed on this writing.

110C ■ TABULATION PRODUCTION MEASUREMENT [30]

Time Schedule
Planning and preparing . . 3′
Timed tabulating production . 20′
Proofreading; computing
n-pram . . . . 7′

If you complete the following problem before 20 minutes are up, start over on a new sheet. Erase and correct all errors. Proofread your work. Deduct 15 words from total words typed for each uncorrected error; divide remainder by 20 to determine *n-pram*.

Full sheet ■ reading position ■ DS data ■ 6 spaces between columns

Each figure is used a minimum of 18 times.

Name	Age	Telephone	Subject	Words in Cols.	Total Words
STUDENT TUTORING SERVICE BUREAU					6
					16
Alexander, John	15	274-9099	Mechanical Drawing	9	26
Belding, Greg	16	393-8477	Social Studies	18	34
Brownstein, Lynda	16	893-0293	Latin	25	41
Castillo, Leticia	14	262-7038	Spanish	32	49
Drury, Kim	15	385-4890	Art	38	54
Franklin, David	15	403-2308	General Business	47	63
Grohs, Frank	17	202-5930	Mathematics	54	71
Hashimoto, Alice	16	802-0584	Shorthand	62	78
Jasperson, William	17	585-4920	Chemistry	70	87
Johnson, Sallie	14	264-9843	English	77	94
Keller, Harvey	17	620-9483	Physics	84	101
Leoni, Edith	16	293-3570	French	91	107
Marcus, Nick	16	574-3928	Biology	97	114
Nelson, Monica	15	474-0937	Business English	106	123
Nostrand, Arnold	17	874-3629	American History	116	132
Oliver, Teddy	16	285-7654	Algebra	122	139
Pearce, Harriet	16	862-8902	Typewriting	130	147
Platz, Ronald	17	850-4677	Computer Science	139	155
Salas, Sarah	15	964-0259	English	146	162
Thornton, Linda	16	385-3875	Office Machines	154	171
Ware, David	16	203-5649	History	160	177

Personal / Business Communications

■ LESSON 52

52A ■ CONDITIONING PRACTICE [8] each line 3 times SS; then 1′ writings on Line 4

Alphabet	Four complex keyboard reviews were quickly organized by Patrick Johns.
Figures	What is the sum of 9 and 12 and 39 and 40 and 48 and 57 and 60 and 93?
Figure/symbol	I ordered 5 copies of #31 @ $4.60 each, 8 copies of #297 @ $7.45 each.
Fluency	To build skill, they take three or four short timed writings each day.

Eyes on copy; start new line quickly

| 1 | 2 | 3 | 4 | 5 | 6 | 7 | 8 | 9 | 10 | 11 | 12 | 13 | 14 |

52B ■ IMPROVING SPEED/CONTROL [32]

Make a list of the page and activity numbers given at the right. Place the list beside your typewriter for easy reference. Place a slip of paper in your book on this page (85) so that you can return to it when you have completed all activities.

PAGE, ACTIVITY	DO
Page 64, 38B: Skill Transfer	1′ writings on each ¶; compare *gwam*
Page 65, 39B: Tabulation Checkup	1′ writings on each line
Page 66, 39C: Skill Comparison	1′ writings on each ¶
Page 66, 39D: 3′ Writings	Type 2 or more 3′ writings

52C ■ ALIGNING AND TYPING OVER WORDS [10] (Line: 60; SS)

LOCATE: Aligning scale (33); variable line spacer (3).

1. Type the following sentence but do not make the return:

   I aligned this copy with little difficulty.

2. Move the carriage (or carrier) so the word *aligned*, *this*, or *with* is above the aligning scale. Note that a vertical line points to the center of the letter *i* in the word.

3. Study the relation of the top of the scale to the bottom of the letters with down stems (g, p, y).

   It is important for you to get an eye picture of the exact relation of the typed line to the top of the scale so you will be able to adjust the paper correctly to type over a word with exactness.

4. Remove the paper; reinsert it. Gauge the line so the bottoms of the letters are in correct relation to the top of the aligning scale. Operate the **variable line spacer (3)** if necessary to move the paper forward or backward. Operate the **paper release (16)** to move the paper to the left or right, if necessary, when centering the letter *i* over one of the lines on the aligning scale.

5. Check the accuracy of your alignment by setting the **ribbon control (22)** for stencil position and typing over one of the letters. If necessary, make further alignment adjustments. *Return the ribbon control to typing position* (black).

6. Type over the words *aligned*, *this*, and *with* in the sentence, moving the paper forward or backward, to the left or right, as necessary for correct alignment.

7. Repeat Steps 1, 3, 4, 5, and 6.

109C ■ BUILDING SUSTAINED TABULATING SKILL 30

Time Schedule

Planning and preparing . .	5'
Timed tabulating production .	20'
Proofreading; determining g-pram	5'

Directions for each problem are given with that problem. If you complete the problems before time is called, start over. Plan and prepare for each problem with a minimum of waste time. Have the materials needed ready so that you can move quickly from one problem to the next.

Problem 1

Full sheet ■ center vertically in reading position ■ DS data ■ 6 spaces between columns ■ center columnar headings over longest columnar items

Alertness Cue: Reset tab stops for Cols. 2 and 3 one space to right for second and following items of table.

Problem 2

Retype Problem 1 but center vertically in exact center

			Words
POPULATION OF FOURTEEN LARGEST			6
STANDARD METROPOLITAN STATISTICAL AREAS*			14
			TS
Metropolitan Area	1960 Census	1970 Census	30
New York City	10,695,000	11,529,000	38
Los Angeles-Long Beach	6,039,000	7,032,000	46
Chicago	6,221,000	6,979,000	52
Philadelphia	4,343,000	4,818,000	58
Detroit	3,762,000	4,200,000	64
San Francisco-Oakland	2,649,000	3,110,000	72
Washington	2,077,000	2,861,000	79
Boston	2,595,000	2,754,000	84
Pittsburgh	2,405,000	2,401,000	91
St. Louis	2,105,000	2,363,000	97
Baltimore	1,804,000	2,071,000	103
Cleveland	1,909,000	2,064,000	109
Houston	1,418,000	1,985,000	114
Newark	1,689,000	1,857,000	120

SS ——————— (type 1½" underline)   123
DS *Figures rounded to nearest thousand.   131

Problem 3

Half sheet ■ long side up ■ center vertically ■ SS data ■ 16 spaces between columns ■ center columnar headings over longest columnar items

Problem 4

Retype Problem 3 with these changes: half sheet ■ short side up ■ DS data ■ 12 spaces between columns

		Words
POPULATION OF TEN LARGEST STATES		7
State	1970 Census	13
California	19,953,134	18
New York	18,190,740	22
Pennsylvania	11,793,909	27
Texas	11,196,730	30
Illinois	11,113,976	34
Ohio	10,652,017	37
Michigan	8,875,083	41
New Jersey	7,168,164	45
Florida	6,789,443	49
Massachusetts	5,689,170	54

■ LESSON 53

53A ■ CONDITIONING PRACTICE [8] each line 3 times SS; then 1' writings on Line 3

Alphabet	Mrs. Joyce Zublick is not quite finished with this expensive training.
Figures	What is the sum of 7 and 10? of 29 and 38? of 46 and 52? of 60 and 79?
Figure/symbol	Their Invoice #85309, dated 12/18, totals $621.30, less 2% in 10 days.
Fluency	The chairman claims that a majority of the members like the amendment.

| 1 | 2 | 3 | 4 | 5 | 6 | 7 | 8 | 9 | 10 | 11 | 12 | 13 | 14 |

NOTE: Remove the paper; reinsert it; gauge the line and letter; type over the last line.

53B ■ IMPROVING SPEED/CONTROL [10]

1. Type three 1' *speed* writings on the ¶. Try to increase your rate by at least 4 to 8 *gwam* from Writing 1 to Writing 3.

2. Type three 1' *control* writings on the ¶. An average goal is 2 errors a minute; a good goal, 1 error; an excellent goal, 0 errors.

1' GWAM

Can you use language to say effectively what you mean, and do you 13
always really mean what you say in social dialogue? Unless a man says 27
precisely what he means and means exactly what he says, he, just like a 42
factory smokestack or an automobile, is needlessly polluting the air. 56

1' GWAM | 1 | 2 | 3 | 4 | 5 | 6 | 7 | 8 | 9 | 10 | 11 | 12 | 13 | 14 |

53C ■ PROBLEM TYPING: INFORMATIONAL MEMORANDUMS [32] (Half sheets; line: 60; SS)

Problem 1: Read the model memorandum illustrated below; then type two copies of it.

```
November 12, 19--
               Operate return mechanism
               4 times (3 blank line spaces)

SUBJECT:  Memorandum on the Block Style
                              DS
This memorandum is typed in what is known as the block style.
When block style is used, all lines (including the date and
the subject lines) begin at the left margin.  Single spacing
is used with double spacing (one blank line space) separating
the paragraphs.
               DS
The use of the block style for typing announcements and memo-
randums in both schools and offices is very common today.  In
addition, its use in typing personal and business letters is
growing as its timesaving features are recognized.
```

53C continued on page 87

LESSON 109

109A ■ CONDITIONING PRACTICE [5] each line 3 times SS: slowly, faster, in-between rate

Alphabet　　John V. Maze is able to type six words faster by using a quick stroke. *Wrists low and relaxed*

Figure/symbol　These fishing boxes (9½" x 8¼" x 14¼") with 6/0 reels sell for $23.75.

Quiet hands　The major exercise for many people comes from jumping to a conclusion.

Fluency　　The successful typewriting student is one who has formed right habits.

| 1 | 2 | 3 | 4 | 5 | 6 | 7 | 8 | 9 | 10 | 11 | 12 | 13 | 14 |

109B ■ GROWTH INDEX: STRAIGHT COPY [15] two 5' writings; determine GWAM; proofread and circle errors

All letters are used.

	GWAM		
	1'	5'	

¶ 1

Education is available in many different sizes and shapes, which 　13 3 | 54
are all an important part of life. Remember when you suddenly realized, 　28 6 | 57
as a child, that your left shoe really didn't fit on your right foot? 　42 8 | 60
Remember when you learned to tie your shoes, to tell time, or to go to 　56 11 | 63
the store alone? These special events represented additions to your learn- 　71 14 | 66
ing and your education. For some persons, getting an education is the 　85 17 | 69
result of just these kinds of day-to-day experiences. For example, the 　100 20 | 72
teen-ager who dents the fender on the family car is getting an education 　114 23 | 74
when he has to use part of his summer pay, or his allowance, to pay for 　129 26 | 77
the repair. 　131 26 | 78

¶ 2

Think of what a loss it is for many millions of good minds to be 　13 29 | 80
bored nightly by television re-runs and old movies. The alert person 　27 32 | 83
eliminates this loss of his time. He does this by getting more educa- 　41 34 | 86
tion––by returning to school. Our educational system is one of the 　55 37 | 89
unique things that make this country different from any other country. 　69 40 | 92
We must not sell education short and we must not neglect it. Your educa- 　84 43 | 95
tion does not end when you are graduated from high school or from college; 　99 46 | 98
education is a lifelong process. Learning is an important part of good 　113 49 | 100
living; the man who stops learning has, in a real way, stopped living. 　127 52 | 103

1' GWAM | 1 | 2 | 3 | 4 | 5 | 6 | 7 | 8 | 9 | 10 | 11 | 12 | 13 | 14 |
5' GWAM | 1 | 2 | 3 |

Problem 2

Type the memorandum given at the right, erasing and correcting your errors as necessary. The line endings are indicated by | in color, but listen for the bell as a signal to return.

Current date on Line 7

(3 blank line spaces)

SUBJECT: Two Methods for Determining the Center of a Column 15

DS

Mechanical Method. Determine the longest item in the column | and 32
position the carriage so that the first character of that | item is 45
at the printing point. Next, space forward once for | each two 57
strokes in the item (ignoring an odd or leftover one). | The col- 70
umn center is the point where the forward spacing ends. 81

DS

Problem 3

Remove Problem 2 from your typewriter. Reinsert it; gauge the line; align the letters and type over the paragraph headings.

Mathematical Method. Determine the longest item and position | the 98
carriage as in the mechanical method. Next, note on the | cylinder 112
scale the figure above the printing point (the begin- | ning of the 124
item). Then move the carriage to the last charac- | ter of the item 137
and note on the scale the figure above the | printing point. Fi- 150
nally, add those two figures and divide the | sum by 2. The result- 163
ing number is the center of the column. 171

◼ LESSON 54

54A ◼ CONDITIONING PRACTICE [8] each line 3 times SS; then 1' writings on Line 2

Alphabet	Zero winds quickly exhausted Mr. Fred Jeffrey, but he did not give up.
Figures	Our group read 45 plays, 186 books, and 203 articles during 1971-1972.
Figure/symbol	Order 1 punch @ $5.40; 72 pencils @ 8¢ each; and 37 erasers @ 9¢ each.
Fluency	Going on a wild goose chase is a rather poor way to feather your nest.

| 1 | 2 | 3 | 4 | 5 | 6 | 7 | 8 | 9 | 10 | 11 | 12 | 13 | 14 |

54B ◼ PROBLEM TYPING/COMPOSING: PERSONAL NOTES [30] (Half sheets; line: 60; SS)

Problem 1

Type a copy of the model personal note illustrated at the right. Note the similarity between arrangement of this note and arrangement of the memorandums typed in Lesson 53. Correct your errors as you type.

Problem 2

Compose and type in the same form a personal note to one of your friends. X-out any errors you make as you type the note.

Problem 3

Proofread and correct the copy prepared in Problem 2; then retype it in usable form.

Line
1
2
3
4
5
6
7
8
9
10
11
12
13
14
15
16
17
18
19
20
21
22
23
24
25
26
27
28
29
30
31
32
33

November 13, 19--

Operate return mechanism
4 times (3 blank line spaces)

Dear Darrell

DS

The big Tech-Roosevelt game will be played here on the 25th. I have four seats at the 50-yard line. I hope you'll come for the game and spend the weekend. Kay will get a date for you for the game and for the post-game festivities.

DS

Several parties are to be given after the game. We'll let Kay and your date decide which we'll attend. All of them should be fun.

DS

Be sure to come for the game. Let me know your flight schedule. I'll be on hand to meet you.

DS

Cordially

Steve

Full sheet ■ clear all stops ■ center table vertically in exact center ■ TS after centered heading ■ DS after columnar headings ■ DS data ■ leave 10 spaces between columns

Type as two-line heading, **SUGGESTED STUDY PROCEDURES** — 5
SS → **FOR WORDS OFTEN MISSPELLED** — 11

NOTE: The color underlines in Column 1 show parts of words where misspellings most frequently occur. Do not type the underlines.

Alertness Cue: Remember that 2 lines are used for columnar headings.

Analyze Each Word	Pronounce by Syllables	Acceptable Divisions	Words
			17 / 29
absence	ab-sence	Avoid dividing	36
accommodate	ac-com-mo-date	accom-mo-date	44
attendance	at-tend-ance	attend-ance	51
business	busi-ness	busi-ness	57
candidate	can-di-date	can-di-date	64
difference	dif-fer-ence	dif-fer-ence	71
enough	e-nough	Do not divide	77
foreign	for-eign	for-eign	82
government	gov-ern-ment	gov-ern-ment	90
graduation	grad-u-a-tion	gradu-ation	97
knowledge	knowl-edge	knowl-edge	104
misspell	mis-spell	mis-spell	109
occurring	oc-cur-ring	occur-ring	116
planned	planned	Do not divide	122
proceed	pro-ceed	pro-ceed	127
quantity	quan-ti-ty	quan-tity	133
receive	re-ceive	Avoid dividing	140
recommend	rec-om-mend	rec-om-mend	146
referring	re-fer-ring	refer-ring	153
separate	sep-a-rate	sepa-rate	159
studying	stud-y-ing	study-ing	165
supersede	su-per-sede	super-sede	172
teacher	teach-er	Do not divide	178

Problem 2: Typing from Dictation

Full sheet ■ center vertically and horizontally ■ TS after centered heading: IMPROVING SPELLING ■ DS data of columns ■ assume longest line of each column has 12 spaces ■ 10 spaces between columns

1. Use the list of words in Column 1 of Problem 1. Type a two-column table from your teacher's dictation (book closed):

Col. 1: Type each word as it should be spelled.

Col. 2: Type each word and show, by hyphens, acceptable divisions of word. If the word cannot be divided, type it whole.

2. Check your spelling and word division; circle each spelling or word division error.

54C ■ SKILL-TRANSFER TYPING: STRAIGHT COPY/STATISTICAL COPY 12 (Line: 70; DS; record scores)

1. Type a 1' speed writing on each of the following ¶s. Compare *gwam.*

2. Type two 1' writings on ¶ 2, trying to equal your *gwam* rate on ¶ 1.

3. Type a 2' writing on each ¶. Determine *gwam* and compare rates. Proofread and circle errors.

All letters and figures are used.

	GWAM
	1' | 2'

¶ 1

Words are the major component of written communication, and the typewriter is a very vital tool we use to put those words on paper with speed and ease. To exchange information effectively, the words we use must be chosen quite carefully and typed in a neatly arranged form. We should keep in mind that the selection of the right word is of greater importance than the size of the word because clarity is crucial.

13 | 6 | 48
27 | 14 | 55
41 | 21 | 62
56 | 28 | 69
70 | 35 | 76
83 | 41 | 83

¶ 2

In a recent survey of a national sample of 2,061 business letters, it was found that 30.5% of all messages were brief (100 words or fewer), 54.5% were medium (101 to 300 words), and 15.0% were long (over 300 words). In another vital study––this one having to do with letter cost–– it was learned that a message of medium length cost about $3.00. From all indications, message cost will be considerably higher in 1971-1980.

13 | 7 | 49
28 | 14 | 56
42 | 21 | 63
56 | 28 | 70
71 | 35 | 76
85 | 42 | 85

1' GWAM | 1 | 2 | 3 | 4 | 5 | 6 | 7 | 8 | 9 | 10 | 11 | 12 | 13 | 14 |
2' GWAM | 1 | 2 | 3 | 4 | 5 | 6 | 7 |

■ LESSON 55

55A ■ CONDITIONING PRACTICE 8 each line 3 times SS

Alphabet   V. J. Brahmford is quite well known as an exceptional zoology scholar.

Figures   If $23 \times 654 - 789 + 190 = 14{,}443$, how much would $32 \times 456 + 109$ equal?

Figure/symbol   Glynn & Waggoner's 10/14 Order #1937 was for 2 5/8-inch pine flooring.

Fluency   Are we working on the solution of our problem, or are we a part of it?

| 1 | 2 | 3 | 4 | 5 | 6 | 7 | 8 | 9 | 10 | 11 | 12 | 13 | 14 |

NOTE: Remove the paper; reinsert it; gauge the line and letter; type over the first line.

55B ■ SKILL-TRANSFER TYPING 12 repeat 54C, above

55C ■ COMPOSING AT THE TYPEWRITER 10 (Half sheet; line: 60; SS; current date)

Compose a 2-paragraph memorandum, summarizing the information presented in 54C, above. Use the subject and paragraph headings given at the right. As you compose your memorandum, x-out errors.

SUBJECT: Written Communication
   (See p. 59 for ¶ heading styles.)
Paragraph 1: Word Choice and Clarity
Paragraph 2: Length and Cost of Business Letters

■ LESSON 108

108A ■ CONDITIONING PRACTICE ⑤ each line three times SS: slowly, faster, in-between rate

Alphabet   B. V. Mark recognized the quaint, jagged flowers with spurred calyxes.   *Quick, snap*
Figure/symbol   The terms of discount on Order #47-2896 dated June 15 were 2/10, n/30.   *stroke; immedi-*
Fingers 3 and 4   The happy porpoise easily leaped through the loop and caught the ball.   *ate key release*
Fluency   The right techniques coupled with the right attitudes aid your typing.
     | 1 | 2 | 3 | 4 | 5 | 6 | 7 | 8 | 9 | 10 | 11 | 12 | 13 | 14 |

108B ■ CENTERING COLUMNAR HEADINGS: LEARNING ⑮ practice solution first; then center on half sheet

Drill 1: Columnar Headings Shorter than Columnar Entries

1. First, center columnar entries horizontally; leave 10 spaces between columns.

2. Then, center, type, and underline the headings on the second space above the columnar entries.

Try the drill without referring to the solutions; then check your solution with those suggested.	Analyze Each Word	Pronounce by Syllables	Acceptable Divisions
	accommodate	ac-com-mo-date	accom-mo-date

Drill 2: Columnar Headings Longer than Columnar Entries

1. When columnar headings are considerably longer than columnar entries (as illustrated below), center the columnar headings horizontally first (in this drill leave 4 spaces between headings).

2. Then, double-space and center longest columnar entry under the heading. Use forward-space, backspace method. Check your solution by the mathematical method (as explained below).

Analyze Each Word	Pronounce by Syllables	Acceptable Division Points
accommodate	ac-com-mo-date	accom-mo-date

Suggested Solutions:
1. Forward-Space, Backspace Method. From the first letter of the column (or columnar heading, if it is used for horizontal centering), space forward (→) 1 space for each 2 spaces in the columnar item (or heading, when it is used for centering), ignoring any extra letters. This point will be the center of the column.

Forward space→1→2→3→4→5 spaces
Illustration: ac|co|mm|od|at

From this point, backspace (←) once for each 2 spaces in the heading to

be centered (or the longest columnar item if it is to be centered under a columnar heading), again ignoring any odd or leftover letter.

Backspace   ←1←2←3←4 spaces
Illustration: Ea|ch|#W|or

From this point, type and underline the second heading line (Drill 1). It will be centered over the column. Next, center and type the first heading line, and the two-line heading will be centered over the column as shown above.

2. Mathematical Method. To the number on the cylinder (platen) or line-of-writing scale immediately under the first letter of the columnar entry (or heading when it is used), add the number shown under the space following the last letter of the columnar entry (or heading). Divide this sum by 2; the result will be the center point. From this point on the scale, backspace to center the heading (or the columnar entry when it is to be centered under the heading). Type and underline the heading, and it will be centered.

108C ■ TABULATING SKILL APPLICATIONS ㉚

Problem 1: Three-Column Table with Columnar Headings (Learning Recall)

Type and arrange table at top of page 166 in proper form. Use the forward-space, backspace method to

center the columnar headings over the *longest line* of each column. Make notes of directions.

55D ■ PROBLEM TYPING: PERSONAL NOTES WITH SPECIAL FEATURES 20 (Half sheets; line: 60; SS; correct your errors)

Problem 1: Note with Centered Line

Type the following personal note in the block style illustrated on page 87. Center the address given as Line 3 of the message. DS above and below it.

	Words
Current date on Line 7	3
Dear Linda	5
We are moving to Fort Lauderdale, Florida,	14
next month. Our new address will be	21
3499 Bayview Drive	25
where the ZIP Code is 33306. Our tele-	33
phone number will be (305) 521-7820.	40
Plan to spend some time with us during	48
your spring holiday. By then you'll be glad	57
to get out of the "Frozen North," and I'll be	66
glad to have you soak up some sunshine with	75
me.	76
Yours	77

Problem 2: Note with Simple Table

Type the following personal note in the style used for Problem 1. Center the 2-line table horizontally with 6 spaces between columns. DS above and below the table.

	Words
Current date on Line 7	3
Dear Jan	5
The two telephone numbers you asked me to	13
send you are listed below:	19
Michael J. Wade 471-2056 SS	24
Candice Morrison 931-4857	29
I'm certain Mike and Candy will appreci-	37
ate a telephone invi- tation to your party.	46
Both will be delightful out-of-town guests.	55
All our friends will enjoy getting to know	63
them, I'm sure.	67
Sincerely	68

■ LESSON 56

56A ■ CONDITIONING PRACTICE 8 each line 3 times SS; then 1' writings on Line 2

Alphabet	Mr. Ed Byron did exceptionally good work for the Java quartz industry.
Figures	We have stores at 247 Opera Place, 3805 Avon Court, and 691 Rich Road.
Figure/symbol	The new rate on Leichty & Pierce's $14,670 note (due 12/19/83) is $5\frac{1}{4}$%.
Fluency	To be proficient in office work, you must find and correct all errors.

| 1 | 2 | 3 | 4 | 5 | 6 | 7 | 8 | 9 | 10 | 11 | 12 | 13 | 14 |

56B ■ MANIPULATIVE PARTS DRILL 8 type twice (Line: exactly 60 spaces)

Lines 1-2: Set tab stops to have 6 spaces between words. Tabulate from column to column.

Lines 3-4: Use the shift keys and lock without moving the hand down or the elbows out.

Lines 5-6: Backspace 5 times to start Line 5; backspace 4 times to start Line 6.

1	*Tabulator*	am	aid	and	also	auto	body	born
2	*and return*	an	air	apt	both	busy	city	down

3 *Shift keys* Epworth took TWA Flight 69 at 3:15; Hahn, AA Flight 72 at 4.
4 *and lock* Mark read the book, DESTINY, but not the review in <u>Newsweek</u>.

5 *Margin release* I have now learned to apply my typing skill to prepare useful papers.
6 *and backspacer* A. She must release the margin and backspace four times to type A.

56C ■ TYPING ON SPECIAL-SIZE PAPER 20 (Line: 40; date on Line 13; return carriage at bell signal)

1. Insert a half sheet, long side at left. Type Problem 1 of 55D, above.

2. Insert a half sheet, long side at left. Type Problem 2, above.

4	Word response	their work, and the work, work with them, when she paid, sign the form He may work with their men when they sign the right form for the city. They wish to go to the city with the chairman to sign the right forms.	✔ Speedy, word-level typing response
5			
6			
7	Combination response	and the tax, only their, but they care, when they read, pay such rates state when they, in the reserve, were you paid, and their opinion then minimum profit, an average problem, reserve a quantity, for the estate	✔ Variable rhythm; uniform stroking
8			
9			
10	Variable rhythm	Quantities of problems are solved for the estates at a minimum profit. She will provide us with a statement of the case and added amendments. A million or more statements are mailed by the union staff each month.	✔ Continuity and rhythm
11			
12			

| 1 | 2 | 3 | 4 | 5 | 6 | 7 | 8 | 9 | 10 | 11 | 12 | 13 | 14 |

107C ■ TABULATING SKILL APPLICATIONS 30

Problem 1: Three-Column Table

Half sheet ■ center vertically ■ DS data ■ 6 spaces between columns ■ check solution with placement cues given at bottom of this page

Problem 2: Skill Building

Retype Problem 1 ■ half sheet ■ short side up ■ 4 spaces between columns

Problem 3: Four-Column Table

Half sheet ■ SS data ■ center vertically ■ 6 spaces between columns ■ note spelling of each word as it is typed

Problem 4: Skill Building

Retype Problem 3 ■ full sheet ■ reading position ■ DS data ■ 10 spaces between columns

Lines Used	WORDS FREQUENTLY MISSPELLED			Words in Cols.	Total Words
1					6
2					
3					
4	accommodate	enforceable	liaison	6	12
5					
6	airmail	facilitate	maintenance	13	18
7					
8	bookkeeping	familiar	miscellaneous	20	25
9					
10	clientele	government	occurred	26	31
11					
12	deferred	irrelevant	similar	31	37
KEY	11	6	11	6	13

SPELLING DEMONS				Words in Cols.	Total Words
					3
copied	copying	tried	trying	6	9
employ	employed	valley	valleys	12	15
gully	gullies	stop	stopping	17	21
confer	conferring	profit	profited	24	27
begin	beginning	useful	using	30	33
desire	desirable	courage	courageous	37	41
notice	noticeable	true	truly	43	46
argue	argument	brief	chief	49	52
either	neither	seize	leisure	54	58
weird	height	neighbor	weigh	60	63

Placement Cues: Problem 1, Above

VERTICAL PLACEMENT

Formula:

$$\frac{\text{Lines Available} - \text{Lines Used}}{2} = \text{Top Margin}$$

$\frac{33 - 12}{2} = 10$ blank lines in top margin (extra line left at bottom)

Proof:
10 + 12 + 11 = 33 (lines available)

HORIZONTAL PLACEMENT

Backspace from center of paper 1 space for each 2 spaces in longest columnar lines and for spaces between columns:

ac|co|mm|od|at|e1|23|45|6e|nf|or|ce|ab|1e|12|34|56|mi|sc|el|la|ne|ou

Learning Recall: Ignore an extra space at the end of the last column. Remember to space forward to determine tab stops for Columns 2 and 3.

56D ■ SKILL-TRANSFER TYPING: SCRIPT/ROUGH DRAFT 14 (Line: 70; DS; listen for bell to return)

1. Type a 1' *speed* writing on each of the following ¶s. Compare *gwam* on each ¶ with that made on ¶ 1, 54C, page 88.

2. Type two 1' writings on each of the following ¶s, trying to equal or exceed your *gwam* rate on ¶ 1, 54C, page 88.

3. Type a 2' writing on each ¶. Determine *gwam* and errors. Compare *gwam* with that made on the 2' straight-copy writing of 54C.

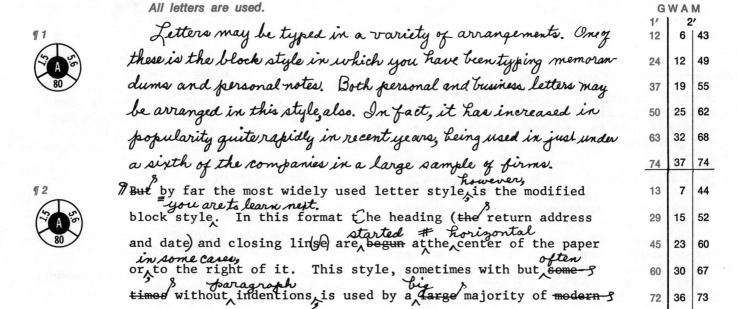

All letters are used.

	GWAM 1'	GWAM 2'	
¶1	12	6	43
	24	12	49
	37	19	55
	50	25	62
	63	32	68
	74	37	74
¶2	13	7	44
	29	15	52
	45	23	60
	60	30	67
	72	36	73
	74	37	74

■ LESSON 57

57A ■ CONDITIONING PRACTICE 8 each line 3 times SS

Alphabet   Judge Bingham was quite vexed when C. K. Zuegendorfer failed to reply.

Figures   These stock numbers need to be replenished: X2938, B10562, and J4702.

Figure/symbol   Terms on Hendrick & Babson's order dated 4/6 for $879.50: 2/10, n/30.

Fluency   Lee found that the elements of the problem are difficult to determine.

| 1 | 2 | 3 | 4 | 5 | 6 | 7 | 8 | 9 | 10 | 11 | 12 | 13 | 14 |

NOTE: Remove the paper; reinsert it; gauge the line and letter; type over the last line.

57B ■ SKILL BUILDING/COMPOSING 12

1. Type two 1' *speed* writings on each ¶ of 56D, above. Determine and compare *gwam* and errors on each pair of writings.

2. Using a 60-space line, compose a 5- to 7-line summary of ¶s 1 and 2 of 56D, above. As you compose your paragraph, x-out errors.

space for each 2 spaces in the longest line in each column and for each 2 spaces to be left between columns. If the last column ends with an extra space, ignore the space. Set the left margin stop at the point where the backspacing ends. From the left margin stop, space forward 1 space for each space in the longest line in the first column and for each space to be left between the first and second columns. Set a tab stop at this point for the second column. Continue procedure for any additional columns.

Spacing between columns. An even number of spaces is usually left between columns (4, 6, 8, 10, or more). The number of spaces to be left between columns is governed by the space available, the number of columns used, and the requirement of ease of reading.

Columnar headings. Columnar headings (when used) are usually centered over the columns.

Other Information

Spacing review. Most typewriters have 6 single line spaces to the vertical inch. Since there are 10 pica-type spaces or 12 elite-type spaces to the horizontal inch, paper 8½ x 11 inches has 66 writing lines of 85 pica or 102 elite spaces. The usual center point for pica-type machines is 42; for elite-type, 50 or 51.

Dollar sign. In a money column, place the dollar sign before the top figure in the column and the total (if shown). The dollar sign may be placed one space to the left of the horizontal beginning point of the longest line in the column, or it may be placed next to the first digit of the top figure in the column, whether this is the longest line in the column or not.

106D ■ COMPOSING ▢15 (1″ side margins; 1½″ top margin; heading: TABULATION)

1. Type *complete sentence answers* in enumerated form to the questions listed at the right. Number your answers with the numbers corresponding to the questions. Single-space, but leave a blank line after each answer. X-out any typing errors you make; then type the word correctly.
2. Proofread your copy. Correct in longhand directly on your copy all misspelled words, errors of correct usage (grammar, capitalization, punctuation, etc.). Check your answers by referring to the copy you typed for 106C; make any additional corrections needed.
3. Using your corrected rough-draft copy of Step 2, retype your answers in proper form. Erase and correct any typing errors.

1. What is meant by tabulating?

2. Give in your own words the steps to follow in centering a table vertically on the page.

3. How many blank lines separate the main heading and the secondary heading of a table?

4. How many blank lines separate the heading lines from the rest of the table?

5. What is meant by reading position in placing a table on a full sheet?

6. Give in your own words the steps to follow in arranging columnar material horizontally on the page.

■ LESSON 107

107A ■ CONDITIONING PRACTICE ▢5 each line 3 times SS: slowly, faster, in-between rate

Alphabet James saw a big gray fox move quickly along a building near the plaza. *Finger-reach*
Figure/symbol He paid $1,830.45 in 1967 for an oriental rug (8′ x 12′) for his home. *action; hands*
Fingers 3 and 4 The plump squaw was coloring wax apples as the zany tourists appeared. *quiet*
Fluency Keep your eyes on the copy and type with continuity to increase speed.
| 1 | 2 | 3 | 4 | 5 | 6 | 7 | 8 | 9 | 10 | 11 | 12 | 13 | 14 |

107B ■ TECHNIQUE IMPROVEMENT ▢15 each line 3 times SS: slowly, faster, top speed

High-frequency words emphasized.

CHECK
1 are you was him best only dear upon date state opinion average minimum ✔ *Finger action;*
2 *Stroke* No, I was not able to get an opinion or to reserve a tax date for you. *fingers curved*
3 *response* We can get him to give an opinion now on only a few extra trade cases. *and upright*
| 1 | 2 | 3 | 4 | 5 | 6 | 7 | 8 | 9 | 10 | 11 | 12 | 13 | 14 |

(Drill continued on page 164)

57C ■ PROBLEM TYPING: PERSONAL/BUSINESS LETTERS IN MODIFIED BLOCK STYLE 30

■ Two class periods will be required to complete the following problems.

Problem 1: Style Letter 1

Type on a full sheet the letter illustrating the *modified block style* with *block paragraphs* and *mixed punctuation* as shown on page 92. Use a 60-space line; begin the return address on Line 16.

Problem 2: Letter with Changes

Type Style Letter 1 (page 92) to the following address. Use an appropriate salutation for the letter.

Dr. Donald J. Newkirk
Department of English
Academy of Fine Arts
Monterey, Calif.   93940

■ Information on ZIP Codes and abbreviations in addresses is presented on pages 104 and 106.

Problem 3: Letter in Unarranged Form

Type in the form of Style Letter 1 (p. 92) the letter given at the right. Full sheet; 60-space line; 6 spaces between columns; begin on Line 18. *Miss* or *Mrs.* is often included with the typed name; *Mr.* never is.

■ *To aid you in typing this first unarranged letter, the line endings are indicated by | in color.*

	Words
3499 Monticello Avenue | New Orleans, La.	8
70118 | November 16, 19–– | Listeners Rec-	16
ord Service | 1220 Avenue of the Americas |	24
New York, N.Y. 10020 | Gentlemen: | (¶ 1)	31
Please send to me by parcel post one copy of	40
each of the fol- | lowing stereo recordings: |	48

		Words
Brahms: Double Concerto	J2147	55
Dionne Warwick: Greatest Hits	M3058	62
Tom Jones: Live in Las Vegas	Z6219	69
Gounod: Romeo and Juliet	C4412	76
The Beatles: Let It Be	N8203	82

	Words
(¶ 2) Charge these to my account, Credit Card	90
#L-214785, and bill | me in the usual man-	97
ner (10 percent discount deducted; parcel |	106
post charges added). | Sincerely yours, | Miss	115
Marsha Donaldson	118

Problem 4: Composing

Using the directions of Problem 3, compose a letter to a friend indicating what you have learned so far in typing. Point out how useful you consider your new skill to be. Proofread; correct; retype the letter.

■ LESSON 58

58A ■ CONDITIONING PRACTICE 8 each line 3 times SS; then 1′ writings on Line 2

Alphabet	Six experts from Brazil drove quickly away from John Greggory's place.
Figures	FOR URGENT CALLS: Fire, 561-7232; Police, 561-7000; Doctor, 841-5839.
Figure/symbol	On May 9, Horton & Todd offered Special "Q" @ 78½¢ a lb. in 500# lots.
Fluency	Stay on your toes, and you can then keep others from stepping on them.

| 1 | 2 | 3 | 4 | 5 | 6 | 7 | 8 | 9 | 10 | 11 | 12 | 13 | 14 |

58B ■ TECHNIQUE PRACTICE: STROKING/SHIFTING 12 type twice

1	Adjacent keys	Sam Frew has pointed out that truth has greater power than we believe.
2		Drew has said that Julia and Sadie Poindexter have done superior work.
3	One-hand	Lonny Hill was as sad as Fred Webster was at your team's great defeat.
4	words	Minny Barber defeated Lilly Hull at darts as Ed Holm beat Tab Stewart.
5	Balanced-	It is also the chairman's duty to aid all of them with their problems.
6	hand words	The city auditor is due by eight, and he may lend a hand to the panel.

| 1 | 2 | 3 | 4 | 5 | 6 | 7 | 8 | 9 | 10 | 11 | 12 | 13 | 14 |

58C ■ PROBLEM TYPING: PERSONAL/BUSINESS LETTERS 30 complete the problems in 57C, above

Tabulation

■ LESSON 106

106A ■ CONDITIONING PRACTICE ⑤ each line 3 times: slowly, faster, in-between rate

Alphabet	This bright jacket has an amazing weave and is of exceptional quality. *Fingers curved*
Figure/symbol	The 6.70 x 15, 2-ply tires (natural rubber) may cost more than $34.89. *and upright*
Long words	Work for typing perfection through thoughtful and purposeful practice.
Fluency	Learn to space quickly between words in order to type with continuity.

| 1 | 2 | 3 | 4 | 5 | 6 | 7 | 8 | 9 | 10 | 11 | 12 | 13 | 14 |

106B ■ TECHNIQUE REFINEMENT: FIGURE REACHES ⑤ four 1' writings

Line: 74 ■ tab stops at 10-space intervals ■ last two digits of each group give word count

EMPHASIZE

Each figure used a minimum of 12 times	3701	7302	4603	6404	5805	8506	9507	5908	✔ Finger-reach action
	3409	7410	6311	8912	6713	9514	8315	7416	
	6517	7218	3819	4920	8921	5622	6823	7924	✔ Quick, tab spacing
	4025	4926	5627	4728	5829	9430	8631	3732	

106C ■ MANUSCRIPT TYPING ㉕ (Margins: 1" side and bottom; 2" top margin, first page; DS; ¶ indention: 5)

NOTES: (1) As a page-end reminder, use a lined backing sheet, or make a light pencil mark at the right edge of the sheet 1 inch from the bottom, and another mark about ¼ inch above the 1-inch mark. Erase marks when page is completed. (2) The backspace-from-vertical-center method is explained on page 78.

TABULATING SUMMARY TS

Tabulating is the arrangement of material in columnar (table) form for ease of reading and reference. The steps to follow, as well as other information, are given below.

Step 1: Vertical Placement of Material DS

Mathematical placement. To determine vertical placement, do this: (1) count the total lines to be used for the table (including the blank spaces between lines if the material is to be typed in double- or triple-spaced form); (2) subtract this figure from the total lines available for use on the sheet; and (3) divide the remainder by 2. This new figure will indicate the number of blank lines to be left at the top of the sheet (ignore any "remainder" lines when dividing by 2). Use the formula: (Total Lines Available Minus Total Lines Used) ÷ 2 = Blank

Lines to Be Left in the Top and in the Bottom Margin.

Spacing after heading lines. When counting the lines to be used, leave 1 blank line (DS) between the main heading and the secondary heading. Leave 2 blank lines (TS) after a main heading if a secondary heading is not used, or after the secondary heading when both a main heading and a secondary heading are used. Leave 1 blank line (DS) after columnar headings (when used).

Reading position. A modern practice in centering material vertically on a full page (8½ x 11 inches) is to center the material in reading position (visual center), a point approximately 2 line spaces above actual vertical center. To center material in reading position, determine the top margin in the usual way, then subtract 2 from the number of lines to be left in the top margin.

Step 2: Horizontal Placement of Columns

Backspace from center. First, move the margin stops to the ends of the scale and clear all tab stops. Then, to arrange the columns horizontally on the sheet, backspace from the center of the sheet 1

(Continued on page 163)

			Words in Parts	Total Words

Tabulate to center point to type return address, date, and closing lines

Return address — Line 16 — 1260 Michigan Avenue — 4 — 4

Dateline — Cincinnati, Ohio 45208 — 9 — 9

November 15, 19-- — *2 spaces* — 13 — 13

Operate return 4 times

Letter address
Mr. Evan K. Hart, Director — 18 — 18
Communication Systems, Inc. — 24 — 24
1027 N. Lakeshore Drive — 28 — 28
Chicago, Illinois 60611 — 33 — 33
DS

Salutation
Dear Mr. Hart: — 37 — 37
DS

Body of letter
For a term paper in English II at Walnut Hills High School, I — 49 — 49
have selected the topic "Rhetoric Versus Grammar in Writing." — 62 — 62
Some members of my class believe that "it doesn't matter how — 74 — 74
you say something as long as you are understood"; but others — 86 — 86
believe that "to write effectively, one must know and observe — 98 — 98
basic rules of grammar." — 103 — 103
DS

I want to support my paper with quotations from authorities — 12 — 115
in general and business communication. As a notable author — 24 — 127
in this field, your viewpoint on the relative importance of — 36 — 139
grammar and rhetoric would strengthen my report immeasurably. — 49 — 152
DS

If you will take the time to give me a brief statement, I — 12 — 163
shall be most grateful. I believe that your comments will — 23 — 175
help me to show that "you can't have one without the other." — 36 — 188
DS

Complimentary close
Sincerely yours, — 39 — 191
Operate return 4 times

Signature
David L. Herzog

Typed name of writer
David L. Herzog — 42 — 194

Mixed Punctuation. In *mixed punctuation*, illustrated in this letter, a colon follows the salutation and a comma follows the complimentary close.

Open Punctuation. In *open punctuation*, no punctuation follows the salutation or complimentary close. Open punctuation is used in the personal note on page 87.

Style Letter 1: Personal/Business Letter in Modified Block Style; Mixed Punctuation

comments. If your time permits, we should like 259
to have you join us at our next Planning Con- 268
ference, which will be held at the Lakeside Inn 278
in Denver, June 15-21. In any event, may we 287
hear from you soon. Your help is urgently 295
needed. | Sincerely yours | John H. Kingston | 304
Your initials | Enclosure (277) 306/319

the enclosed postage free card. At your con- 163
venience, a qualified representative will call to 173
discuss our many services to the homeowner. 182
Remember, we are here to help, so call us soon. | 192
Sincerely yours | James Thompson | *Your initials* | 199
Enclosure (174) 201/214

Problem 2

Current date | Mr. Charles Templeman | 6712 9
Bennett Avenue, So. | Chicago, IL 60649 | 16
Dear Mr. Templeman | (¶ 1) A few months 23
ago we wrote you regarding the sale of your 32
home. Since that time, our office has partici- 41
pated in the sale or lease of many homes 49
throughout the Chicago and suburban areas. 58
(¶ 2) Even though interest rates have not 65
stabilized, there is still a great demand for 74
homes. A true market value opinion of your 83
property by one of our experienced real estate 93
brokers is just one of the many services that the 103
THOMPSON REALTY COMPANY can pro- 109
vide without any obligation on your part. We 118
also offer financing service should you wish to 128
refinance your present home. (¶ 3) You may 135
take advantage of any of our professional ser- 145
vices by telephoning our office or by returning 154

Problem 3

Current date | Mrs. Dorothy Losee | 4596 8
Beachview Drive | Cleveland, OH 44117 | 15
Dear Mrs. Losee | (¶ 1) Asking for money is 23
never a simple or pleasant job. In asking for 32
your contribution to the American Cancer 40
Society, one is tempted to support the request 50
with statistics, with emotional appeals, or even 60
with slogans. But in the final analysis, your 69
contribution must depend upon your own feel- 78
ings regarding the worth of the Society's efforts 88
to win the war against cancer. (¶ 2) I can only 96
assure you that your gift, whether for $5 or 105
$25, will be used carefully and efficiently in 115
the fight against cancer. Won't you please 124
write your contribution check now, payable to 133
the American Cancer Society. A return enve- 142
lope is enclosed for your convenience. | Sin- 150
cerely yours | Mrs. Walter S. Burr | Volunteer 159
Chairman | *Your initials* | Enclosure (131) 163/175

■ LESSON 105

105A ■ CONDITIONING PRACTICE 5 each line 3 times SS: slowly, faster, in-between rate

Alphabet	With amazing dexterity, the jovial squaws plucked the big white fowls.
Figure/symbol	Order No. 8475 for 6 chairs ($39.75 ea.) will be shipped May 19 or 20.
Third row	Jerry Pettie won't quote you a good price on any of those typewriters.
Fluency	Send a draft of the statement to the union at the address on the card.

Type with continuity and rhythm

| 1 | 2 | 3 | 4 | 5 | 6 | 7 | 8 | 9 | 10 | 11 | 12 | 13 | 14 |

105B ■ SKILL BUILDING: STRAIGHT COPY 15

1. Type a 5′ writing on the ¶s of 103B, page 158, on *control level* (try to type with 5 or fewer errors).

2. Type another 5′ writing. If you made the goal of Step 1, increase your speed on this writing.

105C ■ PRODUCTION SKILL MEASUREMENT: LETTERS 30 (Block style; open punctuation; correct your errors)

Time Schedule	
Planning and preparing	4′
Timed production writing	20′
Proofreading; computing *n-pram*	6′

Repeat 104C, page 160, and above. In this timing, however, erase and correct all errors. Proofread your work. Deduct 15 words from total words typed for each uncorrected error; divide remainder by 20 to determine *n-pram* (net production rate a minute—all errors corrected).

■ LESSON 59

59A ■ CONDITIONING PRACTICE 8 each line 3 times SS; then 1' writings on Line 3

Alphabet	Mrs. Alex J. Preble's zeal very quickly influenced those good workmen.
Figures	My Social Security number is 938-27-5026; my work permit number, R415.
Figure/symbol	Their price is 95¢ a copy (less 20% discount on orders of 36 or more).
Fluency	Now is the time to stop pushing for high speed and drive for accuracy.

| 1 | 2 | 3 | 4 | 5 | 6 | 7 | 8 | 9 | 10 | 11 | 12 | 13 | 14 |

59B ■ TECHNIQUE PRACTICE: RESPONSE PATTERNS 7 two 1' writings on each line; determine GWAM

Letter response	Only a few estates were traded after you set a tax rate on my acreage.
Word response	The amendment did signal an end to the rigid social theory of the day.
Combination	The contract with the union may entitle the workmen to a minimum wage.

| 1 | 2 | 3 | 4 | 5 | 6 | 7 | 8 | 9 | 10 | 11 | 12 | 13 | 14 |

59C ■ ASSEMBLING, INSERTING, AND ERASING A CARBON PACK 10 (Full sheets; line: 60; DS)

1. Read ¶ 1 at the right and assemble a carbon pack as directed there.
2. Read ¶ 2, then insert the pack as directed.
3. Type the material as given at the right. Begin on Line 13. *Erase and correct your errors.*

Copy sheet
Carbon paper
Original

ASSEMBLING AND INSERTING A CARBON PACK
TS

TO ERASE ERRORS

1. Pull the original sheet forward and place a 5" x 3" card in front of the carbon sheet. Erase the error on the original with a hard (typewriter) eraser.
2. Remove the card. Then with a soft (pencil) eraser, erase the error on the carbon (file) copy.

Place the sheet on which the carbon (file) copy is to be made flat on the desk; then place a sheet of carbon paper, carbon side down, on top of the paper. Finally, place the sheet for the original on top of the carbon paper.

Pick up the papers and tap them lightly on the desk. Insert the pack into the machine, carbon side toward you as you insert the papers. Roll the pack in far enough for the feed rolls to grip the papers; then operate the paper-release lever to eliminate possible wrinkles.

59D ■ PROBLEM TYPING: BUSINESS LETTERS IN MODIFIED BLOCK STYLE 25

Problem 1: Style Letter 2

Type on a full sheet Style Letter 2, page 94. Use a 60-space line; type the date on Line 16 from the top edge of the paper. *Erase and correct errors.*

Problem 2: Skill Building

Type a 1' writing on the opening lines (date through salutation); determine *gwam*. Then type a 1' writing

on the closing lines (complimentary close through enclosure); determine *gwam.*

Problem 3: Letter with Changes

Type Style Letter 2, page 94, but address it to:

Mr. John A. Marsh, Manager
Pacific Building, Suite 5
Oakland, CA   94612

Prepare a carbon copy; erase and correct errors

LESSON 104

104A ■ CONDITIONING PRACTICE 5 each line 3 times SS: slowly, faster, in-between rate

Alphabet	The brown fox jumped very quickly to grab those excited, fuzzy chicks.	*Quick, snap stroke;*
Figure/symbol	Write checks for these amounts: $41.44, $53.26, $178.90, and $414.45.	*immediate key release*
Double letters	A committee will meet the bookkeeping class to discuss current assets.	
Fluency	The auditor will send a statement to the firm by the end of the month.	

| 1 | 2 | 3 | 4 | 5 | 6 | 7 | 8 | 9 | 10 | 11 | 12 | 13 | 14 |

104B ■ TECHNIQUE IMPROVEMENT: MANIPULATIVE CONTROLS 15 each line 3 times SS: slowly, faster, top speed

EMPHASIZE

1 — and and and, the the the, they they they, then then then, pay them for ✔ *Quick, down-and-in spacing motion*

2 *Space-bar control* — if it is, and the, they may pay, when they try, to help you, the drain

3 — They may pay them when they try to help you clean the old storm drain.

4 — Floyd Flynn, Paul McNeil, and Jack Burred attended the AMS Convention. ✔ *Quick, little finger reach*

5 *Shift-key control* — R. J. Asham, T. O. Black, A. E. Byrd, and Jan Kane made A's in typing.

6 — H. V. McGil, President of McGil & Company, left for Chicago, Illinois.

Center   +   10 = ↓ TAB
A quick return

7 *Return*   of the carriage ————— Tab ————→with an immediate ✔ *Manual: Quick, flick-of-hand reach motion*

start of the new line ————— Tab ————→will result in an ✔ *Electric: Quick, little finger reach*

increased speed rate. ————— Tab ————→(*Repeat as many times as time permits.*)

104C ■ BUILDING PRODUCTION SKILL: LETTERS 30 (Block style; open punctuation; do not correct errors)

Time Schedule	
Planning and preparing	4'
Timed production writing . . .	20'
Proofreading; determining *g-pram*	6'

Type each letter on a separate letterhead or plain sheet. Determine placement: See table, page 144. Make notes of needed directions. If you complete all letters before time is called, start over. When time is called, proofread letters; determine *g-pram* (total words ÷ 20).

Problem 1

Words

Current date | Mr. Henry Abbott | 219 Wana- 8
maker, North | Philadelphia, PA 19139 | 16
Dear Mr. Abbott | (¶ 1) Recently a number of 23
us met to consider the future of America—its 33
land, its cities, and its people. From this meet- 43
ing emerged the enclosed preliminary report 51
of a plan to save our environment. It is an 60
attempt to deal, in a systematic and construc- 70
tive way, with the many and varied problems 78
we face. (¶ 2) I am sure you will be interested 87
in this report. In preparing it, we have not felt 97
bound by any established notions of what 105
"planning" is supposed to be. Instead, we have 115
attempted to determine what it must be, and 124

Words

to indicate why. The report demonstrates that 133
it is indeed quite possible to maintain a pleas- 143
ant environment for everyone and yet permit 152
the utmost opportunity for personal initiative 161
and fulfillment. The close relation of phys- 170
ical and social problems is well known. We 179
have attempted to show how we may seek 187
solutions to these problems under a single, 195
easily understood set of policies and goals. 205
(¶ 3) This preliminary report cannot offer 212
solutions to all problems or answers to every 221
question with which we must deal. It needs 230
careful evaluation and criticism. Therefore, we 240
are asking you to study it, and to send us your 249

(*Continued on page 161*)

CENTURY 21

SCHOOL/OFFICE EQUIPMENT COMPANY

11 GUITTARD ROAD   BURLINGAME, CA 94010   415/697-7050

*Tabulate to center point
to type date and closing lines*

		Words in Parts	5' GWAM
Dateline	*Line 16* November 17, 19--	4	1
	Operate return 4 times		
Letter address	Mr. Dennis R. Knox, Principal	10	2
	Golden Gate High School	14	3
	2800 Turk Boulevard	18	4
	San Francisco, CA 94118	23	5
	DS		
Salutation	Dear Mr. Knox:	26	5
	DS		

Surely you agree that few things are more personal than the   12   8
messages you write. They convey your ideas, your thoughts,   24   10
your ideals. They are you--on paper. But are the messages   37   13
that bear your signature giving you fair representation?   50   15

Body of letter

Study this message for a moment and decide for yourself. Note   62   18
how it is centered upon the page. Then observe that the mar-   74   20
gins are balanced and clearly defined, that the paragraphs are   87   23
well proportioned.   91   23

Note also that every type character is clean-cut, uniform in   103   26
impression, and evenly spaced. The capitals, which in so many   116   28
cases show a tendency to jump above the line, are in perfect   128   31
alignment.   130   31

Compare and see! Let us deliver a new IMPACT ELECTRIC type-   142   34
writer to your office where you can see for yourself how the   155   36
performance of an IMPACT will give you better-looking messages   167   39
for better representation. Your signature on the enclosed   179   41
card is all it takes to arrange an appointment.   188   43

Complimentary close	Sincerely yours, *4 line spaces (3 blank lines)*	3	44
Signature	*J. Marshall Goodwin*		
Typed name of writer	J. Marshall Goodwin	7	44
Official title of writer	Regional Sales Manager	12	45
	DS		
Initials of typist	mhh	13	45
	DS		
Enclosure notation	Enclosure	15	46

Cincinnati   Chicago   Burlingame, California   Dallas   New Rochelle, New York

Style Letter 2: Business Letter in Modified Block Style; Mixed Punctuation

103C ■ SKILL APPLICATIONS 30 (Plain sheets, 8½″ x 11″; half sheet, 8½″ x 5½″)

Problem 1: Personal/Business Letter

Block style ■ open punctuation ■ return address started on Line 16

4298 Browndale Avenue | Minneapolis, Minnesota 55416 | *Current date* | Mr. Robert Sullivan | Century Plaza Square, Suite 1408 | 1169 Avenue of the Stars | Century City, California 90024 | Dear Mr. Sullivan | (¶1) I had the opportunity to hear your inspiring talk entitled "The Brotherhood of Man" at the National Convention of the Future Business Leaders of America. (¶2) After your talk, you said that you would send us copies of the poem entitled "Outwitted" by Edwin Markham and the philosophical statement entitled "I Believe" by John D. Rockefeller, Jr., which you quoted in your talk. (¶3) Will you please send these copies to me. I am enclosing a self-addressed and stamped envelope for your reply. Again, may I thank you for your inspirational talk. | Sincerely yours | William Walton | Enclosure (107)

Problem 2: Business Letter in Block Style with Open Punctuation

Current date | Mr. William Walton | 4298 Browndale Avenue | Minneapolis, MN 55416 | Dear Mr. Walton | (¶1) I am very glad to send you copies of the poem "Outwitted" by Edwin Markham and the philosophical statement "I Believe" by John D. Rockefeller, Jr. (¶2) I am always pleased when I get letters such as yours; I am even more pleased when I learn that many persons are working hard to help others help themselves. Here, I think, our teachers deserve a big vote of thanks. | Cordially yours | Robert Sullivan | (xxx) | Enclosures (73)

NOTE: After you have typed Problems 3 and 4, attach the copies to this letter.

Problem 3: Arranging Material in Theme Form

Full sheet ■ single spacing ■ 1½″ top margin ■ 60-space line ■ ¶ indention: 5

NOTE: Double-space after the last line of the theme and start author's name at center point.

Heading: I BELIEVE (¶1) I believe in the supreme worth of the individual and in his right to life, liberty, and the pursuit of happiness. (¶2) I believe that every right implies a responsibility; every opportunity, an obligation; every possession, a duty. (¶3) I believe that the law was made for man and not man for the law; that government is the servant of the people and not their master. (¶4) I believe in the dignity of labor, whether with head or hand; that the world owes no man a living but that it owes every man an opportunity to make a living. (¶5) I believe that thrift is essential to well-ordered living and that economy is a prime requisite of a sound financial structure, whether in government, business, or personal affairs. (¶6) I believe that truth and justice are fundamental to an enduring social order. (¶7) I believe in the sacredness of a promise, that a man's word should be as good as his bond; that character—not wealth or power or position—is of supreme worth. (¶8) I believe that the rendering of useful service is the common duty of mankind and that only in the purifying fire of sacrifice is the dross of selfishness consumed and the greatness of the human soul set free. (¶9) I believe in an all-wise and all-loving God, named by whatever name, and that the individual's highest fulfillment, greatest happiness, and widest usefulness are to be found in living in harmony with His will. (¶10) I believe that love is the greatest thing in the world; that it alone can overcome hate; that right can and will triumph over might. | --John D. Rockefeller, Jr.

Problem 4: Centering Checkup

Center the poem, vertically and horizontally. Use a half sheet (8½″ x 5½″), long side up. Double-space the lines, but triple-space after the author's name. **NOTE:** Center only the first line of the poem; start other three lines at this same point.

OUTWITTED

by

Edwin Markham

He drew a circle that shut me out--

Heretic, rebel, a thing to flout.

But Love and I had the wit to win:

We drew a circle that took him in!

(Reprinted by permission of Virgil Markham)

LESSON 60

60A ■ CONDITIONING PRACTICE [8] 3 times SS; then 1' writings on Line 1

Alphabet	Y. M. Winlock plans to drive Elizabeth Jeffries to Quebec next August.
Figures	On May 8 she ordered 750 sets of 6-ply NCR paper--No. 294731--for you.
Figure/symbol	Your Policy #NY13967-946-21 (issued February 5, 1970) expires in 1983.
Fluency	If you fall, get to your feet and climb before you skid to the bottom.

| 1 | 2 | 3 | 4 | 5 | 6 | 7 | 8 | 9 | 10 | 11 | 12 | 13 | 14 |

60B ■ IMPROVING LETTER TYPING SKILL [17]

1. Type a 2' writing on the opening lines and ¶ 1 of Style Letter 1, page 92. Try to improve your speed in moving from part to part.

2. Type a 2' writing on the last ¶ and the closing lines of Style Letter 1, page 92. Use the tabulator quickly to improve your speed.

3. Type a 1' writing on the opening lines, then on the closing lines, of Style Letter 2, page 94. Space and indent efficiently.

4. Type a 5' writing on Style Letter 2, page 94. When time is called, proofread and determine *gwam*. Compare *gwam* with your straight-copy *gwam*.

60C ■ PROBLEM TYPING: BUSINESS LETTERS IN MODIFIED BLOCK STYLE [25] (Full sheets; line: 60; SS)

Problem 1: Letter with Centered Line

Words

Current date on Line 16 | Mr. Alan J. Kent, Presi- 8
dent | Central Data Processing Center | 3011 16
West Grand Boulevard | Detroit, MI   48202 | 24
Dear Mr. Kent: | (¶ 1) One of my associates 31
has just written a booklet on the impor- | tant 40
subject of communication. It is called | 48

Writing Out Loud 55

and contains 32 pages of up-to-date, refresh- 64
ing pointers on | one of the most important 72
elements of your job and mine-- | dictating. 81
I should like to send you a complimentary 89
copy | to see whether you find it as helpful 98
as I did and also | whether you agree that 106
most people who dictate could read it | with 115
decided profit. |(¶ 2) Writing Out Loud takes 126
only a few minutes to read and will | almost 134
certainly help you reduce your dictating time. | 144
(¶ 3) Simply fill in and mail the enclosed card, 153
and I shall see | that the booklet reaches you 162
promptly. Your comments will be | most wel- 170
come. | Sincerely yours, | Alexander P. Klein | 178
President | njz | Enclosure 183

Problem 2: Letter with Table

Prepare a carbon copy of the letter in the next column. Erase and correct your errors on both the original and the carbon copy. Listen for the bell for line endings in the body of the letter.

Words

Current date on Line 16 | Dr. Lloyd M. Powell, 7
Superintendent | Columbia Public School Sys- 15
tem | 1002 Range Line | Columbia, MO 22
65201 | Dear Dr. Powell: | (¶ 1) Congratula- 29
tions on the passage of the bond issue that will 39
permit you to build, equip, and staff a new 48
senior high school. (¶ 2) The following book- 56
lets, which you requested, should be of real 65
help in your planning: | 69

6 spaces

Guide to Classroom Layout | Cronin 76
Equipping the Modern School | Stebbens 83
Selection of Business Machines ↓ Marlow 91

(¶ 3) After you have studied the booklets, may 99
we have one of our representatives arrange an 108
appointment to discuss ways in which we may 117
be able to assist you in this new program? 126
Simply fill in and return the enclosed card, 135
and we'll do the rest. | Sincerely yours, | 143
Donald K. Hawley, Jr. | Sales Manager | jlb | 151
Enclosure 153

Problem 3: Letter with Changes

Type the letter of Problem 1 (with carbon copy, your errors corrected), but address it to:

Dr. Eric J. Stoner, Dean
Essex Polytechnic Institute
100 W. Cold Spring Lane
Baltimore, MD   21209

NOTE: Keep these letters for use in Lesson 61.

■ LESSON 103

103A ■ CONDITIONING PRACTICE 5 each line 3 times SS: slowly, faster, in-between rate

Alphabet | Five kind doctors gazed jubilantly at the new hospital annex marquees.
Figure/symbol | A special "J&B" rug (8'10" x 12') sells for $346.79 less 15% discount.
Long reaches | The unusual aluminum bridge is decorated with many bright nylon flags.
Fluency | They plan to see the ancient ornaments when they visit the old museum.

Finger-reach action; hands quiet

| 1 | 2 | 3 | 4 | 5 | 6 | 7 | 8 | 9 | 10 | 11 | 12 | 13 | 14 |

103B ■ GROWTH INDEX: STRAIGHT COPY 15 two 5' writings; determine GWAM; proofread for errors

All letters are used.

GWAM
1' | 5'

¶ 1

For many typing tasks, the typist must use paper, carbon sheets, — 13 | 3 | 59
envelopes, and other items. Often, time may be wasted in using such — 27 | 5 | 62
supplies. For example, supplies may be in utter disarray on or in the — 41 | 8 | 64
typist's desk. The production rate of a typist can be increased by care- — 55 | 11 | 67
ful planning of the order and layout of paper, carbon sheets, envelopes, — 70 | 14 | 70
and other items. In this way, these items can be located quickly and — 84 | 17 | 73
easily as they are needed. A similar principle also applies to erasers, — 99 | 20 | 76
note pads, pencils, pens, and other items that may be used in the task — 113 | 23 | 79
to be completed. "A place for everything with each thing in its place," — 127 | 25 | 82
is a good rule to follow. — 132 | 26 | 83

¶ 2

Another guide to efficiency of work habits relates to the assembly, — 14 | 29 | 85
pickup, and insertion of supplies into the typewriter. Often, the typist — 28 | 32 | 88
may make many waste motions in assembling and inserting a carbon pack — 42 | 35 | 91
into the machine. There is little realization of the time that may be — 57 | 38 | 94
lost with just such a simple task as the insertion of a sheet of paper — 71 | 41 | 97
into the machine. For instance, the typist may fumble the paper, he — 85 | 43 | 100
frequently uses both hands in the pickup of the paper, he may turn the — 99 | 46 | 102
paper several times, he may grind rather than twirl the paper into the — 113 | 49 | 105
machine, and he may make many other waste motions—–each of which results — 128 | 52 | 108
in lost time. This is time that can and should be turned into typing — 142 | 55 | 110
time and increased production rates. — 149 | 56 | 112

1' GWAM | 1 | 2 | 3 | 4 | 5 | 6 | 7 | 8 | 9 | 10 | 11 | 12 | 13 | 14 |
5' GWAM | 1 | 2 | 3 |

■ LESSON 61

61A ■ CONDITIONING PRACTICE ⑧ each line 3 times SS; then 1' writings on Line 3

Alphabet	Dwight Jacobs frequently goes to visit the Phoenix Municipal Park Zoo.
Figures	The letter shows the ZIP Code 45208 and the telephone number 931-6720.
Figure/symbol	On Line 16, type "On 4/18 ship Ward & Sons 72 pens @ $3.90, less 5½%."
Fluency	The problem is big, but a man of determination can certainly solve it.

| 1 | 2 | 3 | 4 | 5 | 6 | 7 | 8 | 9 | 10 | 11 | 12 | 13 | 14 |

61B ■ ADDRESSING SMALL ENVELOPES; FOLDING AND INSERTING LETTERS ⑳

Return Address. Type in block style, single-spaced, the writer's name, street number and name (or box number), city, state (followed by 2 spaces), and ZIP Code in the upper left corner (unless an envelope with a printed address is provided). Begin on the second line space from the top edge and 3 spaces from the left edge.

Envelope Address. Begin about 2 inches (Line 12 or 13) from the top and 2½ inches from the left edge of the envelope. Use block style and single spacing, no matter how many or how few lines are required.

■ Type the city name, state name or abbreviation, and ZIP Code on the last line of the address.

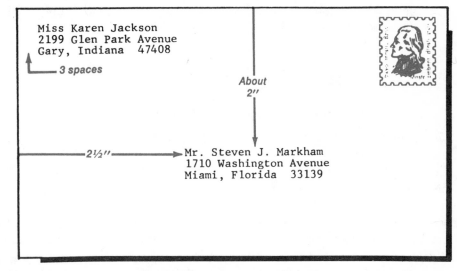

■ In letter and envelope addresses, direction names (North, South, East, and West) may be abbreviated (N., S., E., and W., respectively) to improve the balance of the lines in the address.

Problem 1

■ Type the model envelope illustrated at the right, above; then address an envelope for each letter typed as 60C Problem Typing, page 95. *The envelope address should agree with the letter address in content, style, spacing.*

Problem 2

■ Study the directions and illustrations below for folding and inserting a letter into a small envelope; then fold and insert into their addressed envelopes the letters typed as Problems 1-3, page 95.

Problem 3

■ If time permits, address a small envelope (using your own return address) for a letter to:

Mrs. Elaine Brooks, Principal
Emerson Elementary School
715 Stadium Drive
San Antonio, Texas   78212

FOLDING A LETTER FOR A SMALL ENVELOPE

Step 1: With the letter face up on the desk, fold from the bottom up to ½ inch of the top.

Step 2: Fold right third to left.

Step 3: Folding from left to right, fold left third to ½" of last crease.

Step 4: Insert last creased edge first.

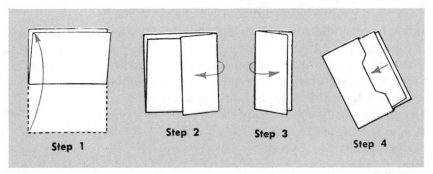

■ LESSON 102

102A ■ CONDITIONING PRACTICE [5] each line 3 times SS: slowly, faster, in-between rate

Alphabet   The juke box music puzzled a gentle visitor from a quaint valley town.   *Finger-reach action; hands quiet*
Figure/symbol He sent $234.98 for the camera and $16.75 for the case (plus 20% tax).
Shift lock   A sample was printed in four colors on BEST Papers PKG #34110 BRISTOL.
Fluency   If they give him a key to the office, he might finish the work for us.
     | 1 | 2 | 3 | 4 | 5 | 6 | 7 | 8 | 9 | 10 | 11 | 12 | 13 | 14 |

102B ■ SKILL BUILDING: LETTER COPY [15]

1. Type a 10' writing on Style Letter 4, page 156. If you complete the letter before time is called, start over on a new sheet.

2. Proofread your copy and circle all errors; determine *gwam* (total words typed ÷ minutes typed). Record your letter-copy rate.

102C ■ SKILL APPLICATIONS [30] (Plain sheets, 8½" x 11")

Problem 1: Block Style; Open Punctuation

Current date | Dr. James C. Bennett | Business Education Department | San Fernando Valley State College | Northridge, CA   91344 | Dear Dr. Bennett | (¶ 1) Quality education is one of our greatest needs in this period of rapid technological and social change. Our educational programs dare not lag behind in meeting the needs of today's youth if they are to have an orderly transition into a complicated fast-moving era. (¶ 2) The evaluation-accreditation program sponsored by the WESTERN ASSOCIATION OF SCHOOLS AND COLLEGES is the nation's best effort in focusing the attention of the entire faculty and student body of a given secondary school on an assessment of quality of both the educational process and the product. When further refined and expanded, this program could well provide the model for a nationwide system of quality assurance in education. (¶ 3) Although each educator is chiefly concerned with the program in his particular school, or schools, his diagnostic judgments and evaluative techniques can be sharpened and enhanced and new concepts developed through participating in the evaluation of other schools. I trust that you will look upon the enclosed invitation as an opportunity to render an outstanding service to the profession and, at the same time, to further develop personal competencies in key areas of educational leadership. | Sincerely yours | L. W. Hedge | Executive Secretary | *Your Initials* | Enclosure (244)

Problem 2: Proofreading; Making Rough-Draft Corrections

Often an executive in a business office will make extensive changes in the original draft of a letter. You are to make such changes in the letter that you typed as Problem 1. (You will need to show most of your longhand corrections in the margins; however, indicate clearly by lines-and-arrows where the changes are to be made or inserted in your original letter.)

¶ 1: In sentence 2, *change* "dare not lag behind in meeting" to "must not fail to meet"; *change* "if they are to have" to "if these young people are to make"; *delete* "fast-moving era" at the end of this sentence, and *add* "and changing world when they graduate." ¶ 3: *Change* sentence 1 to read: "Through participating in the evaluation of other schools, each educator can have his diagnostic judgments and evaluative techniques sharpened and enhanced." (**NOTE:** This change now starts with the ending words of the sentence. Show by means of a line-and-arrow that these words are to be moved to the beginning of the sentence. Indicate the other corrections by drawing lines through words to be deleted.) In sentence 2 *change* "I trust that you will" to "Please"; *change* "as an opportunity" to "as a way"; *change* "to further develop personal" to "as an opportunity to develop your." ¶ 4—*Add* the following as ¶ 4: May I look forward to an affirmative reply from you. Just use the enclosed postal card.

Problem 3: Typing from Rough-Draft Copy

Type the corrected rough-draft copy of Problem 1 in block style with open punctuation. Erase and correct any errors you make as you retype the letter.

61C ■ PROBLEM TYPING: LETTERS IN MODIFIED BLOCK STYLE [22] (Full sheets; line: 60; address envelopes)

Problem 1

	Words
Current date on Line 16 | Mrs. Helen Q. Gibson |	7
Department of Business | St. Ursula High	15
School | 755 Commonwealth Avenue | Boston,	23
MA 02215 | Dear Mrs. Gibson: | (¶1)	29
Whether it's a small dot or a large area, you	38
erase it neatly and quickly with the new	46
ERASOMATIC Electronic Eraser. (¶2) It's	53
as easy to use as a pencil. Just lift the hand-	63
piece and it starts. Put the handpiece back	72
on the cradle and it stops. And a special lock	81
keeps it from being started accidentally. (¶3)	90
When the eraser tip wears down, simply run	98
it across the Trimmer and you have a sharp	107
edge again. Proper tip length is maintained	116
simply by inserting eraser tips into the built-in	126
Renewer. (¶4) Quiet? No more sound than a	134
purring kitten; will not disturb others in the	143
same work area. (¶5) Use the handy order	151
card that is enclosed to order your first	159
ERASOMATIC now. After this first tryout,	167
you'll want one for every work station in your	177
office practice laboratory. | Sincerely yours, |	186
Charles T. LaRue | Regional Sales Manager |	194
ltd | Enclosure	197/218 *

* Includes envelope address.

Problem 2

Type the letter of Problem 1 (with carbon copy, your errors corrected), but address it to:

Miss Rosalie Steinberg
Department of Business
Atlantic High School
31 Clinton Street
Newark, NJ   07102

Change *office practice laboratory* in the last paragraph to *advanced typewriting class.*

Problem 3: Composing

Compose a personal/business letter to Mr. Charles T. LaRue (*of Problem 1*) requesting further information about the ERASOMATIC Electronic Eraser. You might want to know, for example, whether the eraser can operate on batteries as well as electricity, how long it should operate without repair, where it can be repaired, where additional eraser elements can be obtained in your locality. The address of Mr. LaRue is CENTURY 21, School/Office Equipment Co., 512 North Avenue, New Rochelle, NY   10802.

■ LESSON 62

62A ■ CONDITIONING PRACTICE [8] 3 times SS; then 1' writings on Line 3

Alphabet	Helvig d'Aquin visited Mexico, Brazil, and Peru for two weeks in July.
Figures	She worked from 8:45 to 2:30 on June 16; from 9:50 to 5:00 on June 17.
Figure/symbol	Hunter & Muncy's check for $697.80 (Check #1435) was cashed on July 2.
Fluency	Was your auditor skeptical of the authenticity of this last signature?

| 1 | 2 | 3 | 4 | 5 | 6 | 7 | 8 | 9 | 10 | 11 | 12 | 13 | 14 |

62B ■ PERSONAL/BUSINESS COMMUNICATIONS: REVIEW [42]

Make a list of the following page numbers and problem references. Place the list alongside your typewriter for easy reference. Type as many of the problems as you can. Prepare a carbon copy of each problem. Work quickly but carefully, correcting your errors.

Page 86, 53C, Problem 1
Page 87, 54B, Problem 1
Page 91, 57C, Problem 3
Page 95, 60C, Problem 1
Page 97, 61C, Problem 2 (Address envelope.)

If you complete all the problems before time is called, compose a paragraph of several lines interpreting the meaning of the following quotation:

> The dogmas of the quiet past are inadequate to the stormy present . . . . As our case is new, so we must think anew and act anew. We must disenthrall ourselves.
>
> ——Abraham Lincoln

Proofread and correct your copy; then retype it in correct form, erasing and/or correcting your errors as you type.

One Victory Boulevard, S.

Burbank, California 91502

Telephone 483-2759

Typewriters   Adding Machines   Calculators   EDP-IDP Equipment

	Words
March 28, 19--	3
Dr. Lyn R. Clark, President	9
Systems Design Corporation	14
11463 Wilshire Blvd.	18
Los Angeles, CA 90024	23
Dear Dr. Clark	26

Today many business firms use the block style letter for   37
their correspondence. This letter is an example of that   49
style. You will note that all lines start at the left   60
margin. The advantage of this style is that the mechan-   71
ical process of indenting opening and closing lines, or   82
paragraphs, is eliminated. This practice saves typing   93
time as well as space.   98

Open punctuation is used with this letter. Punctuation   109
marks are omitted after the date, address, salutation,   120
and complimentary close unless an abbreviation is used.   131
In this case the period is typed as a part of the abbre-   143
viation. Elimination of these punctuation marks helps   154
to increase letter production rates. Another recommended   165
timesaving feature is to type only the typist's initials   177
for reference when the dictator's name is typed in the   188
closing lines.   191

As you can see, the block style letter gives good place-   202
ment appearance. Because many extra typing strokes and   213
motions are eliminated, the use of this style does help   225
to increase letter production rates. It is the letter   236
style I recommend for use in the business office.   246

Sincerely yours   249

Scott M. Sellwood

Scott M. Sellwood   253
Communications Consultant   258

lwe   258

Style Letter 4: Block Style with Open Punctuation

UNIT 16 (Lessons 101-105) Business Letters   **LESSON 101 / PAGE 156**

LESSON 63

63A ■ CONDITIONING PRACTICE [8] 3 times SS; then 1′ writings on Line 4

Alphabet   Jackson, Fieldor & Quigley will build their plant in Veracruz, Mexico.

Figures   These typewriters need repair: E 13-601252; J 14-859720; M 15-214938.

Figure/symbol   Does Mr. Chambord's Policy #163045 for $7,500 expire on June 29, 1978?

Fluency   Did he question the authority of those who make such profits possible?

| 1 | 2 | 3 | 4 | 5 | 6 | 7 | 8 | 9 | 10 | 11 | 12 | 13 | 14 |

63B ■ GROWTH INDEX [8] one 5′ writing; determine GWAM and errors

All letters are used.

		GWAM	
		1′	5′

¶ 1   Even though you may be in only the eighth or ninth grade, it is not   14   3 | 36

too early to begin thinking about your eventual career. Whether you se-   28   6 | 39

lect business or some other area, typing skill will prove valuable to   42   8 | 42

you. Should you select office work, ability to type will be essential.   56   11 | 45

¶ 2   Your teachers or a guidance counselor can give you very valuable   13   14 | 47

information about the various kinds of jobs, specific work requirements,   27   17 | 50

and the size of salary you may expect as a beginner and to which you may   42   20 | 53

aspire. There are also good books about careers you may want to read.   56   22 | 56

¶ 3   An excellent way to begin exploring career fields is to work after   13   25 | 59

school or during the summer. This is a safe, yet quick, method of find-   28   28 | 62

ing out whether a certain kind of activity is to your liking. Just as   42   31 | 65

crucial, it offers you an opportunity to discuss careers with others.   56   34 | 67

1′ GWAM | 1 | 2 | 3 | 4 | 5 | 6 | 7 | 8 | 9 | 10 | 11 | 12 | 13 | 14 |
5′ GWAM | 1 | 2 | 3 |

63C ■ PROBLEM TYPING MEASUREMENT: PERSONAL/BUSINESS COMMUNICATIONS [34]

                                                   Words

(Half and full sheets; line: 60; SS)

Current date on Line 7   3

SUBJECT: Typing on Postal Cards   10

Problem 1: Informational Memorandum

Type the memorandum given at the right in block style. Use a half sheet. Correct your errors. Refer to the model on p. 86.

NOTE: Continue with Problem 2, page 99.

← 29 →

Vertical Space. A postal card is 5½ by 3¼ inches and has a   24
total of 19 lines. Since the top and bottom margins take 2   36
or 3 lines each, however, there will be just 12 to 14 lines   48
for typing.   51

Horizontal Space. Each line on a postal card has 55 pica or   66
66 elite spaces, but the left margin will take 3 or 4 spaces   78
and the right margin 2 or 3 spaces. The writing line, then,   91
is limited to 48 to 50 pica or 59 to 61 elite spaces.   101

Business Letters

■ LESSON 101

101A ■ CONDITIONING PRACTICE [5] each line 3 times SS: slowly, faster, in-between rate

Alphabet
Figures
Shift key
Fluency

Exquisite lace was found in the Topaz Village Market by the jolly man.
Will you enter machine Nos. 12-93-45 and 10-87-36 on the repair cards.
The salesmen are from Dow and Co., J&B Products, Inc., and Lynn & Son.
The proper keystroke is made with your fingers held close to the keys.

Quick, shift-key reach with little finger

| 1 | 2 | 3 | 4 | 5 | 6 | 7 | 8 | 9 | 10 | 11 | 12 | 13 | 14 |

101B ■ TECHNIQUE IMPROVEMENT: STROKING [15] each line 3 times SS with emphasis on technique goals

FINGERS CURVED   **FINGERS UPRIGHT**   **FINGER-REACH ACTION**

Technique Goals →

1 *Home row*   J. J. Hall has had half a dish of hash. Ask the lads to wash glasses.
2 *3d row*   Are you trying to type on the upper row by reaching with your fingers?
3 *1st row*   Aza C. Bonham calmed an excited lynx as the men carried it to the van.

4
5 *Fingers 3 and 4*
6
  Cool-as-a-breeze cottons, in the popular new azure color, are on sale.
Six zebra were seen eating wet, waxy poppy pods in the quaint old zoo.
Wally was appalled by the zealous opinion expressed by the quaint man.

7
8 *Long, direct reaches*
9
  A number of union members may be at the unveiling of the unique mural.
An eccentric man bought bright, unique bronze statues at the ceremony.
A musical ceremony will have precedence over the unique presentations.

10
11 *Double letters*
12
  A ragged puppy looked quizzically at the kitten sitting on the pillow.
Miss Booth will tell them to keep all supplies needed for class drill.
Betty will sell glass balls for a drill meet next week in Mississippi.

| 1 | 2 | 3 | 4 | 5 | 6 | 7 | 8 | 9 | 10 | 11 | 12 | 13 | 14 |

101C ■ SKILL APPLICATIONS [30] (Plain sheets, 8½" x 11")

Problem 1: Learning

Type Style Letter 4, page 156, in block style with open punctuation as shown (words in body: 220).

Use standard spacing after each letter part. Type the letter at rough-draft speed; x-out or strike-over any errors you make.

Problem 2: Proofreading and Making Rough-Draft Corrections

Proofread the letter you typed as Problem 1. Indicate by handwritten corrections any changes that you need to make in the copy. Use standard proofreaders' marks to indicate the needed corrections.

Problem 3: Skill Building

Using your corrected rough-draft copy, retype the letter in block style. As you type, make the corrections indicated in your copy.

Erase and correct neatly any errors you make as you retype the letter. Compare your copy with the style letter.

Problem 2: Personal Note in Rough Draft

Type a corrected copy of the following personal note on a half sheet.
(The lines in your note will not be the same as those shown below.)

Words

Current date   3

Single-space the ¶s

Dear Paul: 5

Believe it or not, I survived the Qualifying Round for the City   18
Golf Championship. You can't be more surprised than I am or half   31
as happy.   33

The semi-finals are scheduled for two weeks from saturday, and   45
I'd like to have you come over to cheer me on. The finals will be held on the   60
following Saturday, but I may not be lucky enough to qualify for them.   75

Can you come for the week end of the semifinals? That's when   87
I'll need your support!   92

Cordially   94

Problem 3: Personal/Business Letter

Full sheet with carbon copy; line: 60; begin return address on Line 16; leave 3 blank line spaces between the date and the letter address. Address an envelope. Correct your errors.

Words

1157 W. Summit Avenue | Pueblo, Colorado   8
81005 | November 17, 19-- | Mr. J. D. Byers,   16
Director | Frontier Placement Service | 1515   24
Cleveland Place | Denver, Colorado   80202 | 32
Dear Mr. Byers: | (¶1) The members of the   39
Pueblo FBLA Chapter have authorized me to | 48
invite you to address our group on the topic | 57

"New Frontiers in Careers"   62

at 7:30 Wednesday evening, January 10, at   71
our annual Career | Day banquet. We have   79
reservations from over fifty business | stu-   87
dents who are eager to peer into the future   96
with you to see | what lies ahead in job oppor-   104
tunities. (¶2) You are acquainted with   113
FBLA and Pueblo, I believe; for our | sponsor,   121
Mr. Wellington, has indicated that you have   130
had a | very warm reception here on two pre-   138
vious occasions. | (¶3) It will be a real plea-   146
sure for me to tell our members that you | 154
will be with us as a guest at our banquet. May   164
I hear from | you soon? | Sincerely yours, | 172
Miss Margot Fontaine | FBLA Secretary   179/211

Problem 4: Business Letter

Full sheet with carbon copy; line: 60; current date on Line 16 followed by 3 blank line spaces; center the table with 6 spaces between columns. Address an envelope. Correct your errors.

Words

Current date | Mr. Ray W. Chamberlain | Stu-   8
dent Store Manager | College Preparatory   16
School | Des Moines, IA   50309 | Dear Mr.   24
Chamberlain: | (¶1) Here is our check for   31
$45 to cover the amount of your recent over-   40
payment of the following invoices: 47

| M-4096 | $171.20 | 50
| N-1025 | 238.50 | 53
| N-1138 | 95.46 | 56

(¶2) These three invoices total $505.16. Your   65
check, however, was issued for $550.16--a   73
simple transposition error. We think you would   83
prefer the refund to a credit balance with us.   93
(¶3) Thank you very much for continuing to   100
stock your student store with our Century 21   109
line of products. | Sincerely yours, | Louis B.   118
Perrino | Credit Manager | wmc | Enclosure   126/144

Problem 5

If you complete all problems before time is called, repeat Problem 2.

LESSON 100

100A ■ CONDITIONING PRACTICE 5 each line 3 times SS: slowly, faster, then at in-between rate for CONTROL

Alphabet	Jack Voguel expected to find a buzzing atmosphere in West Quincy, N.H.
Figure/symbol	Order #6890 for 2 gross of buttons totals $3.72 (24 doz. @ 15½¢ each).
Shift key	Joseph J. Tymczyszym won the London Conservatory of Music Scholarship.
Fluency	The town chairman is delighted to learn that he will get an endowment.

| 1 | 2 | 3 | 4 | 5 | 6 | 7 | 8 | 9 | 10 | 11 | 12 | 13 | 14 |

100B ■ TECHNIQUE EVALUATION 15 repeat 99C, page 153; try to improve your typing techniques

100C ■ SKILL-TRANSFER TYPING: STATISTICAL COPY 15

1. Type two 5′ writings on the following paragraphs. Determine *gwam*; circle your errors.

2. Compute % of transfer: statistical-copy rate divided by straight-copy rate of 99D, page 153. Record your better 5′ rate and % of transfer score.

All letters and figures are used.

¶ 1   Recently you requested some estimates of costs to produce a letter. Research studies reveal that some typists take as long as 10 minutes, or even more, to type an average letter of, say, 125, 167, or 190 words. If the typist is paid from $1.80 to $2.40 an hour, this indicates that the letter costs from 30 to 40 cents to produce in terms of the typist's time alone. When other factors are evaluated, the ordinary letter may cost from $1.80 to $2.94 to produce. This finding is a rather startling statistic, isn't it?

¶ 2   Information storage costs, too, should be considered. On the average, it costs 6½ cents to store one copy of a business letter in the files for one year. Just to file the copy costs a cent. It costs $7.50 annually to maintain one cubic foot of records in the business office, exclusive of employee costs. It costs $196 a year to maintain a 4-drawer file, including personnel. It has been estimated that it costs $6,200 just to create and file the contents of a 4-drawer file. Add these cost factors to the letter production expenses, and the ordinary business letter may really cost as much as $1.93 to $3.08 to produce and retain.

	GWAM 1′	5′
	14	3 / 49
	28	6 / 52
	43	9 / 55
	57	11 / 58
	71	14 / 61
	86	17 / 64
	100	20 / 66
	104	21 / 67
	13	23 / 70
	27	26 / 73
	42	29 / 76
	56	32 / 78
	71	35 / 81
	85	38 / 84
	100	41 / 87
	114	44 / 90
	128	46 / 93

1′ GWAM | 1 | 2 | 3 | 4 | 5 | 6 | 7 | 8 | 9 | 10 | 11 | 12 | 13 | 14 |
5′ GWAM | 1 | 2 | 3 |

100D ■ LETTER TYPING EVALUATION 15

Words in letter body: 232
Modified block, indented ¶s
Current date
Mixed punctuation
Erase and correct errors

1. Using the paragraphs of 100C, above, as the body of the letter, type a letter to the address given in Column 2.

Opening lines:

Mr. John Barrons | Apollo Corporation | 4659 Radcliffe Road | Boston, MA 02178 | Dear Mr. Barrons: |

Closing lines:

Sincerely yours, | Charles Parker | Your initials for reference.

2. Since a record is to be made of the time it takes you to produce

a letter, start typing the letter when your teacher tells you to start. When you have completed the letter, proofread it carefully to be sure the letter is acceptable; then raise your hand and your teacher will give you the total time to that point.

3. Record this time on your letter; then determine your *words a minute rate* by dividing your time into 260 (total words).

Themes / Outlines / Report Manuscripts

■ LESSON 64

64A ■ CONDITIONING PRACTICE [5] each line twice SS

Alphabet	Dave bought a quaint zircon pin for Sue; Jack, an onyx ring for Wilma.
Figures	Marilyn Suzuki has library card number H-483190, locker number B-2756.
Figure/symbol	On December 31 Lee found that 65% of Arvin & Orr's bills were overdue.
Fluency	These social problems may be as long in the solution as in the making.

Fingers upright, deeply curved

| 1 | 2 | 3 | 4 | 5 | 6 | 7 | 8 | 9 | 10 | 11 | 12 | 13 | 14 |

NOTE: Remove the paper; reinsert it; gauge the line and letter; type over the last line.

64B ■ IMPROVING SPEED/CONTROL [20]

1. Type a 1' writing for speed and a 1' writing for control on each of the following ¶s.

2. Type a 3' *exploration-level* writing on the ¶s. Try to equal your best 1' *gwam*.

3. Type a 5' *control-level* writing on the ¶s. Determine *gwam* and errors. Compare 1', 3', and 5' *gwam*.

All letters are used.

	GWAM 1'	3'	5'

¶ 1   Of the three vital steps in planning a theme or report, selecting — 13 | 4 | 3
a topic is not merely the first but also the most important one. It is — 28 | 9 | 6
essential that you choose a subject about which you have something to — 42 | 14 | 8
say or in which you are sufficiently interested to do the research needed — 56 | 19 | 11
to speak with quiet authority. Knowledge is crucial. — 67 | 22 | 13

¶ 2   The next step is to limit the topic so that you can treat the sub- — 13 | 27 | 16
ject adequately within the space and time limitations that have been — 27 | 31 | 19
set. It is not easy, for instance, to say much of importance about a — 41 | 36 | 22
social problem such as pollution, polarization, or the generation gap — 55 | 41 | 24
in a short theme. Therefore, cover just one or two aspects. — 67 | 45 | 27

¶ 3   The last step requires deciding upon and listing the major ideas — 13 | 49 | 29
you wish to pursue. From this list you can easily type an outline to — 27 | 54 | 32
guide you as you write, eliminating the need to muddle through a maze — 41 | 58 | 35
of random ideas. The outline ought to consist of a heading for each — 55 | 63 | 38
main division, with subheadings for all the supporting ideas. — 67 | 67 | 40

1' GWAM	1	2	3	4	5	6	7	8	9	10	11	12	13	14
3' GWAM		1		2		3		4		5	
5' GWAM		1		2		3	

64C ■ TYPING A THEME [25] (Full sheet; line: 65 [center − 33; center + 32 + 3 to 7]; DS; ¶ indention: 5)

1. Center and type the heading PLANNING A THEME on Line 13; triple-space; then type the ¶s of 64B, above, as a double-spaced theme.

2. Proofread your copy carefully; indicate needed corrections with proofreaders' marks (see p. 59). Retype the theme, erasing as necessary.

99C ■ TECHNIQUE EVALUATION $\boxed{15}$ 1' writing on each sentence as your teacher evaluates techniques; repeat as time permits

Keystroking	✔ Curved, upright fingers ✔ Quick, snappy keystrokes ✔ Hands quiet
Continuity/Rhythm	✔ Continuous keystroking ✔ Rhythm varies according to copy difficulty
Return	✔ Quick return ✔ Eyes on copy ✔ New line started immediately

1 Balanced   The map of the ancient land forms may aid them when they work with us.
2 Combination Please reserve a quantity of the forms and statements for the estates.
3 One hand   I was asked to refer a minimum number of weavers to the union address.
| 1 | 2 | 3 | 4 | 5 | 6 | 7 | 8 | 9 | 10 | 11 | 12 | 13 | 14 |

Shift Key	✔ Little finger reach—other fingers in home position ✔ No pauses

4   Jack McNeil will meet Elvis C. O'Brien tomorrow in Idaho Falls, Idaho.
5   Order the Damp Proof Red Primer from Bartons & Delaney, New York, N.Y.
| 1 | 2 | 3 | 4 | 5 | 6 | 7 | 8 | 9 | 10 | 11 | 12 | 13 | 14 |

Space Bar	✔ Right thumb curved—on or close to space bar ✔ Quick, down-and-in spacing stroke

6   If it is so, then he may do the work for us and the men from the city.
7   Please pay them when they have the plan for the map room for John May.
| 1 | 2 | 3 | 4 | 5 | 6 | 7 | 8 | 9 | 10 | 11 | 12 | 13 | 14 |

99D ■ GROWTH INDEX: STRAIGHT COPY $\boxed{15}$ two 5' writings; determine GWAM; proofread for errors; record your scores fo future comparison

All letters are used.

	GWAM	
	1'	5'

¶ 1

The business letter is, in an important sense, the personal envoy | 13 | 3
of the business office that produces it. All business firms give careful | 28 | 6
attention to the content of the letter so that it will be as effective | 42 | 8
as possible; however, if the letter is carelessly typed or poorly placed | 57 | 11
on the page, much of its effect may be lost. Depending upon the first | 71 | 14
impression a letter makes, it tends to give a good or a poor image of the | 86 | 17
company that sends it. Every typist should recognize that good placement | 101 | 20
of the letter on the letterhead page is, then, of primary importance. | 114 | 23

¶ 2

A letter must be carefully proofread before it is removed from the | 13 | 26
typewriter. Just be sure that you acquire this necessary proofreading | 28 | 28
habit. Given here is an idea of some of the basic steps to follow: | 41 | 31
First, observe the placement and the format of the letter. It should | 56 | 34
be well placed on the page, and it should look much like a picture in a | 70 | 37
frame. Every keystroke should be even or uniform. Second, be sure that | 85 | 40
every figure and amount are exact. Check to be sure that the address is | 99 | 43
correct. Lastly, verify the content of the letter; also, the grammar | 113 | 45
and spelling. Be certain that every typing error has been neatly cor- | 127 | 48
rected, and that there are no errors of word division. | 138 | 50

1' GWAM | 1 | 2 | 3 | 4 | 5 | 6 | 7 | 8 | 9 | 10 | 11 | 12 | 13 | 14 |
5' GWAM | 1 | 2 | 3 |

LESSON 65

65A ■ CONDITIONING PRACTICE [5] each line twice SS

Alphabet	Jackie Marvel did type the next history quiz for Mrs. Biggs last week. *Quick, snap strokes*
Figures	Census figures in 1960 showed a population of 48,572; in 1970, 63,479.
Figure/symbol	A contract (#19370), signed April 28, raised the hourly rate to $4.65.
Fluency	The auditor reports that the tax bill amendment will affect all of us.

| 1 | 2 | 3 | 4 | 5 | 6 | 7 | 8 | 9 | 10 | 11 | 12 | 13 | 14 |

NOTE: Remove the paper; reinsert it; gauge the line and letter; type over the last line.

65B ■ IMPROVING SPEED/CONTROL [20]

1. Type a 1' writing for speed and a 1' writing for control on each of the following ¶s.

2. Type a 3' *exploration-level* writing on the ¶s, trying to reach your best 1' gwam.

3. Type a 5' *control-level* writing on the ¶s. Determine *gwam* and errors. Compare 1', 3', and 5' gwam.

All letters are used.

			GWAM		
			1'	3'	5'
¶ 1		After you have selected a topic, limited the number of points to be	14	5	3
		covered, and prepared an outline, you are ready to begin to search for	28	9	6
		data and read for authoritative statements to support the ideas you wish	42	14	8
		to convey. Gathering facts takes time, but it is time well spent. It	57	19	11
		is one evidence of real effort and adds credibility.	67	22	13
¶ 2		The next step is to prepare a rough draft of the report. Organize	13	27	16
		the material into a series of related paragraphs, each with a topic	27	31	19
		statement to announce its major idea. Arrange the sentences in each of	41	36	22
		the paragraphs to expand the thought of the main statement or to support	56	41	25
		it with an important fact or with an appropriate quote.	67	45	27
¶ 3		As soon as the rough copy is done, read it with very close atten-	13	49	29
		tion to the accuracy of its content, the continuity of the ideas in the	27	54	32
		sentences of each paragraph, the order of the paragraphs, and the clar-	42	59	35
		ity of each statement. Read it a second time for accuracy of its spell-	56	63	38
		ing, punctuation, and style. Then type the final draft.	67	67	40

1' GWAM	1	2	3	4	5	6	7	8	9	10	11	12	13	14
3' GWAM		1		2		3		4		5				
5' GWAM		1			2			3						

65C ■ TYPING A THEME [25] (Full sheet; line: 65; DS; ¶ indention: 5)

1. Center and type the heading PREPARING A RE-PORT on Line 13; triple-space; then type the ¶s of 65B, above, as a double-spaced theme.

2. Proofread your copy carefully; indicate needed corrections with proofreaders' marks. Retype the theme in correct form, erasing as necessary.

Performance Evaluation

■ Lessons 99-100 provide activities that will help you evaluate your typing skill. They may, also, indicate areas where you need improvement.

■ LESSON 99

99A ■ CONDITIONING PRACTICE [15] each line 3 times SS: slowly, faster, then at in-between rate for CONTROL

Alphabet
Figure/symbol
Quiet hands
Fluency

This quick quiz will cover exceedingly important factors of job skill.
Is the total charge on Order No. 2378, dated June 10, $45.69 or $4.56?
Purposeful repetition leads to rapid improvement of stroking patterns.
She may go with them down the lane to the shale rocks by the big lake.
| 1 | 2 | 3 | 4 | 5 | 6 | 7 | 8 | 9 | 10 | 11 | 12 | 13 | 14 |

Type with continuity and rhythm

99B ■ SKILL-TRANSFER TYPING: ROUGH DRAFT [5] (Line: 70)

1. Type two 5′ writings. Determine *gwam*; proofread for errors.
2. After typing straight copy of 99D, page 153, com-

pute % of transfer: rough-draft rate divided by straight-copy rate. Record your better 5′ rate and % of transfer score.

All letters are used.

	GWAM	
	1′	5′

¶ 1

It is amazing how much ~work~ efficiency can be increased by ^the^ careful — 14 | 2
~planning and~ organizing all work tasks. This is as true for class room work as — 33 | 3
is it for work in the office area. ^In the office,^ The trend is toward work simpli- — 49 | 10
fication and #the utilization of time and motion principles. ^in all work^ Office — 65 | 13
workers learn to increase their efficiency by grouping ^similar^ taks. They — 80 | 16
adjust their work pace to the ^difficulty of the^ job task. They try to reduce waste — 97 | 19
motions by having ^all^ materials need ^d^ for the job, ^they are to do^ within easy reach — 114 | 23
~and arranged for quick use.~ — 119 | 24

¶ 2

In the typewriting classroom, you should ^organize^ plan all work and — 13 | 26
work in ^an organized^ the right way. In using the typewriter, this right way of — 27 | 29
operating means that you type with good ^technique and~ form, that you work for a — 41 | 32
fluent key stroking pattern with the reach action limited to the — 54 | 35
fingers only, that you eliminate all unnecessary motions and that you ~so that you will be able to keep the hands quiet. Additionally, it means~ — 72 | 38 — 83 | 40
operate with an increasing sense of relaxation ^as your skill increases.^ Then, too, boys and — 102 | 44
girls who are learning to type must make a real effort to improve. — 115 | 47
~As is true for the right way of working,~ — 124 | 49
^A^ real effort to improve is an essential element of success. — 136 | 51

■ LESSON 66

66A ■ CONDITIONING PRACTICE [5] each line twice SS; then 1' writings on selected lines

Alphabet	J. K. Roxy and Q. W. Lutz are captains of Voight High's football team.
Figures	Type figures 1, 2, 3, 4, 5, 6, 7, 8, 9, and 10; Roman numerals I to X.
Figure/symbol	FOR RENT: two 4-room apartments @ $130; two 5-room apartments @ $176.
Fluency	The six workmen kept a log of the time spent on each phase of the job.

Shift quickly but firmly

| 1 | 2 | 3 | 4 | 5 | 6 | 7 | 8 | 9 | 10 | 11 | 12 | 13 | 14 |

66B ■ ALIGNING ARABIC AND ROMAN NUMERALS [15] type twice

■ Align columns of Arabic and Roman numerals at the right. Set a tab stop for the digit in each column (after the first) that requires the least forward and backward spacing.

DO: Move the margin stops to the ends of the scale; clear all tabulator stops; set the left margin stop and tab stops for spacing as indicated by the key.

MARGIN ↓	TAB ↓	TAB ↓	TAB ↓	TAB ↓	TAB ↓
1	I	6	VI	15	XV
2	II	7	VII	40	XL
3	III	8	VIII	50	L
4	IV	9	IX	60	LX
5	V	10	X	100	C

KEY |1| 4 |3| 10 |2| 4 | 4 | 10 |3| 4 |2|

66C ■ PROBLEM TYPING: OUTLINES [30]

Problem 1 (Half sheet; line: 70; exact vertical center; spacing as indicated)

	Words
TOPIC OUTLINES	3

Space forward once from margin ↓   TS

	Words
I. CAPITALIZING HEADINGS IN TOPIC OUTLINES DS	12

↑ 2 spaces

Reset margin →

	Words
A. ↓ Title of Outline in ALL CAPS (May Be Underlined)	26
B. Major Headings in ALL CAPS (Not Underlined)	36
C. Important Words of First-Order Subheadings Capitalized	47
D. Only First Word of Second-Order Subheadings Capitalized	59

↓ ─Backspace   DS

	Words
II. SPACING TOPIC OUTLINES	66

DS

	Words
A. Horizontal Spacing	71

1st tab stop →

	Words
1. Title of outline centered over the writing line	81
2. Identifying numerals for major headings aligned at the	93

2d tab stop →

	Words
left margin, followed by 2 spaces	100
3. Identifying letters and numerals for each subsequent level	113
of subheading aligned beneath the first word of the pre-	125
ceding heading, followed by 2 spaces	133
B. Vertical Spacing	137
1. Title of outline followed by 2 blank spaces	147
2. Major headings (except the first) preceded by 1 blank	158
space; all followed by 1 blank space	166
3. All subheadings single-spaced	173

■ LESSON 98

98A ■ CONDITIONING PRACTICE [5] each line 3 times SS: slowly, faster, then at in-between rate for CONTROL

Alphabet	Have you ever watched a quick jet zoom past as a bird in exact flight?
Figures	Please ship Order No. 750 for 36 typewriters, 49 desks, and 128 lamps.
Figure/symbol	What is the sum of 16 7/8 and 23 3/4 and 45 1/2 and 10 8/9 and 90 1/4?
Fluency	The authenticity of the ancient amendment may help them gain clemency.

Uniform keystroking

| 1 | 2 | 3 | 4 | 5 | 6 | 7 | 8 | 9 | 10 | 11 | 12 | 13 | 14 |

98B ■ BUSINESS LETTER PHRASES [15] two 1' writings on each sentence; compare rates

1 We would be pleased to send the box to you if you would be there soon.
2 Your letter has been forwarded by the post office to our Ogden office.
3 It is true that the mail from the college is late and we know of this.
4 Attached is a copy of a report I have in our files as a safety design.
5 This is, as you are aware in this case, my only copy and I can use it.
6 He can be there this week, but do not schedule a meeting of the group.

Variable rhythm and continuity

| 1 | 2 | 3 | 4 | 5 | 6 | 7 | 8 | 9 | 10 | 11 | 12 | 13 | 14 |

98C ■ PRODUCTION MEASUREMENT [30] (Modified block; indented ¶s; mixed punctuation; use letterheads or plain sheets)

Time Schedule	
Planning and preparing	4'
Timed production writing	20'
Proofreading; determining *g-pram*	6'

If you complete both letters before time is called, start over. Type on the *control level*; do not correct errors. When time is called, proofread each letter. Determine *g-pram* (gross production rate a minute). G-PRAM = Total words ÷ minutes typed.

Problem 1

Words

Current date | Mr. Wilmert Perkins | 3689   8
Benedict Drive | Dallas, TX   75214 | Dear   16
Mr. Perkins: | (¶ 1) Here's the material on in-   24
vesting that you requested. We're happy to   33
send it to you. It contains information that   42
will help you understand the particular advan-   51
tages and disadvantages in stocks, mutual   60
funds, municipal bonds, commodities, and the   69
like. This information should help you decide   78
which of these investment opportunities can   87
best meet your personal investment objectives.   96
(¶ 2) To make sure that our information is   104
accurate and up to date, we utilize the talent   113
and findings of our Research Department. We   122
have the latest in computerized equipment to   131
store and retrieve information for us and our   140
clients. In addition to Dow Jones, we have   149
our own private news wire. Our offices are   158
linked by over 340,000 miles of private lines.   168
Every account executive in our brokerage firm   177
has quick access to the latest facts and figures   187
through this nationwide communications net-   195
work. And these services are available to you   205
at any time, whether you have an account with   214
us or not. (¶ 3) Again, thank you for writing   222

Words

to us. We'll be glad to help you with your   231
investment problems in any way we can. Just   240
give us a call at 825-2620. | Sincerely   248
yours, | Lloyd Fredericks, Director | Infor-   256
mation Bureau | (xxx) | Enclosures (226)   262/273

Problem 2

April 25, 19–– | Mr. Peter Lumsdaine | 11756   8
Bordeaux Place | Orlando, FL   32808 | Dear   16
Mr. Lumsdaine: | (¶ 1) Don't miss the next   24
meeting of the Central Florida Realty Board,   32
Orlando Division, which will be held at 12:00   41
noon, Monday, May 3, at the Florida Club   49
Restaurant, 1108 Taylor Avenue, Orlando.   58
(¶ 2) The speaker will be Mr. Alan Wunsch.   65
During the past five years, he has sold over   74
10 million dollars worth of homes. Mr.   82
Wunsch, who is only 29 years old, is the top   91
salesman for the Orlando Realty Company.   100
He will present his unique methods of selling   109
and listing. It will be a stimulating and in-   118
formative talk. (¶ 3) Plan now to be with us.   126
Just return the enclosed card to confirm your   136
reservation. | Sincerely yours, | James Crews,   144
Chairman | (xxx) | Enclosure | (120)   149/161

Problem 2 (Full sheet; line: 65; exact vertical center; SS)

1. Space forward once from margin to type Roman numeral I. Reset margin 2 spaces to the right of the period in "I." for subheadings **A.** and **B.**

2. Set first tab stop 2 spaces to the right of "**A.**"; second stop, 2 spaces to the right of "**1.**". Use the margin release and backspace to type II.

	Words
UNBOUND MANUSCRIPTS	8
ᴛꜱ	
I. Margins and Spacing *all caps*	13
A. Margins *and bottom* *approximately*	15
1. Side margins: (minimum of 1" #	25
2. Top margin, first page: pica, 1½"; elite, 2"	35
3. Top margin, additional pages: 1"	43
B. Spacing (:)	45
1. Body of manuscript, double	52
2. Paragraph indentions: 5 or 10 spaces uniform*e*ly	62
3. Quoted paragraph	67
a. Four lines or more	72
(1) Single-spaced	76
(2) Indented 5 spaces from *each* margins	85
(3) Quotation marks may be used--*not required*	95
b. Fewer than four lines	100
(1) Quotation marks *used*	105
(2) Not separated *and indented from text margins*	116
II. NUMBERING PAGES #	121
DS A. First Page: (Numbered Centered ½" from Bottom *Edge*	131
B. Other Pages: Number Typed Even with Right Margin,	144
½" from) Top *Edge of Paper*	148

NOTE: Space once after closing parenthesis

■ LESSON 67

67A ■ CONDITIONING PRACTICE 5   each line twice SS; then 1' writings on selected lines

Alphabet	Evan Wykle quizzed the top men about the next golf match set for June.
Figures	There were 40,632 paid admissions the first month; 51,987, the second.
Figure/symbol	Mr. Robb owes a total of $3,475, of which $620 must be paid by May 19.
Fluency	I wish to do their work so the men may go with them to make the signs.

| 1 | 2 | 3 | 4 | 5 | 6 | 7 | 8 | 9 | 10 | 11 | 12 | 13 | 14 |

67B ■ TYPING FROM SCRIPT 10

1. Type the following paragraph as two 2' writings, using a 60-space line and double spacing. Indent the paragraph the usual 5 spaces.

2. Next, set the margin stops to have 1" side margins (10 pica spaces, 12 elite). Retype the paragraph with these margins.

	GWAM		
	1'	2'	
Whether you use pica or elite type, you have up to now	11	5	47
typed all copy with the line length stated in spaces. This	23	11	53
was done to simplify your learning to type. You are now to	35	18	59
learn to follow standard conventions of report layout. For	47	24	65
unbound manuscripts, 1-inch side margins are used (12 elite	59	30	71
or 10 pica spaces). As a result, an elite line will contain	71	36	77
78 spaces while a pica line will contain only 65 spaces.	83	41	83

Alertness Training: Supply needed punctuation, capitalization, or missing letter parts as you type. Be alert! Use mixed punctuation with all letters.

Problem 1: Modified Block with Indented ¶s

	Words
Mr. Robert Neches, President │ Fleetwood	11
Manufacturing Company │ 330 Aurora	18
Avenue, N.W. │ Atlanta, GA 30314 │ *(Supply*	25
an appropriate salutation) │ (¶ 1) Every day liter-	31
ally millions of letters are typed and mailed.	40
Letters are one of the ways business firms use	50
to communicate with their customers, pros-	58
pects, and associates. Obviously, letters carry	68
a great variety of messages, but they also con-	77
vey to the recipient an image of the writer and	87
the business firm he represents. (¶ 2) When	95
we speak to someone in person, the words we	104
use are often modified by our attitude, our	112
facial expression, the tone of our voice, and	122
our appearance. A letter, however, cannot	130
smile; its words must speak for themselves. The	140
appearance of the letter, the words we use, and	150
the clarity of our expression, therefore, become	159
very important. If the tone of our letters is	169
warm and friendly, the recipients will usually	178
get a favorable impression of us. (¶ 3) We	186
have prepared a booklet to assist you in your	195
letter writing. Of course, the suggestions it con-	205
tains are only a guide, for your letters should	215
reflect you and your personality. Neverthe-	224
less, hundreds of businessmen who have used	232
this letter-writing booklet have commented	241
that it has helped them write better letters--	250
letters that foster an image of their company	259
as helpful and eager to serve, as businesslike	269
and efficient, and as friendly and courteous.	278
The booklet sells for only a dollar. A sample	288
copy is enclosed for your review. I know you	297
will want to order a booklet for each of the	305
persons in your organization who write the let-	315
ters that represent your company. It is a small	325
investment that will pay big dividends. │ *(Supply*	335
a complimentary close) │ John R. Perry, Man-	340
ager │ (xxx) │ Enclosure (304)	344/365

Problem 2: Modified Block with Indented ¶s

	Words
dr. allien russon │ 1145 east fourth street │ salt	13
lake city, ut 84102 │ (¶ 1) Going places?	20
You'll go three times as far in the new Midas	29
98 Compact. Yes, one gallon of gasoline will	38
take you 36 or more miles even in city driving.	48
(¶ 2) Going places? You'll have more money	56

	Words
to spend if you invest in the best buy of all	65
compacts--the Midas 98. The price is only	74
$1,795. You'll have more money to spend, too,	83
because the new Midas 98 is really a miser	92
with gasoline on the open road. (¶ 3) Going	99
places? Then go right to the nearest mailbox	109
with the enclosed postal card. Just indicate	118
the most convenient time for your free-trial	127
demonstration. The supply of new Midas 98	135
Compacts is going fast, so you had better	144
hurry. │ joseph p. sansone │ sales manager	152/165
(127)	

Problem 3: Personal/Business Letter; Modified Block; Reference: Page 92

	Words
24065 Ocean Avenue │ Torrance, Calif.	7
90505 │ *Current date* │ mr. john r. perry, man-	16
ager │ communication consultants, inc. │ 840	24
madison avenue │ new york, new york 10022 │	33
(¶ 1) I have just learned that your organiza-	40
tion publishes a letter-writing booklet that has	50
been used with success in the business world.	60
(¶ 2) Please send me one of these booklets and	68
bill me at the address shown above for the cost	77
of the booklet and any mailing charges. Thank	88
you. │ Mrs. Mercedes Henderson │ (55)	93/122

Problem 4: Personal/Business Letter; Modified Block with Indented ¶s

	Words
315 Mountain Street │ Winnipeg, Manitoba │	8
Current date │ Mr. Sam Stewart, Manager │	16
the phoenix inn │ 360 wagon wheel drive, w. │	24
phoenix, arizona 85021 │ (¶ 1) Recently I	32
had the pleasure of staying at the Phoenix Inn.	41
I should like to commend the management and	50
staff for making my stay so enjoyable and	58
comfortable. The friendly atmosphere and the	68
good food are still vivid in my mind. (¶ 2)	75
Since my return home, I have been unable to	84
locate a book that I had at the Inn. The title	94
of the book and the author are listed below:	103
Venture to the Interior by Laurens van der Post	117
(¶ 3) Since this book was a personally auto-	125
graphed copy that I received from the author,	134
it has considerable personal value to me. I	143
shall be grateful to you if you would have	152
someone at the Inn make a search for the	160
book. │ very sincerely, │ Robert E. Under-	168
wood │ (131)	168/194

■ Type the following first page of a report in unbound report form. Use 1″ side and bottom margins; a 2″ top margin for elite, a 1½″ top margin for pica. Center the title and TS after it; DS the body of the report. Type from the copy below, *not from the models at the right.* Do not correct errors.

■ As this is page 1 of a report to be completed in Lesson 68, center and type the figure **1** a half inch above the bottom edge of the sheet (on the fourth line space, pica; or third line space, elite, below the last typed line of the report).

■ Proofread your copy, using proofreaders' marks to indicate corrections; then retype the report, erasing and correcting errors as necessary.

PICA   1

ELITE   1

	Words
ELECTRONIC MAIL SORTING	5

3

The ZIP Code system of sorting mail was begun in 1963. ZIP (Zoning Improvement Plan) divides the country into delivery units, each given a 5-digit number. The first digit represents one of ten geographic areas; the second, a certain part of a geographic area; the third, one of the sectional center areas for sorting mail; the last two, a zone number for internally zoned cities or the delivery station for smaller ones.

ZIP coding was only one step in a massive program designed to bring efficiency to the chaotic condition of mail handling. This coding system foresaw the eventual use of the Optical Character Reader (an electronic mail sorter) that depends upon a numeric language (the ZIP Code) for maximum efficiency in handling mail.

The marriage of ZIP and OCR occurred in 1967 when the Optical Character Reader began full-time operation in the Detroit Post Office. Since then, the OCR has been installed in at least ten major cities, including New York, Los Angeles, and Chicago.

The OCR has peculiar reading habits. For example, it first scans from <u>right to left</u> to find the beginning of the address lines on the envelope; then it reads from <u>left to right</u>, starting with the bottom line and reading toward the top. Thus, addresses on envelopes must appear within a specified "read zone"; otherwise, the envelopes will be rejected and will have to be manually sorted.

Addressing guides supplied by the U.S. Postal Service are recommended for both personal and business mail.

Words count column: 21, 38, 56, 73, 90, 106, 123, 141, 154, 170, 186, 204, 222, 239, 260, 278, 287, 303, 308

96C ■ APPLICATION SKILL BUILDING: LETTERS [30] (Modified block style; 5-space ¶ indention; 2″ margins)

1. Type a 3′ writing on the letter to establish a base rate. If you finish before time is called, start over.
2. Determine *gwam*. To this rate add 8 *gwam* to set a new goal. Divide the goal rate into four equal segments; note these quarter-minute check points for guided writings.
3. *Leave proper spacing between let-*

ter parts, but begin the letter (date-line) near the top of the sheet. Beginning with the date, type three 1′ guided writings on the opening parts of the letter and ¶ 1. *Begin the second and third writings a double space below the last line of the preceding writing.*
4. Repeat Step 3, using ¶ 2 and the

closing lines of the letter.
5. Type another 3′ writing on the complete letter. Try to maintain your new goal rate for this writing. Determine *gwam* and compare it with the rate you attained in Step 1.
6. Type the letter from your teacher's dictation.

	Words in Parts	3′ GWAM
September 30, 19–– | Mr. David Barton | 1199 Riverview	10	3
Drive | Des Moines, Iowa 50313 | Dear Mr. Barton: |	20	7
(¶ 1) We want to be sure to give you credit, but not the kind of credit which is	15	12
usually given by a credit manager. We mean the kind of credit which is defined	31	17
by Webster as "praise or approval to which a person is entitled."	44	21
(¶ 2) The way you have handled your account with us during the past year cer-	14	27
tainly merits our praise. We appreciate the promptness with which you pay your	30	31
account. So we want to say thank you, and "give credit where credit is due."	46	37
It is a pleasure to be of service to you.	54	39
Sincerely yours, | Robert Hall, Credit Manager | lwe (98)	10	42

■ LESSON 97

97A ■ CONDITIONING PRACTICE [5] each line 3 times SS: slowly, faster, then at in-between rate

Alphabet	Jay will make executive organizational plans for the old Quebec firms.
Figures	Please notice Rule 36 on page 210 as well as Rule 85 on pages 479-482.
Figure/symbol	Her check showed 45 men and 26 women on TWA's Flight #718 at 9:30 a.m.
Speed	The clansmen got into the dory by the shale rock and circled the lake.

Finger-reach action; hands quiet

| 1 | 2 | 3 | 4 | 5 | 6 | 7 | 8 | 9 | 10 | 11 | 12 | 13 | 14 |

97B ■ SKILL BUILDING: LETTER PARTS [10] 1′ writings (Plain paper, 8½″ x 11″; 2″ margins)

1. Using 96C, above, type three 1′ writings on the opening lines. Determine *gwam*.
2. Using the same letter, type three 1′ writings on the closing lines. Determine *gwam*.
3. Type a 1′ writing on each of the ¶s of the letter. Determine *gwam*. Compare your 1′ rates.

■ LESSON 68

68A ■ CONDITIONING PRACTICE 5 each line twice SS; then 1' writings on selected lines

Alphabet	Jan seized the wheel very quickly as big cars pulled out from an exit.
Figures	Supply him with 14 hats, 79 shirts, 38 scarves, 60 ties, and 25 coats.
Figure/symbol	Derek's boat sold for $1,750, which gave him a 10% profit on the sale.
Fluency	The panel may then work with the problems of the eight downtown firms.

Reach, don't "leap" to figure keys

| 1 | 2 | 3 | 4 | 5 | 6 | 7 | 8 | 9 | 10 | 11 | 12 | 13 | 14 |

68B ■ LINE FINDER (RATCHET RELEASE) 10

■ A *superscript* is a figure or symbol typed above the line of writing; a *subscript*, a figure or symbol typed below. Use the **automatic line finder** or **ratchet release (6)**; then turn the platen so that the paper is properly positioned.

To Type a Footnote Reference Figure (Superscript): (1) Operate the ratchet release **(6)**; (2) turn the cylinder *backward* (toward you) a half space; (3) type the figure, then return the ratchet release and cylinder to normal position.

To Type a Chemistry Symbol (Subscript): (1) Operate the ratchet release; (2) turn the cylinder *forward* (away from you) a half space; (3) type the figure and return the ratchet release and cylinder to normal position.

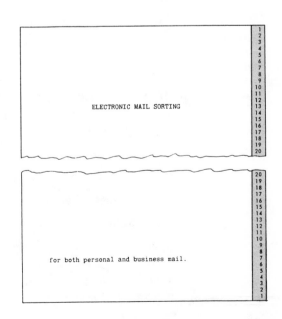

DRILL PROCEDURE (Line: 60)

1. Type a 2½″ line, using the underline key; then center and type your name on the line.

2. Operate the ratchet release; turn the cylinder *forward* (away from you) about 1″; type the current date centered under your name.

3. Return the lever to normal position; turn the cylinder back to your name; type over your name.

4. Type the sentences given below, typing the superscripts and the subscript as directed at the left.

According to a Typewriting News article, "The ZIP Code should appear on the line with the names of the city and state."[1]

Water (H_2O) freezes at 32° Fahrenheit.

68C ■ PREPARING A PAGE LINE GAUGE 10

■ You can use a page line gauge as a guide when typing manuscripts, determining top and bottom margins, and placing footnotes correctly.

To Make a Page Line Gauge: Type the figure *1* in the first line space below the top edge and near the right edge of a full sheet; then number the lines consecutively through 33. For the lower half of the page, type 33 down to 1 on consecutive lines (33 will appear twice on the page line gauge).

Drill Using Page Line Gauge

Place the gauge back of and extending slightly to the right of a full sheet; insert both into machine; space forward to Line 13 from the top. Center horizontally and type

ELECTRONIC MAIL SORTING

as a main heading. Then space forward to Line 7 from the bottom and type

for both personal and business mail.

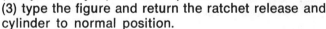

Problem 1: Skill Building

Words

Current date on Line 14 | Professor David Foley | 8
Business Education Department | California 16
State Polytechnic College | Pomona, CA 23
91766 | Dear Professor Foley: | (¶ 1) Our 30
generation has seen major changes in educa- 38
tion, and the rate of change is still accelerating. 49
Our Committee of Educators has become con- 57
vinced that political and socio-economic forces 67
will influence future educational methods and 76
the kinds of programs that are offered. We 85
believe all educators at every level of respon- 94
sibility should make every effort to become 103
fully acquainted with current thinking about 112
all aspects of public policy. (¶ 2) Many of us 121
in the area have chosen to join Town Hall 129
because at its meetings we can hear a broad 138
cross-section of the nation's leaders. We know 147
of no better way to keep abreast of the signifi- 157
cant issues of our times, and we would like to 166
have you join us. If you are not already 175
acquainted with Town Hall, the enclosed bro- 184
chure will give you the basic information. 192
(¶ 3) If you share our convictions, why don't 200
you complete the enclosed application card 209
and become a part of Town Hall, one of the 218
nation's most influential public forums. Dues 227

Words

and contributions are tax deductible, of course. | 237
Cordially yours, | Raymond McKelvey | Chair- 245
man | ake | Enclosures | (208)   249/**270**

Problem 2: Skill Building

Current date on Line 16 | Mr. Thomas McDonnell | 7
14041 East Light Street | Whittier, CA 15
90605 | Dear Mr. McDonnell: (¶ 1) Without 22
theater and without music, the world would be 31
like a tree without leaves! The performing arts 41
bring grace to our lives. And Channel 28 49
brings all the arts to you––just for the tuning. 59
For six years KCET has encouraged cultural 68
arts appreciation in Southern California. Thou- 77
sands have been introduced to music and 85
drama, some for the first time. (¶ 2) Channel 94
28 truly belongs to the people. It is kept alive 104
and humming by its members in the com- 111
munity. If you are not yet a member, I hope 120
you will join us. As a member, your share of 129
this year-round theater is about the price of a 139
pair of tickets to just one performance. Mem- 148
bership begins at $15 a year. (¶ 3) Please send 157
your check today and become a member of 165
Channel 28. It will be good to welcome you to 174
our performing arts group. | Sincerely yours, | 183
John W. Luhring, President | jys | (158)   189/**202**

■ LESSON 96

96A ■ CONDITIONING PRACTICE ⑤ each line 3 times SS: slowly, faster, then at in-between rate

Alphabet	By his frequent adjustments, an amazing executive kept their goodwill.
Figures	The zoo ordered 785 birds, 4 bears, 20 bison, 9 lions, and 163 snakes.
Figure/symbol	Jud & Co.'s order read: "Ship 12 doz. #45 cups; 39 gr. #6780 plates."
Fluency	The authenticity of the six amendments may torment the skeptical boys.

Quick, snap stroke; immediate key release

| 1 | 2 | 3 | 4 | 5 | 6 | 7 | 8 | 9 | 10 | 11 | 12 | 13 | 14 |

96B ■ BUSINESS LETTER PHRASES* ⑮ two 1' writings on each sentence; compare rates

1   We are aware of his need, and we thank you for sending us a statement.

2   You will note that I will be in the city for your tour of the factory.

3   On the first, we will go to the bank with the auditor of our business.

4   It is a fact that we have to be there for the installation of the men.

5   I am glad that you have a copy of the letter in your file at the desk.

6   Thank you for the books and the letters that you sent for my birthday.

| 1 | 2 | 3 | 4 | 5 | 6 | 7 | 8 | 9 | 10 | 11 | 12 | 13 | 14 |

* The sentences of 96B, above, and of 98B, page 151, contain all of the 50 most frequently used business letter phrases.

68D ■ PROBLEM TYPING: REPORT MANUSCRIPT (Page 2) ▢25

■ Type the following copy (the second page of the report begun in Lesson 67) in unbound report form. Use 1″ top and side margins. Type the page number at the right on the fourth line space from the top edge. DS the body of the report; SS the table with 8 spaces between columns.

■ Type from the script copy given below, *not from the models at the right*. Do not correct errors.

■ Proofread your copy, using proofreaders' marks to indicate needed corrections; then retype the copy, erasing and correcting errors as necessary.

PICA

ELITE

Words

Although the OCR can read speedily and accurately state names — 12
spelled in full or abbreviated in the standard manner, the — 24
U.S. Postal Service prefers the use of 2-letter (without periods — 37
and spaces) ZIP abbreviations -- but only if ZIP Codes — 48
are used with them. The names, standard abbreviations, — 59
and special 2-letter ZIP abbreviations of the ten most — 70
populous states are given below as examples: — 79

California	Calif.	CA	83
New York	N.Y.	NY	87
Pennsylvania	Pa.	PA	91
Texas	Tex.	TX	94
Illinois	Ill.	IL	97
Ohio	Ohio	OH	100
Michigan	Mich.	MI	103
New Jersey	N.J.	NJ	107
Florida	Fla.	FL	110
Massachusetts	Mass.	MA	115

The 2-letter abbreviations for all states are available from — 127
the local post office in POD Publication 114. Furthermore, — 139
because businesses so often use mechanical addressing — 150
devices which limit the number of spaces that can be — 160
typed per line, the U.S. Postal Service also provides standard — 173
abbreviations for city and street names in POD Publication — 185
59. — 185

One Victory Boulevard, S.

Burbank, California 91502

Telephone 483-2759

✱ELECTRA CORPORATION

Typewriters   Adding Machines   Calculators   EDP-IDP Equipment

	Words in Parts	Total Words
Start at center point of paper		

Dateline — Line 16   February 15, 19-- | 4 | 4 |

4 line spaces (3 blank lines)

Letter address

	Words in Parts	Total Words
Mr. Mark Brown, President	9	9
Associated Industries, Inc.	14	14
1078 California Avenue	19	19
Seattle, WA 98116	23	23
DS		

Salutation   Dear Mr. Brown: | 26 | 26 |
DS

Body of letter

	Words in Parts	Total Words
Often the effectiveness of a letter is reduced if it	11	36
is poorly placed on the page. Good letter placement has	22	48
eye appeal. A letter that is properly placed on the page	34	59
gets the kind of positive attention that leads to action	45	71
as your customer reads your message.	53	78
Our Research Division has just completed an intensive	63	89
study of letter placement problems. They have developed	75	101
a new letter placement guide that assures good placement	86	112
every time. Several copies of this new guide are enclosed.	98	124
Why not have your typists try it. I know you will be	109	135
pleased with the very attractive "picture frame" place-	120	146
ment it will give your letters.	127	153
This letter placement guide is another of the free	137	163
services we offer to the busy executive who must depend	148	174
upon his typing staff for proper letter placement. It is	160	186
always good to have an occasion to be of service to you.	171	197

Start at center point of paper   DS

Complimentary close   Sincerely yours, | 3 | 200 |

4 line spaces (3 blank lines)

Signature

Richard Krisher

Typed name and official title   Richard Krisher, Manager | 8 | 205 |
DS

Reference initials   sae | 9 | 206 |
DS

Enclosure notation   Enclosures | 11 | 208 |

Style Letter 3: Modified Block with Indented Paragraphs and Mixed Punctuation

LESSON 69

69A ■ CONDITIONING PRACTICE [5] each line twice SS; then 1' writings on selected lines

Alphabet	Quite a few very big men like to jump and do exercises on the trapeze.
Figures	The main feature will be shown at 7:05, 8:16, 9:24, and 10:38 tonight.
Figure/symbol	Doesn't a half-paid amount of $8 mean 50% is still due from Hix & Son?
Fluency	The five girls spent their profit on an ancient memento of the island.

Keep the hands and arms quiet

| 1 | 2 | 3 | 4 | 5 | 6 | 7 | 8 | 9 | 10 | 11 | 12 | 13 | 14 |

69B ■ TECHNIQUE PRACTICE: MACHINE MANIPULATIONS [5] each line twice

Line 1: Set tab stops to have 8 spaces between columns.

Line 2: Use the ratchet release to type the subscripts.

Line 4: Backspace to begin line 2 spaces into left margin.

Tabulator	20% #391 403# 10:45 $129.57 641,270
Ratchet release	The formula for sodium carbonate is Na_2CO_3; for hydrogen sulfide, H_2S.
Shift lock	I may underline a book title, as in Topaz; or all cap it, as in TOPAZ.
Margin release	Metzger & Reid, Inc., is selling copies of Moon Walk for $6.25 (less 10%).

69C ■ TYPING SUPERIOR FIGURES AND FOOTNOTES [15] twice as illustrated with 1" side margins

■ Use a superior figure (superscript) in the text for each footnote reference. To type a superior figure: (1) operate the **automatic line finder** or **ratchet release (6)**; (2) turn the cylinder back (toward you) a half space; (3) type the figure; (4) return the ratchet release and cylinder to normal position.

■ In planning a manuscript page, save 2 lines for the divider line and the spaces before and after it; 3 or 4 lines for each footnote to be typed on the page; and 6 lines for the bottom margin.

■ Type a footnote on the same page with its corresponding superior figure. After typing the last line of text on a page, SS and type a 1½" divider line; then DS and type the footnote with single spacing and a ¶ indention. If two or more footnotes are to be typed on the same page, DS between them. Authorities differ on details of typing footnotes, but the illustrations given here are in acceptable form.

DO: Place your page line gauge back of a full sheet with the line numbers extending to the right; insert the two sheets; then type the following drill, beginning on Line 22 (pica) or on Line 19 (elite) from the bottom of the page to have a 1" bottom margin.

According to one statement, "Job changes are expected several times in each worker's life."[1] Moreover, as Aurner and Burtness have said, "Your personal skill in telling what you can do is your best insurance for job security."[2]

---

[1] Walter L. Blackledge, Ethel H. Blackledge, and Helen J. Keily, You and Your Job (Cincinnati: South-Western Publishing Co., 1967), p. iii.

[2] Robert R. Aurner and Paul S. Burtness, Effective English for Business Communication (6th ed.; Cincinnati: South-Western Publishing Co., 1970), p. 501.

PICA

ELITE

94D ■ APPLICATION SKILL BUILDING 25 (Plain sheets, 8½″ x 11″)

Problem 1: Learning

Type Style Letter 3, page 147, in modified block style with 5-space ¶ indentions as shown (171 words).

In typing the letter in correct form, be guided by the placement and spacing notations given in color.

Type the letter at rough-draft speed (exploration level); x-out or strikeover any typing errors.

Problem 2: Proofreading and Making Rough-Draft Corrections

Proofread the letter you typed as Problem 1. Indicate by handwritten corrections any changes that you need to make in the copy.

Use the standard proofreaders' marks you learned (Reference: pages 59 and x) to make the needed handwritten corrections.

Problem 3: Skill Building

Using your corrected rough-draft copy, retype the letter. As you type, make the corrections you have indicated in your copy.

Type on the *control level*; erase and correct neatly any errors you make as you retype the letter. Compare your letter with Style Letter 3.

■ LESSON 95

95A ■ CONDITIONING PRACTICE 5 each line 3 times SS: slowly, faster, then at in-between rate

Alphabet   A jovial man in this plaza fixed Will's bicycle during a quick squall. *Wrists low and relaxed*

Figures   Is American Flight 738 scheduled to arrive at 9:25 a.m. or 10:46 p.m.?

Double letters   The difference between success and luck may well be a matter of pluck.

Fluency   If they do the work, they may go to the lake to fish and to dig clams.

| 1 | 2 | 3 | 4 | 5 | 6 | 7 | 8 | 9 | 10 | 11 | 12 | 13 | 14 |

95B ■ SKILL BUILDING: LETTER PARTS 15 1′ and 3′ writings (Plain paper; margins: 1½″)

1. Using Style Letter 3, page 147, type four 1′ writings on the opening parts (date through salutation). When you have typed through the salutation, DS, indent for the date, and repeat the drill. Type these lines as many times as you can during the 1′ timings. Determine *gwam*.

2. Using the same letter, type four 1′ writings on the closing parts (complimentary close through enclosure notation). When you have typed through the enclosure notation, DS, indent for the complimentary close, and repeat the drill. Type on the *speed level*. Determine *gwam*.

3. On another sheet of paper, type a 3′ writing on the body of the letter. Determine *gwam* by dividing the total words typed by 3.

■ *On which of the timed writings did you make the highest speed: opening lines? closing lines? body of the letter? Why?*

95C ■ PRODUCTION SKILL BUILDING: LETTERS 30 (Plain paper, 8½″ x 11″)

Type the two letter problems on page 148 as directed below:

Style: Modified block, 5-space ¶ indentions, mixed punctuation; date and closing lines started center.

Placement: Use the Letter Placement Table, page 144. The number of words in the letter body is indicated by the number in parentheses at the end of the letter.

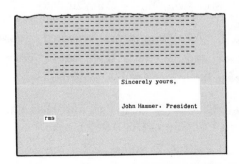

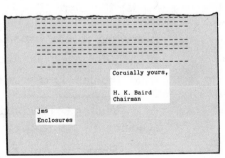

Placement of Official Title in Closing Lines

69D ■ PROBLEM TYPING: MANUSCRIPT WITH LISTED ITEMS AND FOOTNOTES [25]

Type the following one-page unbound manuscript: side and bottom margins, 1″; top margin, 2″ elite or 1½″ pica. SS and indent the listed items 5 spaces from the left margin. Do not type a page number.

Words

COMMUNICATION AND EMPLOYMENT
6

A good job is a major goal of almost everyone at least once in his life. According to one statement, "Job changes are expected several times in each worker's life."[1] Employment involves three phases: (1) locating a job, (2) getting it, and (3) keeping it. 23 / 40 / 58

A variety of sources may be used in obtaining part- or full-time or summer employment. Some of them can aid as follows: 74 / 83

    1.   Relatives and friends can provide job leads. 93
    2.   Teachers and counselors have employment contacts. 104
    3.   Local newspapers carry help-wanted advertisements. 115
    4.   Local employment agencies have many job listings. 126
    5.   Local companies have employment offices. 135

Once a job contact is made, both oral and written communications become important. As Aurner and Burtness have said, "Your personal skill in telling what you can do is your best insurance for job security."[2] Their statement implies that communication is vital in both securing and keeping a job. A personal interview is an essential step in getting a job, and it requires primarily oral communication. Often an application letter is required, and a data sheet is generally requested, too. Each of these is a test of your skill in writing effectively. 152 / 170 / 187 / 205 / 223 / 240 / 246

Keeping the job once you have been hired is as much a matter of personal attitude and behavior as it is of performance skill. 263 / 272 / 276

    [1] Walter L. Blackledge, Ethel H. Blackledge, and Helen J. Keily, You and Your Job (Cincinnati: South-Western Publishing Co., 1967), p. iii. 295 / 307

    [2] Robert R. Aurner and Paul S. Burtness, Effective English for Business Communication (6th ed.; Cincinnati: South-Western Publishing Co., 1970), p. 501. 333 / 347

■ LESSON 70

70A ■ CONDITIONING PRACTICE [5] each line twice SS; then 1′ writings on selected lines

Alphabet	Evelyn explained that the quilted warm-up jacket was Bob Graft's size. *Keep the carriage moving*
Figures	The captains recorded 30 typhoons and 46 hurricanes from 1958 to 1972.
Figure/symbol	Jergens & Reed Co. spent $384,650 for antipollution equipment in 1972.
Fluency	May I go with them to see if the boys or girls will do the job for me?

   | 1 | 2 | 3 | 4 | 5 | 6 | 7 | 8 | 9 | 10 | 11 | 12 | 13 | 14 |

70B ■ TYPING FOOTNOTES [10] retype 69C, page 107, as directed there

94B ■ MANUSCRIPT TYPING [15] (Full sheets)

1" side and bottom margins ■ 1½" top margin first page ■ DS ¶ 1 ■ SS the enumerated items ■ DS after each item ■ 1" top margin second page ■ number of second page approximately ½" from top edge and even with right margin

After typing the first paragraph, reset the margin stops to indent the enumerated items 5 spaces from the left and right margins.

Reset the left margin: (1) at the figure position with a tab stop for the lines of copy; OR (2) at the beginning of the lines of copy and use the margin release and backspace to position the figures.

SPECIAL LETTER PLACEMENT POINTS
TS

Certain points must be kept in mind when using a letter placement table. First, check the placement of the paper guide so that the horizontal centering of the letter will be accurate. The left and right margins should be approximately equal. Special letter placement points are listed below: DS

1. Dateline. The horizontal placement of the dateline varies according to the letter style used. Its vertical placement is governed by the length of the letter.   DS

2. Address lines. When the letter is addressed to a person, his official title may be placed on the first or the second line of the address, whichever gives a better balance to the lines. The first address line is started on the fourth line (3 blank lines) below the dateline.

3. Salutation. The salutation is typed on the second line (DS) below the last address line.

4. Body of letter. The body of the letter is typed in paragraph style, with the first paragraph starting on the second line (DS) below the salutation (or the subject line, when one is used).

5. Complimentary close. The horizontal placement of the complimentary close varies according to the letter style used. It is typed on the second line below the last line of the body of the letter.

6. Typed name and official title. The name of the person who dictated the letter and his official title are typed on the fourth line (3 blank lines) below the complimentary close, or on the fourth line below the

typed company name when it is used. When both the dictator's name and the official title are used, they may be typed on the same line, or the official title may be typed on the line below the typed name.

7. Reference initials. The reference initials (usually only the initials of the typist are used) are typed at the left margin on the second line below the typed name or official title.

8. Enclosure notation. The enclosure notation (spelled in full or abbreviated to Enc.) is typed at the left margin on the second line below the reference initials.

9. Carbon copy notation. The carbon copy notation (usually abbreviated as cc) and the name of the person who is to receive the copy are typed at the left margin on the second line below the reference initials or the last closing line. (*See model on page 214 with "Copy to," which equals "cc."*)

10. Attention line. When an attention line is used, it is usually typed on the second line below the last address line. (*See model on page 203.*)

11. Subject line. The subject line, when used, may be typed on the second line below the salutation. It may be centered or typed at the left margin. (*See model, page 203.*)

12. Company name. Sometimes the company name is typed in the closing lines. When used, it is typed in all CAPITAL LETTERS on the second line below the complimentary close. The modern practice is to omit the company name in the closing lines; this is especially true when letterhead paper is used. (*See model, page 214.*)

13. Two-page letters. If a letter is too long for one page, at least two lines of a paragraph should be typed at the bottom of the first page and at least two lines should be carried to the next page. The bottom margin on the first page should be approximately equal to the side margins. The second page of a letter, or any additional pages, requires a proper heading. Either of two forms may be used for typing the extra-page heading. (*See model, page 203.*)

94C ■ ACTION LEARNING (Observation) [5]

Using the manuscript prepared in 94B, study and relate as many of the items as possible to Style

Letter 3, page 147. Note the use of the word "Enclosures" to indicate the inclusion of separate items.

70C ■ PROBLEM TYPING: ROUGH-DRAFT MANUSCRIPT WITH LONG QUOTATION ⌷35⌷

LEARN: Quoted material of 4 or more lines is single-spaced and indented 5 spaces from the left and right margins. Double-space above and below the quoted material.

■ Be sure to use your page line gauge to note where the divider line should be typed to have a 1″ bottom margin.

DO: Type the following rough draft as a 1-page manuscript. Side and bottom margins: 1″; top margin: 2″ elite and 1½″ pica. *Do not correct your errors as you type.* Remove the paper; proofread and mark the copy for correction; then retype the manuscript from your marked copy, erasing and correcting *all* errors as you type.

	Words
Habits ̿ TS	1
[We are a *society of* people with habitual behavio*r* ~~called~~ *known as* "customs." These are	18
learned responses to specific sit*u*ations; such as, bru*s*hing our teeth *after* ~~at least~~	33
~~twice a day~~ *meals* or greeting an a*c*quaintance by saying *̲g̲*ood morning."	45
Many ~~of our~~ *such* habits, whether learned *inadvertently* ~~accidentally~~ or by imitation or	58
practiced deliberately, ar*e* a ~~valuable~~ desirable me⌒ans of conserving our	71
higher mental ~~processes~~ *powers* for more demanding task*s*. *a number* ~~Some~~ of our habits,	85
~~however~~ *though*, have ~~harmful~~ *detrimental* (social *and* personal) consequences. As pointed ou*t*	100
by Boehm:	103
Compulsive eaters, chain smokers, heavy drinkers (including	115
coffee drinkers), dru*g* addicts--they're all hooked on something	127
called a habit, easy to acquire, hard to kick. Breaking ou*t* is	140
like breaking out of a maze.[1]	147
A *great* ~~tremendous~~ amount of energy ~~as well as~~ *and* money is being poured into	158
an all-out ~~fight~~ *rebellion* against such habits. The gover*n*ment*,* is waging war on *at every level,*	176
d*r*ug use and abuse. Cigarette advertising has come under ~~increasing~~ *intense*	189
fire. Thousands *of people* are joining the ranks of ~~A.A.'s~~ *AA (Alcoholics Anonymous)* and W.W.'s (Weight	208
Watchers). Books, articles *and* films by the ~~hundreds~~ *score* fo*r*cus on "re-	221
habilitation" centers, "panaceas," and "cures." It has been estimated	235
that perhaps half of ~~the~~ adult American*s* ~~population is~~ *are* determined (or at	247
least *embarrassingly* committed) to do something a⌒bout over-eating, overdrinking, over-	264
smoking, (*no*) overdoing something else.	272
	276
[1]George A. W. Boehm, "Habits: Easy Come, Not-So-Easy Go,"	288
Think (November/December, 1969), p. 8.	297

PHASE 4: PERSONAL/BUSINESS APPLICATIONS

■ As you apply your basic typing skill in various problem-and-production situations, you will make the greatest skill gains if you plan your work and type with good technique and a minimum of waste motion.

UNIT 14 LESSONS 94-98

Personal/Business Letters

Stationery: Business letters are usually typed on 8½- by 11-inch letterheads which have the name and address of the company and sometimes other information printed at the top.

If a letter is longer than one page, plain paper of the same size, color, and quality as the letterhead is used for the additional pages. Special paper (onionskin or manifold-copy paper) is used for carbon copies.

Smaller letterheads (usually 8½ by 5½ or 5½ by 8½ inches) may be used for short letters.

Margins and Vertical Placement:
Some offices use standard margins (a set line length) for all letters. Other offices vary the margins according to letter length.

A placement table will help you place letters properly. As you gain skill, you should be able to estimate letter length and place letters correctly without this "aid."

Notes About the Placement Table:

1. Vertical placement of the dateline varies according to letter length. The address is always typed on the fourth line (3 blank line spaces) below the date.

2. Letters with special lines (attention, subject, etc.) or unusual features (tables, extra lines in address or closing) may require adjustment in dateline placement. If a deep letterhead makes it impossible to type the date on the designated line, type it on the second line below the last letterhead line.

LETTER PLACEMENT TABLE

Letter Classification		5-Stroke Words in Letter Body	Side Margins	Margin Description	Dateline Position (From Top Edge of Paper)
Short		Up to 100	2″	Wide	Line 20
Average	1	100 – 150	1½″	Standard	18
	2	151 – 200	1½″	"	16
	3	201 – 250	1½″	"	14
	4	251 – 300	1½″	"	12
Long		301 – 350	1″	Narrow	12
Two-page		More than 350	1″	Narrow	12

■ LESSON 94

94A ■ CONDITIONING PRACTICE [5] each line 3 times SS; slowly, faster, then at in-between rate for CONTROL

Alphabet	Jack's brevity always complements his quietly expressed zeal for good. *Fingers curved and upright*
Figures	Do Problems 6, 7, 8, and 9 on page 4, and Problems 2 and 3 on page 50.
Figure/symbol	Is Check #1576 for $48.90, dated May 23, made out to McNeil & O'Brien?
Fluency	The eight men handled the historical ornament with the utmost caution.

| 1 | 2 | 3 | 4 | 5 | 6 | 7 | 8 | 9 | 10 | 11 | 12 | 13 | 14 |

■ LESSON 71

71A ■ CONDITIONING PRACTICE [5] twice SS; then 1' writings on selected lines

Alphabet	James quickly paid a ticket received for a wrong turn by the zoo exit.
Figures	The Orioles won the last 4 games by scores of 5-2, 7-6, 10-9, and 8-3.
Figure/symbol	Hertz & Poe's check for $2,873.45 (less 10%) is an overpayment of $96.
Fluency	The chairman did name the eight men to handle such big civic problems.

Work for continuity of stroking

| 1 | 2 | 3 | 4 | 5 | 6 | 7 | 8 | 9 | 10 | 11 | 12 | 13 | 14 |

71B ■ SPECIAL CHARACTERS AND SYMBOLS [10] each line twice SS

1 *Single quote* Emory said, "My teacher quoted, 'Poetry is the language of the soul.'"

2 *Abbreviations* The C.O.D. shipment to Reynolds & Lane, Inc., was sent f.o.b. Detroit.

3 *Feet/inches* Use ' for feet and " for inches. Sue bought a rug that is 18'9" long.

4 *Minutes/seconds* My class typed 45 <u>gwam</u> on a 2' writing with the call of the 15" guide.

5 *Equations* Use x for times, – for minus, and = for equals: 290 x 8 – 457 = 1863.

6 *Degrees* The freezing point of water is 32° F. and the boiling point is 212° F.

7 *Roman numerals* Use capital letters for Roman numerals: I II IV V VI X XI XII XX XXI.

8 *Subscripts* The formula for antimonous nitrate is $Sb(NO_3)_3$; that for methane, CH_4.

71C ■ FOOTNOTES ON PARTIALLY FILLED PAGE; ELLIPSIS [10] (1" side margins)

Partially Filled Page with Footnotes: Between the last line of the text and the divider line above the footnotes, leave enough space to drop the footnotes to have an approximate 1" (6-line) bottom margin. Use your page line gauge for placing the divider line.

Ellipsis: The ellipsis is used to indicate omission of words from a quotation. It is shown by 3 alternating periods and spaces, or by 4 if the end of a sentence is included in the omission.

    You may write . . . if it seems desirable.

Type on Line 28 from bottom of page; 1" side margins

Aurner and Burtness, using the **AIDA** formula, list four basic steps in the application procedure: "attracting attention, arousing interest, stimulating desire . . . and getting action."[1] This was my guide for getting my summer job, but I failed at first to follow its advice. As another writer has said: "Looking for a job is a job."[2]

Space down as necessary to have a 1-inch bottom margin

---

   [1] Robert R. Aurner and Paul S. Burtness, <u>Effective English for Business Communication</u> (6th ed.; Cincinnati: South-Western Publishing Co., 1970), p. 507.

   [2] M. Jean Herman, <u>The Job Interview</u> (New York: Alumnae Advisory Center, Inc., 1966), p. 4.

93C ■ IMPROVING STROKING: COMMON WORD BEGINNINGS AND ENDINGS [10] each line 3 times SS: slowly, faster, at top speed

TECHNIQUE CUES

1	*Common*	invest instruct increase request regard subject submit prevail perhaps	*Fingers curved and upright; space quickly*
2	*word*	exercise programs | provide experience | concert committee | almost complete	
3	*beginnings*	When it is convenient, a committee should inspect the file completely.	
4	*Common*	rated fitted passed rating asking having highly previously application	*Eyes on copy; concentrate on drill lines*
5	*word*	possible actions | active sessions | practical education | technical ability	
6	*endings*	I could be relatively satisfied with this varied teaching opportunity.	
7	*Beginnings*	being regional recently questions situation consider anxious dictation	*Quick, snappy keystroking; finger action*
8	*and endings*	medical authority | following inquiry | public policies | available solution	
9		According to the manager, our division should proceed as you directed.	

93D ■ TECHNIQUE CHECKUP [20] each line 3 times as you give special attention to the Technique Cues; then 1' writings on Lines 1-6, as time permits

	Points to check:	
Keystroking	1. Fingers curved and upright 2. Fingers close to keys; hands quiet 3. Wrists low and relaxed	4. Quick, snap keystroke with immediate key release; finger action

	Points to check:	
Continuity and Rhythm	1. Continuous keystroking; no pauses or breaks in the typing	2. Smooth, fluent rhythm pattern which varies according to copy difficulty

	Points to check:	
Return	1. Return made quickly at ends of lines	2. New line started without pause 3. Eyes kept on copy

1	It was necessary to make an orderly progression from beginning to end.
2	I suppose you appreciate the difficulty of processing the new payroll.
3	With this background information, headquarters will welcome estimates.
4	The letterhead printing did not represent high quality of workmanship.
5	In depreciating assets, do not deviate from this straight-line method.
6	Yesterday, we were asked to certify the insurance forms and estimates.

| 1 | 2 | 3 | 4 | 5 | 6 | 7 | 8 | 9 | 10 | 11 | 12 | 13 | 14 |

	Points to check:	
Shift Key Control	1. Quick, little finger reach; other fingers in typing position	2. No pauses or breaks before or after shift-key reach

7	Jan C. McNeil and Paula O'Brien will speak at the Key West Convention.
8	Jack Flood, Mary E. Langs, and C. O. Quaile work for Black & Williams.

	Points to check:	
Space Bar Control	1. Right thumb curved, on or close to space bar at all times	2. Quick, down-and-in-motion of right thumb 3. No pause before or after spacing stroke

9	At the end of the day, please try to have the form work in good order.
10	Jim and Amy may try to help John Jay Meany with the new typing lesson.

71D ■ PROBLEM TYPING: MANUSCRIPT WITH SIDE HEADINGS 25

LEARN: Long reports are often divided into two or more sections by the use of side headings. Such headings are typed at the left margin and underlined; important words are capitalized. Triple-space above and double-space below the side headings.

DO: Type the following 2-page manuscript as an unbound manuscript. Side and bottom margins: 1″; top margin: 2″ elite and 1½″ pica on page 1 and 1″ elite and pica margins on page 2. Place each footnote on the page on which its reference figure appears in the text. SS and indent the quoted paragraph 5 spaces from each margin.

Alertness Cue: The second page is a partially filled page.

PICA   1

ELITE   1

	Words
POLLUTION OF OUR ENVIRONMENT	6

TS

Pollution is the act or process of making | 14
soil, water, or the atmosphere unhealthful by | 23
the discharge of harmful waste material or | 32
noxious substances. Most, if not all, of us are | 42
big polluters, and a majority are concerned | 51
about the pollution of our once-clean environ- | 60
ment--especially our water and air. The grow- | 69
ing alarm about pollution is well justified, but | 78
alarm alone will not eliminate it. | 86

TS

War on Water Pollution | 95

DS

According to *Fortune*, "Efforts to combat | 104
water pollution are intensifying, with Con- | 113
gress appropriating $800 million for waste- | 121
water treatment plants in the current fiscal | 130
year alone . . . ."[1] Nevertheless, it is still a | 140
limited war. Industry, too, is contributing to | 150
the antipollution campaign. Many firms report | 159
they are spending 10 percent of their capital | 168
budgets on pollution control, and some say | 177
they are spending between 20 and 30 percent. | 186
Even so, we may ultimately have to purify our | 195
water just before we drink it or purify waste | 205
water before we throw it away. Increasingly, | 214
we will have to emphasize the latter approach, | 223
which is far more desirable for man and for | 232
nature--or so it is said by some. | 239

	Words
War on Air Pollution	247

The word "smog" once was a source of amus- | 255
ing comments on radio and television and | 264
"seemed" to exist primarily in Los Angeles. | 273
Air pollution today is no laughing matter, | 281
whether it is identified as smog or something | 290
else or whether it exists in Los Angeles or | 299
in Zap, North Dakota. According to the *En-* | 308
cyclopaedia Britannica: | 318

Air pollution, like other forms of en- | 325
vironmental pollution, is directly related | 334
to fuel usage, increased industrialization, | 342
and growing urban populations. This his- | 350
torical relationship is perhaps somewhat | 359
more direct and apparent for atmospheric | 367
than for water pollution.[2] | 372

The automobile is considered to be a major | 381
source of air pollution in most large cities. | 390
Concentrated effort of the auto industry as a | 400
result of coaxing by the U.S. Government | 408
promises to reduce auto-engine pollution by | 417
one third within the next fifteen years, accord- | 426
ing to authoritative opinion. | 432

[1] "Fortune's Wheel," *Fortune* (February, 1970), p. 2.   (16 words)

[2] "Pollution," *Encyclopaedia Britannica* (1968), 18, 184.   (20 words)

1. Type a 5' writing. Determine *gwam*; proofread for errors.
2. Type a 1' writing on ¶ 1 for speed.
3. Type a 2' writing on ¶ 1 and try to maintain Step 2 rate.
4. Repeat Steps 2 and 3 with ¶ 2.
5. Type another 5' writing. Determine *gwam*; proofread for errors. Record your better 5' rate.

All letters are used.

	GWAM		
	1'	2'	5'

¶ 1 Just what does it mean to be young and when is a person young? To be young is perhaps a feeling or disposition, a particular manner of looking at things and responding to them. To be young is never a chronological period or time of life, although it might be a young person examining some material with fascination and pleasure or the Composer Verdi in his eighties writing his best opera. To be young might be a person hanging "ten" on a surfboard, or swinging to a musical composition. To be young might be Einstein in his seventies still working with his field theory, sailing his boat, or playing his cherished fiddle.

1'	2'	5'	
13	7	3	49
27	14	5	52
41	21	8	55
55	28	11	58
69	35	14	60
83	42	17	63
97	49	19	66
112	56	22	69
126	63	25	72

¶ 2 To be young is never the monopoly of youth. It flourishes everywhere visionaries have stimulated our thinking or amazed us. To be young in nature is quite desirable whether you are a young person, a middle-aged person, or a chronologically old person. To be young should be respected whether the beard is soft and curly or stiff and gray. To be young has no color; it seems always translucent with its own imaginative light. There is no generation space between the young of any age because they see things as they ought to be.

1'	2'	5'	
13	7	28	74
28	14	31	77
42	21	33	80
56	28	36	83
70	35	39	86
85	42	42	88
99	50	45	91
107	53	46	93

1' GWAM | 1 | 2 | 3 | 4 | 5 | 6 | 7 | 8 | 9 | 10 | 11 | 12 | 13 | 14 |
2' GWAM | 1 | 2 | 3 | 4 | 5 | 6 | 7 |
5' GWAM | 1 | 2 | 3 |

■ LESSON 93

93A ■ CONDITIONING PRACTICE [5] each line 3 times: slowly, faster, in-between rate

Alphabet Pecquoix Avenue was a bizarre jungle of many colored, blinking lights.

Quick, snappy keystroking; hands quiet

Figures In 1972, we had 83 office chairs, 40 office desks, and 56 work tables.

Figure/symbol He bought 80 pencils @ 6¢ each; 23 erasers @ 9¢ each; 1 punch @ $4.75!

Fluency If you do all your work in the right way, the work will be easy to do.

| 1 | 2 | 3 | 4 | 5 | 6 | 7 | 8 | 9 | 10 | 11 | 12 | 13 | 14 |

93B ■ IMPROVING SPEED/CONTROL [15] type two 5' writings on 92D, above

Inventory / Measurement

■ LESSON 72

72A ■ CONDITIONING PRACTICE 5 each line twice SS; then 1' writings on selected lines

Alphabet	Lt. J. W. Knox of "B" Company organized the bivouac squads at Ft. Ord.	Keep stroking action in fingers
Figures	They purchased 205 pines, 167 firs, and 83 blue and 49 silver spruces.	
Figure/symbol	Check #8 (dated 5/1) for $23 covers Invoice #74 less the 10% discount.	
Fluency	It is your social duty to rush to your neighbor's aid when he is sick.	

| 1 | 2 | 3 | 4 | 5 | 6 | 7 | 8 | 9 | 10 | 11 | 12 | 13 | 14 |

72B ■ SKILL-COMPARISON INVENTORY 10 two 1' writings on each line; compare GWAM

Consecutive-direct	Cecil Marvin produced Marilyn Frederick's great new play off Broadway.	Hands quiet, fingers curved
One-hand	D. J. West, a union steward, gave a rare opinion based on a few facts.	
Combination	Their information is unfit for admission in the Nesbit abduction case.	
Balanced-hand	The policy of the giant firm may entitle the chairman to an endowment.	

| 1 | 2 | 3 | 4 | 5 | 6 | 7 | 8 | 9 | 10 | 11 | 12 | 13 | 14 |

72C ■ INVENTORY OF BASIC TYPING ACTIVITIES 35 (Line: 50; full sheet: Items 1-6; half sheets: Items 7-10)

1. Beginning on Line 10, type the figures and periods **1.** to **10.** in a column at the left margin, SS.

2. Return to Line 10; reset left margin 10 spaces to the right and type Roman numerals and periods **I.** to **X.** opposite Arabic figures **1.** to **10.**

3. Reset margin; type sentence; supply missing figures:

   A vertical inch has __ line spaces; a horizontal inch has __ pica or __ elite spaces.

4. Type the symbol for the italicized words in the following sentences:

   Ship Ibsen *and* Hamma 250 *pounds at* 70 *cents.*
   I typed for *2 minutes* with the 15 *second* call.

5. Type the periods for abbreviations and initials in the following sentences. Use correct spacing.

   R J Luke finished the project at 2:45 p m.
   Mr Abner received a C O D package from Taiwan.

6. Type each of these sentences, correcting errors in spacing, punctuation, and capitalization:

   Give mr apgar 10 # for # 8. 75
   (less 10 %).
   His two- part article, "automation,"
   appears in Today's business.

7. Center the following table vertically and horizontally. Leave 10 spaces between columns.

   REGIONAL SALES ESTIMATES
   (Based on Current Economic Conditions)

Region	This Year	Next Year
Northern	$9,150,000	$10,825,000
Southern	7,462,700	8,350,500

8. Center the problem vertically and horizontally. Type each word with a hyphen to show the first acceptable division if bell rings on typing of first letter; leave 10 spaces between columns.

refer	puzzle	certainly
around	obvious	regulate
steady	yielded	winning
smaller	neutral	probable
likely	omitted	radical

9. Beginning on Line 4, type in modified block style, mixed punctuation, the letter address and salutation for the following addressee; address an envelope for it, using your own return address.

   mrs j r seiwert   118 kenmore avenue, apt 6
   syracuse new york   13205

10. Beginning on Line 21, type in modified block style, mixed punctuation, an appropriate *complimentary close*, your name, and your initials as reference for Item 9.

■ LESSON 92

92A ■ CONDITIONING PRACTICE ⑤ each line 3 times: slowly, faster, in-between rate

Alphabet   The kind queen received extra jewels from a dozen brave young pirates. *Fingers curved and upright*

Figures   I have read 127 books, 364 magazines, 50 newspapers, and 89 pamphlets.

Figure/symbol Mr. Jay asked us to check this total: $123 - 56 + 90 - 148 \times 75 = 675$.

Fluency   If they are to go with us to the big city, we shall be there at eight.
           | 1 | 2 | 3 | 4 | 5 | 6 | 7 | 8 | 9 | 10 | 11 | 12 | 13 | 14 |

92B ■ IMPROVING STROKING: COMMON 2-, 3-, AND 4-LETTER COMBINATIONS ⑩ each line 3 times SS: slowly, faster, at top speed

TECHNIQUE CUES

1   had look real than miss more give seem help mate feel made been little *Continuity; quick, snappy keystroking*

2   exert effort | sent thanks | heavy package | current yield | first court order

3   The dealer received a dozen of the custom machines for corps projects.

4   well mail ache fowl exit upon sing just much tent spot does week lists *Eyes on copy; space quickly*

5   short quote | employ labor | mental growth | evident success | regular charter

6   Each military detail moved slowly through the full length of the city.

7   cost take vary disc find size type felt does items large rough adjusts *Fingers curved and upright; finger-reach action*

8   involves respect | sincere student | business telegram | select and describe

9   After several years, our stock enters a major upswing for five months.

92C ■ RELATED LEARNING CHECKUP: PUNCTUATION GUIDES ⑩ (Line: 74; correct as you type)

* See page 126, if necessary, for code explanation.

1-2:128; 22:134*	1. Mr. Jahn said_ _Spectrum colors include red, yellow, blue, and green._
33:137; 23:134	2. Mary_s article_ I believe_ was titled _Woodrow Wilson, the President._
6:129; 17:132; 5:128	3. On a hot_ humid summer day_ July 15, 1971_, I left Newark_ New Jersey.
7:129; 13:131	4. On April 9_ 1,500 boy scouts participated in the 1_30 p.m. dedication.
20:132; 9:129	5. Did he read the book Megacity_ which was listed in the New York Times_
33:137; 10:131	6. John_s new car_ a red Jaguar_ was the most impressive thing about him.
6:129; 15:131; 11:131	7. These are her favorite modern_day poets_ Frost, McKuen, and Sellwood.
11,14:131	8. Spell these numbers_ sixteen, twenty_nine, forty_six, and fifty_four.
16:132	9. All of us were asked to tutor first_, second_, and third_grade pupils.
18:132	10. Grade these techniques: _1_ stroking, _2_ continuity, and _3_ rhythm.
2:128; 22:134	11. Kin Hubbard said_ _Lots of folks confuse bad management with destiny._
27:135	12. He cannot work today_ therefore, you must be sure to do his work, too.
31:137	13. I didnt see John today; yet I know that he cant do this work for us.
35:138; 33:137	14. The boys_ baseball team will play the mens_ baseball team on Saturday.

LESSON 73

73A ■ CONDITIONING PRACTICE ⑤ each line twice SS; then 1' writings on selected lines

Alphabet   Jay G. Bux made a quick trip to Switzerland; Van F. Heald chose Italy.   *Shift firmly; return quickly*

Figures   On May 19, 67 men will be interviewed between 8:30 a.m. and 12:45 p.m.

Figure/symbol   Please order 5 doz. #1828MB pencils @ 60¢; 4 doz. #597BP pens @ $3.00.

Fluency   It is better to try to do well and not succeed than not to try at all.

| 1 | 2 | 3 | 4 | 5 | 6 | 7 | 8 | 9 | 10 | 11 | 12 | 13 | 14 |

73B ■ SKILL-TRANSFER INVENTORY ⑩ (Line: 60) two 1' writings on each line; compare GWAM

Rough draft   Lieutenant Adcock signaled *Dubuque* headquarters, *his* replacements *for reinforcements.*

Script   *Mystery director Hitchcock did spend his boyhood in Britain.*

Statistical   The Bayh Co. check (#1293) for $1,047.59 paid Invoice #2836.

Straight copy   Winford keeps his outboard cabin cruiser at Kirkdale Marina.

| 1 | 2 | 3 | 4 | 5 | 6 | 7 | 8 | 9 | 10 | 11 | 12 |

73C ■ GROWTH INDEX ⑧ (Line: 70) one 5' writing; determine GWAM and errors

		GWAM 1'	GWAM 5'	

¶ 1   *All letters are used.*

Some people can find something good in virtually every situation.   13   3 | 43

Even when things go wrong, they believe every dark cloud hides a silver   28   6 | 46

lining. No matter what the source of this point of view, it results in   42   8 | 49

the power of positive thinking. A great deal of praise should be given   57   11 | 52

the person who can be identified as a positive thinker.   68   14 | 54

¶ 2   Have you acquired the power of positive thinking? When the going   13   16 | 57

gets difficult at school or at home, can you recognize some good in the   28   19 | 59

situation? When you get an unsatisfactory comment on a paper in one of   42   22 | 62

your classes, do you adjudge the teacher unjust? This is the typical   56   25 | 65

reaction of many a person who does not think positively.   67   27 | 67

¶ 3   A positive thinker would accept a poor mark he received on a paper   13   30 | 70

and develop it into something of value. He would evaluate each of the   28   32 | 73

suggestions on a paper and employ it in his very next attempt to make   42   35 | 76

the work a praiseworthy job. He would realize that the comments sug-   55   38 | 78

gested a need to improve learning or increase performance.   67   40 | 81

1' GWAM | 1 | 2 | 3 | 4 | 5 | 6 | 7 | 8 | 9 | 10 | 11 | 12 | 13 | 14 |

5' GWAM | 1 | 2 | 3 |

91C ■ IMPROVED STROKING: COMMON 2-, 3-, AND 4-LETTER COMBINATIONS │10│ each line 3 times SS: slowly, faster, at top speed

1 add addition cop copy pay pays payments war aware forward once concern

Eyes on copy; finger action, hands quiet

2 copy the address │ she wishes payment │ a number of sheets │ already payable

3 A number of shipments from my warehouse were forwarded to his address.

4 owe power however who whole whose get together forget gain gains again

Fingers close to keys; quick spacing

5 show me the budget │ replace the folder │ place it carefully │ gain in power

6 If the budget folder is full, open another and place the two together.

7 rod production win winner way away always air fair airman hang hanging

Quick, snappy keystroking; variable rhythm

8 the product │ repair the highway │ attend a benefit │ attached profit report

9 The attached profit report on that product tends to indicate a winner.

91D ■ SKILL-TRANSFER TYPING: SCRIPT │25│ (Line: 70)

1. Type a 5' writing. Determine *gwam*; proofread for errors.
2. Type a 1' writing on ¶ 1 for speed.
3. Type a 2' writing on ¶ 1 and try

to maintain Step 2 rate.
4. Repeat Steps 2 and 3 with ¶ 2.
5. Type another 5' writing. Determine *gwam*; proofread for errors.

6. Compute % *of transfer*: script copy rate divided by straight-copy rate of 88D. Record better 5' rate and % of transfer score.

All letters are used.

		GWAM		
		1'	2'	5'

¶ 1 The beginning worker has to cope with many difficult problems in — 13 | 7 | 3 | 38

the business office. Not the least of these enigmas is the art of get- — 27 | 14 | 5 | 41

ting along with others. A significant solution to the problem of — 40 | 20 | 8 | 44

human relations is to do your own work in the right way. This precise — 55 | 27 | 11 | 47

mode of working is one identification of the mature person. A mature — 69 | 34 | 14 | 49

person does not make the same mistakes again and again, and he — 81 | 41 | 16 | 52

reasons with other employees instead of punching them in the nose. — 95 | 47 | 19 | 55

¶ 2 Just practicing good manners at home or in school, with your — 12 | 6 | 21 | 57

family or with others, will help you gain poise and quiet confidence. — 26 | 13 | 24 | 60

Being well-mannered means following the recognized rules of behav- — 40 | 20 | 27 | 62

ior which aid in making your contacts more genial. A basis of good — 53 | 27 | 30 | 65

manners is kindness and a deep concern for every person. You must — 67 | 33 | 32 | 68

like or respect everyone, and then be sure to make an extra effort — 80 | 40 | 35 | 71

to relate to them. — 84 | 42 | 36 | 71

73D ■ PROBLEM TYPING MEASUREMENT: CENTERING/TABLES ⌷27⌷

Problem 1

Center the following announcement vertically on a half sheet, DS; center each line horizontally.

	Words
The Junior Chamber of Commerce	6
Cordially Invites You to Attend Their	14
ANNUAL INTERNATIONAL BAZAAR	19
December 5, 7-10 p.m.	24
Yates Junior High School Auditorium	31
Admission: Adults 75¢; Children Free	39
Proceeds Will Go to the Band Uniform Fund	47

Problem 2

Center the following table vertically and horizontally on a half sheet; DS; 14 spaces between columns.

		Words
DELINQUENT ACCOUNTS		4
(December 31, 19––)		8
Yielding Cookware Corp.	$218.45	15
KC Bakery Utensils, Inc.	92.57	21
Kaupneur Products, Ltd.	163.50	27
Tucson Pottery Company	87.20	33
Albuquerque Gift Shoppe	149.62	39

Problem 3

Center the following table vertically and horizontally on a half sheet; DS; 6 spaces between columns.

Correct the errors indicated in the copy. In addition, erase and correct errors you make as you type.

			Words
STEERING COMMITTEES FOR SENIOR CLASS ACTIVITIES			10
Yearbook	Prom	Banquet	18
Joy Bowdon, Chairman	Mae Yingst, Chairman	Tye Haygood, Chairman	30
Emma Kirkpatrick	Barbara Kapmeier	Leah Kashfir	40
Evalyn Mansford	Darleen Lemming	Denice Koghue	49
Gerald Tupman	Dwight McDonough	Barry Lipmann	59
Richard Topmiller	Marie Rodrigues	Margot Mansfield	68
Jo Ann Yingling	George Wstphall	Tommy McNulty	77

LESSON 74

74A ■ CONDITIONING PRACTICE ⌷5⌷ each line twice SS; then 1' writings on selected lines

Alphabet	Did Jean Glick get Stewart Phelps to fix my map of Mozambique for Eve?
Figures	Our 6 winning scores were: 7-6, 23-14, 25-19, 30-21, 34-28, and 16-0.
Figure/symbol	The $1,000 Dwyer Water Authority $4\frac{1}{4}$% bond, due 6/20/87, sold for $953.
Fluency	A formal audit of all departments may be made by the end of the month.

| 1 | 2 | 3 | 4 | 5 | 6 | 7 | 8 | 9 | 10 | 11 | 12 | 13 | 14 |

74B ■ IMPROVING SPEED/CONTROL ⌷15⌷ two 5' writings on 73C, page 113

90D ■ SKILL-TRANSFER TYPING: ROUGH DRAFT [25]

1. Type a 5′ writing. Determine *gwam*; proofread for errors.
2. Type a 1′ writing on ¶ 1 for speed.
3. Type a 2′ writing on ¶ 1 and try to maintain Step 2 rate.
4. Repeat Steps 2 and 3 with ¶ 2.
5. Type another 5′ writing. Determine *gwam*; proofread for errors.
6. Compute % *of transfer*: rough-draft copy rate divided by straight-copy rate of 88D. Record your better 5′ rate and % of transfer score.

	GWAM		
	1′	2′	5′

¶ 1

Some material from which you type in the business office may be in — 13 | 7 | 3 | 52
copy similar to this copy.
rough draft form, the copy will contain various kinds of corrections, — 32 | 16 | 6 | 55
In some situations,
which usually ~~will be~~ *are* handwritten. These corrections may be difficult — 49 | 25 | 10 | 59
busy executive
to read as they may been (have) written hurriedly by a ~~business person~~ as — 64 | 32 | 13 | 62
and revises
he changes the copy. Often, too, your employer may ask you to type a — 81 | 40 | 16 | 65
or report *When this request is made,*
letter in rough-copy from. Your employer may be in a hurry for the rough — 103 | 51 | 21 | 69
*or x-out*
copy; therefore, he may tell you to strike over any typewriting errors — 119 | 59 | 24 | 72
you make. *If readable, such rough copy is satisfactory for use.* — 131 | 66 | 26 | 75

¶ 2

this
The employer then uses ~~the~~ rough draft as a way to evaluate the — 13 | 6 | 29 | 78
or report, Often, *handwritten*
content of the letter. He will make many changes and other corrections — 33 | 17 | 34 | 82
or
before he returns the copy to you. You will be expected to make the — 54 | 27 | 37 | 86
As you type from the rough draft,
corrections indicated. You will need to read it ~~carefully~~ to be certain — 76 | 38 | 41 | 90
make *corrected* *with care*
you ~~understand~~ all corrections and that the copy makes good sense. ~~As a~~ — 90 | 45 | 44 | 93
~~final step~~ you will proofread carefully the final copy that you *have* — 102 | 51 | 47 | 95
prepared before submitting it to your employer. *for his approval.* — 114 | 57 | 49 | 98
When the copy is returned to you,

■ LESSON 91

91A ■ CONDITIONING PRACTICE [5] each line 3 times: slowly, faster, in-between rate

Alphabet — Some Hi-Fi fans adopt with zeal or absorb quickly an extensive jargon. *Type with continuity*

Figures — Today he typed 40 letters, 15 reports, 369 orders, and 278 statements.

Figure/symbol — Pay Lee & Co.'s bill for $137.56 before you pay Al & Ed's for $248.90.

Fluency — They lent the ancient ornament to their neighbor by the big city dock.
| 1 | 2 | 3 | 4 | 5 | 6 | 7 | 8 | 9 | 10 | 11 | 12 | 13 | 14 |

91B ■ TYPING FROM ROUGH DRAFT [10] repeat Steps 2-4 of 90D, above

74C ■ PROBLEM TYPING MEASUREMENT: PERSONAL/BUSINESS COMMUNICATIONS 30

Problem 1: Personal Note

Use a half sheet, short side at left; 60-space line; SS; block style, open punctuation. Correct your errors.

Be guided by the warning bell to return the carriage (carrier) at the end of the line. (See page 87.)

	Words
Current date	3

Dear Sandra — 5

You'll be happy to hear that The Whitmills are organizing a sight-seeing [20] tour next summer for high school students in this area. This will be the [35] sixth tour they have sponsored. [41]

Carlsbad Caverns, the Grand Canyon, and Disneyland will be the features [56] of the tour; and since you have always wanted to see these tourist attrac- [70] tions, I couldn't wait to let you know about the trip. [81]

If you think your parents will let you join the tour, be sure to contact [96] R. C. Whitmill for further information. I understand that the group will [111] be limited to 35 students, so it's important that you get your reservation [126] in early. [128]

Sincerely — 130

Problem 2: Personal/Business Letter

Modified block style; mixed punctuation; 60-space line; current date on Line 16, preceded by the return address. Leave 3 blank line spaces between the date and letter address. Indent the quotation 5 spaces from left and right margins. *Erase and correct your errors.* Address an envelope.

	Words
3147 Oaktree Street, N.E. | Kansas City, Missouri 64118 | (Current date) | Dr. Marybeth Hepburn | Department of Psychology | University of Kansas | Lawrence, Kansas 66044 | Dear Dr. Hepburn: | (¶1) In a recent issue of the Kansas City Star, you were quoted as saying:	8 / 17 / 24 / 32 / 40 / 52 / 53

> Once firmly established, a habit per- [61]
> vades so many corners of a person's [68]
> psychic and physical being that to [75]
> root it out is equivalent to slaying [82]
> the hydra, the mythical nine-headed [89]
> monster. [91]

(¶2) As a clinician in a local hospital that [99] treats many patients with emotional and men- [108] tal problems, I try to keep informed about [117] harmful habits and their causes and cures. [125] (¶3) I should like to obtain a reading list that [134] includes the most recent thinking in this field. [144] I shall be most appreciative if you will send [153] me a list of reading references that might be [163] helpful. \| Sincerely yours, \| Mrs. James W. [171] Lemmon [172/205]

Problem 3: Business Letter

Modified block style; mixed punctuation; 60-space line; current date on Line 16, followed by 3 blank line spaces; 10 spaces between columns; *erase and correct your errors.* Address an envelope.

	Words
Current date | Mr. Arnold J. Buck, Manager | Star Optical Company | 217 Swayne Avenue | Ft. Worth, TX 76111 | Dear Mr. Buck: | (¶1) In reply to your inquiry of December 21, we have narrowed our choices of three-bedroom homes. When you arrive next week, we think you will be interested in seeing those listed below:	9 / 16 / 24 / 32 / 39 / 48 / 58 / 61

		Words
563 Crabtree Avenue	$21,750	66
841 Sweetbriar Street	23,500	72
1202 Jacqueline Avenue	26,250	79

(¶2) When it's convenient upon your arrival [86] in the city, please drop by our office and I'll [96] take you out to see these homes. They are all [105] situated in fine neighborhoods and appear to [114] have the features you desire. (¶3) I am look- [123] ing forward to assisting you further in secur- [132] ing a new home in this area for you and your [141] family. \| Sincerely yours, \| Harold E. Swillin- [149] ger \| Residential Specialist \| (Your initials for [155/172] reference)

LESSON 90

90A ■ CONDITIONING PRACTICE [5] each line 3 times: slowly, faster, in-between rate

Alphabet	Murky haze enveloped a city as jarring quakes broke forty-six windows.	*Space quickly— down-and-in motion of right thumb*
Figures	The inventory includes 96 pamphlets, 1,827 books, and 3,450 magazines.	
Figure/symbol	Jerry Trane said, "Dan's Policy 123-756, due in 1983, is for $50,000."	
Fluency	He may sign the usual form by proxy if they make an audit of the firm.	

| 1 | 2 | 3 | 4 | 5 | 6 | 7 | 8 | 9 | 10 | 11 | 12 | 13 | 14 |

90B ■ IMPROVED STROKING: COMMON 2-, 3, AND 4-LETTER COMBINATIONS [10] each line 3 times SS: slowly, faster, slowly

TECHNIQUE CUES

1   use useful because now known off offices turn turning return returning   *Fingers curved and upright*

2   factory income | my assistant | comes understanding | manufacturing standard

3   It is useful to know that factory income is now in an upturn, however.

4   new news renew renewal car carry carbons sit visit hesitate ours hours   *Quick, snappy keystroking action*

5   lower the sign | furnish a design | below the signature | it is our position

6   Most newspapers furnish a renewal form that requires only a signature.

7   urn return day days today son person persons eat feature what whatever   *Continuity of typing; quick spacing*

8   great person | seven owners | toward town | great event | whatever the weather

9   Whatever the weather, the seven owners will return for the main event.

90C ■ RELATED LEARNING: PUNCTUATION GUIDES (End of Series) [10] use a new sheet of paper

34. Apostrophe—To show possession, add the apostrophe and s to a proper name of one syllable which ends in s.

35. Apostrophe—To show possession, add the apostrophe only after (a) plural nouns ending in s and (b) a proper name of more than one syllable which ends in s.

36. Apostrophe—To show possession, add the apostrophe after the last noun in a series to indicate joint or common possession of two or more persons.
NOTE: Separate possession of two or more persons is indicated by adding the possessive to each of the nouns; as, the manager's and the treasurer's reports.

34 *Learn*   Do not pay Charles's bill for $230 today, but pay 75 cents at Jones's.
   Apply   Was it Bess' hat, Ross' shoes, or Chris' watch that was lost today?

35 *Learn*   Those lawyers' offices were about 15 miles from Anthony Roberts' home.
   Apply   The boys camp counselor said that he will visit the Adams home soon.

36 *Learn*   Men's hats and boys' shoes will be on sale at Levy and Stover's store.
   Apply   Jerrys and Philips bicycles were found at my aunt's and uncle's house.

     (separate possession)   *(common possession)*

LESSON 75

75A ■ CONDITIONING PRACTICE [5] each line twice SS; then 1' writings on selected lines

Alphabet   Liz and Paul Davis quickly got a new house near Jane and Bix Folsom's.

Figures   Their GWAM rates are: 10, 40-48; 27, 33-39; 38, 23-32; and 15, 16-22.

Figure/symbol His 6/30/72 note for $15,280 will be paid 6/30/82 (plus 7½% interest).

Fluency   They have a right to be proud of the skills they have built this term.
      | 1 | 2 | 3 | 4 | 5 | 6 | 7 | 8 | 9 | 10 | 11 | 12 | 13 | 14 |

75B ■ PROBLEM TYPING MEASUREMENT: OUTLINES/MANUSCRIPTS [45]

Problem 1: Outline from Rough Draft

Line: 53. Center and type in *reading position* on a full sheet the following outline. Correct all errors indicated in the copy as well as those you make as you type.

	Words
Automation] center	2
I. Economics of Automation	8
A. Investment and Productivity	14
B. Impact (n) National economy	20
1. Productivity	24
2. Employment stability	29
3. Earnings	32
II. Impact on Employment and Earnings	40
A. Effects of Some Innovations ~~Changes~~	47
1. Computers and clerical work	53
2. Computer systems and data communication	60, 63
B. Skills and Education ~~Training~~	68
1. Social background and education	75
2. Distinction between education and skills	82, 85
a. Professional and technical	91
b. Workers Foremen and craftsmen	99
c. Laborers	102

Problem 2: Unbound Manuscript

Type the copy in the right-hand column as an unbound manuscript. Be alert to the extra space that may need to be left between the body of the report and the divider line.

	Words
THE MEANING OF SERENDIPITY	5

Have you ever gone to the dictionary to look up a word and discovered the meaning of a new word which happened to be on the same page? Have you ever turned to a certain volume in a set of encyclopedia to read about a particular topic only to discover information pertaining to a new and interesting subject about which you knew nothing before you opened the volume? For that matter, have your parents ever browsed around in an antique shop and come across a good buy on a priceless object of art? 13 22 31 40 49 58 67 75 83 92 100 105

If you have ever experienced these or similar incidents, then you should be able to understand what is meant by the word "serendipity." The word takes its meaning from the Per fairy tale The Three Princes of Serendip. One modern dictionary defines the word as: "the faculty of making fortunate and unexpected discoveries by accident."[1] 114 123 133 142 157 167 175 179

Some of our greatest discoveries in this world have come about as the result of the process of serendipity. Alert and intelligent scientists, or other well-known scholars, bent on studying one particular set of phenomena have uncovered new facts which have opened up wide areas for further exploration. You can be sure that the process of serendipity is at work as we probe into outer space. 187 196 205 215 224 232 242 251 258 261

[1] William Morris (ed.), The American Heritage Dictionary of the English Language (Boston: American Heritage Publishing Co., Inc., and Houghton Mifflin Company, 1969), p. 1183. 272 289 298 306 307

Problem 3: Page 2 of Unbound Manuscript

Type the last two paragraphs and the footnote of Problem 2 as page 2 of an unbound manuscript.

89C ■ SKILL-TRANSFER TYPING: STATISTICAL COPY [25]

1. Type a 5′ writing. Determine *gwam*; proofread for errors.
2. Type a 1′ writing on ¶ 1 for speed.
3. Type a 2′ writing on ¶ 1 and try

to maintain Step 2 rate.
4. Repeat Steps 2 and 3 with ¶ 2.
5. Type another 5′ writing. Determine *gwam*; proofread for errors.

6. Compute % *of transfer*: statistical copy rate divided by straight-copy rate of 88D. Record your better 5′ rate and % of transfer score.

All figures are used.

		GWAM		
	1′	2′	5′	

¶ 1   In the period of the 70's the labor force will grow from 85 million 14 | 7 | 3 | 51
in 1970 to 100 million in 1980, a growth element of about 17.6 percent. 28 | 14 | 6 | 54
The female labor force will grow virtually 23.4 percent, from 30 million 43 | 21 | 9 | 57
to 37 million. The teen-age work force will grow 11 percent, but there 57 | 29 | 11 | 60
will be a dramatic expansion in the labor force in the 25-34 years age 71 | 36 | 14 | 63
category. The array of workers in this age area will grow by 49 percent. 86 | 43 | 17 | 66
The overall tally of white-collar workers will continue to grow. It 100 | 50 | 20 | 68
will be roughly 50 percent higher than the overall number of blue-collar 115 | 57 | 23 | 71
workers; yet the latter group will jump from 29 to 31 million. 127 | 64 | 25 | 74

¶ 2   The number of farm workers will decrease from 4.2 million to 3.2 13 | 6 | 28 | 76
million by 1980. It is forecast, too, that the number of government 27 | 13 | 31 | 79
workers will grow from a tally of 9.1 to 13.8 million at the state and 41 | 20 | 34 | 82
local levels, and from 2.7 to 3.0 million at the Federal level. There 55 | 27 | 36 | 85
will be about 21.1 million workers in what may be termed the professional 70 | 35 | 39 | 88
area; 5.5 million in the building area; 4.6 million in the finance area; 85 | 42 | 42 | 91
20.5 million in what may be termed the trade area; 22.4 million in produc- 99 | 50 | 45 | 94
tion; 0.6 million in the mining sector; and 5.3 million in all other areas. 114 | 57 | 48 | 97

1′ GWAM	1	2	3	4	5	6	7	8	9	10	11	12	13	14
2′ GWAM		1		2		3		4		5		6		7	
5′ GWAM			1				2				3				

89D ■ RELATED LEARNING: PUNCTUATION GUIDES [10] reinsert paper used for typing 88C, page 135

31. **Apostrophe**—Use the apostrophe as a symbol to indicate the omission of letters or figures (as in contractions or figures).

32. **Apostrophe**—Use the apostrophe and s to form the plural of most figures, letters, and words (6's, A's,

five's). In market quotations, form the plural of figures by the addition of s only.

33. **Apostrophe**—To show possession, add the apostrophe and s to (a) a singular noun and (b) a plural noun which does not end in s.

31 *Learn* Shouldn't we pay tribute to the "Spirit of '76" in celebrating July 4?
    Apply Cant the class of 72 meet today? We shouldnt upset our scheduling.

32 *Learn* Be sure your f's don't look like 7's. Boston Fund 4s are due in 1977.
    Apply Cross your ts and dot your i s. Be sure to sell United 6's this week.

33 *Learn* A boy's bicycle has been found, but the men's shoes are still missing.
    Apply Buy the girls dress today; childrens toys will be on sale Wednesday.

PHASE 3: IMPROVING BASIC TYPING SKILLS

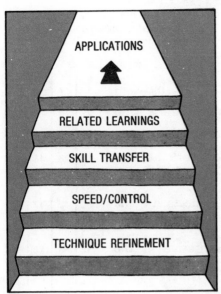

APPLICATIONS

RELATED LEARNINGS

SKILL TRANSFER

SPEED/CONTROL

TECHNIQUE REFINEMENT

■ You have a dual goal in the 18 lessons of Phase 3.

■ Your primary goal is to maximize your basic typewriting skill. Make an effort to improve through purposeful practice at appropriate practice levels (sometimes for speed, often for technique improvement, and at other times for control or accuracy).

■ Your second goal (but an important one) is to improve your basic communication skills. Do this by careful study of the number, capitalization, and punctuation guides and by thoughtful practice on the Learn and Apply sentences.

Machine Checkup and Adjustments
(for each lesson of Cycle 2)

1. Set paper guide at 0 on most typewriters.
2. Set paper-bail rolls to divide paper into thirds.
3. Set ribbon control for typing on upper portion of ribbon.

USE:
70-space line and single spacing.
5-space paragraph indention.
Double spacing for all timed writings of more than 1 minute.
Double spacing after each single-spaced group of drill lines.
Triple spacing after drills.

UNIT 11 | LESSONS 76-81

Improving Typing Techniques / Related Learnings

■ LESSON 76

76A ■ CONDITIONING PRACTICE [8] use the following practice plan for Lessons 76-150

Type each line 3 times SS as directed at the right; then, as time permits, retype selected lines.

First Writing: Type at a slow, well-controlled pace as you give close attention to good stroking technique.

Second Writing: Type for speed.
Third Writing: Type for accuracy with as much speed as possible.

Alphabet   Just work for improved basic techniques to maximize your typing skill.   *Fingers curved*
Figures   We received 129 chairs, 30 typewriters, and 75 desks on Order No. 648.   *and upright*
Continuity   a;sldkfj (Repeat this pattern for a full line without spacing; use quick, snappy strokes.)
Fluency   The map of the ancient land forms may aid them when they work with us.
       | 1 | 2 | 3 | 4 | 5 | 6 | 7 | 8 | 9 | 10 | 11 | 12 | 13 | 14 |

76B ■ FINGER POSITION ANALYSIS [5] check finger position with illustrations; retype Fluency line above

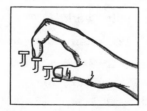

PROPER CURVE OF FINGERS
1. Fingers curved at first and second joints.
2. Thumb curved and resting lightly on the space bar.
3. Wrists low and relaxed.

IMPROPER FINGER ALIGNMENT
Result: Direction of stroke results in a glancing stroke causing clashing and jamming of keys. Turn hand inward to get proper finger alignment.

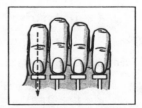

PROPER FINGER ALIGNMENT
Result: Direction of stroke enables typist to strike keys with a direct, quick snap stroke with an immediate release of the key. Less clashing or locking of keys.

88D ■ SKILL-TRANSFER TYPING: STRAIGHT COPY [25]

1. Type a 5' writing. Determine *gwam*; proofread for errors.
2. Type a 1' writing on ¶ 1 for speed.
3. Type a 2' writing on ¶ 1 and try to maintain Step 2 rate.
4. Repeat Steps 2 and 3 with ¶ 2.
5. Type another 5' writing. Determine *gwam*; proofread for errors. Record your better 5' rate.

All letters are used.

		GWAM	
	1'	2'	5'

¶ 1

	1'	2'	5'	
There are two kinds of typists who rarely achieve in the business	13	7	3	54
office––those who cannot do what they are directed to do and those who	27	14	5	57
can do little else. One of the important things every student must learn	42	21	8	60
to do is to proofread quickly and accurately every piece of work he pro-	57	28	11	63
duces on the typewriter. The letter, report, or memorandum with every	71	35	14	66
error neatly corrected represents a pride in work that reflects to the	85	42	17	69
credit of the typist who produced it. Nearly all of us need to be re-	99	49	20	71
minded that the work we produce is our personal representative in the	113	56	23	74
eyes of others. Often, it is the primary basis on which quality judg-	127	63	25	77
ments are made.	130	65	26	78

¶ 2

	1'	2'	5'	
It is important to find and correct neatly all errors before the	13	6	29	80
finished copy is given either to the teacher to grade or to the execu-	27	13	31	83
tive in the business office to use. Some typists fail to find their	41	20	34	86
errors because they are careless. They often do not realize the impact	55	28	37	89
an error may have on those who evaluate the finished copy. In proof-	69	34	40	91
reading your copy, be very careful to verify the accuracy of each date,	83	42	43	94
figure, and amount. Check, too, to ascertain if all words are divided	98	49	46	97
correctly at the ends of lines. Then read the copy carefully to be	111	56	48	100
certain that each word is spelled correctly and that each typing error	125	63	51	103
is corrected.	128	64	52	103

1' GWAM	1	2	3	4	5	6	7	8	9	10	11	12	13	14
2' GWAM		1		2		3		4		5		6		7	
5' GWAM			1			2			3						

■ LESSON 89

89A ■ CONDITIONING PRACTICE [5] each line 3 times: slowly, faster, in-between rate

Alphabet	Just strive for maximum progress by quickly organizing the daily work.	*Quick, snappy keystroking; finger action*
Figures	The shipment included 132 divans, 156 lamps, 48 desks, and 790 chairs.	
Figure/symbol	The 6¼% rate (on his 1973 note for $24,850) is to be increased to 7½%.	
Fluency	The efficient way to gain speed is to type with continuity and rhythm.	

| 1 | 2 | 3 | 4 | 5 | 6 | 7 | 8 | 9 | 10 | 11 | 12 | 13 | 14 |

89B ■ IMPROVING SPEED/CONTROL [10] type two 1' writings on each line of 89A: once for SPEED; then once for CONTROL

76C ■ TECHNIQUE IMPROVEMENT [17] each line 3 times SS: slowly, faster, slowly

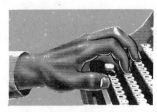

TECHNIQUE GOAL:
Improved Keystroking

CHECK:
1. Fingers curved and upright.
2. Quick, snap keystroke.
3. Finger-action reaches; hands quiet.
4. Wrists low and relaxed.

1	*Home keys*	all hall fall shall dad lad glad ask asks lash gash sash flash jag lag
2	*Third row*	or worry to tow row we were top yet too it tire retire quit quip equip
3	*Both*	You said that the old warehouse was quite adequate for these supplies.
4	*Home keys*	asks all lads; a jag; a fall fad; add gas; all shall; add half a glass
5	*Bottom row*	can van manx cabs ban banks act back dazzle access plant chance change
6	*Both*	Buzz, Bix, and Jack have come back from the plant in a big moving van.

7 *Top row:*   Figure-symbol checkup: 2", 3#, 4$, 5%, 6, 7&, 8', 9(, 0), ¢, @, ½, ¼.
  Figure/symbol   <u>Electric:</u> 2@, 3#, 4$, 5%, 6¢, 7&, 8*, 9(, 0), ½, ¼, ' ".
8 *emphasis*   TYPE these <u>figures and symbols</u>: ($4.50); 7 + 8 = 15; 5%; 8' × 12'; 3!

76D ■ RELATED LEARNING: NUMBER GUIDES [20] follow Study-Learn-Apply procedure given below

Machine Adjustments:
1. 74-space line; single spacing.
2. 1½" top margin on first page of each series of guides (number, capitalization, etc.); 1" top margin on all other pages.
3. Bottom margin of about 1" on all pages that are full.

DO: 1. Study explanatory guide.
2. Type the guide number (with period), space twice, then type the **Learn** sentence, noting rule application at color underlines.
3. Type **Apply** sentence, making all needed corrections; then DS. *Points that may need correction*

are noted by color underline.

After completing each series:
1. Assemble sheets in order.
2. Number all pages (except first) in upper right corner even with right margin ½" from top of sheet.
3. Staple sheets in upper left corner and turn them in.

1. Spell numbers from one to ten except when used with numbers above ten.*

2. Always spell a number beginning a sentence even though figures are used later in the sentence.

3. As a general rule, spell the shorter of two numbers used together.

4. Spell isolated fractions in a sentence, but type a series of fractions in figures. Use the diagonal (/) for "made" fractions.

———————

* A common practice in business is to use figures for all numbers, except those which begin a sentence. This practice makes number recognition much easier and verification more sure.

(Center) **SERIES 1: NUMBER GUIDE EXAMPLES**   *Retain paper for use in next lesson*

TS

1 *Learn* He ordered 72 books on English, 8 on mathematics, and 36 on geography.   SS
  Apply About 150 delegates, 225 observers, and seven guests were at the assembly.

DS

2 *Learn* Eighty-six applications were received, but only 15 persons were hired.   SS
  Apply 8 of the men were here yesterday; the other 16 will come tomorrow.

3 *Learn* Order No. 1350 called for ten 50-gallon drums and 350 ten-gallon cans.
  Apply We may need 340 3-pound boxes and 15 75-pound drums tomorrow.

4 *Learn* About two thirds of the work is done. Type 1/8, 1/2, 1/4, and 15 7/8.
  Apply 1/3 of the work is completed. Add one half, 3/4, six 5/8, and 13 5/16.

Improving Skill Transfer/Related Learnings

■ LESSON 88

88A ■ CONDITIONING PRACTICE [5] each line 3 times SS: slowly, faster, in-between rate

Alphabet	With the expert advice of Judge Jackson, I may be able to do the quiz.	*Make a quick, shift-key reach*
Figures	Today Vi sold 34 dresses, 56 hats, 78 ties, 90 shirts, and 12 jackets.	
Figure/symbol	Use finger-reach action (hands quiet) to type #1032, #4658, and #7920.	
Fluency	Both of them will help the city auditor with the work that is pending.	

| 1 | 2 | 3 | 4 | 5 | 6 | 7 | 8 | 9 | 10 | 11 | 12 | 13 | 14 |

88B ■ IMPROVING STROKING: COMMON 2-, 3-, AND 4-LETTER COMBINATIONS [10] each line 3 times SS: slowly, faster, slowly

1 par parts separate red reduce offered art articles each reach teachers
2 start to teach | know each part | that particular teacher | locate a catalog
3 Each teacher knows the reduced articles offered in these art catalogs.

TECHNIQUE CUES
Wrists low and relaxed
Finger-reach action

4 can cancel cannot has purchased man manner demand chairman thin within
5 insure their shipment | consider our side | the purchase is surely assured
6 Sureton has presided in a manner to command trust from the membership.

Continuity of typing; quick spacing

7 ore store before ant want antique quantity rate rates operate operates
8 to cooperate | it is pleasant | my units | rate advantage | a united community
9 To operate an antique store in a united community is an advantage now.

Fingers close to keys; eyes on copy

88C ■ RELATED LEARNING: PUNCTUATION GUIDES [10] reinsert paper used for typing 87D, page 134

27. Semicolon—Use a semicolon to separate independent clauses when they are joined by a conjunctive adverb (however, consequently, nevertheless, etc.).

28. Semicolon—Use a semicolon to separate a series of phrases or clauses (especially if they contain commas) that are introduced by a colon.

29. Semicolon—Place the semicolon outside the final quotation mark; the period, inside the quotation mark.

30. Apostrophe—Use the apostrophe as a symbol for "feet" in billings or tabulations, or as a symbol for "minutes." **NOTE:** The quotation mark may be used as a symbol for "seconds."

27 *Learn* He did not follow the rule; consequently, he made many serious errors.
   Apply He had good typewriting techniques consequently, he typed with speed.

28 *Learn* Our sales were: 1970, $1,125,840; 1971, $1,531,450; 1972, $1,935,976.
   Apply These are the new officers: John Van, President Dee Ford, Secretary.

29 *Learn* Mr. Carr spoke on "Building Speed"; Mr. Brown, on "Building Accuracy."
   Apply They cannot use "therefore;" expenses will not increase "necessarily".

30 *Learn* The billing was as follows: 15' x 18'. Robert ran the mile in 3'54".
   Apply The apostrophe may be used to express feet in billings; as, 20 ft. x 24 ft.

LESSON 77

77A ■ CONDITIONING PRACTICE 8 each line 3 times as directed on page 117

Alphabet	Will Jim realize that excellent skill develops by refining techniques?	*Quick, snap strokes*
Figures	Type 1 and 2 and 3 and 4 and 5 and 6 and 7 and 8 and 9 and 10 and 213.	
Third row	u uj r rf y yj t tf i ik e ed o ol w ws p p; q qa typewriter quote try	
Fluency	She may pay the firm for the work when they sign the right audit form.	

| 1 | 2 | 3 | 4 | 5 | 6 | 7 | 8 | 9 | 10 | 11 | 12 | 13 | 14 |

77B ■ TECHNIQUE IMPROVEMENT 10 each line 3 times SS: slowly, faster, slowly

EMPHASIZE

1	Adjacent	are read area era every her here ask easy please prior radio we weight	*Read ahead to speed up keystroking*
2	keys	part north report post export try trial open hope say sale same sample	
3		Please try to read a copy of her safety report before the trial opens.	
4	Consecutive-	used credit center recent piece specific loan along amount color great	*Quick, finger-action reaches; hands quiet*
5	direct	any many freight number premium annual minute survey serve kind mutual	
6	reaches	Any loan handled by our mutual credit centers is checked once a month.	
7	Outside	quite please second repair period totals groups stores explain against	*Fingers curved and upright; Quick, snap strokes*
8	keys	short course | always close | best quality | special schedule | promptly place	
9		Our company plans to place six thousand shares of stock on the market.	

77C ■ RELATED LEARNING: NUMBER GUIDES (End of Series 1)* 12

1. Reinsert sheet used for typing sentences of 76D, page 118.

2. Follow directions outlined in 76D, page 118.

3. Align copy properly and continue with Guide 5 sentences.

5. Usually express in figures numbers preceded by nouns.
6. Express measures (also weights and dimensions) in figures.
7. Use the percent sign (%) when it is preceded by definite figures. "Percent" (spelled) is preferred with approximations and in formal writing.
8. Spell names of small-numbered avenues and streets (ten and under). Type house numbers in figures except for house number *One*.

5	Learn	We found the exact quotation in Volume VIII, Section 4, pages 210-213.	SS
	Apply	Rule six can be found in Monograph one, Chapter ten, page 136, Paragraph one.	
			DS
6	Learn	The box I sent to Ralph measured 6 ft. 9 in. and weighed 72 lbs. 2 oz.	
	Apply	James Kane, who is only 16 years old, is nearly six ft. three in. in height.	
7	Learn	This interest rate of 5½% will be changed to 7¼% on your future loans.	
	Learn	Approximately 50 percent of the students have completed all this work.	
	Apply	Nearly 40% of all mortgage loans last week were made at 6 3/8 percent.	
8	Learn	The factory is at 18 First Street; the store, at 164 West 59th Street.	
	Learn	They moved their office from One Lexington Avenue to 270 Fifth Avenue.	
	Apply	We plan to move our store from 264 4th Street to 3975 6th Avenue.	

*In these concise guides, not every acceptable alternative is included—to do so would merely lead to confusion. The guides given, however, can be used with confidence as they represent basic guides of good usage.

87C ■ IMPROVING STROKING: COMMON 2-, 3-, AND 4-LETTER COMBINATIONS 〔12〕 each line 3 times: slowly, faster, slowly

CHECK

1   her here otherwise per permit proper time sometime very every delivery   ↙ *Fingers curved and upright*

2   over all six departments | part of your coverage | notice the price of ice

3   Every person must practice in the proper way; otherwise, he will fail.

4   any many company end ends extend year yearly midyear cent cents recent   ↙ *Quick, snap strokes*

5   send his letter | complete the booklet | everyone wants service | her advice

6   A recent bulletin indicates that a new policy was endorsed by midyear.

7   act acted facts contact out outline south about rest arrest interested   ↙ *Finger action; hands quiet*

8   some damage | general agents | operate an agency | some say it was wholesome

9   The general agent was somewhat dismayed with the outcome of that suit.

87D ■ RELATED LEARNING: PUNCTUATION GUIDES 〔13〕 reinsert sheet used for typing 86C, page 132

21. Underline—Use the underline (as you may use quotation marks) to call attention to special words or phrases. **NOTE:** Use a continuous underline unless each word is to be considered separately from the rest; as, He misspelled steel, occur, and weird.

22. Quotation Marks—Use quotation marks to enclose direct quotations. **NOTE:** When the question mark applies to the entire sentence, it is typed outside the quotation mark.

23. Quotation Marks—Use quotation marks to enclose

titles of articles, poems, plays, and the like.

24. Quotation Marks—Use quotation marks to enclose special words or phrases (for emphasis).

25. Quotation Marks—Use single quotation marks (the apostrophe) to indicate a quotation within a quotation.

26. Semicolon—Use a semicolon to separate two or more independent clauses in a compound sentence when the conjunction is not expressed.

21   *Learn*   There is a difference between blazing a trail and burning up the road.

     Apply   A girl translated the Latin phrase nemo non venit as "everybody came."

22   *Learn*   Was it Emerson who said, "The only way to have a friend is to be one"?

     Apply   He quoted Samuel's statement, _ The electorate is the jury writ large.

23   *Learn*   Did any of you read Peter's latest article, "Frontier Thinking Today"?

     Apply   The musical Song of Norway won a top rating in the Atlantic Monthly.

24   *Learn*   The difficult "problem of space" is still that space between our ears!

     Apply   It is only by scratching for the facts that we arrive at real truth.

25   *Learn*   I think I wrote, "We must have, as Tillich said, 'the courage to be.'"

     Apply   I said, "We must be, as the poet said, One for all and all for one."

26   *Learn*   To be critical is easy; to be constructive and helpful is not so easy.

     Apply   We cannot live on past glory we must strive to improve and go onward.

77D ■ APPLYING IMPROVED TECHNIQUES: GUIDED WRITING ☐20

1. Type a 2' writing on ¶ 1 (at a controlled pace and with good stroking techniques).
2. Determine *gwam*. To this rate add

8 *gwam*. Determine quarter-minute goals for 1' writings at new rate (Example *48*: 12, 24, 36, 48).
3. Type three 1' writings on ¶ 1 at

goal rate as your teacher calls the quarter-minute guides.
4. Repeat Steps 1-3 with ¶ 2. Give attention to improved techniques.

All letters are used.

		•	4	•	8	•	12

¶ 1
Home-, third-, and bottom-row keys

Jack and Zeno will try to quote their best price on new electric
typewriters. You are aware that as many as five or six new typewriters
may be purchased to replace the quaint old machines that Zack and Ben
have been using. We shall be quite happy to know that our peer group
will have new typewriters. Indeed, we view this purchase as a bonanza
for a number of us. Having these five or six new machines will make
learning to type a joy.

EMPHASIZE
Curved, upright fingers; quick, snappy keystrokes

¶ 2
Outside keys, adjacent keys, and direct reaches

A number of credit centers have recently been formed to service
union members who need specific loans. Paul and Aza were requested to
bring us a report on this lending activity. Paul said that every effort
would be made to review the annual report of each credit center as they
prepare their special paper. We were quite pleased to learn that their
report would be prepared promptly. Our company expects to make special
loans to unions.

EMPHASIZE
Finger-reach action; quiet hands; wrists low and relaxed

■ LESSON 78

78A ■ CONDITIONING PRACTICE ☐8

Alphabet   Six skaters jumped grotesquely in a veritable frenzy of wacky rhythms.

Figures   Order 75 pencils, 36 pens, 12 desk pads, 48 desk sets, and 90 erasers.

Third row   Type upper-row keys properly by making quick reaches with the fingers.

Fluency   They may use eight or more of the angle forms in order to do the work.

| 1 | 2 | 3 | 4 | 5 | 6 | 7 | 8 | 9 | 10 | 11 | 12 | 13 | 14 |

Type without breaks or pauses; space quickly

78B ■ APPLYING IMPROVED TECHNIQUES ☐20 repeat 77D, above; improve keystroking technique

86D ■ GROWTH INDEX [20]

1. Type a 5' writing. Determine *gwam*; proofread for errors.
2. Type a 2' writing on each ¶. Select

a goal of either speed or control according to your need.

3. Type another 5' writing and try to

improve your Step 1 score. Determine *gwam*; proofread for errors. Record your better 5' rate.

All letters are used.

		GWAM		
	1'	2'	5'	

¶ 1

The greatness of America is that more people have achieved the good | 14 | 7 | 3 | 57
things of life than anywhere else in the world today or at any time in | 28 | 14 | 6 | 60
history because of the countless opportunities that exist for the person | 42 | 21 | 8 | 63
who is ready and willing to work. A person's responsibility for his own | 57 | 28 | 11 | 66
life is fundamental in a free, civilized society such as ours. In the | 71 | 36 | 14 | 69
world of work, your own work skills and talents are the best guarantee | 85 | 43 | 17 | 72
that you can secure a job when you need it. To an ever-increasing degree, | 100 | 50 | 20 | 75
work skills are based on a sound education; and, because the problems of | 115 | 57 | 23 | 78
unemployment are greatest among individuals with the least skill, a suit- | 130 | 65 | 26 | 81
able education is the best single investment you can make in your own | 144 | 72 | 29 | 83
future. | 145 | 73 | 29 | 84

¶ 2

In school, your teachers are interested in you as an individual and | 14 | 7 | 32 | 86
as a student. They are interested in helping you achieve your potential. | 29 | 14 | 35 | 89
In the world of work, an employer will be more interested in what you can | 43 | 22 | 38 | 92
produce in return for the salary that you command. Your opportunities | 58 | 29 | 41 | 95
for advancement in the world of work will be quickly enhanced if you will | 72 | 36 | 44 | 98
recognize that a promotion will necessitate a resolute attempt on your | 87 | 43 | 46 | 101
part to utilize your talents. Employers want alert workers who can get | 101 | 50 | 49 | 104
a task finished when it needs to be done, who can work under pressure | 115 | 57 | 52 | 107
when the need arises, and who can add something extra to the job. | 128 | 64 | 55 | 109

1' GWAM		1		2		3		4		5		6		7		8		9		10		11		12		13		14	
2' GWAM			1			2			3			4			5			6			7	
5' GWAM				1					2					3	

■ LESSON 87

87A ■ CONDITIONING PRACTICE [5] each line 3 times: slowly, faster, in-between rate

Alphabet
Figure/
shift lock
Related
learning
Fluency

Steven was intrigued by the quizzical expression on Judge Mark's face. *Eyes on copy;*
These 1,258 men have had FORTRAN, IBM 7094, and SYSTEM 360 experience. *type with*
continuity
True discipline is not enslaving--the disciplined man is the free man.
The six men may go down to the rifle field to fix the eight-day dials.

| 1 | 2 | 3 | 4 | 5 | 6 | 7 | 8 | 9 | 10 | 11 | 12 | 13 | 14 |

87B ■ IMPROVING SPEED/CONTROL [20] repeat 86D, above, as directed there

78C ■ TECHNIQUE IMPROVEMENT □12

1. Type each line 3 times at gradually increased rates. Give attention to points to be emphasized.

2. As time permits, type from dictation the lines with the flag (|▶) before them.

The color bars (⎯⎯⎯) under words indicate *word response*. Read and type these words, word groups, or word parts as units or wholes.

The color dots (. . . .) under words indicate *stroke* or *letter response*. Read and type letter by letter.

			EMPHASIZE
1	*Letter response*	as in at on be no ad up ax my re oh we you are him was oil few joy saw	*Speedy, stroking response; finger action*
2		act ink get ply tax pop were join card only ages pump ever upon stated	
3		Are you able to state only a best date for a start on those tax cases?	
4	*Word re-sponse*	▶ he an or to is of it me us so am if do by go ox ah the and for men wit	*High-speed word response; quick spacing*
5		▶ end key but sit may own pen pay bus she fir tie rod aid fit aid thrown	
6		▶ If it is so, then I may go with them and make them do the work for us.	
7	*Combina-tion response*	and was | men are | pay him | aid you | she sat | big tax | may eat | did get | within	*Variable rhythm; uniform stroking*
8		go into | maybe they | sit forward | within six | race toward | inland waterways	
9		Maybe he can see the race if he sails into the inland waterway at six.	

78D ■ RELATED LEARNING CHECKUP: NUMBER GUIDES □10 correct as you type

The sentences below are in problem form. To type them correctly, you must recall the number guides. A guide code is given before each sentence. Use it to check the rule, if you are uncertain about the cor-rections (1-2:118—Guides 1-2, page 118). **NOTE:** The color underline indicates a possible point of correc-tion. It is used to "cue" you and to test your ability to make "correct decisions" as you type.

Number and type the sentences in correct form; use a 74-space line.

1-2:118
3:118
4:118

1 5 of the 126 checks on out-of-town banks were returned to the firm.
2 Did Order No. 15 call for one hundred ten-gallon cans or 10 100-gallon drums?
3 Only 1/2 of the work is done. Add 1/8, three fifths, 1/4, 1 1/2, and 5/6.

5-6:119
7:119
8:119

4 Check Guides five and six, page 119. John Quincy is six feet 9 in. in height.
5 Nearly 100% of the banks have reduced the prime rate to 7 1/2 percent.
6 Please send my check to 1350 5th Avenue rather than 1 Polk Street.

■ LESSON 79

79A ■ CONDITIONING PRACTICE □8

Alphabet	Liza picked several exquisite flowers which grew by the jungle swamps.	*Strike and release keys quickly*
Figures	I ordered 720 pencils, 36 pens, 49 erasers, and 185 cardboard folders.	
First row	m mj v vf n nj b bf , ,k c cd . .l x xs / /; z za / /; z za . .l xs .l	
Fluency	I may work with them or their friends in the ancient city by the lake.	

| 1 | 2 | 3 | 4 | 5 | 6 | 7 | 8 | 9 | 10 | 11 | 12 | 13 | 14 |

79B ■ TECHNIQUE IMPROVEMENT □12 repeat 78C, above

■ LESSON 86

86A ■ CONDITIONING PRACTICE [5] each line 3 times SS: slowly, faster, in-between rate

Alphabet   Maxine was puzzled by the lack of interest in the five good quay jobs.   *Quick, snap*
Figures   In 1972, 583 new employees were added. Read pages 20, 42, 62, and 98.   *strokes; finger-*
Adjacent keys   To permit emotions to control actions seriously hampers use of reason.   *action only*
Fluency   Pay the man for the form and ask the auditor to make the usual checks.

| 1 | 2 | 3 | 4 | 5 | 6 | 7 | 8 | 9 | 10 | 11 | 12 | 13 | 14 |

86B ■ IMPROVING STROKING: COMMON 2-, 3-, AND 4-LETTER COMBINATIONS [12] each line 3 times: slowly, faster, at top speed

1   the their either another you your young yourself and land handle stand
2   your demand | many thousands | only the best | all the rest | your course will
3   If they meet all your demands, you will have to choose another course.

4   for form inform force ate date rate water ill will willing with within
5   work with ease | please lease that land | what bill | they are still without
6   Please inform them if the due date of the last bill is still the same.

7   are aware careful men mentioned amend women able table unable valuable
8   port of call | important export | have you ever | several are there, however
9   Several women at this table have recommended that we amend the report.

86C ■ RELATED LEARNING: PUNCTUATION GUIDES [13] use a new sheet to continue typing the guides

16. Hyphen—Use the hyphen after each word or figure in a series of words or figures that modify the same noun.

17. Parentheses—Use parentheses to enclose parenthetical or explanatory matter and added information. **NOTE:** Commas or dashes may also be used.

18. Parentheses—Use parentheses to enclose letters or figures used to identify enumerated items.

19. Parentheses—Use parentheses to enclose figures following amounts which are expressed in words (when added clarity or emphasis is desired).

20. Underline—Use the underline to indicate titles of books and names of magazines and newspapers. **NOTE:** Such titles may be typed in ALL CAPS, also.

16 *Learn*   First-, second-, and third-class mail is to be sorted before 9:30 a.m.
   Apply   All 6_, 7_, and 8_foot boards are to be used during the 10-day period.

17 *Learn*   The contracts (Exhibit A) and the mortgages (Exhibit B) were enclosed.
   Apply   Nelson's memoirs _published by Pacific Press_ were read with interest.

18 *Learn*   He stressed these factors: (1) speed, (2) accuracy, and (3) neatness.
   Apply   Check these techniques: _1_ stroking, _2_ rhythm, and _3_ continuity.

19 *Learn*   The undersigned agrees to pay the sum of three hundred dollars ($300).
   Apply   A balance of four hundred sixty-two dollars $462 is due and payable.   *(Make needed corrections—cues omitted in Apply sentences.)*

20 *Learn*   The book New Learning was reviewed in Harper's and the New York Times.
   Apply   Did you read the review of Learning to Learn in the Los Angeles Times?

79C ■ APPLYING IMPROVED TECHNIQUES: GUIDED WRITING (Progressive Difficulty Paragraphs) [20]

1. Type a 1' writing on ¶ 1 using your best keystrok-ing techniques. Divide this rate by 4 for ¼' goals.
2. Type three 1' guided writings on ¶ 2 at Step 1 rate. Repeat step for ¶ 3. **Goal:** Good keystroking action.

3. Type two 1' writings on ¶ 1 for speed. **Goal:** Improved speed with finger action and continuity of writing. Repeat step for ¶s 2 and 3 and try to maintain ¶ 1 rate.

¶ 1
Balanced-hand
words = 60%

In typing, all of us should make as our first goal typing with the right form. When we use the right form at the typewriter, the work is much easier. Also, the right form pattern may help us solve the problem of typing with speed and accuracy which is an end goal of typewriting.

Fingers curved and upright; Quick, snap strokes

¶ 2
Balanced-hand
words = 26%
One-hand words
= 14%
Combination
words = 60%

One of the first ways by which you are usually judged is on your appearance. It seems safe to say that a well-groomed person makes a much better impression on others than a person who is not. In addition, he begets an impression of a person who is competent and sure of himself.

¶ 3
One-hand
words = 60%

Were you aware that after that date only a minimum number of the area abstracts can be saved? In my opinion, you should reserve these extra area abstracts for the trade union. You may recall that the trade union group saw this request after we were able to reverse the tax rate.

79D ■ RELATED LEARNING: CAPITALIZATION GUIDES [10] as directed in 76D, page 118

1. Capitalize the first word of every sentence and the first word of every complete direct quotation.
2. Do not capitalize fragments of quotations.
3. Do not capitalize a quotation resumed within a sentence.

NOTE: Type the comma or period before the ending quotation mark.
4. Capitalize the first word after a colon if that word begins a complete sentence. **NOTE:** Space twice after the colon.

SERIES 2: CAPITALIZATION GUIDE EXAMPLES

1 *Learn* She said, "There is no substitute for hard work in attaining success."
  Apply kahlil Gibran once wrote, "i have learned silence from the talkative."

2 *Learn* Among other things, he stressed the importance of "a sense of values."
  Apply His basic thesis seemed to be that the teacher "Affects all eternity."

3 *Learn* "When all else fails," a unique sign read, "try following directions."
  Apply "I'll toot your horn", she said impatiently, "While you start my car".

4 *Learn* These are the directions: Use a 5-space indention and double spacing.
  Apply Do this daily: check the ribbon control and set the paper guide at 0.

85C ■ IMPROVING STROKING: COMMON 2-, 3-, AND 4-LETTER COMBINATIONS [12] each line 3 times at gradually increasing speed

1	*Word*	mat mate material estimate store restore storage cause because caustic	*Finger action;*
2	*building*	us fuse using write writing written since sincere grade graded upgrade	*hands quiet*
3		Four guides tried to upgrade the quality of written answers they gave.	

4	*Double*	too off will shall took small speed stress shipper carry better ballot	*Uniform*
5	*letters*	too little | feels well | allow her | puzzled look | took a loss | missed a week	*keystroking*
6		Bill was puzzled by the number of errors between your account and his.	

7	*Letter response*	few imply | set a date | union case | minimum wage | oil taxes | opinion or fact	*Push for*
8	*Word response*	and the | and then | and if they | and if they go | and if they go to the city	*speed*
9	*Combination*	A date for the case will be agreed upon when they restate the problem.	

85D ■ RELATED LEARNING: PUNCTUATION GUIDES [13] reinsert sheet used for typing 84C, page 129

10. Dash—Use a dash (a) for emphasis; (b) to indicate a change of thought; (c) to introduce the name of an author or a reference when it follows a direct quotation; and (d) for other special purposes. **NOTE:** Type two hyphens for the dash, without space before or after.

11. Colon—Use the colon to introduce an enumeration or a listing.

12. Colon—Use the colon to introduce a question or a long direct quotation.

13. Colon—Use the colon between hours and minutes expressed in figures. **NOTE:** Use figures with *a.m.* or *p.m.*

14. Hyphen—Use the hyphen to join compound numerals from twenty-one to ninety-nine.

15. Hyphen—Use the hyphen to join compound adjectives preceding a noun they modify.

10	*Learn*	The icy road--slippery as a silver-scaled fish--made driving a hazard.
	Learn	"To read good books is to enjoy life's greatest treasures."--Thompson.
	Apply	These field trips, to offices, banks, and stores, are least expensive.

| 11 | *Learn* | Here are the reasons for his success: courage, industry, and honesty. |
| | *Apply* | She bought three items at the store a coat, a dress, and a suitcase. |

| 12 | *Learn* | The question is this: Are you using good technique at the typewriter? |
| | *Apply* | Ask John to answer this question Does inconsistency lead to failure? |

| 13 | *Learn* | When it is 4:30 p.m. in New York City, it is 1:30 p.m. in Los Angeles. |
| | *Apply* | Will the ceremony start at 1-30 p.m. on Friday, January 23, next year? |

| 14 | *Learn* | Spell these figures in this sentence: four, eighty-five, sixty-eight. |
| | *Apply* | At twenty three, I never realized that I would live to be ninety nine. |

| 15 | *Learn* | The good-natured teacher asked them to read only the best-known books. |
| | *Apply* | In the last five year period, our business has increased tremendously. |

LESSON 80

80A ▪ CONDITIONING PRACTICE ⑤

Starting with this lesson, a maximum of 5 minutes will be given for the conditioning practice lines.

Do not waste time, keep the carriage moving, and it should be easy to reach this goal.

Alphabet   Jack found seven quaint game boxes at the new little bazaar in Waypol.

Use finger-action reaches; hands quiet

Figures   They sold 40 watches, 128 rings, 93 clips, 56 tie pins, and 27 clocks.

First row   Six brave men helped Aza C. Bonman carry an excited lynx to a zoo van.

Fluency   She may make the goal if she works with vigor and with the right form.

| 1 | 2 | 3 | 4 | 5 | 6 | 7 | 8 | 9 | 10 | 11 | 12 | 13 | 14 |

80B ▪ IMPROVING SPEED AND ACCURACY: GUIDED WRITING ⑫ repeat 79C, page 122, as directed below

1. Type a 1′ writing on ¶1 for speed. Determine rate; subtract 8 to determine *control rate* for Step 2.

2. Type two 1′ guided writings on ¶1 at *control rate* determined in Step 1. **Goal:** Not over 1 error on

each writing. **Practice Guide:** Type with continuity and without hurry to reach this goal.

3. Repeat Steps 1 and 2 with ¶2; then with ¶3. Be sure to try to type with good keystroking techniques.

80C ▪ RELATED LEARNING: CAPITALIZATION GUIDES ⑩ reinsert paper used for typing 79D, page 122

5. Capitalize first and last words and all other words in titles of books, articles, periodicals, headings, and plays, *except* words of four letters or less used as articles, conjunctions, or prepositions.

6. Capitalize an official title when it immediately precedes a name. When used elsewhere, type it without the capital unless it is a title of high distinction.

7. Do not capitalize business or professional titles used without the name of the person.

8. Capitalize all proper nouns and their derivatives.

9. Capitalize the names of the days of the week, months of the year, holidays, periods of history, and historic events.

5 *Learn* Have you read the new book by Thomas Booth, The Value of an Education?

    Apply The article "wonders of the space age" should be on your reading list.

6 *Learn* On Tuesday, President Fairbanks of the Ottawa Company will address us.

    Apply John DeJur is the Executive Assistant to president James R. O'Connell.

7 *Learn* The doctor will be here at 10 a.m. The attorney is studying the case.

    Apply The Dean will see him soon. Dr. Owen is the new Professor of history.

8 *Learn* John wrote an interesting report on European and American folk dances.

    Apply They plan to attend the canadian Shakespearean Festival during August.

9 *Learn* Capitalize these words: Tuesday, May, Labor Day, and the Middle Ages.

    Apply On friday, november 10, we will have a test on the restoration Period.

84D ■ IMPROVING SPEED/CONTROL: SKILL COMPARISON (Progressive Difficulty Paragraphs) 20

1. Speed. Type three 1′ writings on each ¶ for *speed*. Do this by proper reading of the copy and by keeping the stroking action in your fingers. As you type ¶s 2 and 3, try to maintain the rate of ¶ 1. Your teacher will guide your writing on ¶s 2 and 3 by calling each quarter-minute interval.

2. Control. Type three 1′ guided writings on each ¶ for *control* (not over 1 error each minute). Select a rate that is 4 to 8 *gwam* below your speed rate. Try to type exactly at this rate as your teacher guides your writing by calling each quarter-minute interval. Type with continuity and without hurry.

¶ 1

There are many types of effort. You use effort to run or walk. You use effort just to sit and think. You use a great amount of effort to type the words on this page. As you gain in typing skill, you will expend less effort and still type more words in the same period of time.

¶ 2

As you improve competence, you observe that it seems easier to relax; but this condition does not mean that you are using less physical and mental energy. On the other hand, such energy is needed; and you must make the effort to improve proficiency as you remain free of tension.

¶ 3

As you refine typing competency, measurable growth in relation to every practice effort may seem to diminish. It is important not to relax your energy in this area. Accept this challenge to higher excellence, as you recall that mankind has a tremendous potential for excellence.

■ LESSON 85

85A ■ CONDITIONING PRACTICE 5 each line 3 times SS: slowly, faster, in-between rate

Alphabet   The proud man quickly won five prizes in the high jumping exhibitions. *Make a quick, little finger*

Figures   Jack and Jim labeled 12,967 illustrations, 450 tables, and 38 figures. *reach to the shift key*

Shift keys   R. H. Dalton, of Ault, Moore & Wallace Company, is visiting in Newark.

Fluency   If they pick the eight fowls for the widow, she will pay them in cash.

| 1 | 2 | 3 | 4 | 5 | 6 | 7 | 8 | 9 | 10 | 11 | 12 | 13 | 14 |

85B ■ IMPROVING SPEED/CONTROL: SKILL COMPARISON 20 retype 84D, above, as directed below

1. Speed. Type three 1′ writings on each ¶ for *speed*. **Goal:** To improve 84D rates and to force speed to new levels. Think each word as you type it, type with continuity, and let the fingers do the typing.

2. Control. Type three 1′ guided writings on each ¶ for *control*. Select a rate that is 4 to 8 *gwam* below your Step 1 speed rate. **Goal:** To improve control as you maintain good typing techniques.

80D ■ TECHNIQUE IMPROVEMENT [15] each line 3 times; note the technique cues

Technique Cues	1. Right thumb curved and in spacing position—on or close to space bar. 2. Avoid up-and-down movement of right hand on words ending in *y, n, m*. 3. Reach with the fingers. Space quickly: down-and-in motion toward palm.

Space bar

and the and the (repeat for full line; space quickly and keep carriage moving)

pay them | pay them when | pay them when they work | pay them when they work

Jim may question many men and women as they try to leave the map room.

Technique Cues	Keep your fingers in typing position and make the reach to the shift key by extending the little finger. Work for good timing to avoid "floating caps."

NOTE: *Book titles may be typed in all caps or with the underline.*

Shift key and shift lock

Ja Ja Ja Jack Jack Jack; F; F; F; Floyd Flynn; Paul McNaulty; Al Dyane

Jack, Frank, Paul, and Quinn read the book HOW TO SUCCEED IN BUSINESS.

Kate Sutton and Jane McNeil wrote the book How to Succeed in Business.

Technique Cues	Manual Return: Quick, flick-of-the-hand motion. Start new line quickly. Electric Return: Extend little finger and tap the return key.

Clear tabs—Center + 10 = TAB

Carriage (or carrier) return

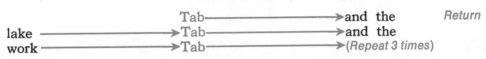

lake ——————→Tab————————→and the   *Return*
——————→Tab————————→and the
work ——————→Tab————————→(*Repeat 3 times*)

Application Checkup	Type the following paragraph, giving attention to quick and proper use of the space bar, shift lock, shift keys, and backspacer.

UNDERLINE the next three words: Type with Speed. Did you use the backspacer to move the carriage back for the underline? It may be quicker to push the carriage back with the left hand, and then use the space bar to position the words to be underlined. Use the backspacer, however, when it is necessary to backspace ONLY A FEW SPACES.

80E ■ GROWTH INDEX [8] type a 5' writing on 81D, page 125; determine GWAM; proofread

■ LESSON 81

81A ■ CONDITIONING PRACTICE [5]

Alphabet   These children were amazed by the quick, lively jumps of the gray fox.

Learning*   one, 1; forty, 40; one, twenty-seven, 127; twelve, seventy-three, 1273

Outside keys   A plucky polo player amazed us as he zigzagged crazily down the field.

Fluency   When he paid for the land, he also signed the audit form for the firm.

| 1 | 2 | 3 | 4 | 5 | 6 | 7 | 8 | 9 | 10 | 11 | 12 | 13 | 14 |

* Read, think, and type figures in two-digit sequences, whenever possible

81B ■ TECHNIQUE IMPROVEMENT [15] repeat 80D, above, as directed there

81C ■ IMPROVING ACCURACY [5] type a 1' writing on each line of 81A, above; work for accuracy

■ LESSON 84

84A ■ CONDITIONING PRACTICE [5] each line 3 times SS: slowly, faster, in-between rate

Alphabet	The unique weave of the blue-gray jacket pleased many zealous experts.	*Type with continuity*
Figures	The fishermen caught 84 albacore, 3,215 barracuda, and 7,690 mackerel.	
Adjacent keys/ direct reaches	A source of wisdom which is denied none is experience and observation.	
Fluency	She may go with them to the town by the lake to do work for the widow.	

| 1 | 2 | 3 | 4 | 5 | 6 | 7 | 8 | 9 | 10 | 11 | 12 | 13 | 14 |

84B ■ TECHNIQUE IMPROVEMENT: RESPONSE PATTERNS [15] each line 3 times SS: slowly, faster, top speed; then lines marked with ▶ from dictation

EMPHASIZE

1 *Letter*   rare link debt pink edge pulp ease kiln aware nylon eager union faster   *Fingers curved and upright*
2 *response*   we are | my data | you were | get him | oil tax | at best | saw no cards | at my age
3   As you are aware, we read union data based on defect tests in my area.

4 *Word*   ▶ also body dual fork hang iris lens turn goals risks shape vigor height   *Think the word or phrase; then type it with speed*
5 *response*   ▶ if it is | to do so | and the | with them | their work | such form | both men wish
6   Eight of the title firms may sign the amendment by the end of the day.

7 *Combination*   the date | they were | to the pin | for the case | and the address | the opinion   *Type with a variable rhythm pattern and uniform stroking*
8 *response*   sign the agreement | held the statement | join the union | state the problem
9   They gave the statement to the union at the address shown on the card.

84C ■ RELATED LEARNING: PUNCTUATION GUIDES [10] reinsert sheet used for typing 83D, page 128

6. Comma—Use the comma to separate two or more parallel adjectives (adjectives that could be separated by the word "and" instead of a comma).

7. Comma—Use the comma to separate (a) unrelated groups of figures which come together and (b) whole numbers into groups of three digits each (however, policy, year, page, room, telephone, and most serial numbers are written without commas).

8. Exclamation Mark—Use an exclamation mark after emphatic interjections and after phrases or sentences that are clearly exclamatory.

9. Question Mark—Use a question mark at the end of a sentence that is a direct question; however, use a period after a question which is in the form of a request.

6 *Learn* That old-fashioned stove kept them warm on long, cold winter evenings.
  Apply They traded the new solid-gold watch for that big friendly black dog.

7 *Learn* During 1967, 1,649 cars, insured under Policy 80-643207, were damaged.
  Apply In 1972 1256 new $100000 policies, Series 1348-92,015, were written.

8 *Learn* What a beautiful view! How lucky they are to be able to go to school!
  Apply Oh, if we could only go_ She typed 80 wam today_ Hurrah, you did it_

9 *Learn* When are you leaving? May we have your check for $15.75 before May 8.
  Apply How old is your uncle_ Will you please do this work before you leave_

81D ■ GROWTH INDEX 15 two 5' writings; determine GWAM; proofread for errors

All letters are used.

	GWAM	
	1'	5'

¶ 1

An important problem of our time is the exacting question of beauty | 14 | 3 | 50
and its relationship to each person. There is beauty of attitude and | 28 | 6 | 52
spirit on the one hand, and beauty of the environment on the other. | 41 | 8 | 55
These two divisions of beauty cannot really be separated. The problem | 56 | 11 | 58
concerning beauty of spirit and the way we feel about the world we live | 70 | 14 | 61
in originates from the violence this world has done and is doing to its | 84 | 17 | 64
environment. This destruction and pollution of the world around us have | 99 | 20 | 67
in turn changed the spirit and attitude of each of us. Isn't it time | 113 | 23 | 69
to start to clean up this infectious disease? | 122 | 24 | 71

¶ 2

We have to recognize that with the new problem of urbanization, and | 14 | 27 | 74
with people compressed into urban centers, a completely new dimension of | 28 | 30 | 77
problems and responsibilities has emerged. We no longer have the free- | 42 | 33 | 80
dom to clutter our environment with a variety of rubbish. The need for | 57 | 36 | 83
beauty in the environment can no longer be thought of as impractical. | 71 | 39 | 85
Each of us, also, must remember that we make up and are a part of this | 85 | 41 | 88
world that now stands accused for the destruction of the beauty of the | 99 | 44 | 91
environment. We just must take action now or it may be too late. | 112 | 47 | 94

1' GWAM | 1 | 2 | 3 | 4 | 5 | 6 | 7 | 8 | 9 | 10 | 11 | 12 | 13 | 14 |
5' GWAM | 1 | 2 | 3 |

81E ■ RELATED LEARNING: CAPITALIZATION GUIDES (End of Series) 10

10. Capitalize the seasons of the year only when they are personified.
11. Capitalize geographic regions, localities, and names. Do not capitalize points of the compass when used to indicate direction or in a descriptive sense.
12. Capitalize such words as street, avenue, company, etc., when used with a proper noun.
13. Capitalize names of organizations, clubs, and buildings.
14. Usually capitalize a noun preceding a figure. Common words, as line, page, and sentence, may be typed with or without a capital.

10 Learn   This winter seems very cold; the icy fingers of Winter are everywhere.
   Apply   Each of the four seasons--Fall, Winter, Spring, Summer--has its charm.

11 Learn   I live in the East, but I plan to move west to Squaw Valley next year.
   Apply   At one time Andrew lived in the south; he now lives on the west coast.

12 Learn   Is 123 Fifth Street or 123 Fifth Avenue the address of Dowe & Company?
   Apply   Is this the Street where you live, or do you live on Tennessee avenue?

13 Learn   The Boy Scouts will meet at the Commercial Club at 4 p.m. on Saturday.
   Apply   The future business leaders of america may meet at the fairmont hotel.

14 Learn   He read Judge Baxter's decision in Volume III, Section 123, page 1049.
   Apply   J. D. Morgan & Company uses style 34 as shown on Page 12 of catalog 5.

83C ■ TECHNIQUE IMPROVEMENT: STROKING ⌷15⌷ each line 3 times SS: slowly, faster, slowly; repeat if time permits

1 *Double*   fill been pass good happy staff sorry shall added manner indeed summer   *Uniform*
2 *letters*   all accept | need apply | add staff | shall carry | will suggest | school office   *keystroking*
3   My assistant arranged for all the staff to attend these meetings, too.

4 *Long*   gym debt once myth curve under bring doubt number column beyond around   *Finger-action*
5 *reaches*   beyond doubt| my sympathy| column numbers| curb my debts| many a gymnasium   *reaches;*
6   Without doubt, the symphony brings a number of celebrities every year.   *hands quiet*

7 *Outside*   else glad touch leave wrote stand control answer estate dollar station   *Fingers curved*
8 *reaches*   a home | most people | spare parts | come through | delivery sheet | sale on oil   *and upright;*
9   Should your club be unable to take that course, I may specify another.   *quick stroking*

83D ■ RELATED LEARNING: PUNCTUATION GUIDES ⌷10⌷ as directed in 76D, page 118

1. **Comma**—Use the comma after (a) introductory words, phrases, or clauses and (b) words in a series with a conjunction.

2. **Comma**—Use the comma to set off short, direct quotations.

3. **Comma**—Use the comma to set off (a) words in apposition (words which come together and refer to the same person, thing, or idea) and (b) words of direct address.

4. **Comma**—Use the comma to set off nonrestrictive clauses (not necessary to meaning of sentence). Do not use commas to set off restrictive clauses (necessary to meaning).

5. **Comma**—Use the comma to separate the day from the year and the city from the state.

SERIES 3. PUNCTUATION GUIDE EXAMPLES

1 *Learn*   After he leaves Atlanta, he will visit Richmond, New York, and Boston.
  Apply   If they leave early_they will have bacon and eggs_toast_and coffee.

2 *Learn*   I asked, "When are you leaving?" She replied, "I plan to leave soon."
  Apply   H. D. Thoreau once said_"Be not simply good: Be good for something."

Note different meaning

3 *Learn*   Mr. King, the owner, is out today. Yes, Dr. Felder, the owner is out.
  Apply   The manager_Mr. Jeffrey_said, "Ask my assistant_Mr. Lange_for it."

4 *Learn*   His story, which no one believed, was told in detail to many visitors. *(nonrestrictive)*
  Apply   Chapters 7 and 8_which relate to this problem_are very well written.

  Learn   All students_who practice with a purpose_will be successful in typing. *(restrictive)*
  Apply   The building will have to be repaired, unless good care is taken of it.

5 *Learn*   He was born September 20, 1953, and lived in Lexington, Massachusetts.
  Apply   They may plan to go to Stockholm_Sweden, on or about August 26_1980.

Improving Speed and Control / Related Learnings

■ LESSON 82

82A ■ CONDITIONING PRACTICE ⑤

Alphabet	Visitors did enjoy the amazing water tricks of six quaint polar bears.	*Anticipate stroking by reading ahead*
Figures	I may buy 15 jackets, 289 blankets, 74 kits, 360 lamps, and 110 tires.	
Shift keys	J. C. McNeil, Vice-President of Roxy's, Inc., is now in New York City.	
Fluency	They wish to go to the city with the chairman for the profit due them.	

| 1 | 2 | 3 | 4 | 5 | 6 | 7 | 8 | 9 | 10 | 11 | 12 | 13 | 14 |

82B ■ TECHNIQUE IMPROVEMENT ⑫ each line 3 times SS; slowly, faster, top speed; repeat as time permits

TECHNIQUE GOALS

1 *Fingers curved*
2 *Fingers upright*
3 *Finger-reach action*

1 *Consecutive-* urge branch junior often liked policy payment news thus why buy obtain
2 *direct* gaze enjoy carbons length mortgage government performance organization
3 *reaches* The performance of our economy often makes news for other governments.

4 *Outside* aqua point acquit policy review claim details amounts zealous equipped
5 *keys* quite short | sound economy | sales group | detailed schedule | initial desire
6 The new program chairman initially wanted to invite only two speakers.

82C ■ RELATED LEARNING CHECKUP: CAPITALIZATION GUIDES ⑬ (Line: 74; correct as you type)

*1:122**	1	heed well Samuel Johnson's advice, "what is easy is seldom excellent."
2:122	2	i was impressed by what she said about "A dedication to quality work."
3:122	3	"if at first you do succeed," he said, "Try something more difficult."
4:122	4	this is what the sign said: take the santa ana freeway to disneyland.
5:123	5	i have just finished the book by lewis, how to read better and faster.
6:123	6	i understand that president kerr is scheduled to speak at the meeting.
7-8:123	7	the general gave an interesting report on roman and grecian mythology.
9:123; 10:125	8	i announced that school would open on monday, september 11, next fall.
11-12-13:125	9	the century club is on sixth street, just east of the new civic plaza.
14:125	10	check lines 14, 16, and 29, on page 37, in volume v, for the solution.

*If you are uncertain about corrections, use the code to check the rule (1:122—Guide 1, page 122). The color underline indicates a *possible* point of correction.

82D ■ IMPROVING SPEED/CONTROL: GUIDED WRITING 20

1. Type a 1′ writing on ¶ 1 for *speed*. Determine rate. To this base rate add 8 words. Determine quarter-minute goals for this new rate.
2. Type two 1′ guided writings on ¶ 1 at new rate determined in Step 1.

3. Repeat Steps 1 and 2 with ¶ 2.
4. Type a 1′ writing on ¶ 1 for *control*. **Goal:** Not over 1 error.
5. Type two 1′ guided writings on ¶ 1 at Step 4 rate if you made over 1 error. If you met the goal, increase your rate by 4 *gwam*.

6. Repeat Steps 4 and 5 with ¶ 2.
7. Type a 3′ writing using both ¶s. **Goal:** To maintain basic rate of Steps 4 and 5 with not more than 3 errors. Determine *gwam*; circle errors.

All letters are used.

	4	8	12	3′ G W A M

¶ 1

Every typing student needs to make a personal evaluation of his — 4 | 55
typewriting ability. A first step in building a better performance is — 9 | 60
to give attention to the techniques you use as you type. Do you keep — 14 | 64
your fingers well curved and upright so that you can type with snappy — 18 | 69
keystroking action? Do you let the fingers do the typing and keep your — 23 | 74
hands and arms quiet and relaxed? — 25 | 76

¶ 2

What are other elements that are indispensable to good performance? — 30 | 81
It is essential to keep the right thumb curved and close to the space — 35 | 85
bar so as to space quickly after every word. Realize, also, that you — 39 | 90
lose skill if you look away from the copy to the typewriter. Just make — 44 | 95
the return quickly at the end of every line. Every technique refinement — 49 | 100
will lead to higher skill. — 51 | 101

3′ GWAM | 1 | 2 | 3 | 4 | 5 |

■ LESSON 83

83A ■ CONDITIONING PRACTICE 5 each line 3 times SS: slowly, faster, in-between rate

Alphabet Fools won't likely adopt the unique economizing objectives of experts. *Make the return quickly; start new line without a pause*

Figures Jack typed 15 letters, 48 envelopes, 73 tags, 29 labels, and 60 cards.

Adjacent keys/ direct reaches If one chooses to be a knocker, he needs neither brains nor education.

Fluency The eight girls wish to go with me when I pay the firm for their work.
| 1 | 2 | 3 | 4 | 5 | 6 | 7 | 8 | 9 | 10 | 11 | 12 | 13 | 14 |

83B ■ IMPROVING SPEED/CONTROL: GUIDED WRITING 20 retype 82D, above, as directed there

TYPEWRITER OPERATIVE PARTS

■ Typewriters have similar operative parts, the names of which vary somewhat from typewriter to typewriter even when the function is the same. These similar operative parts are identified in the four segments of a typewriter given below and on page ii. Each segment is a composite and not an exact segment of any one typewriter. For this reason, the exact location of a part identified in the segment may be slightly different from that on your typewriter; but the differences are, for the most part, few and slight.

Extra parts that are peculiar to the typewriter you operate and not common to most typewriters can be identified by reference to the instructional booklet distributed by the manufacturer of the typewriter that you are using. This booklet can be very helpful to you because the information it contains has been written to apply specifically to the one make of machine.

In using the illustrations, follow the line from the number to the part location. Know the function of each part, as explained in the textbook, and learn to operate it with maximum efficiency. This effort will enable you to type more skillfully.

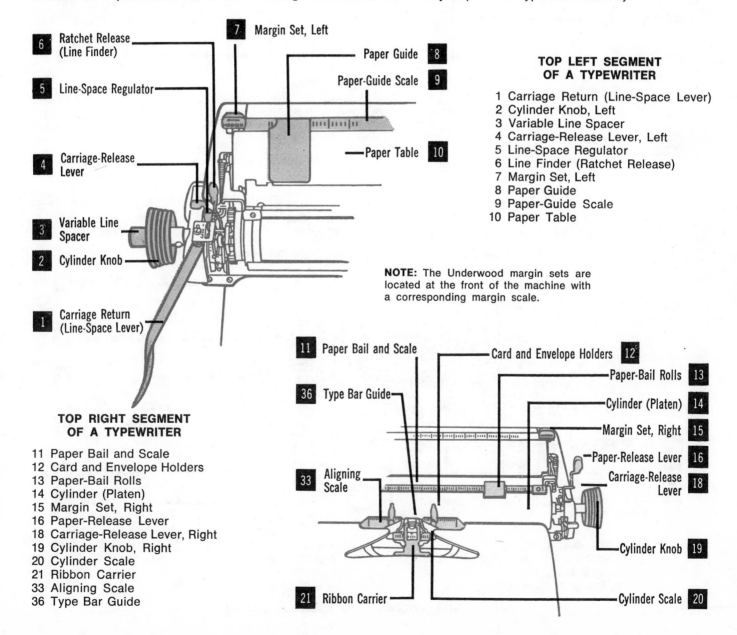

TOP LEFT SEGMENT OF A TYPEWRITER

1 Carriage Return (Line-Space Lever)
2 Cylinder Knob, Left
3 Variable Line Spacer
4 Carriage-Release Lever, Left
5 Line-Space Regulator
6 Line Finder (Ratchet Release)
7 Margin Set, Left
8 Paper Guide
9 Paper-Guide Scale
10 Paper Table

NOTE: The Underwood margin sets are located at the front of the machine with a corresponding margin scale.

TOP RIGHT SEGMENT OF A TYPEWRITER

11 Paper Bail and Scale
12 Card and Envelope Holders
13 Paper-Bail Rolls
14 Cylinder (Platen)
15 Margin Set, Right
16 Paper-Release Lever
18 Carriage-Release Lever, Right
19 Cylinder Knob, Right
20 Cylinder Scale
21 Ribbon Carrier
33 Aligning Scale
36 Type Bar Guide

LOWER SEGMENT OF A MANUAL TYPEWRITER

22 Ribbon Control and Stencil Lock
23 Tab Set Key
24 Tabulator Bar or Key
25 Margin-Release Key

26 Shift Key, Right
27 Space Bar
28 Shift Key, Left
29 Shift Lock, Left and Right

30 Backspace Key
31 Tab Clear Key
32 Ribbon Reverse
34 Touch Regulator

LOWER SEGMENT OF AN ELECTRIC TYPEWRITER

1 Carriage Return (Line-Space Key)
7 Margin Reset Key
15 Margin Reset Key
17 Electric Switch
22 Ribbon Control and Stencil Lock
23 Tab Set Key

24 Tabulator Key
25 Margin-Release Key
26 Shift Key, Right
27 Space Bar
28 Shift Key, Left
29 Shift Lock

30 Backspace Key
31 Tab Clear Key
32 Ribbon Reverse
34 Touch Regulator (Shown in X-Ray View)
35 Impression Control

> CHECK YOUR TYPEWRITER AND SEE IF:
> 1. The position is different for: ¢ @ * _ (underline)
> 2. These keys have "repeat" action: *backspace, space bar, carriage return, hyphen-underline*
> 3. Extra keys are used: + = ! 1

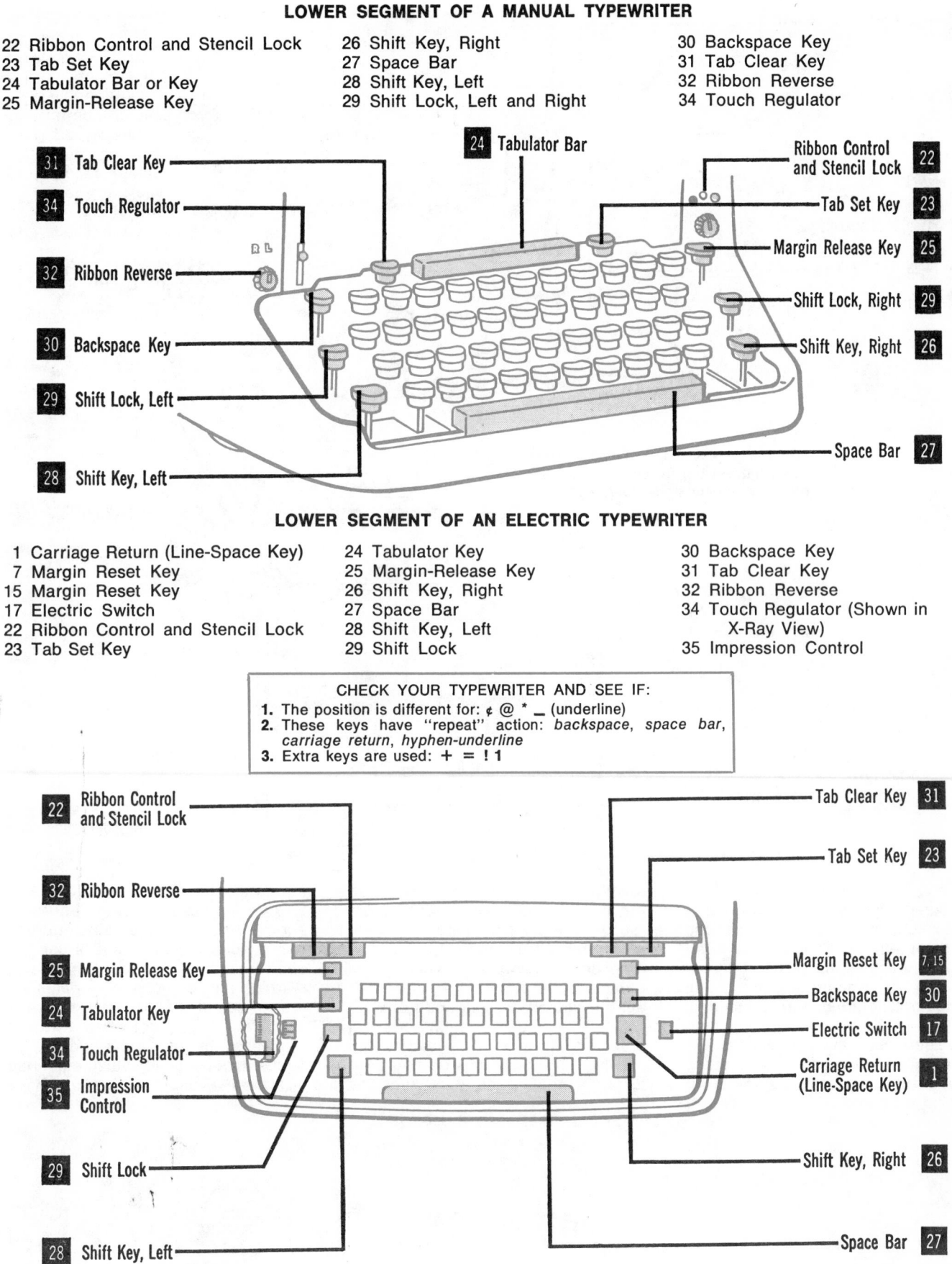

SETTING THE PAPER GUIDE; CENTERING THE PAPER

Olympia, R. C. Allen, Royal, Smith-Corona. Set the paper guide **(8)** so the indicator at the left will point to *0* on the paper-guide scale **(9)**, which is on the paper table **(10)**. When paper of standard size (8½″ by 11″) is inserted with the guide at *0*, the centering point will be:

```
42 for machines with pica type
```

```
50 or 51 for machines with elite type
```

(Note the difference between pica and elite type illustrated in the two lines above. Compare this type with the type on the machine you are using.)

IBM. Insert the paper with the left edge at *0* on the margin scale (Selectric) or the lower platen (cylinder) scale of the standard electric. Move the paper guide so that it is alongside the left edge of the paper. Note the position of the paper guide on the paper table, and always set the guide in this position.

Olivetti Underwood. Insert the paper with the left edge at *0* on the paper-bail scale. Move the paper guide so that it is alongside the left edge of the paper. Note the position of the paper guide on the paper-guide scale, and always set the guide in this position.

Remington. Insert the paper with the left edge at *0* on the bottom carriage scale. Move the paper guide so that it is alongside the left edge of the paper. Note the position of the paper guide on the paper table, and always set the guide in this position.

NOTE: Remington, Smith-Corona, and Olivetti Underwood typewriters have special centering devices. If your instructor wishes to have you use the centering devices, he will give you appropriate instruction.

PLANNING THE MARGIN STOPS

■ To have the typed material centered horizontally, set stops for the left and right margins. Typewriters differ in their mechanical adjustments and the bell rings at different points on different typewriters, but the carriage locks at the point where the right margin stop is set. After the bell rings, there will be from 6 to 11 or more spaces before the carriage locks, some machines allowing more but none fewer than 6 spaces.

Test out your typewriter and determine the number of spaces the bell rings before the carriage (or car-

rier) locks. Take this into consideration when setting the right margin stop. Since the ringing of the bell is a cue to return the carriage, set the right stop 3 to 7 spaces beyond the desired line ending so the bell will ring approximately 3 spaces before the point at which you want the line to end.

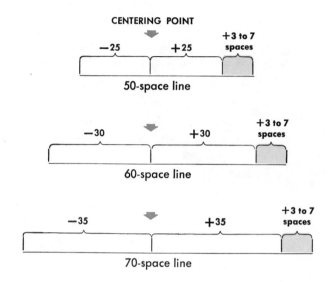

MECHANICS OF SETTING THE MARGIN STOPS

Royal Standard and Electric. *To set the left margin stop*, place your left index finger behind the left "Magic" margin control and move it forward; move the carriage to the desired position; then return the margin control to its original position. *To set the right margin stop*, move the right "Magic" margin control forward; move the carriage to the desired position; then return the margin control to its original position.

IBM Electric. *To set the left margin stop*, move the carriage until it is against the left margin stop; depress and hold down the margin set key as you move the carriage to the desired new position; then release the set key. *To set the right margin stop*, move the carriage until it is against the right margin stop; depress and hold down the margin set key as you move the carriage to the desired new position; then release the set key.

IBM Selectric. With the element carrier approximately centered, move stops to desired position. This is easy to do by relating their location to the keyboard. As there is no movable carriage as on other typewriters, stops can be moved left or right as the line length requires.

R. C. Allen and Olympia. *To set the left margin stop,* depress the left margin stop, move the carriage to the desired position, and set and then release the stop. Use the same procedure for setting the stop for the right margin.

Remington Standard and Electric. *To set the left margin stop,* move the left margin stop to the desired position to begin the line of writing. Move the stop for the right margin to the desired position to set the stop for the right margin.

Smith-Corona Standard. *To set the left margin stop,* press the left margin set button to the left in the direction of the arrow as you move the carriage to the desired position; then release the margin set button. *To set the right margin stop,* press the right margin set button to the right in the direction of the margin set button as you move the carriage to the desired position; then release the margin set button.

Smith-Corona Electric. *To reset the left margin,* depress the left carriage-release button and the left margin button, move the carriage to the right to the desired location, and release the two buttons simultaneously. The same operation is used to reset the right margin.

Olivetti Underwood. Set both right and left margins simultaneously. You do not have to move the carriage. The margin indicators (shaded geometric shapes) on the front scale indicate balanced margin set positions.

KNOW YOUR TYPEWRITER. Your machine may have timesaving features not included in this discussion of operating parts. Learn these features from a study of the manufacturer's pamphlet which describes and illustrates the operating parts of the typewriter you are using. You can get this pamphlet without cost from the manufacturer of your typewriter. The pamphlet will have many ideas for your operative improvement.

CHANGING TYPEWRITER RIBBONS

■ The technique for changing ribbons is not the same for all machines, but in no case is it particularly difficult. The basic steps for changing the ribbon are listed:

1—*Wind the ribbon on one spool,* usually the right.

2—*Raise and lock the ribbon carrier* (21). Do this by pressing down the shift lock (29), moving the ribbon control (22) for typing on the lower portion of the ribbon, and by depressing and locking any two central keys, such as y and u.

3—*Remove the ribbon from the carrier* (21) and remove both spools.

4—*Hook the new ribbon to the empty spool* and wind several inches of the new ribbon on it. Be sure that the ribbon winds and unwinds in the proper direction.

5—*Place both spools on their holders* and thread the ribbon through the ribbon carrier.

6—*Release the shift lock,* and return the ribbon indicator to the position for typing on the upper portion of the ribbon. Unlock the two type bars, and the typewriter will be ready for use.

7—*Clean the keys, if necessary.* When a new ribbon is first used, it may be necessary to clean the keys so that all typed letters will be clear and bright.

NOTE: The Selectric typewriter uses a special ribbon cartridge that makes the foregoing steps unnecessary.

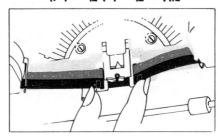

Ribbon Threaded Through the Ribbon-Carrier Mechanism

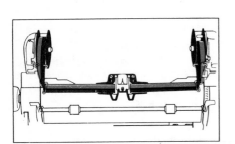

IBM Ribbon

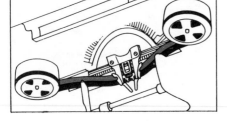

Path of the Ribbon as it Winds and Unwinds on the Two Spools

August 24, 19--

Mr. Roy C. Butterworth
Hilltop Research, Inc.
81 Hamilton Street
Paterson, NJ 07505

Dear Mr. Butterworth

Today many business firms use the block style letter for
their correspondence. This letter is an example of that
style. You will note that all lines start at the left
margin. The advantage of this style is that the mechanical
process of indenting opening and closing lines, or paragraphs, is eliminated. This practice saves time and space.

Open punctuation is used with this letter: Punctuation
marks are omitted after the date, address, salutation,
and complimentary close unless an abbreviation is used,
in which case the period is typed as a part of the abbreviation. Elimination of these punctuation marks helps
to increase letter production rates. Another recommended
timesaving feature is to type only the typist's initials
for reference when the dictator's name is typed in the
closing lines.

As you can see, the block style letter gives good placement appearance; and, because many extra typing strokes
and motions are eliminated, its use does help to increase
letter production rates. It is the letter style that I
recommend for use in the business office.

Sincerely yours

J. Scott Miller

J. Scott Miller
Communications Consultant

rfb

Block, Open

January 15, 19--

Dr. John Cosgrove, President
Cosgrove Business College
Pullman, WA 99163

Dear Dr. Cosgrove:

This letter is an example of the modified block style.
It is one of the most popular business letter styles in
use today. As you will observe, it differs from the block
style in that the dateline and the closing lines (the
complimentary close and the typed name and title) are
indented and blocked. Mixed punctuation is frequently
used with this letter style: a colon after the salutation
and a comma after the complimentary close.

When the modified block style is used, letter production
efficiency dictates that the dateline, the complimentary
close, and the typed name and title be started at the
same point. Actual practice in the business office, however, varies widely. For instance, the dateline may be
centered, it may be typed so that it ends at the right
margin, or it may be given special placement in relation
to the letterhead. Similarly, the closing lines may be
started five spaces to the left of center or may be typed
so that they end approximately at the right margin.

Although the modified block style gives good placement
appearance, it is difficult to account for its popular
appeal since, as compared with the block style, additional
typing motions are involved in the placement of the various
parts. The problem may be that no one has really given
serious consideration to the effect of the letter style
used on letter production efficiency.

Cordially yours,

John E. Homan

John E. Homan, Director

dcr

cc Mr. Ralph Armstrong

Modified Block, Mixed

September 13, 19--

St. Marys School
St. Marys, AK 99658

Attention Manager, Bookstore

Gentlemen:

Thanks for your inquiry about letter styles. This
letter is arranged in the modified block style with 5-space
paragraph indentions. Business letters are usually typed
on 8½- by 11-inch letterhead stationery which has the name
of the company sending the letter, as well as other iden-
tifying information, at the top of the sheet.

The position of the dateline is varied according to
the length of the letter. More space is left before the
dateline for short letters than for long letters. The
address is typed on the fourth line (3 blank lines) below
the date. Some business offices use standard margins (a
set line length) for all letters; others adjust the margins
according to the length of the letter.

Other questions about letter placement are answered
in the letter style booklet which is enclosed with this
letter. Don't hesitate to write to us if there is any
other information you need. Good luck to you and the
other students at your school with your typing service.

Sincerely,

Steven Osborn

Steven Osborn
Communications Consultant

amv

Enclosure

Modified Block, Indented ¶s, Mixed

December 3, 19--

Miss Anne C. Mayes, Chairman
Business Education Department
Biloxi Technical School
Biloxi, MS 39533

AMS SIMPLIFIED LETTER STYLE

The unique Simplified letter style for business correspondence is
sensible, streamlined, and effective. It is a simplified "block
style" with all lines beginning at the left margin. Other features
are listed below:

1. The address is typed 3 or more blank lines below the date.

2. The salutation and complimentary close are omitted.

3. A subject heading in all capitals is typed a triple space below
   the address.

4. Unnumbered listed items are indented 5 spaces, but numbered
   items are typed flush with the left margin.

5. The dictator's name and title are typed in capitals 5 line
   spaces (4 blank lines) below the body of the letter.

6. Reference initials consist of the typist's initials only.

7. Copy notations are typed a double space below the reference
   lines.

Because of the timesaving features of this AMS Simplified style
letter, its use will reduce your letter-writing costs and give your
letters a distinctive "eye appeal." Try it. You will like it.

Lee Clark

LEE CLARK - SECRETARY

hje

AMS Simplified

ADDRESSING ENVELOPES

Envelope Address. Set a tab stop (or margin stop if a number of envelopes are to be addressed) 2½" from the left edge for a small envelope or 4" from the left edge for a large envelope. Start the address here 2" from the top edge of a small envelope and 2½" from the top edge of a large one.

Style. Type the address in *block style*, single-spaced, without punctuation at the ends of lines, except when an abbreviation ends a line. Type the city name, state name or abbreviation, and ZIP Code on the last address line. The ZIP Code is usually typed 2 spaces after the state name.

Addressee Notations. Type addressee notations, such as *Hold for Arrival*, *Please Forward*, *Personal*, etc., a triple space below the return address and about 3 spaces from the left edge of the envelope. These notations may be underlined or typed in all capitals. If an *attention line* is used, type it immediately below the company name in the address lines.

Mailing Notations. Type mailing notations, such as AIRMAIL, SPECIAL DELIVERY, and REGISTERED, below the stamp and at least 3 line spaces above the envelope address. Type these notations in all capital letters.

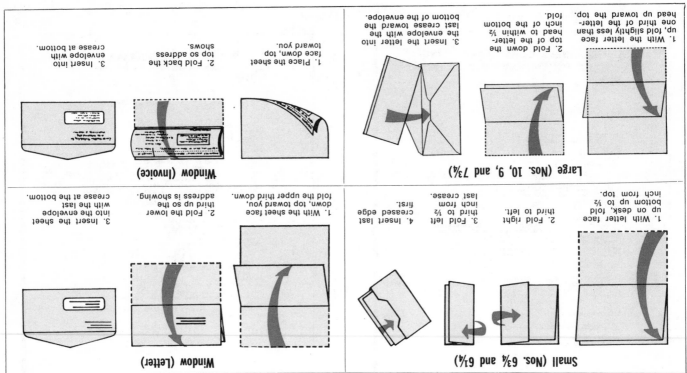

Large Envelope

BUSINESS CONSULTANTS, inc.
21943 BEVERLY STREET • DETROIT, MI 48237

REGISTERED

Gibson & Stewart, Inc.
817 - 16th Street, N.W.
Washington, DC 20006

Airmail envelope with *Registered* notation

Small Envelopes

AIRMAIL

Laughlin, Crews, and Hart
Attention Mr. Ronald Crews
320 South Clark Street
Chicago, IL 60604

Envelope with typed *Airmail* notation and *Attention line*

PLEASE FORWARD

Mrs. L. B. Johnson
3674 Stettinius Avenue
Cincinnati, Ohio 45208

Envelope with typed return address, *Please Forward* notation, and *In Care of* notation

Mr. Carl Howlson
c/o Euclid Publishers, Inc.
23710 Lake Shore Boulevard
Euclid, Ohio 44123

FOLDING-AND-INSERTING PROCEDURE FOR ENVELOPES

Large (Nos. 10, 9, and 7¾)

1. With the letter face up on desk, fold one third of the letter-head up toward the top.

2. Fold down the top of the letter-head to within ½ inch of the bottom fold.

3. Insert the letter into the envelope with the last crease toward the bottom of the envelope.

Window (Invoice)

1. Place the sheet face down, top toward you.

2. Fold back the top so address shows.

3. Insert into envelope with crease at bottom.

Small (Nos. 6¾ and 6¼)

1. With letter face up, fold bottom up to ½ inch from top.

2. Fold right third to left.

3. Fold left third to ½ inch from last crease.

4. Insert last creased edge first.

Window (Letter)

1. With the sheet face down, top toward you, fold the upper third down.

2. Fold the lower third up so the address is showing.

3. Insert the sheet into the envelope with the last crease at the bottom.

Paper-Guide Placement. Check the placement of the paper guide so that the horizontal centering of the letter will be accurate.

Margins and Date Placement. Use the following guide:

5-Stroke Words in Letter Body	Side Margins	Date-line
Up to 100	2″	20
101 - 300	1½″	18-12 *
Over 300	1″	12

*Dateline is moved up 2 line spaces for each additional 50 words.

Horizontal placement of date varies according to the letter style.

Address. The address is typed on the fourth line (3 blank line spaces) below the date. A personal title, such as **Mr., Mrs., Miss,** or **Ms.** (if the marital status of a woman is unknown), should precede the name of an individual. An official title, when used, may be typed on the first or the second line of the address, whichever gives better balance.

Attention Line. An attention line, when used, is typed on the second line (a double space) below the letter address.

Subject Line. A subject line is typed on the second line (a double space) below the salutation. It may be either centered or typed at the left margin.

Company Name. Sometimes the company name is typed in the closing lines. When this is done, it is typed in *all capital letters* 2 lines (a double space) below the complimentary close. The modern practice is to omit the company name in the closing lines, particularly if a letterhead is used.

Typewritten Name and Official Title. The name of the person who dictated the letter and his official title are typed 4 lines (3 blank lines) below the complimentary close, or 4 lines below the typed company name when it is used. When both the name and official title are used, they may be typed on the same line or the official title may be typed on the next line below the typed name.

Unusual Features. Letters having unusual features, such as tabulated material, long quotations, or an unusual number of lines in the address or the closing lines, may require changes in the adjustments normally used for letters of that length.

Two-Page Letters. If a letter is too long for one page, at least 2 lines of the body of the letter should be carried to the second page. The second page of a letter, or any additional pages, requires a proper heading. Either the vertical or the horizontal form may be used for the heading; each is followed by a triple space.

Second-Page Headings

```
Dr. J. W. Orr
Page 2          Vertical Form
May 14, 19--
```

Horizontal Form

```
Dr. J. W. Orr    2    May 15, 19--
```

GUIDES FOR WORD DIVISION

1. Divide a word between syllables only. Type a hyphen at the end of the line to indicate the division. Type the rest of the word on the succeeding line.

2. Do not divide a word of five or fewer letters.

3. Do not divide from the remainder of the word:

a. A one-letter syllable at the beginning or end of a word; as, *around, steady.*

b. A syllable without a vowel; as, *wouldn't.*

c. A two-letter syllable at the end of a word; as, *greatly.*

4. Avoid dividing after a two-letter syllable at the beginning of a word. Try to divide elsewhere in the word; as, *express-ing.*

5. Avoid dividing initials, abbreviations, numbers, and proper names; but a surname may be separated from the initials or given name, when necessary.

6. Divide after a one-letter syllable within a word, as *sepa-rate,* unless the one-letter syllable is followed by the ending syllable *ble, bly, cle,* or *cal*; as, *depend-able.* If two one-letter syllables come together, divide between the vowels; as, *gradu-ation.*

7. When dividing words, type *cial, tial, cion, sion,* or *tion* as a unit; as, *impar-tial, impres-sion.*

8. If the final consonant in a word is doubled when a suffix is added, divide between the double letters; as, *control-ling*; but when a syllable is added to a word that ends in double letters, divide after the double letters; as, *express-ing, unwill-ing.*

9. Divide hyphened or compound words only at the hyphen that connects the two parts; as, *self-explanatory.*

10. If separating the parts of the date is unavoidable, separate between the day of the month and the year.

11. Avoid dividing words at the ends of more than two successive lines, or the final word on a page.

CARBON-PACK ASSEMBLY METHODS

DESK-TOP ASSEMBLY METHOD

1. Assemble letterhead, carbon sheets (dull side up), and one second sheets. Use one carbon and one second sheet for each copy desired.

2. Grasp the carbon pack at the sides, turn it so that the letterhead faces away from you, the glossy side of the carbon faces you, and the top edge of the pack face down. Tap the sheets gently on the desk to straighten.

3. Hold the sheets firmly to prevent slipping; insert pack into typewriter. Hold pack with one hand; turn platen with the other.

Tip for Wrinkle-Free Assembly

Start pack into typewriter with paper-release lever forward; then rest the paper-release lever and turn pack into the machine.

MACHINE ASSEMBLY METHOD

1. Assemble paper for insertion (original on top; second sheets beneath). Turn the "pack" so original faces away from you and the top edge faces down.
2. Insert sheets until the tops are gripped by the feed rolls; then pull the bottom of all sheets ex-cept the last over the top (front) of the typewriter.
3. Place carbon paper between sheets, glossy side toward you. Flip each carbon sheet back (away from you) as you add each carbon sheet.
4. Roll pack into typing position.

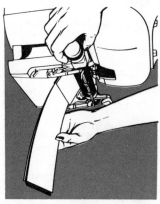

Removing Carbon Sheets

Hold the left edge of the letterhead and second sheets; remove all carbons at one time with the right hand.

Inserting the Pack with a Trough

To keep the carbon pack straight when feeding it into the typewriter, place the pack in the fold of a plain sheet of paper (paper trough) or under the flap of an envelope. Remove the trough or envelope when the pack is in place.

SLOTTED DRAWER ASSEMBLY METHOD

LETTERHEADS
CARBON SHEETS
SECOND SHEETS
ENVELOPES

1. With sheets correctly arranged in slotted drawer, pick up a letterhead with left hand and a sheet of carbon paper with right hand; pull sheets slightly forward; grasp both sheets with left hand as right hand reaches and pulls second sheet into position.
2. Pull sheets from slots. Straighten pack by tapping gently on desk as the sides of the sheets are held loosely by both hands.
3. Add extra sets (a second sheet and a carbon) for any additional copies that may be needed.
4. Insert into typewriter as with desk-top assembly method.

FRONT FEEDING SMALL CARDS AND LABELS

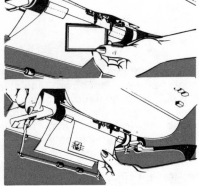
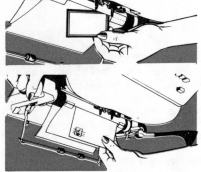